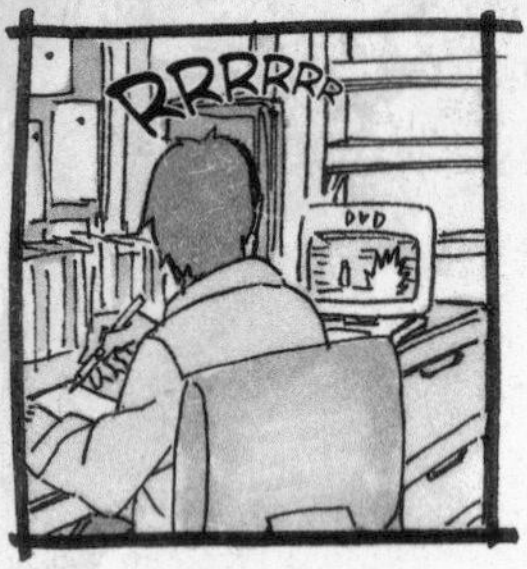
RRRRRRR
DVD

岸本斉史

Recently, because I get lonely when I am working alone, I keep movies playing continuously while I work. I'll occasionally glance at the movie while focusing on work, but then I'll suddenly realize that I'm focused on the movie and just occasionally scribbling on the paper. It's especially bad when it comes to trilogies!

Seriously... (beads of sweat)

—*Masashi Kishimoto, 2010*

Author/artist Masashi Kishimoto was born in 1974 in rural Okayama Prefecture, Japan. After spending time in art college, he won the Hop Step Award for new manga artists with his manga **Karakuri** (Mechanism). Kishimoto decided to base his next story on traditional Japanese culture. His first version of **Naruto**, drawn in 1997, was a one-shot story about fox spirits; his final version, which debuted in **Weekly Shonen Jump** in 1999, quickly became the most popular ninja manga in Japan.

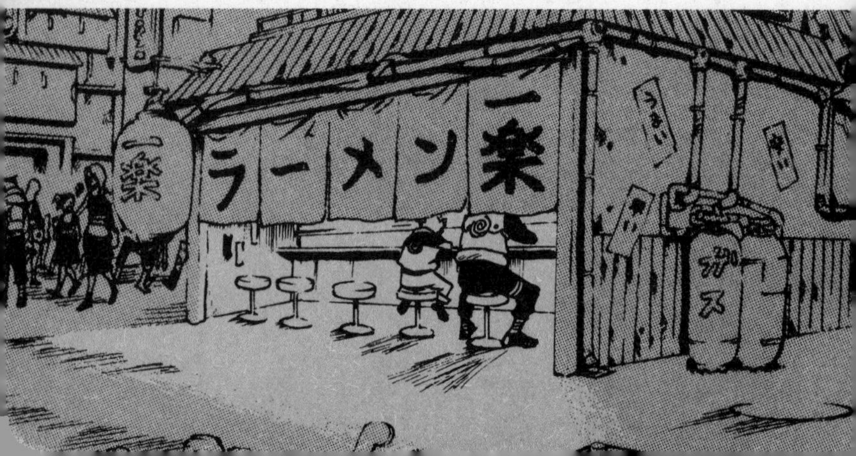
一楽
ラーメン一楽

NARUTO VOL. 49
SHONEN JUMP Manga Edition

This graphic novel contains material that was originally published in English
in SHONEN JUMP #85–88. Artwork in the magazine may have been
slightly altered from that presented here.

STORY AND ART BY MASASHI KISHIMOTO

Translation/Mari Morimoto
Series Touch-up Art & Lettering/Inori Fukuda Trant
Additional Touch-up Art & Lettering/Sabrina Heep
Design/Sean Lee
Series Editor/Joel Enos
Graphic Novel Editor/Megan Bates

VP, Production/Alvin Lu
VP, Sales & Product Marketing/Gonzalo Ferreyra
VP, Creative/Linda Espinosa
Publisher/Hyoe Narita

Printed in the U.S.A.

Published by VIZ Media, LLC
P.O. Box 77010
San Francisco, CA 94107

10 9 8 7 6 5 4 3 2 1
First printing, October 2010

THE WORLD'S
MOST POPULAR MANGA

www.shonenjump.com

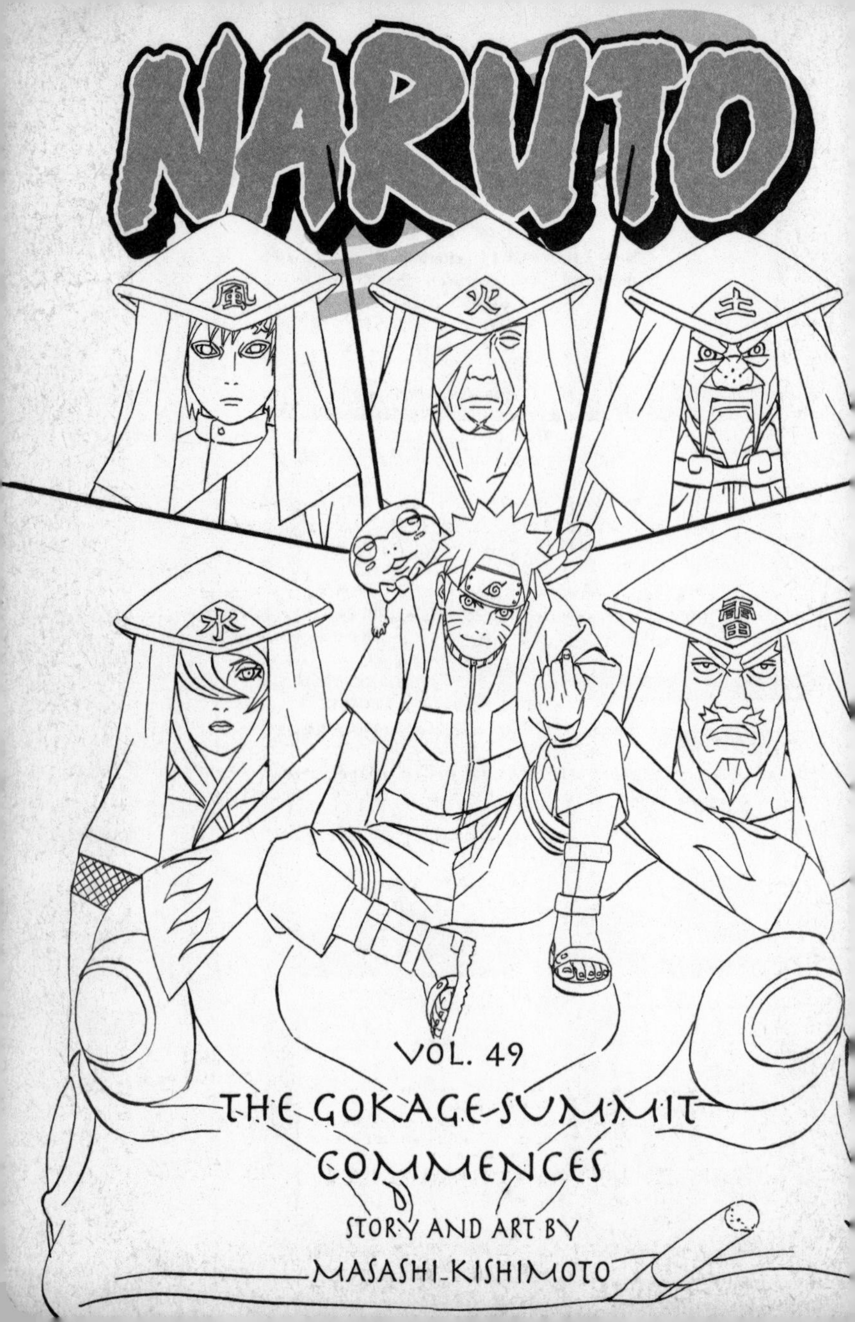
NARUTO
VOL. 49
THE GOKAGE SUMMIT COMMENCES
STORY AND ART BY
MASASHI KISHIMOTO

CHARACTERS

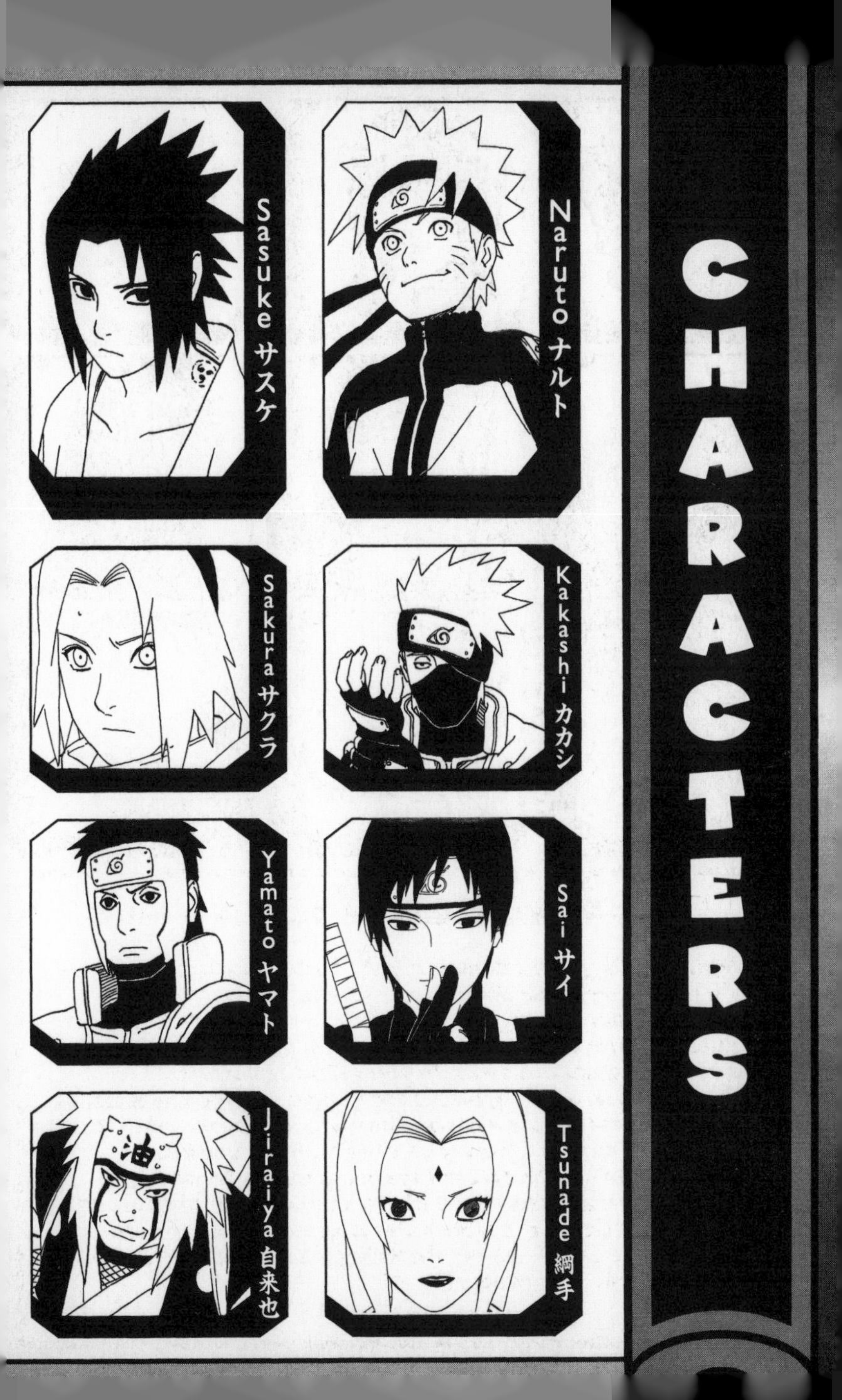
Naruto ナルト
Sasuke サスケ
Kakashi カカシ
Sakura サクラ
Sai サイ
Yamato ヤマト
Tsunade 綱手
Jiraiya 自来也

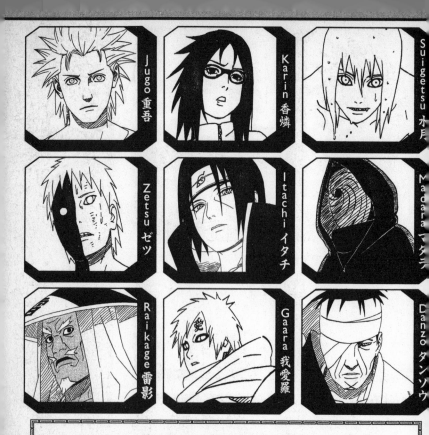

Jugo 重吾

Karin 香燐

Suigetsu 水月

Zetsu ゼツ

Itachi イタチ

Madara マダラ

Raikage 雷影

Gaara 我愛羅

Danzo ダンゾウ

——— THE STORY SO FAR... ———

Naruto, the biggest troublemaker at the Ninja Academy in the Village of Konohagakure, finally becomes a ninja along with his classmates Sasuke and Sakura. They grow and mature through countless trials and battles. However, Sasuke, unable to give up his quest for vengeance, leaves Konohagakure to seek Orochimaru and his power...

Two years pass. Naruto grows up and engages in fierce battles against the tailed beast-targeting Akatsuki. Elsewhere, after winning the heroic battle against Itachi and learning his older brother's true intentions, Sasuke allies with the Akatsuki and sets out to destroy Konoha!

Thanks to Naruto's actions, the crisis of the village's destruction comes to an end, but Danzo of the Black Ops is appointed Sixth Hokage in Tsunade's place. Amidst all this, the Raikage's summons goes out and a Gokage Summit is set to begin!

NARUTO

VOL. 49
THE GOKAGE SUMMIT COMMENCES

CONTENTS

Number 454: Enter the Gokage...!!

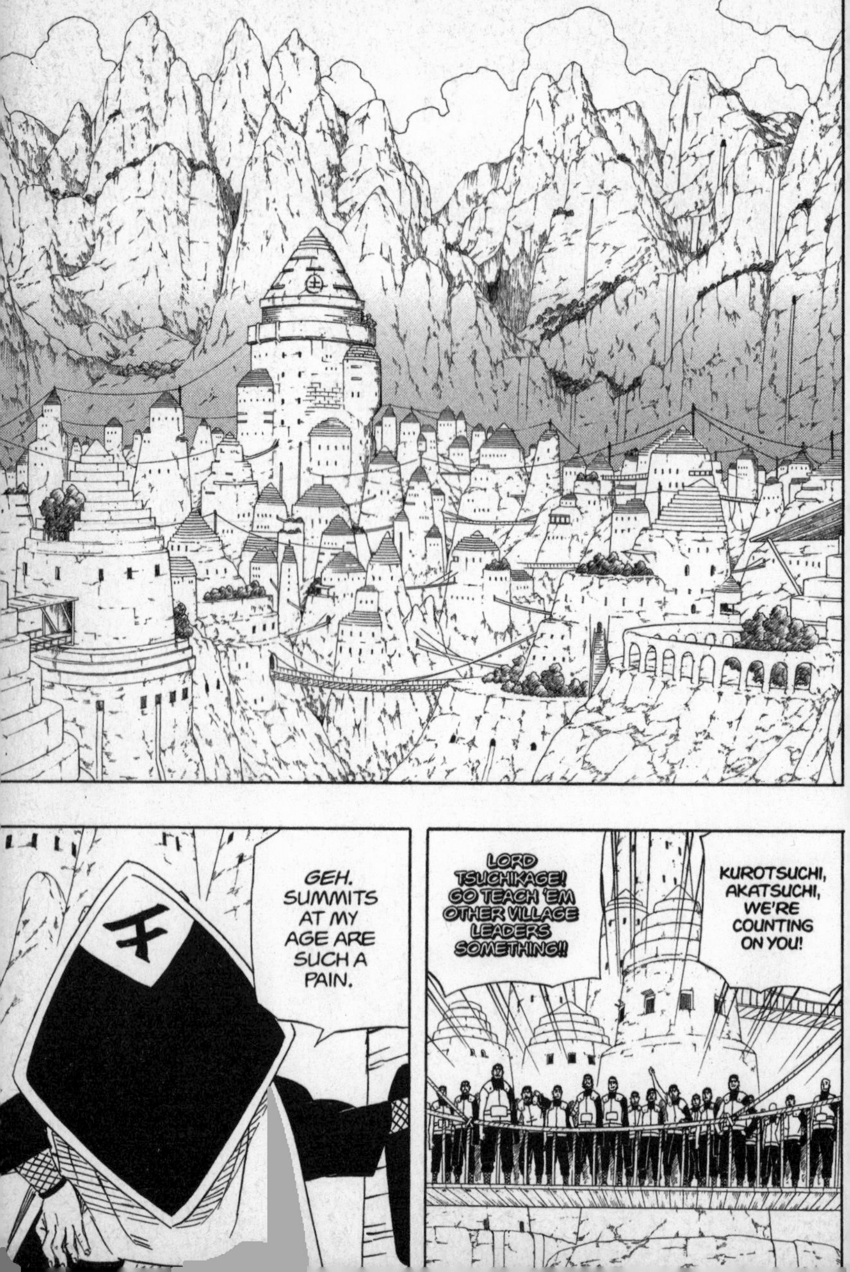
KUROTSUCHI, AKATSUCHI, WE'RE COUNTING ON YOU!
LORD TSUCHIKAGE! GO TEACH 'EM OTHER VILLAGE LEADERS SOMETHING!!
GEH. SUMMITS AT MY AGE ARE SUCH A PAIN.

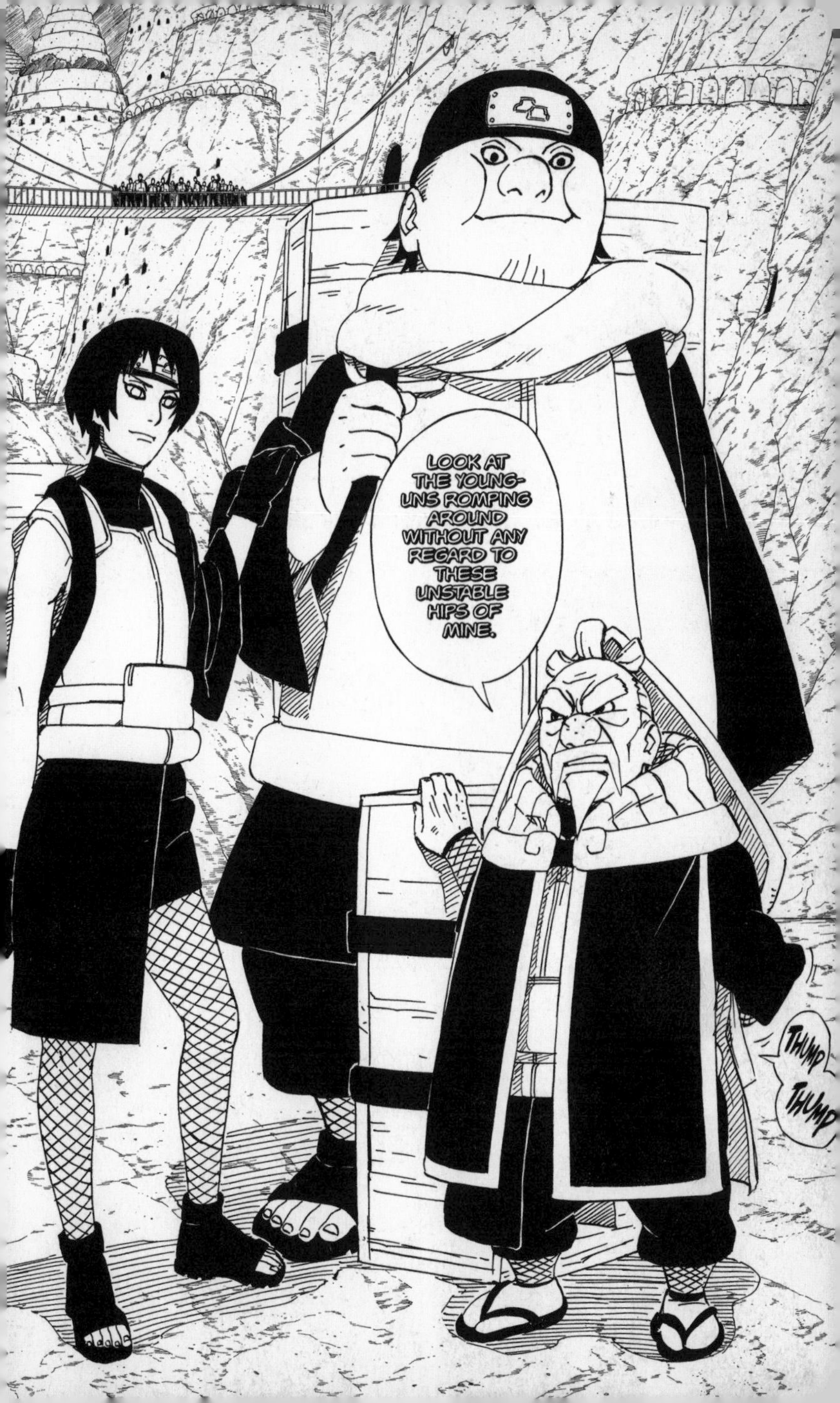
LOOK AT THE YOUNG-UNS ROMPING AROUND WITHOUT ANY REGARD TO THESE UNSTABLE HIPS OF MINE.
THUMP
THUMP

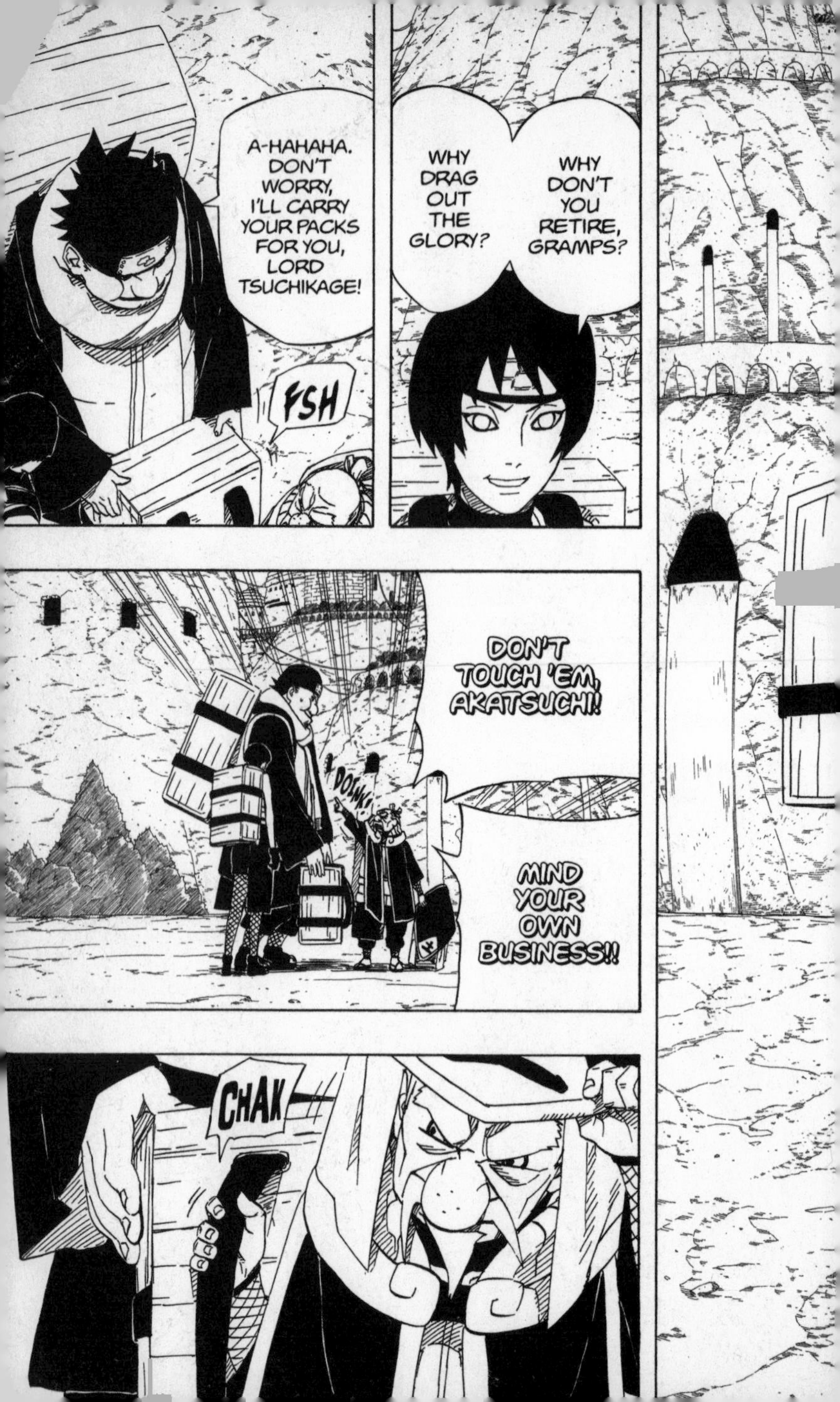
WHY DON'T YOU RETIRE, GRAMPS?
WHY DRAG OUT THE GLORY?
A-HAHAHA. DON'T WORRY, I'LL CARRY YOUR PACKS FOR YOU, LORD TSUCHIKAGE!
FSH
DON'T TOUCH 'EM, AKATSUCHI!!
MIND YOUR OWN BUSINESS!!
DOINK
CHAK

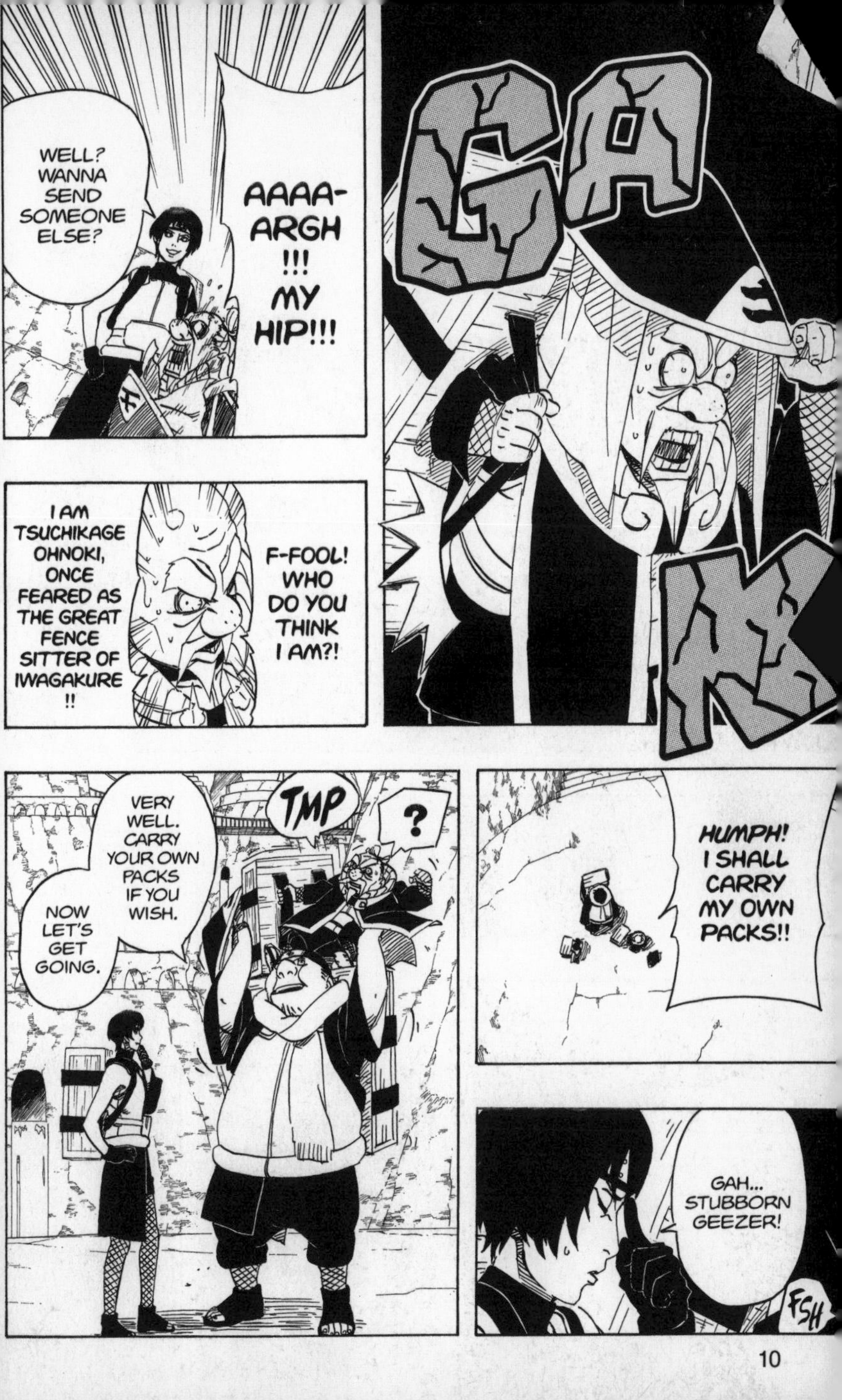
GAK
AAAA-ARGH!!! MY HIP!!!
WELL? WANNA SEND SOMEONE ELSE?
F-FOOL! WHO DO YOU THINK I AM?!
I AM TSUCHIKAGE OHNOKI, ONCE FEARED AS THE GREAT FENCE SITTER OF IWAGAKURE!!
HUMPH! I SHALL CARRY MY OWN PACKS!!
GAH... STUBBORN GEEZER!
FSH
?
TMP
VERY WELL. CARRY YOUR OWN PACKS IF YOU WISH.
NOW LET'S GET GOING.

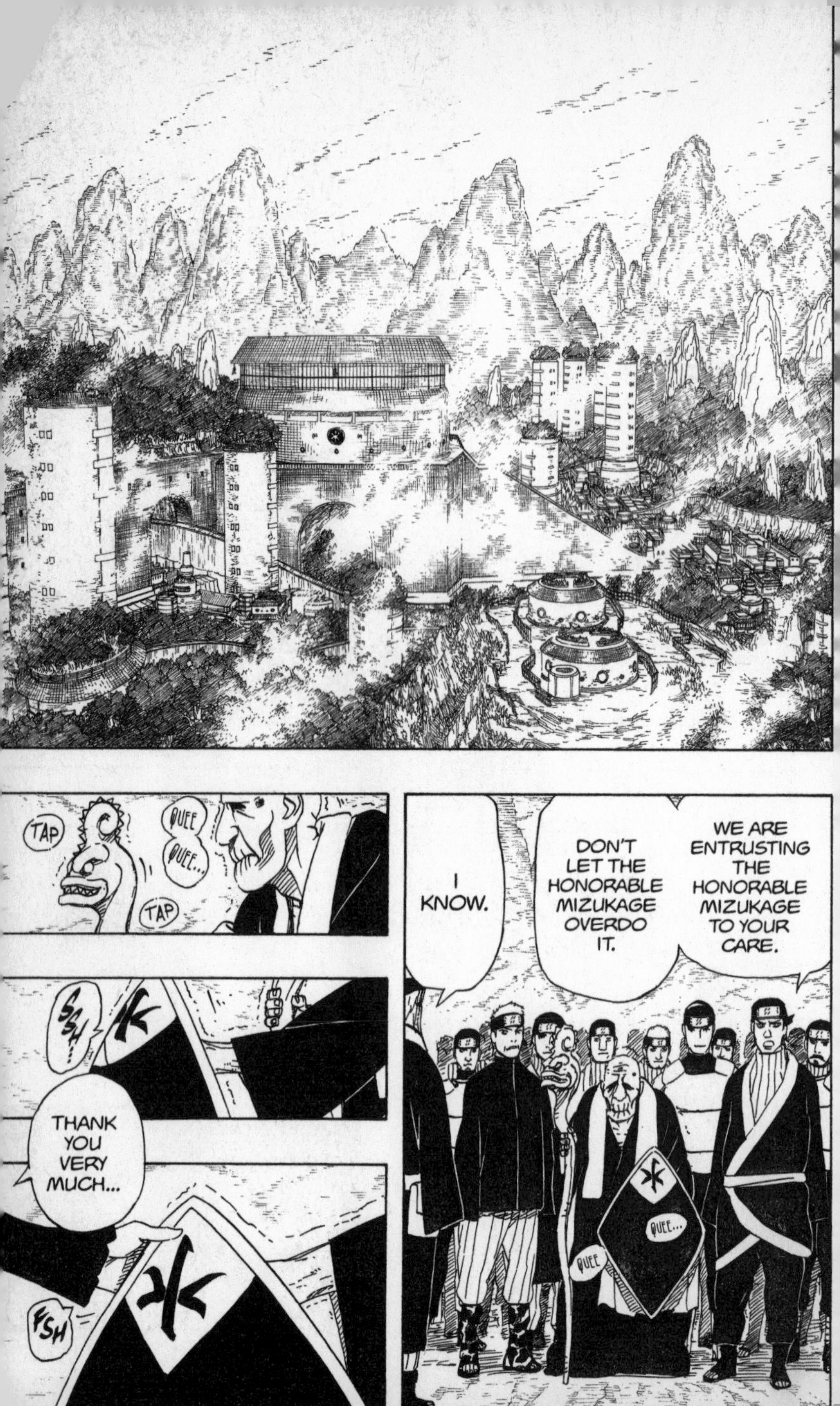
WE ARE ENTRUSTING THE HONORABLE MIZUKAGE TO YOUR CARE.
DON'T LET THE HONORABLE MIZUKAGE OVERDO IT.
I KNOW.
QUEE...
QUEE
TAP
QUEE
QUEE...
TAP
SSH
THANK YOU VERY MUCH...
FSH

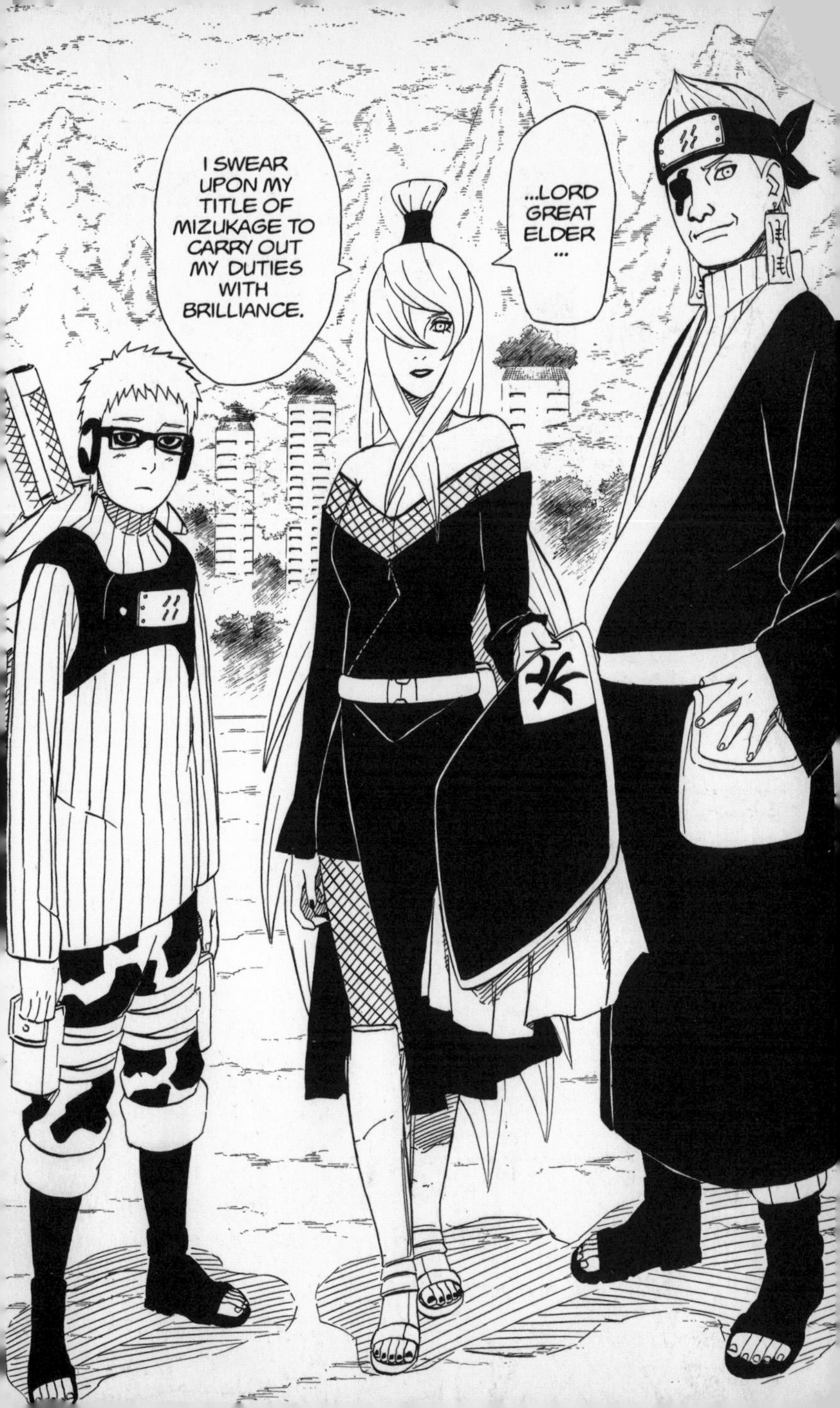
...LORD GREAT ELDER ...
I SWEAR UPON MY TITLE OF MIZUKAGE TO CARRY OUT MY DUTIES WITH BRILLIANCE.

READ THIS WAY

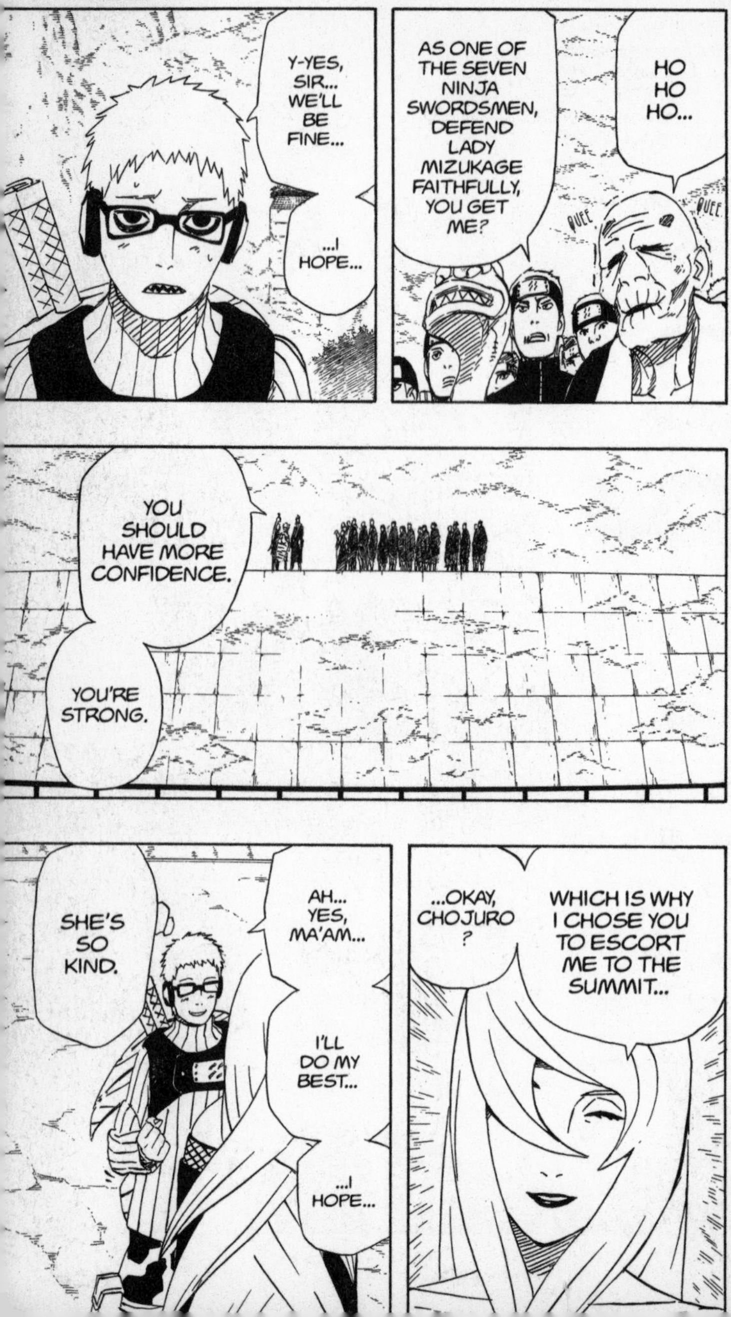
HO HO HO...
QUEE
QUEE
AS ONE OF THE SEVEN NINJA SWORDSMEN, DEFEND LADY MIZUKAGE FAITHFULLY, YOU GET ME?
Y-YES, SIR... WE'LL BE FINE...
...I HOPE...
YOU SHOULD HAVE MORE CONFIDENCE.
YOU'RE STRONG.
WHICH IS WHY I CHOSE YOU TO ESCORT ME TO THE SUMMIT...
...OKAY, CHOJURO?
AH... YES, MA'AM...
I'LL DO MY BEST...
...I HOPE...
SHE'S SO KIND.

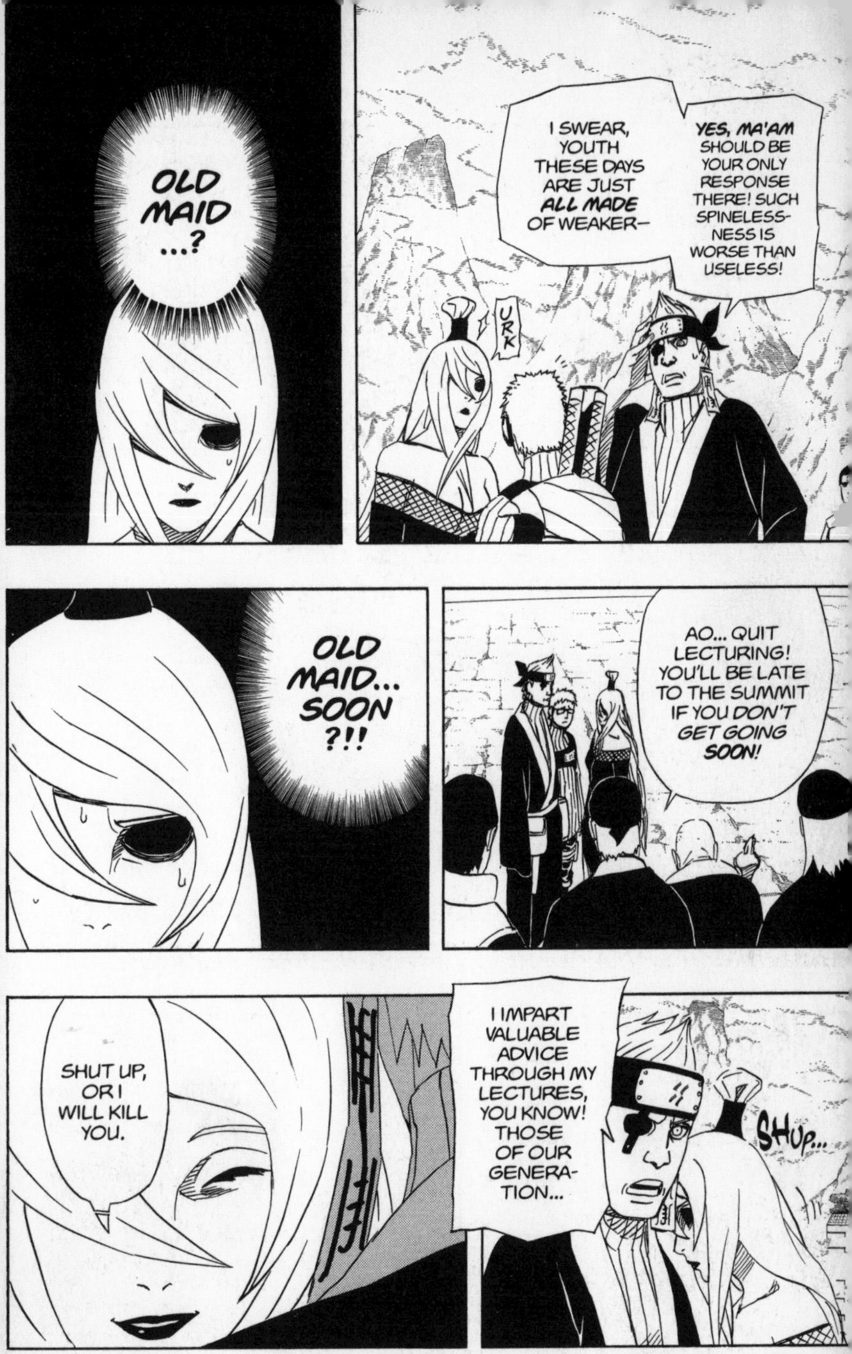
YES, MA'AM SHOULD BE YOUR ONLY RESPONSE THERE! SUCH SPINELESSNESS IS WORSE THAN USELESS!
I SWEAR, YOUTH THESE DAYS ARE JUST ALL MADE OF WEAKER—
URK
OLD MAID ...?
AO... QUIT LECTURING! YOU'LL BE LATE TO THE SUMMIT IF YOU DON'T GET GOING SOON!
OLD MAID... SOON ?!!
SHUP...
I IMPART VALUABLE ADVICE THROUGH MY LECTURES, YOU KNOW! THOSE OF OUR GENERATION...
SHUT UP, OR I WILL KILL YOU.

READ THIS WAY

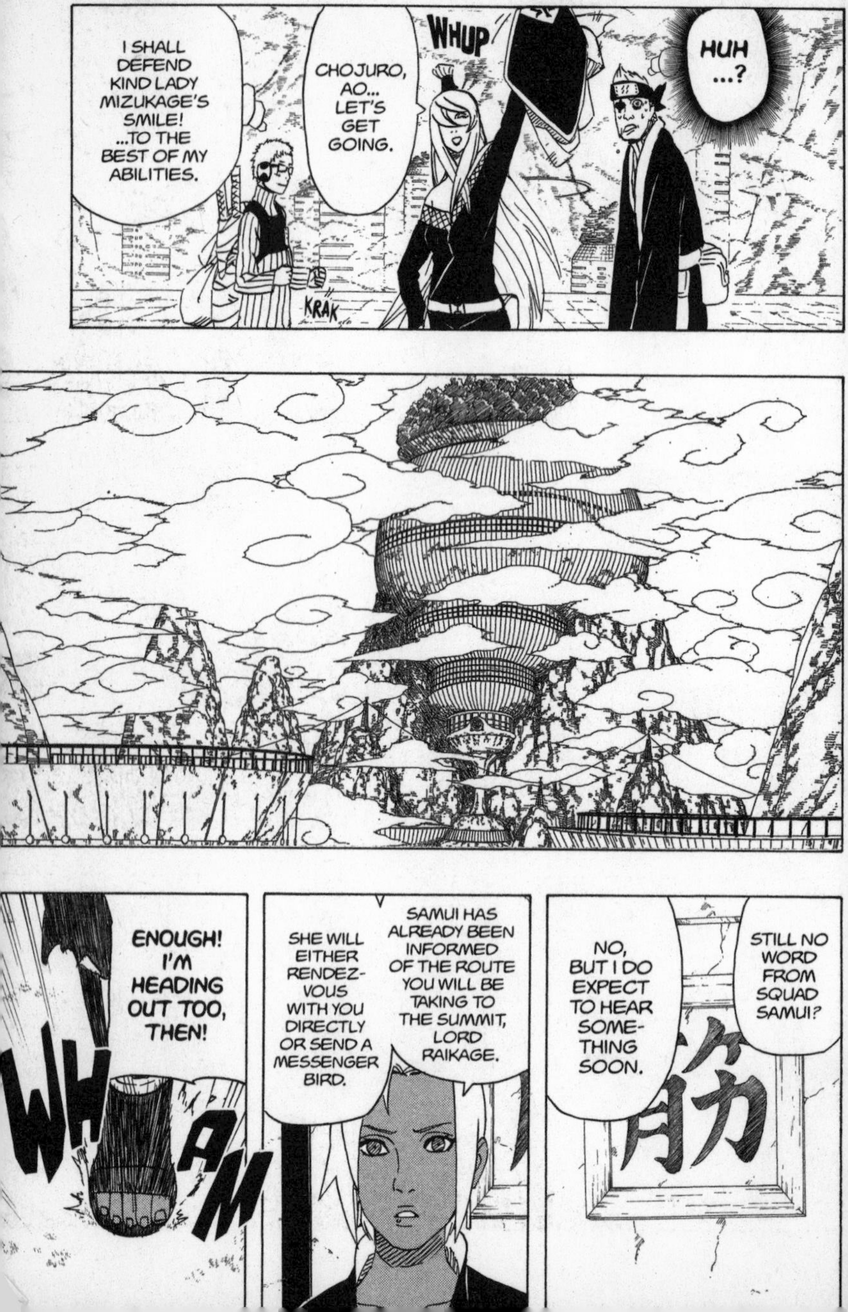
HUH ...?
WHUP
CHOJURO, AO... LET'S GET GOING.
I SHALL DEFEND KIND LADY MIZUKAGE'S SMILE! ...TO THE BEST OF MY ABILITIES.
KRAK
STILL NO WORD FROM SQUAD SAMUI?
NO, BUT I DO EXPECT TO HEAR SOME-THING SOON.
SAMUI HAS ALREADY BEEN INFORMED OF THE ROUTE YOU WILL BE TAKING TO THE SUMMIT, LORD RAIKAGE.
SHE WILL EITHER RENDEZ-VOUS WITH YOU DIRECTLY OR SEND A MESSENGER BIRD.
ENOUGH! I'M HEADING OUT TOO, THEN!
WHAM

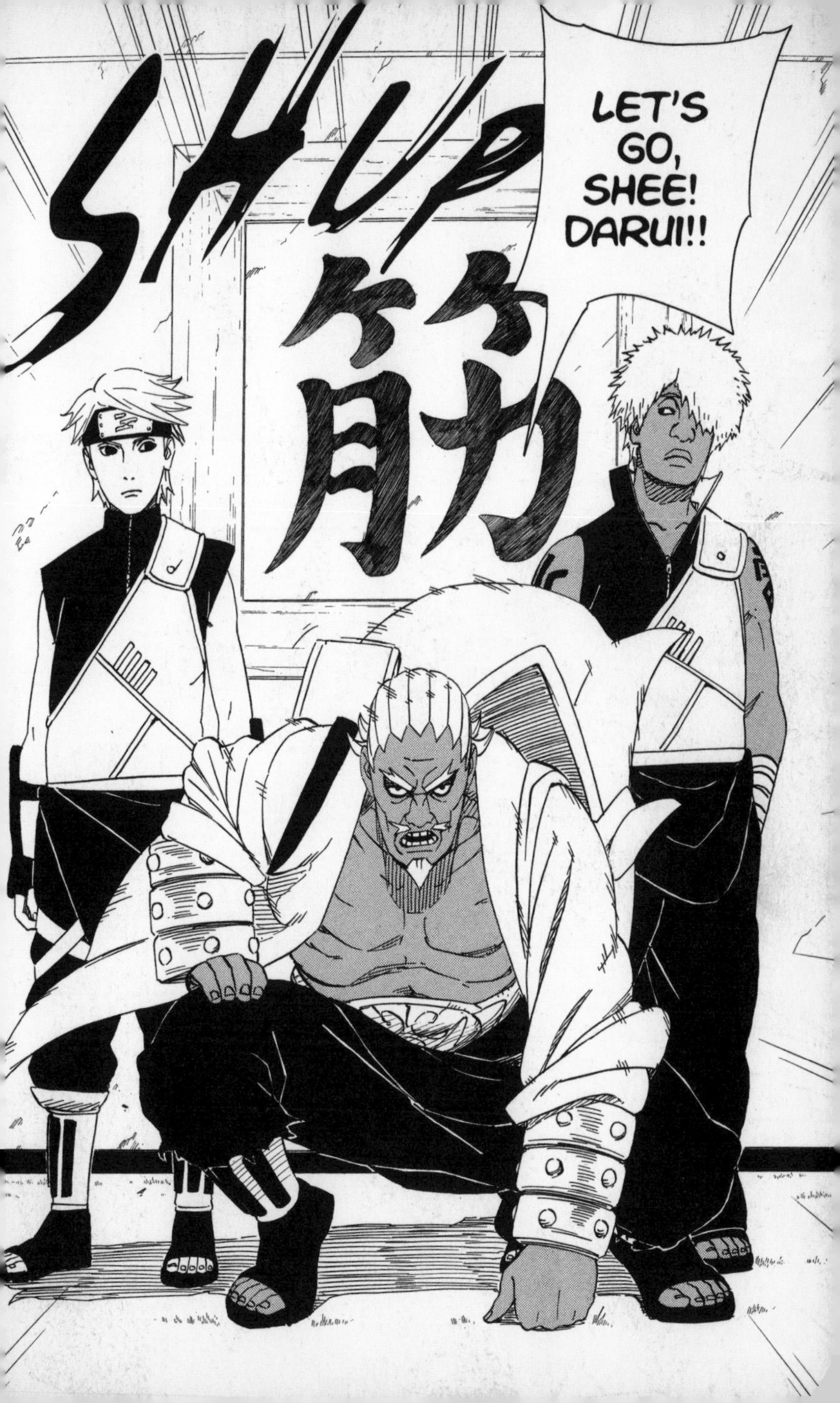
SHUP
LET'S GO, SHEE! DARUI!!

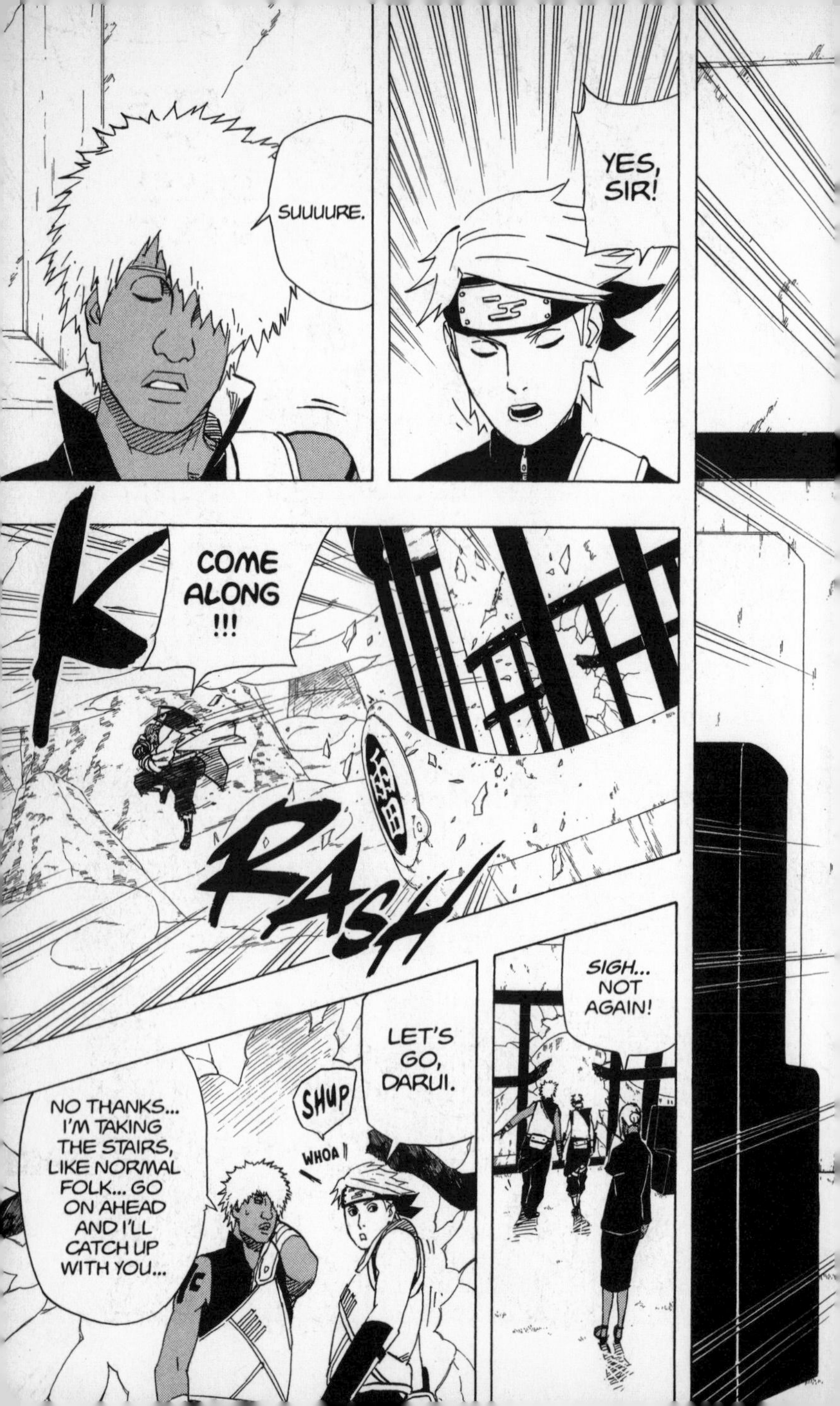
YES, SIR!
SUUUURE.
COME ALONG!!!
K
RASH
SIGH... NOT AGAIN!
LET'S GO, DARUI.
SHUP
WHOA!!
NO THANKS... I'M TAKING THE STAIRS, LIKE NORMAL FOLK... GO ON AHEAD AND I'LL CATCH UP WITH YOU...

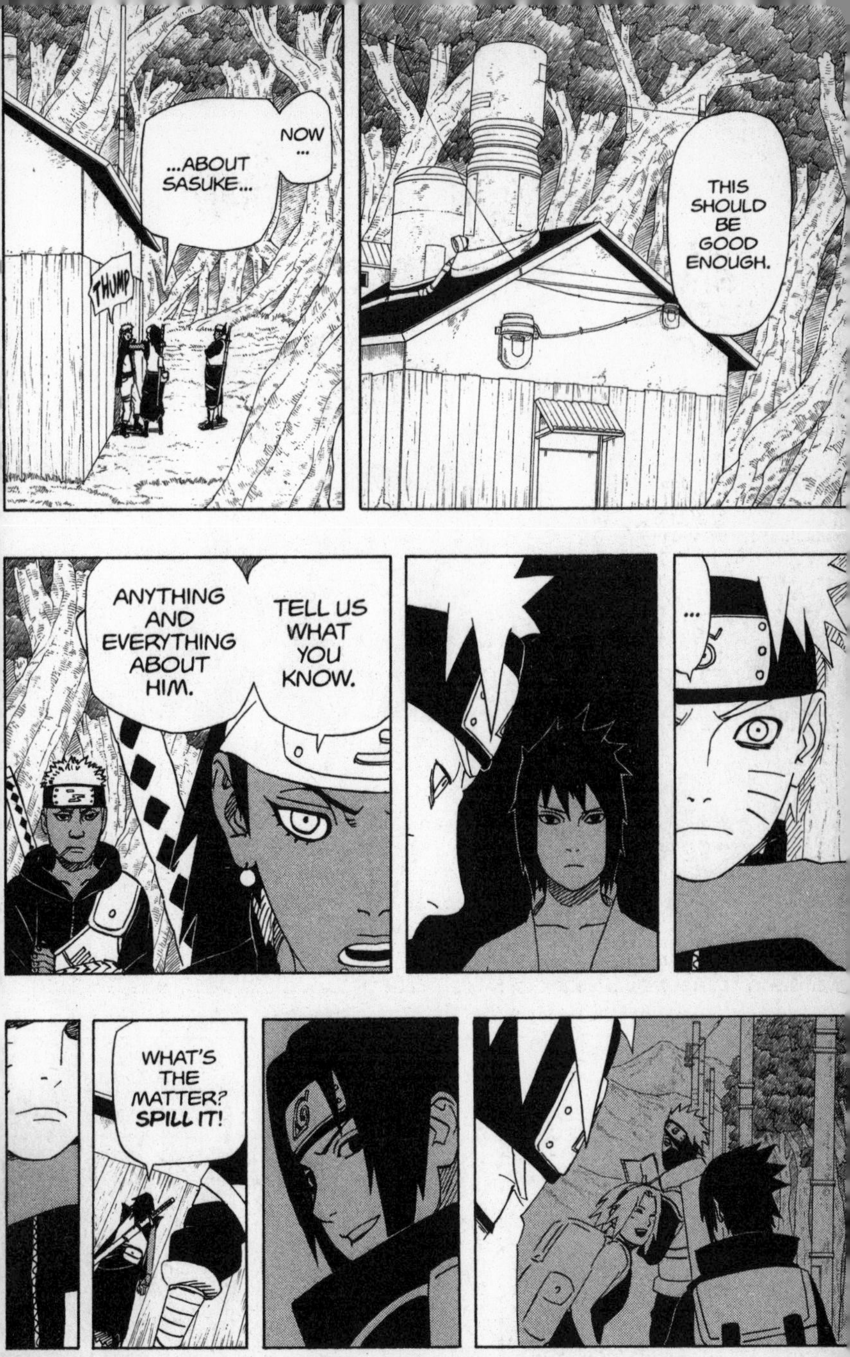
THIS SHOULD BE GOOD ENOUGH.
NOW...
...ABOUT SASUKE...
THUMP
...
TELL US WHAT YOU KNOW.
ANYTHING AND EVERYTHING ABOUT HIM.
WHAT'S THE MATTER? **SPILL IT!**

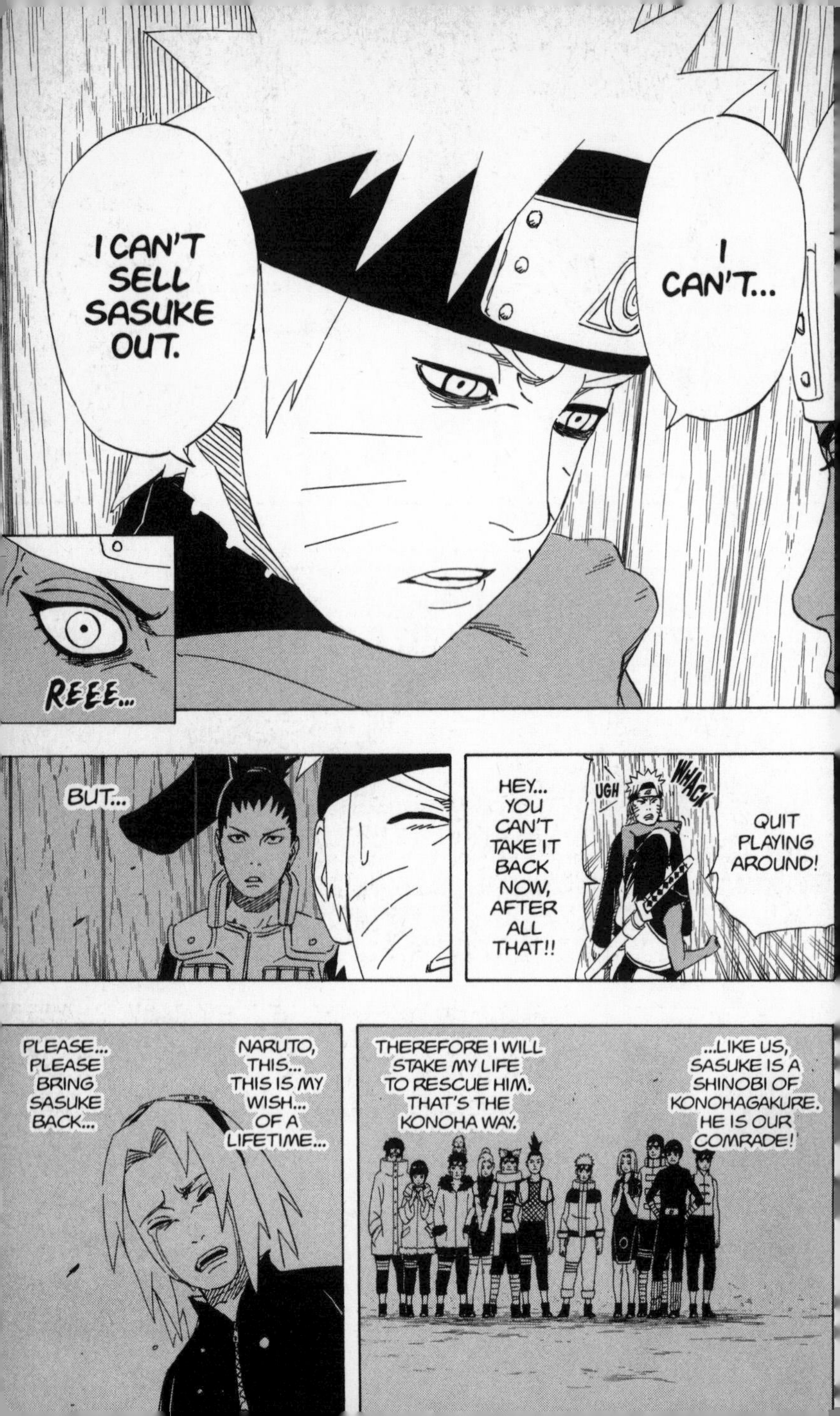
I CAN'T...
I CAN'T SELL SASUKE OUT.
REEE...
WHACK
QUIT PLAYING AROUND!
UGH
HEY... YOU CAN'T TAKE IT BACK NOW, AFTER ALL THAT!!
BUT...
...LIKE US, SASUKE IS A SHINOBI OF KONOHAGAKURE. HE IS OUR COMRADE!
THEREFORE I WILL STAKE MY LIFE TO RESCUE HIM. THAT'S THE KONOHA WAY.
NARUTO, THIS... THIS IS MY WISH... OF A LIFETIME...
PLEASE... PLEASE BRING SASUKE BACK...

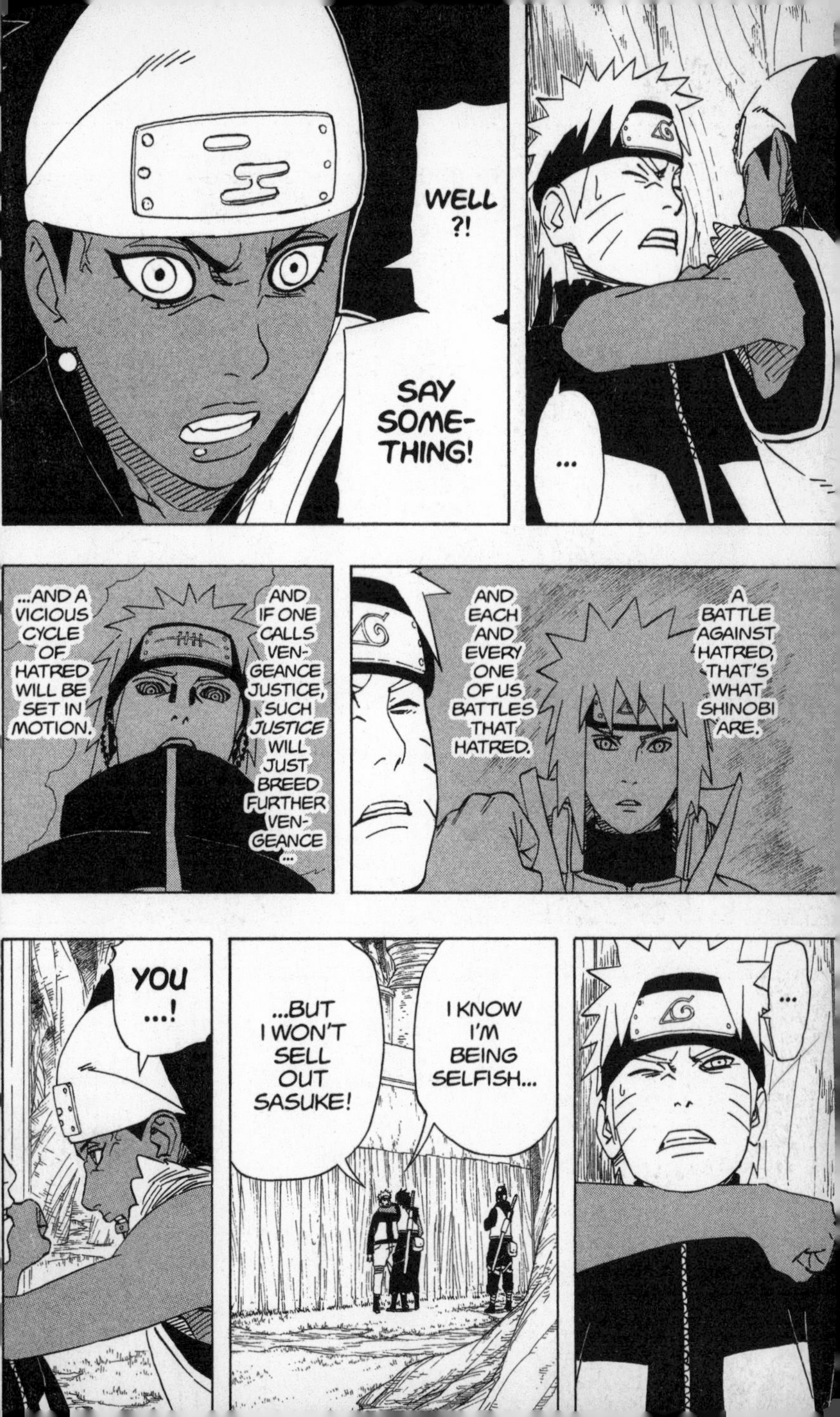

...
WELL ?!
SAY SOME-THING!
A BATTLE AGAINST HATRED, THAT'S WHAT SHINOBI ARE.
AND EACH AND EVERY ONE OF US BATTLES THAT HATRED.
AND IF ONE CALLS VEN-GEANCE JUSTICE, SUCH JUSTICE WILL JUST BREED FURTHER VEN-GEANCE ...
...AND A VICIOUS CYCLE OF HATRED WILL BE SET IN MOTION.
...
I KNOW I'M BEING SELFISH...
...BUT I WON'T SELL OUT SASUKE!
YOU ...!

READ THIS WAY

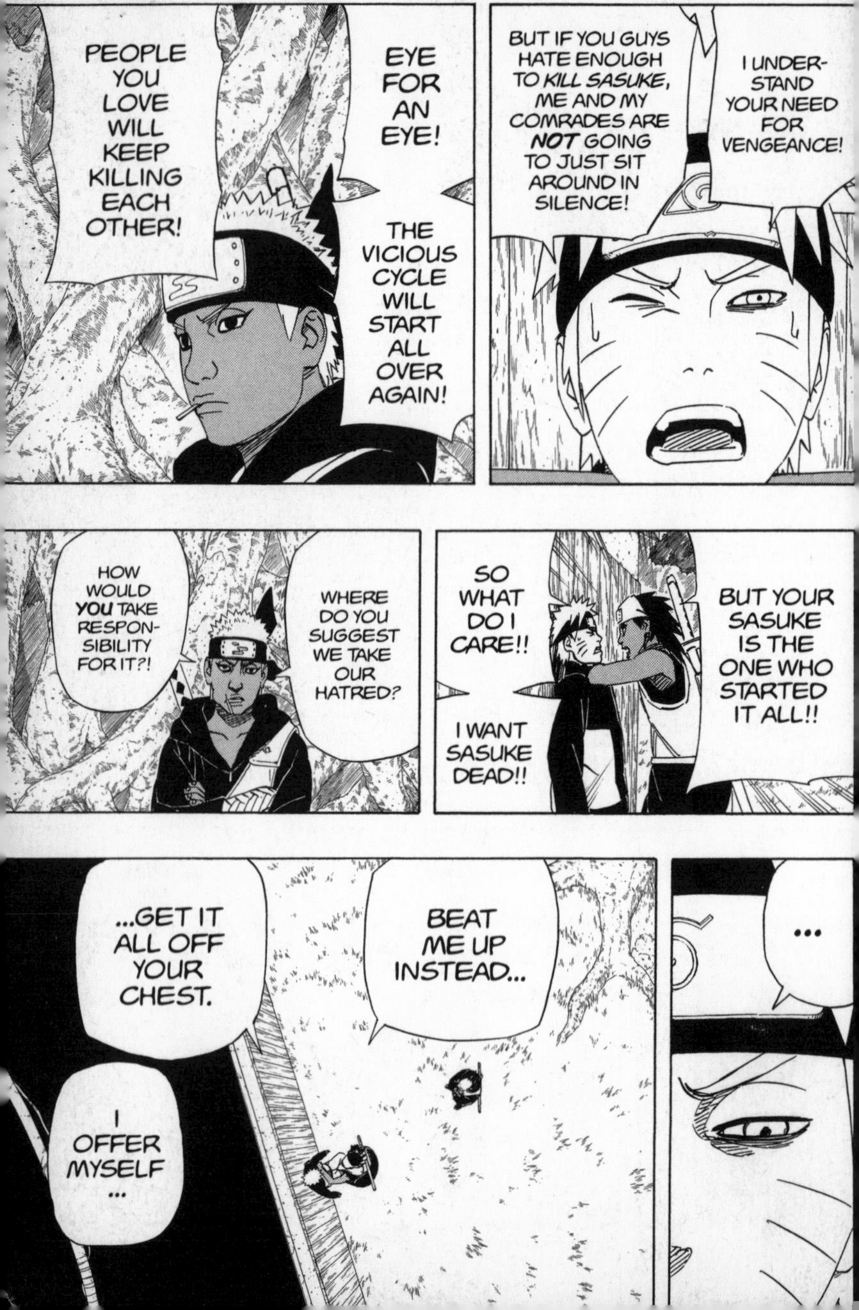
I UNDER-STAND YOUR NEED FOR VENGEANCE!
BUT IF YOU GUYS HATE ENOUGH TO KILL SASUKE, ME AND MY COMRADES ARE NOT GOING TO JUST SIT AROUND IN SILENCE!
EYE FOR AN EYE!
THE VICIOUS CYCLE WILL START ALL OVER AGAIN!
PEOPLE YOU LOVE WILL KEEP KILLING EACH OTHER!
BUT YOUR SASUKE IS THE ONE WHO STARTED IT ALL!!
SO WHAT DO I CARE!!
I WANT SASUKE DEAD!!
WHERE DO YOU SUGGEST WE TAKE OUR HATRED?
HOW WOULD YOU TAKE RESPON-SIBILITY FOR IT?!
...
BEAT ME UP INSTEAD...
...GET IT ALL OFF YOUR CHEST.
I OFFER MYSELF ...

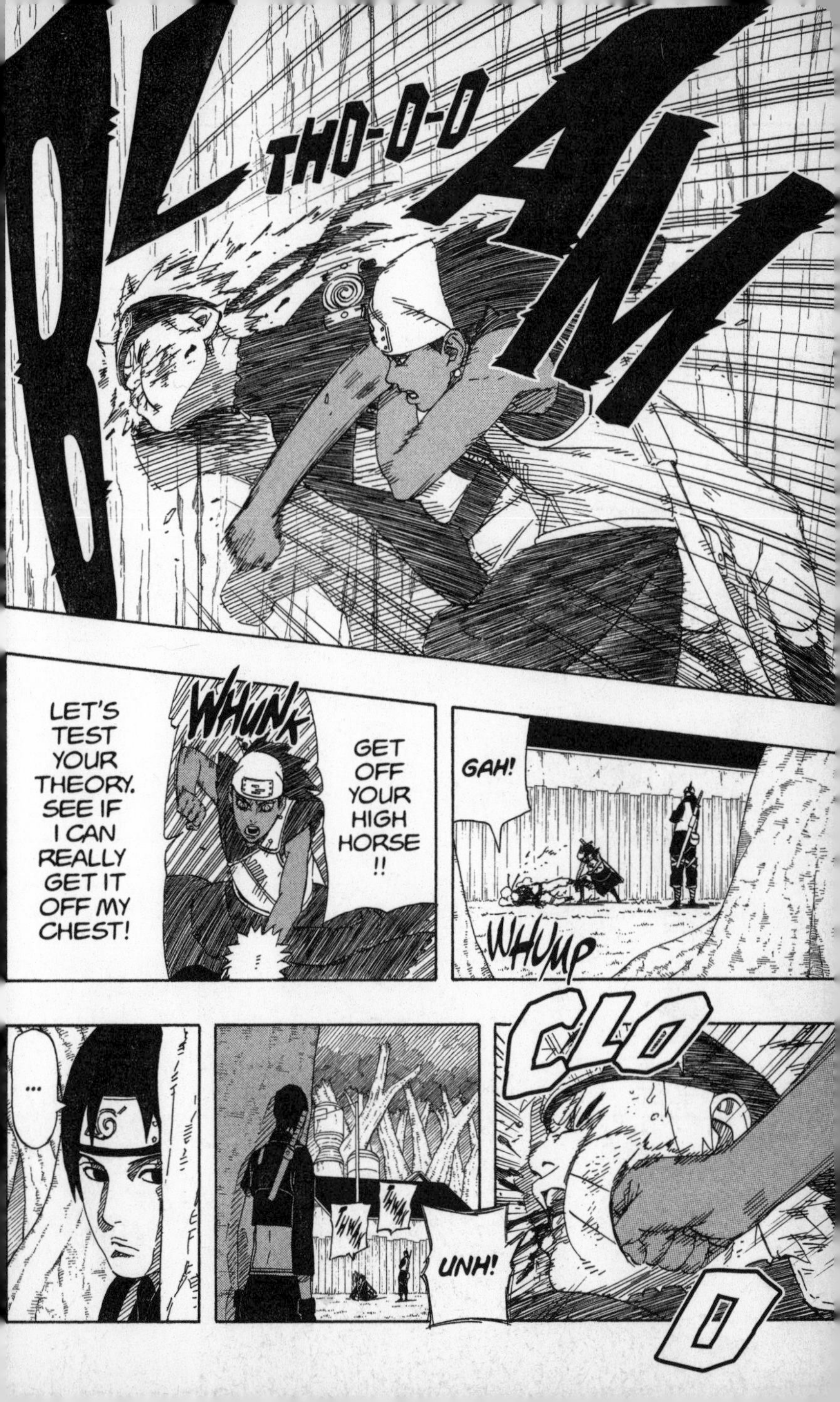
BLAM
THO-O-O
GAH!
WHUMP
WHUNK
GET OFF YOUR HIGH HORSE!!
LET'S TEST YOUR THEORY. SEE IF I CAN REALLY GET IT OFF MY CHEST!
CLOD
UNH!
THWAK
THWAK
THWAK
...

READ THIS WAY

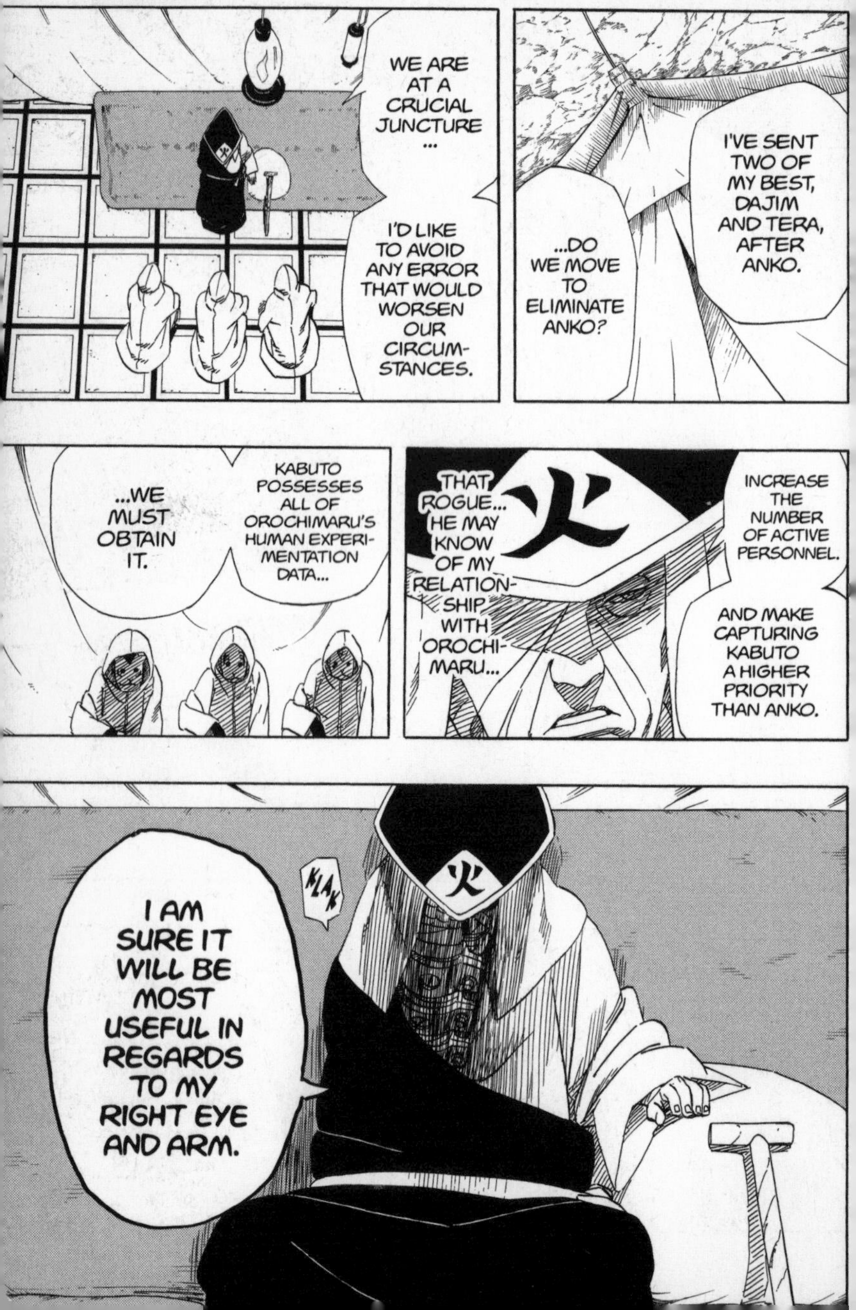
I'VE SENT TWO OF MY BEST, DAJIM AND TERA, AFTER ANKO.
...DO WE MOVE TO ELIMINATE ANKO?
WE ARE AT A CRUCIAL JUNCTURE ...
I'D LIKE TO AVOID ANY ERROR THAT WOULD WORSEN OUR CIRCUM-STANCES.
INCREASE THE NUMBER OF ACTIVE PERSONNEL.
AND MAKE CAPTURING KABUTO A HIGHER PRIORITY THAN ANKO.
THAT ROGUE... HE MAY KNOW OF MY RELATION-SHIP WITH OROCHI-MARU...
KABUTO POSSESSES ALL OF OROCHIMARU'S HUMAN EXPERI-MENTATION DATA...
...WE MUST OBTAIN IT.
KLAK
I AM SURE IT WILL BE MOST USEFUL IN REGARDS TO MY RIGHT EYE AND ARM.

Number 455: Links...!!

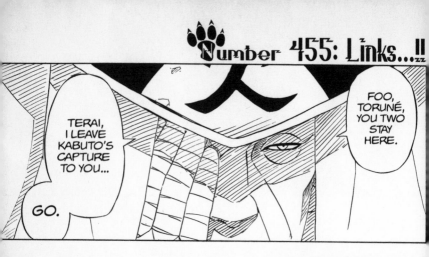

FOO, TORUNÉ, YOU TWO STAY HERE.
TERAI, I LEAVE KABUTO'S CAPTURE TO YOU...
GO.
YES, SIR!
SWSH
NOW... I MUST HEAD OUT TO THE GOKAGE SUMMIT.
EXCEPT IN SPECIAL CASES, WE ARE ONLY PERMITTED TO BRING A MAXIMUM OF TWO RETAINERS TO THE SUMMIT.
I HAVE DECIDED THAT THOSE TWO SHALL BE YOU, WHO ARE THE TWO BEST EVEN AMONG THE FOUNDATION.
FSH
MASKS ARE FORBIDDEN. REMOVE THEM.
KLAK
SSH
WAP

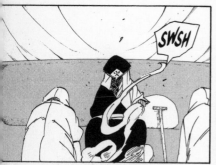

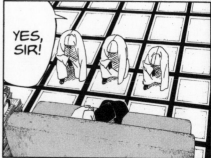

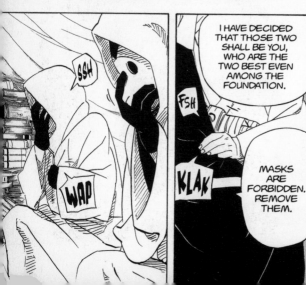

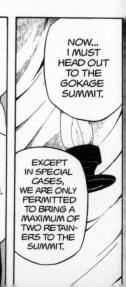

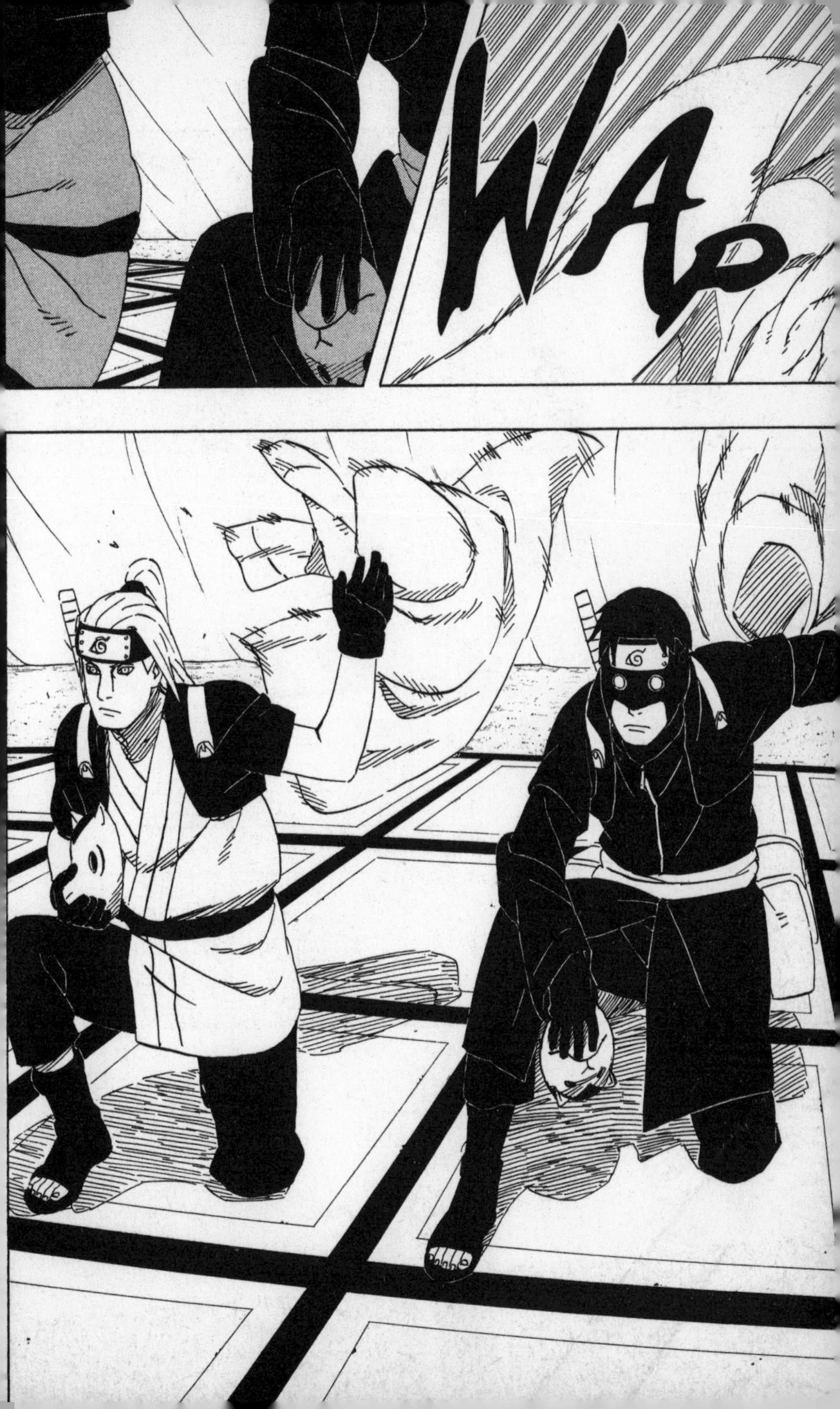
WAP

READ THIS WAY

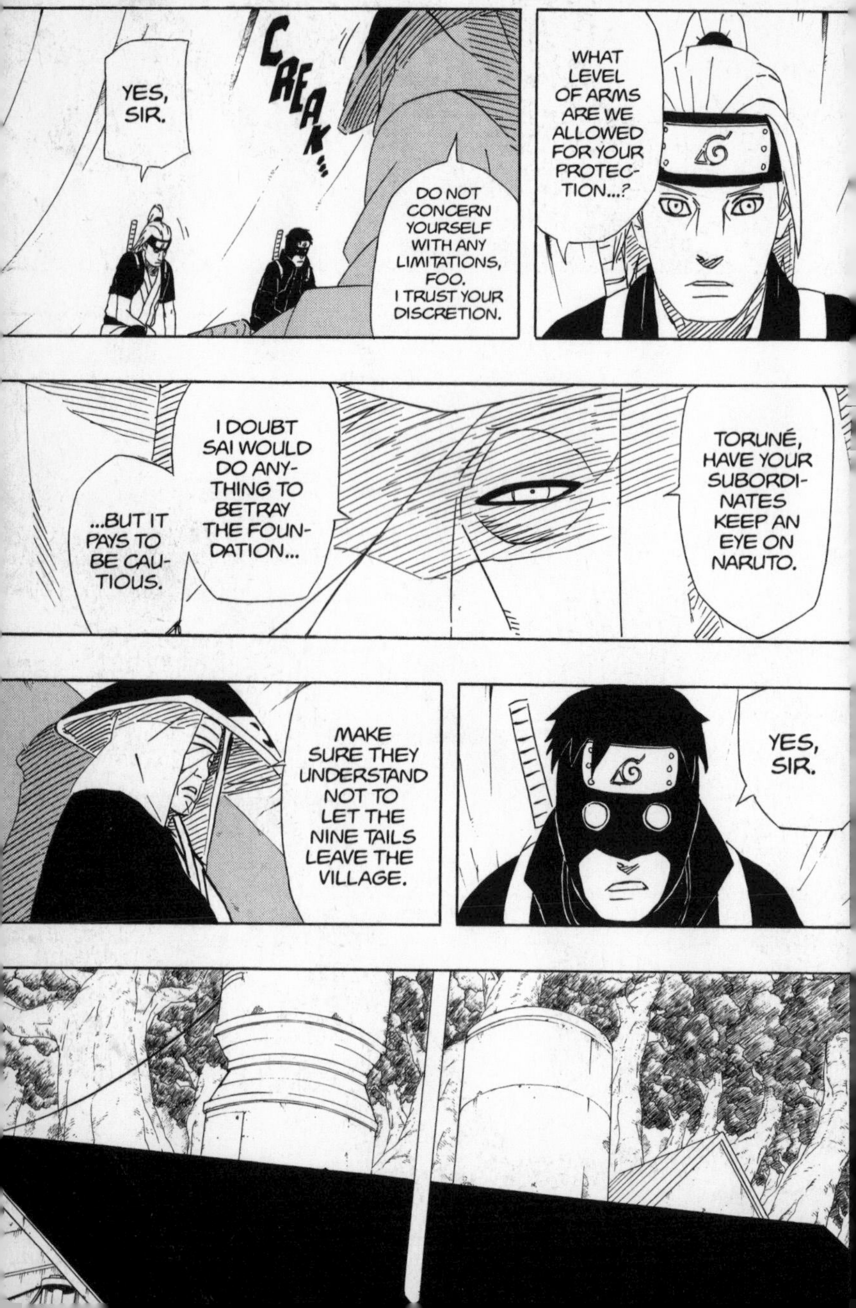
WHAT LEVEL OF ARMS ARE WE ALLOWED FOR YOUR PROTECTION...?
DO NOT CONCERN YOURSELF WITH ANY LIMITATIONS, FOO. I TRUST YOUR DISCRETION.
CREAK...
YES, SIR.
TORUNÉ, HAVE YOUR SUBORDINATES KEEP AN EYE ON NARUTO.
I DOUBT SAI WOULD DO ANYTHING TO BETRAY THE FOUNDATION...
...BUT IT PAYS TO BE CAUTIOUS.
YES, SIR.
MAKE SURE THEY UNDERSTAND NOT TO LET THE NINE TAILS LEAVE THE VILLAGE.

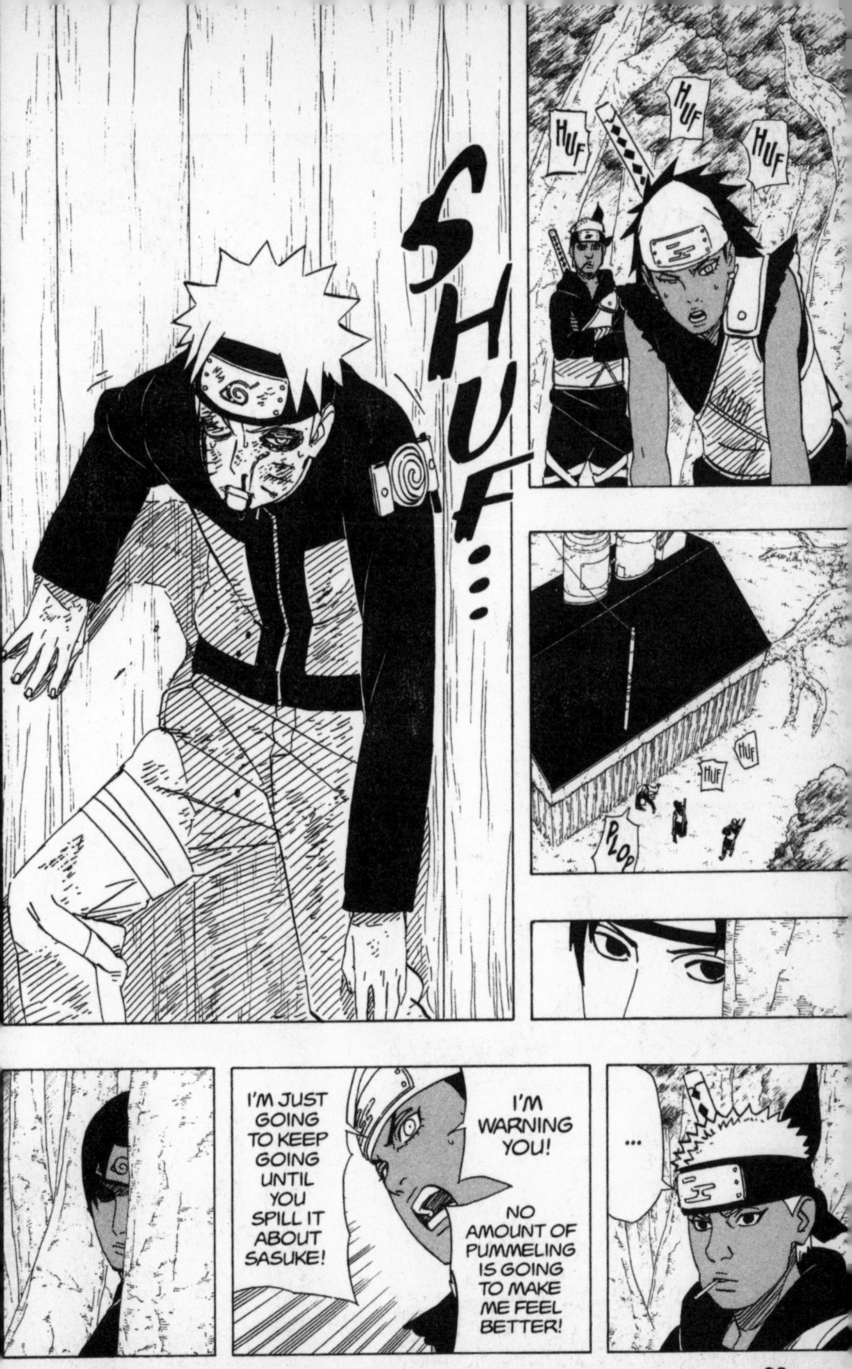
HUF
HUF
HUF
HUF
HUF
PLOP
SHUF...
...
I'M WARNING YOU!
NO AMOUNT OF PUMMELING IS GOING TO MAKE ME FEEL BETTER!
I'M JUST GOING TO KEEP GOING UNTIL YOU SPILL IT ABOUT SASUKE!

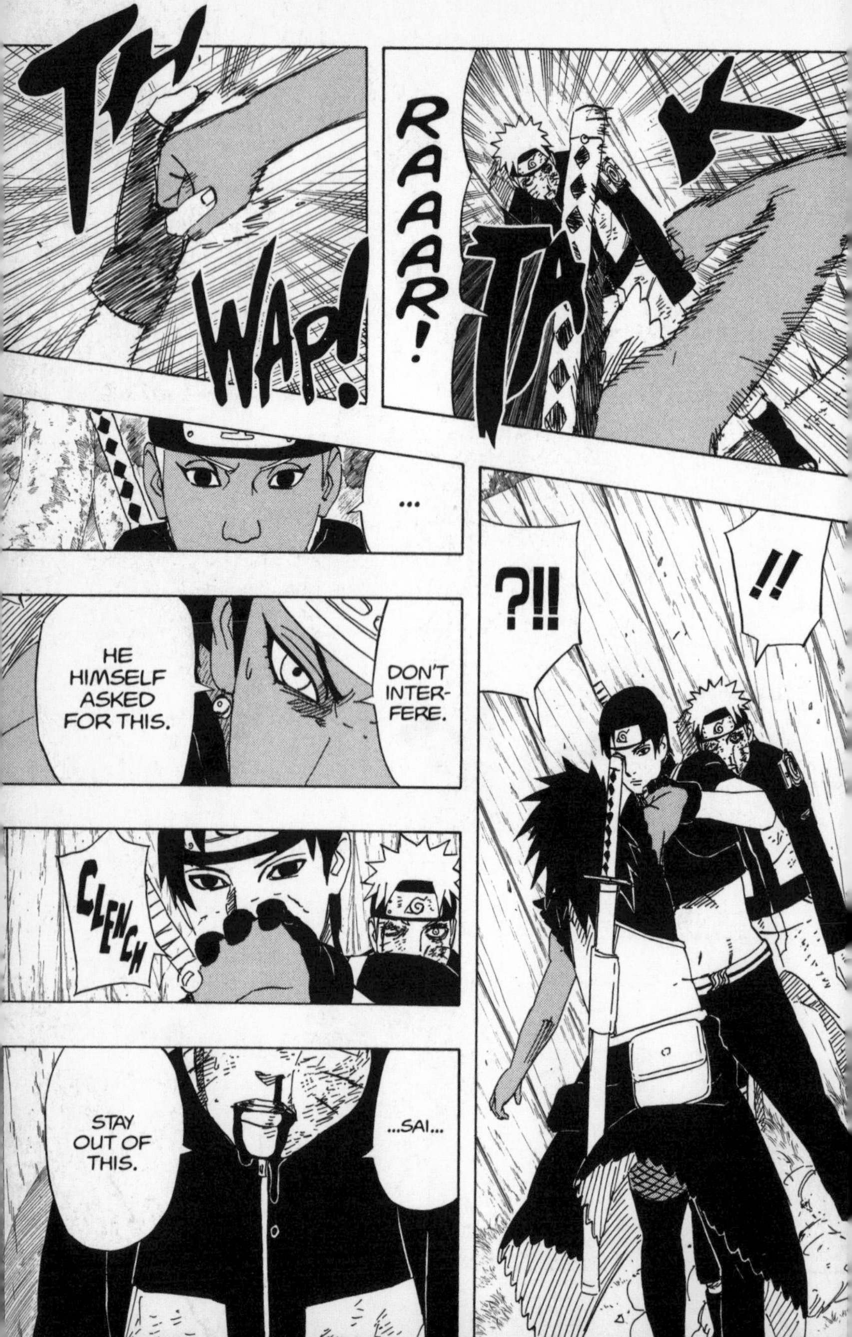
TAK
RAAAAR!
THWAP!
!!
?!!
...
DON'T INTER-FERE.
HE HIMSELF ASKED FOR THIS.
CLENCH
...SAI...
STAY OUT OF THIS.

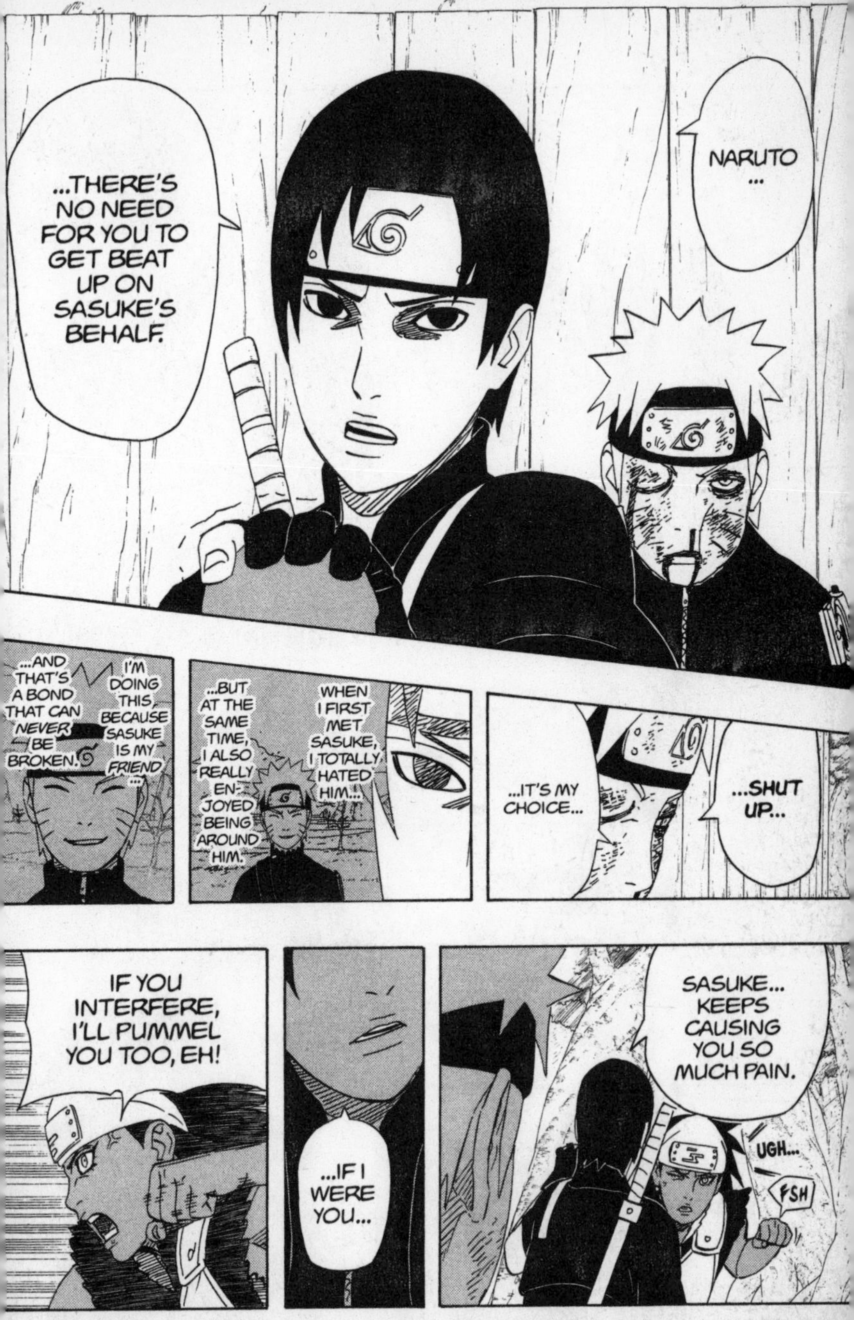

NARUTO...
...THERE'S NO NEED FOR YOU TO GET BEAT UP ON SASUKE'S BEHALF.
...SHUT UP...
...IT'S MY CHOICE...
WHEN I FIRST MET SASUKE, I TOTALLY HATED HIM...
...BUT AT THE SAME TIME, I ALSO REALLY ENJOYED BEING AROUND HIM.
I'M DOING THIS, BECAUSE SASUKE IS MY FRIEND...
...AND THAT'S A BOND THAT CAN NEVER BE BROKEN.
SASUKE... KEEPS CAUSING YOU SO MUCH PAIN.
UGH...
FSH
...IF I WERE YOU...
IF YOU INTERFERE, I'LL PUMMEL YOU TOO, EH!

READ THIS WAY

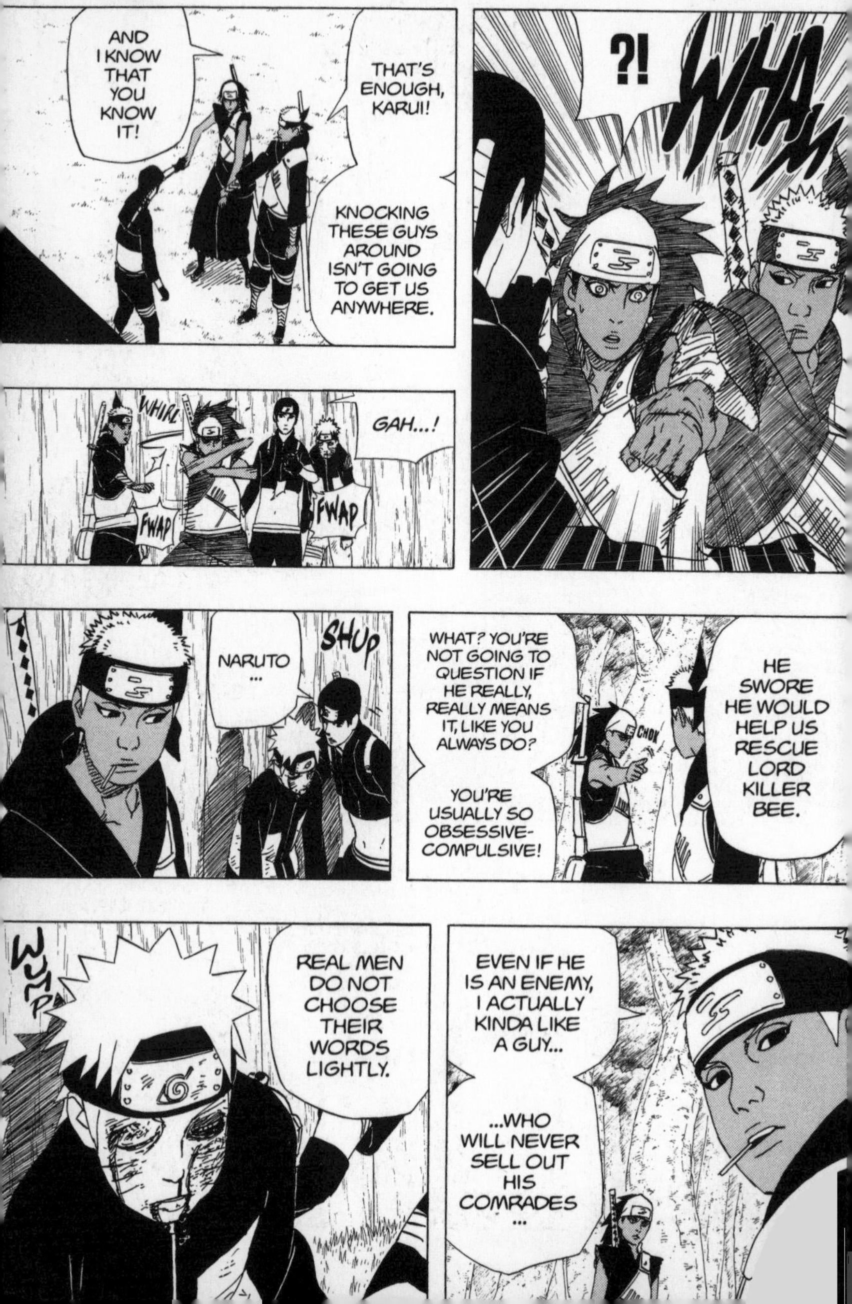
?!
WHA
THAT'S ENOUGH, KARUI!
KNOCKING THESE GUYS AROUND ISN'T GOING TO GET US ANYWHERE.
AND I KNOW THAT YOU KNOW IT!
GAH...!
WHIRL
FWAP
FWAP
HE SWORE HE WOULD HELP US RESCUE LORD KILLER BEE.
WHAT? YOU'RE NOT GOING TO QUESTION IF HE REALLY, REALLY MEANS IT, LIKE YOU ALWAYS DO?
YOU'RE USUALLY SO OBSESSIVE-COMPULSIVE!
CHOK
SHUP
NARUTO ...
EVEN IF HE IS AN ENEMY, I ACTUALLY KINDA LIKE A GUY...
...WHO WILL NEVER SELL OUT HIS COMRADES ...
REAL MEN DO NOT CHOOSE THEIR WORDS LIGHTLY.
WUMP

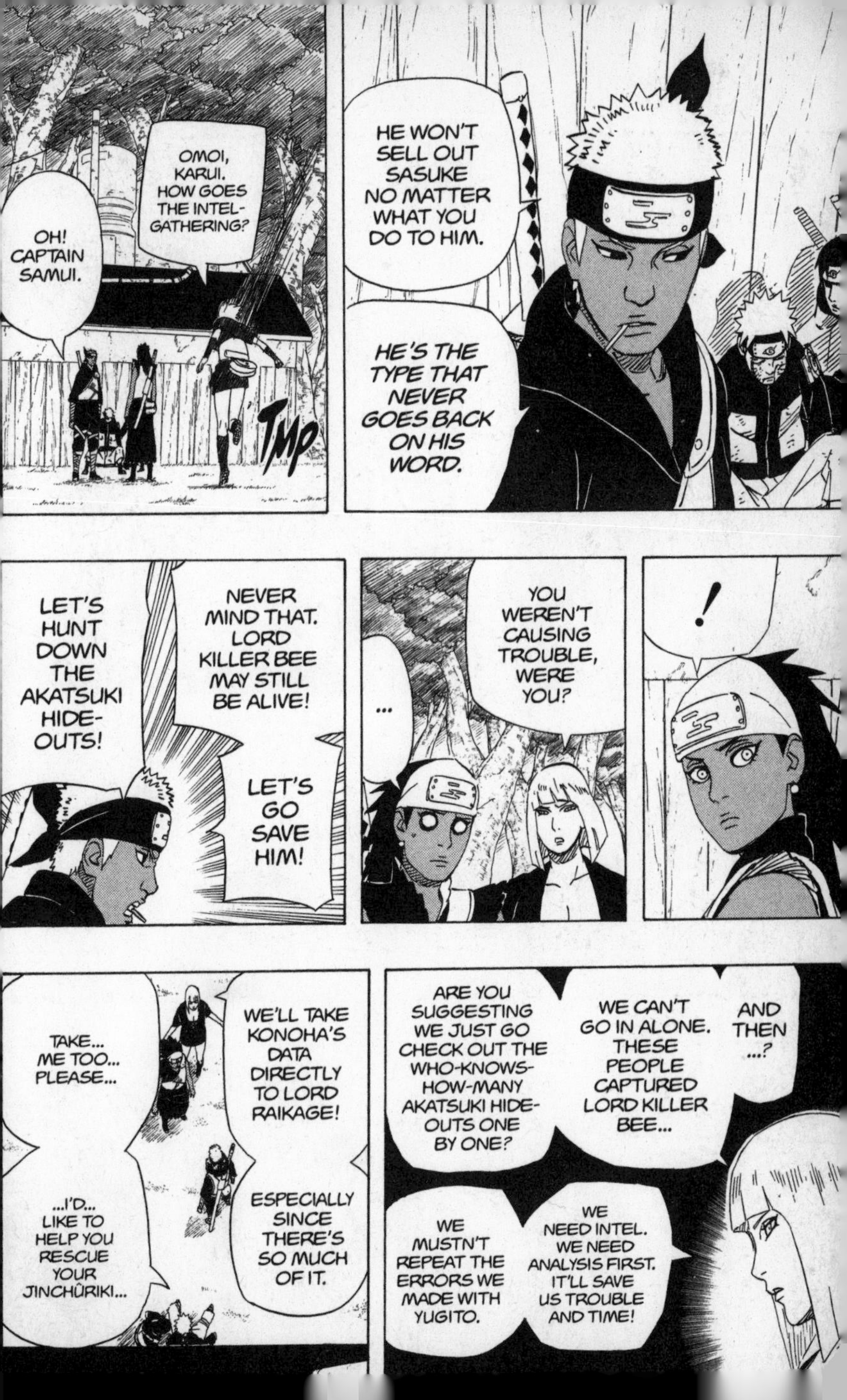
HE WON'T SELL OUT SASUKE NO MATTER WHAT YOU DO TO HIM.
HE'S THE TYPE THAT NEVER GOES BACK ON HIS WORD.
OMOI, KARUI. HOW GOES THE INTEL-GATHERING?
OH! CAPTAIN SAMUI.
TMP
!
YOU WEREN'T CAUSING TROUBLE, WERE YOU?
...
NEVER MIND THAT. LORD KILLER BEE MAY STILL BE ALIVE!
LET'S HUNT DOWN THE AKATSUKI HIDE-OUTS!
LET'S GO SAVE HIM!
AND THEN ...?
WE CAN'T GO IN ALONE. THESE PEOPLE CAPTURED LORD KILLER BEE...
ARE YOU SUGGESTING WE JUST GO CHECK OUT THE WHO-KNOWS-HOW-MANY AKATSUKI HIDE-OUTS ONE BY ONE?
WE NEED INTEL. WE NEED ANALYSIS FIRST. IT'LL SAVE US TROUBLE AND TIME!
WE MUSTN'T REPEAT THE ERRORS WE MADE WITH YUGITO.
WE'LL TAKE KONOHA'S DATA DIRECTLY TO LORD RAIKAGE!
TAKE... ME TOO... PLEASE...
ESPECIALLY SINCE THERE'S SO MUCH OF IT.
...I'D... LIKE TO HELP YOU RESCUE YOUR JINCHŪRIKI...

READ THIS WAY

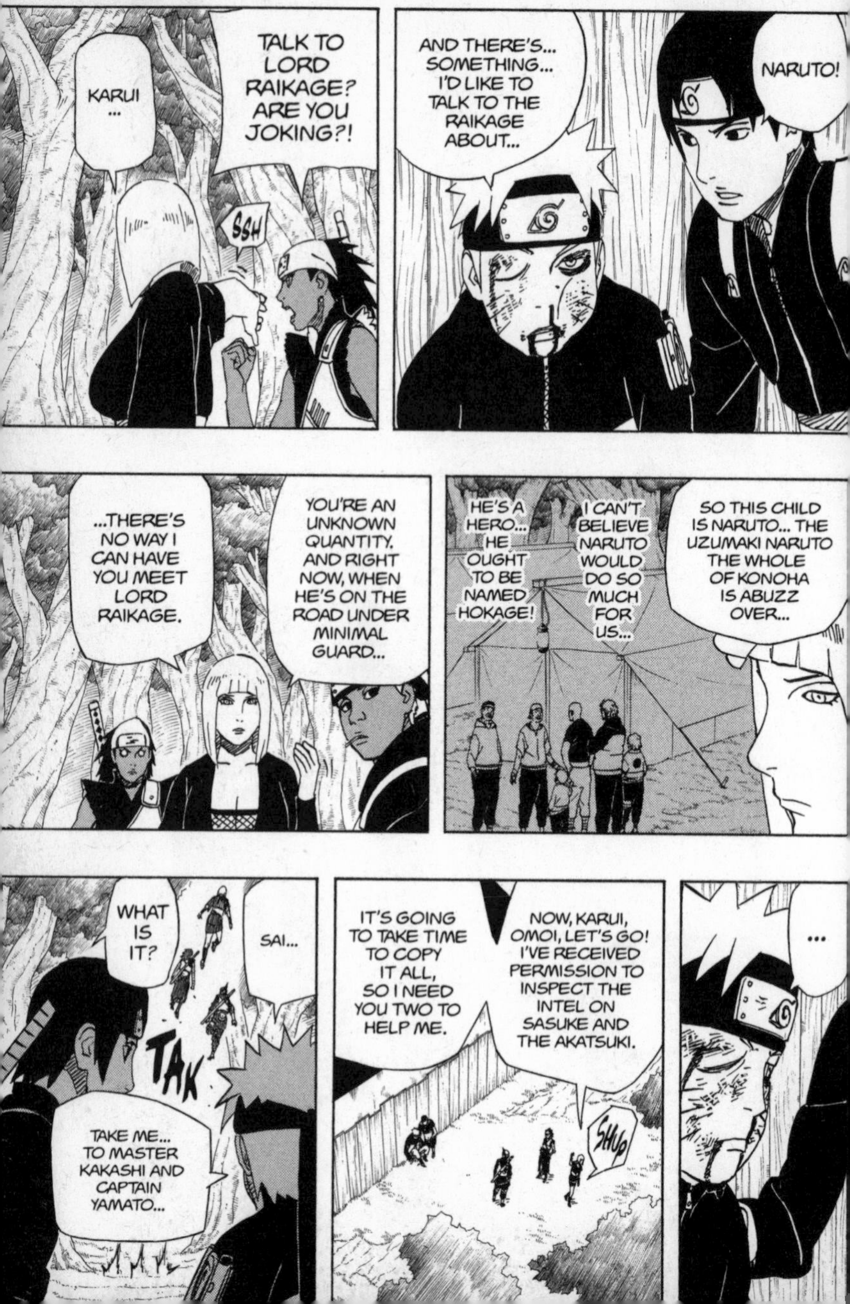
NARUTO!
AND THERE'S... SOMETHING... I'D LIKE TO TALK TO THE RAIKAGE ABOUT...
TALK TO LORD RAIKAGE? ARE YOU JOKING?!
KARUI ...
SSH
SO THIS CHILD IS NARUTO... THE UZUMAKI NARUTO THE WHOLE OF KONOHA IS ABUZZ OVER...
I CAN'T BELIEVE NARUTO WOULD DO SO MUCH FOR US...
HE'S A HERO... HE OUGHT TO BE NAMED HOKAGE!
YOU'RE AN UNKNOWN QUANTITY. AND RIGHT NOW, WHEN HE'S ON THE ROAD UNDER MINIMAL GUARD...
...THERE'S NO WAY I CAN HAVE YOU MEET LORD RAIKAGE.
...
NOW, KARUI, OMOI, LET'S GO! I'VE RECEIVED PERMISSION TO INSPECT THE INTEL ON SASUKE AND THE AKATSUKI.
IT'S GOING TO TAKE TIME TO COPY IT ALL, SO I NEED YOU TWO TO HELP ME.
SHUP
SAI...
WHAT IS IT?
TAK
TAKE ME... TO MASTER KAKASHI AND CAPTAIN YAMATO...

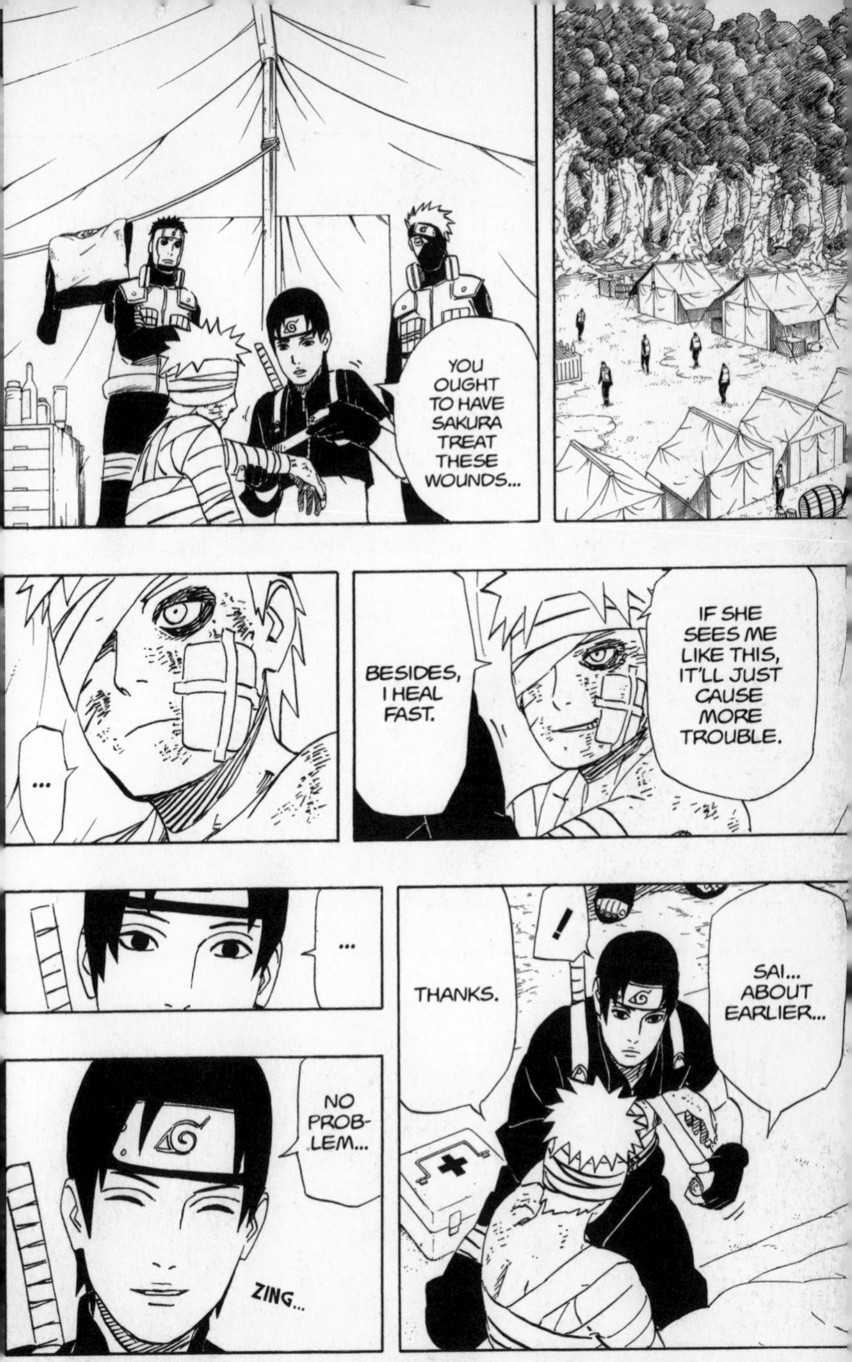
YOU OUGHT TO HAVE SAKURA TREAT THESE WOUNDS...
IF SHE SEES ME LIKE THIS, IT'LL JUST CAUSE MORE TROUBLE.
BESIDES, I HEAL FAST.
...
SAI... ABOUT EARLIER...
!
THANKS.
...
NO PROB-LEM...
ZING...

READ THIS WAY

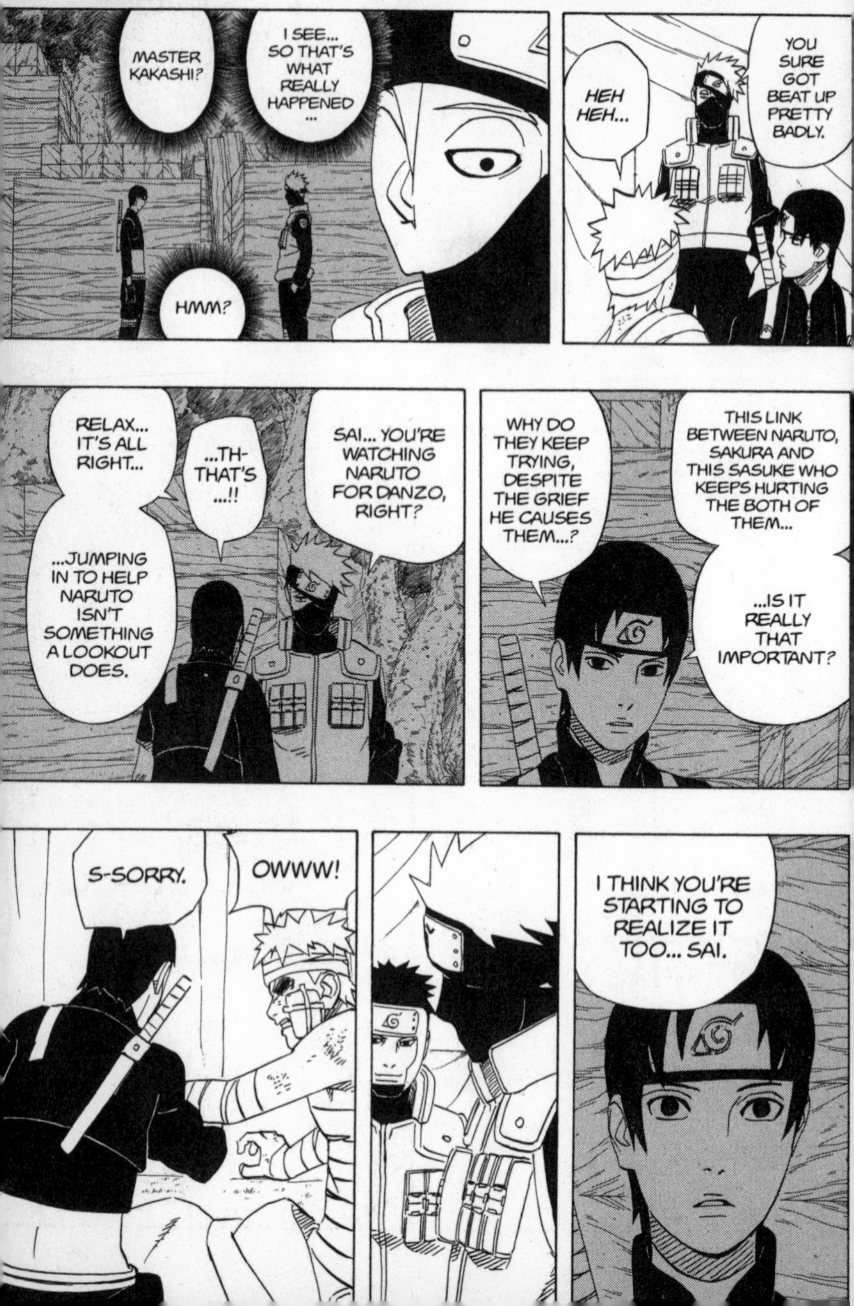
YOU SURE GOT BEAT UP PRETTY BADLY.
HEH HEH...
I SEE... SO THAT'S WHAT REALLY HAPPENED...
MASTER KAKASHI?
HMM?
THIS LINK BETWEEN NARUTO, SAKURA AND THIS SASUKE WHO KEEPS HURTING THE BOTH OF THEM...
...IS IT REALLY THAT IMPORTANT?
WHY DO THEY KEEP TRYING, DESPITE THE GRIEF HE CAUSES THEM...?
SAI... YOU'RE WATCHING NARUTO FOR DANZO, RIGHT?
...TH-THAT'S...!!
RELAX... IT'S ALL RIGHT...
...JUMPING IN TO HELP NARUTO ISN'T SOMETHING A LOOKOUT DOES.
I THINK YOU'RE STARTING TO REALIZE IT TOO... SAI.
OWWW!
S-SORRY.

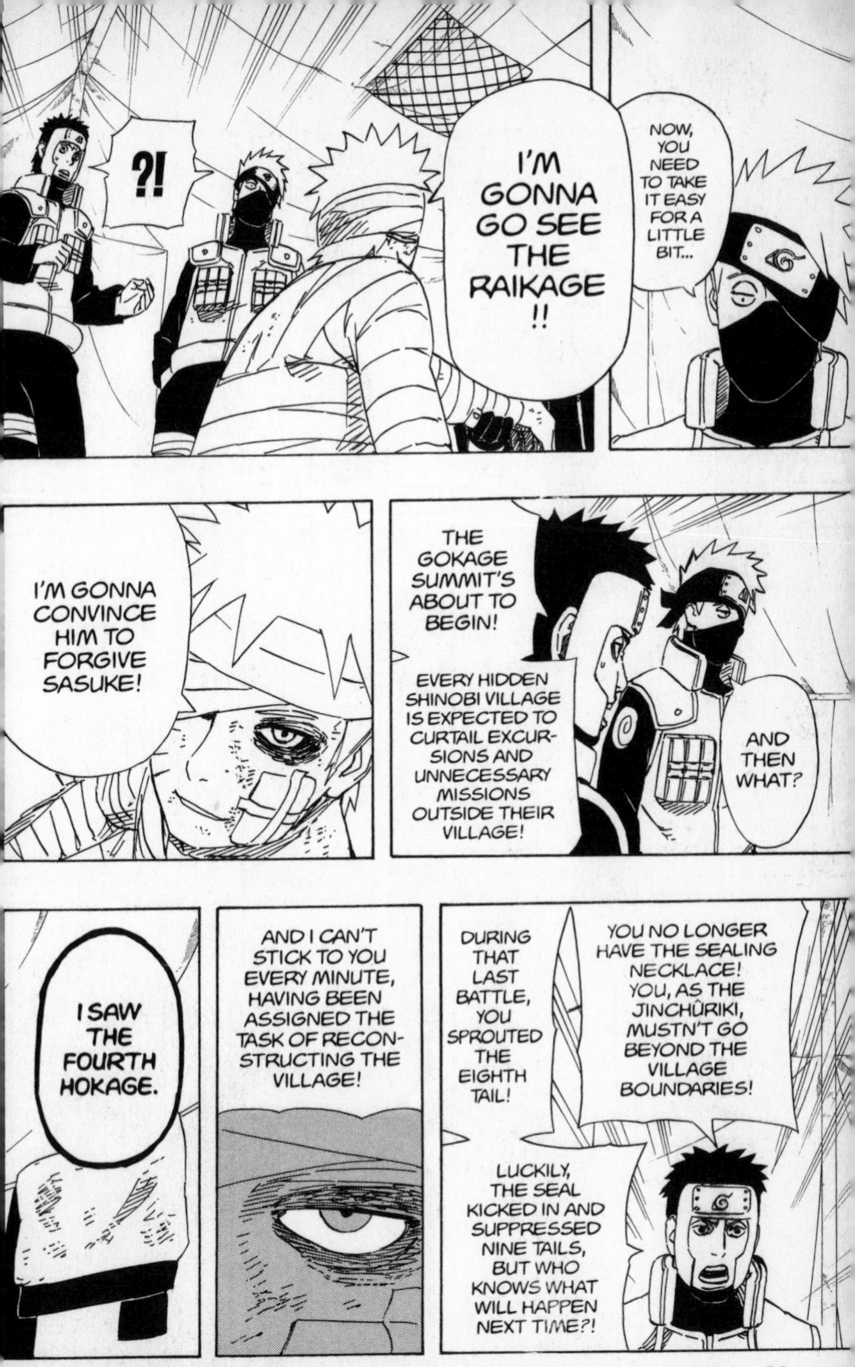
NOW, YOU NEED TO TAKE IT EASY FOR A LITTLE BIT...
I'M GONNA GO SEE THE RAIKAGE!!
?!
THE GOKAGE SUMMIT'S ABOUT TO BEGIN!
EVERY HIDDEN SHINOBI VILLAGE IS EXPECTED TO CURTAIL EXCURSIONS AND UNNECESSARY MISSIONS OUTSIDE THEIR VILLAGE!
AND THEN WHAT?
I'M GONNA CONVINCE HIM TO FORGIVE SASUKE!
YOU NO LONGER HAVE THE SEALING NECKLACE! YOU, AS THE JINCHÛRIKI, MUSTN'T GO BEYOND THE VILLAGE BOUNDARIES!
DURING THAT LAST BATTLE, YOU SPROUTED THE EIGHTH TAIL!
LUCKILY, THE SEAL KICKED IN AND SUPPRESSED NINE TAILS, BUT WHO KNOWS WHAT WILL HAPPEN NEXT TIME?!
AND I CAN'T STICK TO YOU EVERY MINUTE, HAVING BEEN ASSIGNED THE TASK OF RECONSTRUCTING THE VILLAGE!
I SAW THE FOURTH HOKAGE.

READ THIS WAY

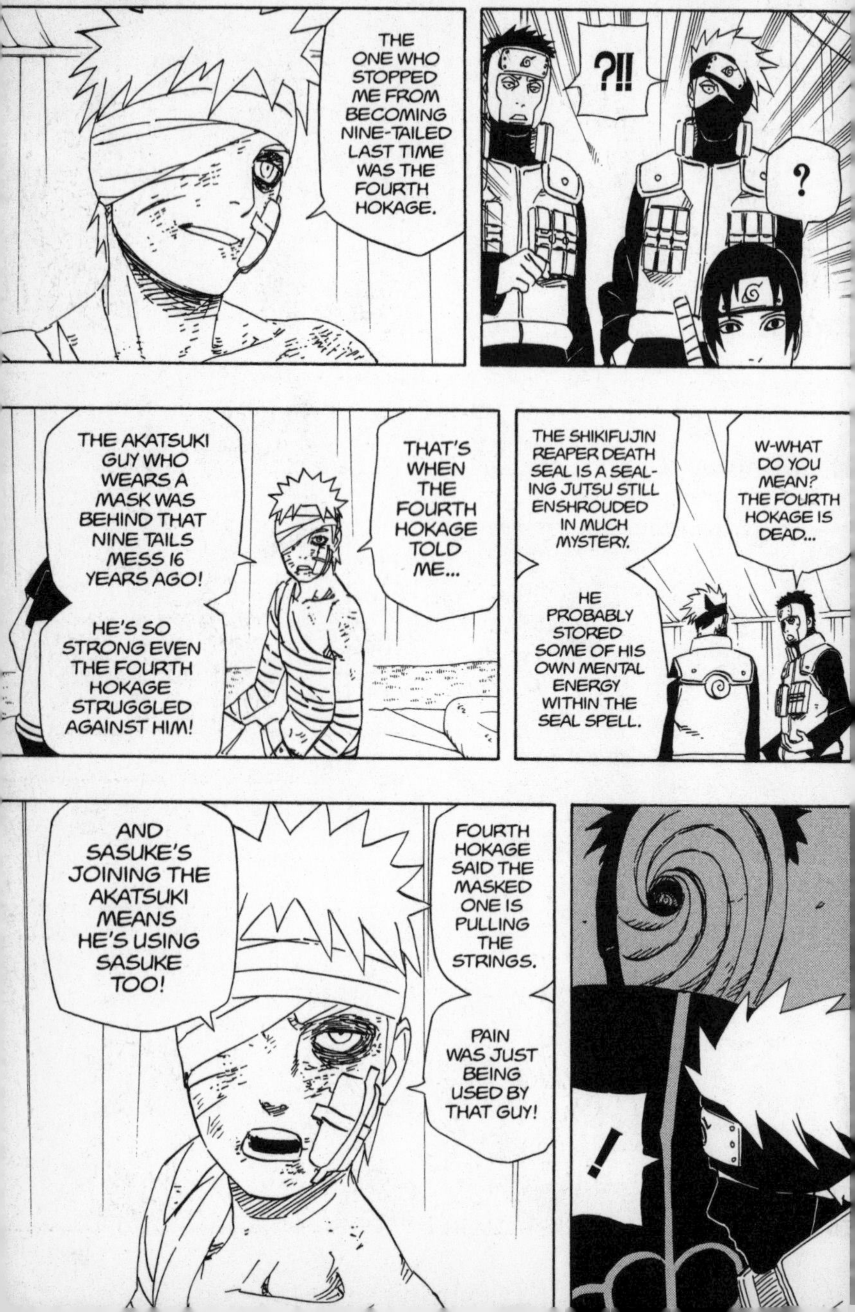

?!!
?
THE ONE WHO STOPPED ME FROM BECOMING NINE-TAILED LAST TIME WAS THE FOURTH HOKAGE.
W-WHAT DO YOU MEAN? THE FOURTH HOKAGE IS DEAD...
THE SHIKIFUJIN REAPER DEATH SEAL IS A SEALING JUTSU STILL ENSHROUDED IN MUCH MYSTERY.
HE PROBABLY STORED SOME OF HIS OWN MENTAL ENERGY WITHIN THE SEAL SPELL.
THAT'S WHEN THE FOURTH HOKAGE TOLD ME...
THE AKATSUKI GUY WHO WEARS A MASK WAS BEHIND THAT NINE TAILS MESS 16 YEARS AGO!
HE'S SO STRONG EVEN THE FOURTH HOKAGE STRUGGLED AGAINST HIM!
!
FOURTH HOKAGE SAID THE MASKED ONE IS PULLING THE STRINGS.
PAIN WAS JUST BEING USED BY THAT GUY!
AND SASUKE'S JOINING THE AKATSUKI MEANS HE'S USING SASUKE TOO!

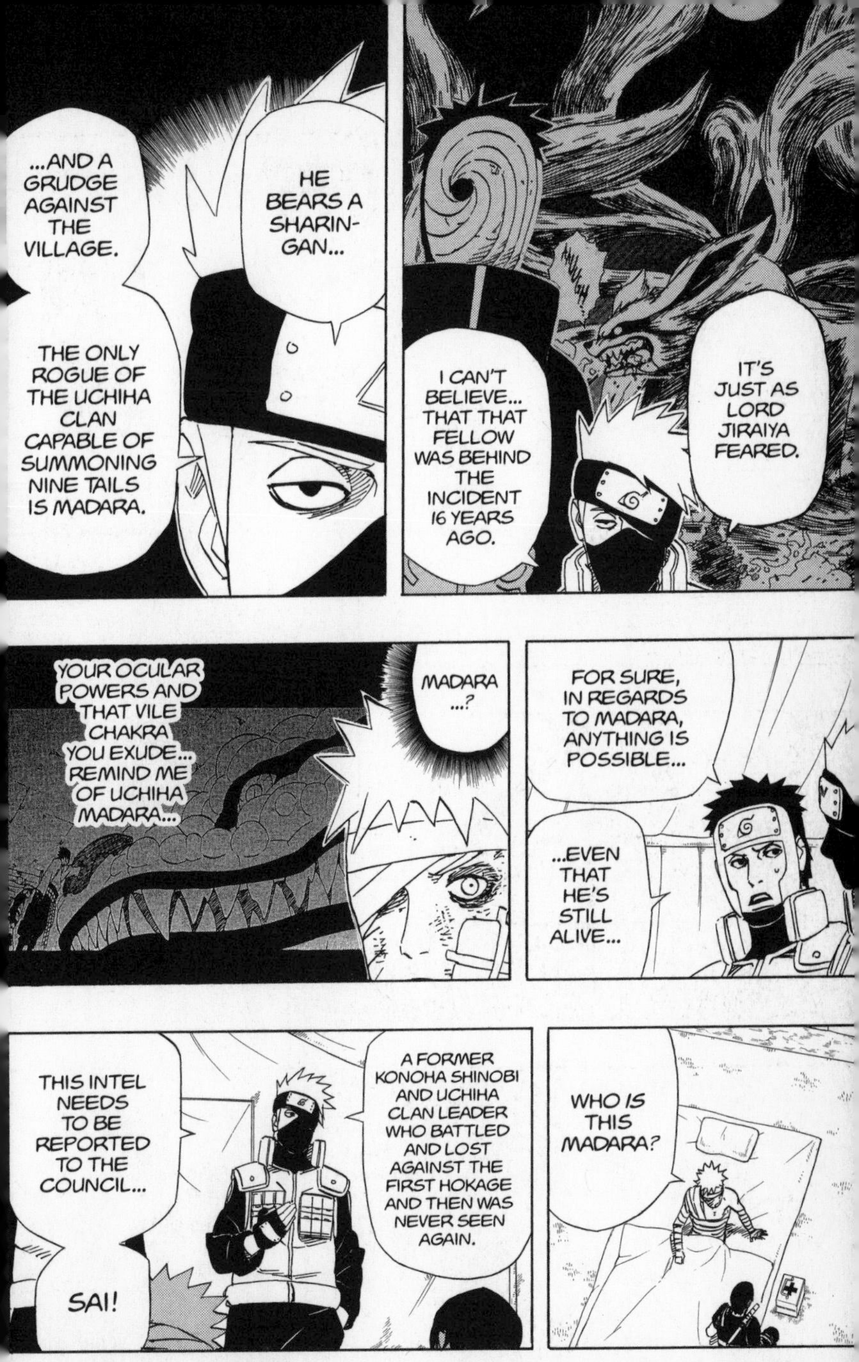
IT'S JUST AS LORD JIRAIYA FEARED.
I CAN'T BELIEVE... THAT THAT FELLOW WAS BEHIND THE INCIDENT 16 YEARS AGO.
HE BEARS A SHARINGAN...
...AND A GRUDGE AGAINST THE VILLAGE.
THE ONLY ROGUE OF THE UCHIHA CLAN CAPABLE OF SUMMONING NINE TAILS IS MADARA.
FOR SURE, IN REGARDS TO MADARA, ANYTHING IS POSSIBLE...
...EVEN THAT HE'S STILL ALIVE...
MADARA ...?
YOUR OCULAR POWERS AND THAT VILE CHAKRA YOU EXUDE... REMIND ME OF UCHIHA MADARA...
WHO IS THIS MADARA?
A FORMER KONOHA SHINOBI AND UCHIHA CLAN LEADER WHO BATTLED AND LOST AGAINST THE FIRST HOKAGE AND THEN WAS NEVER SEEN AGAIN.
THIS INTEL NEEDS TO BE REPORTED TO THE COUNCIL...
SAI!

READ THIS WAY

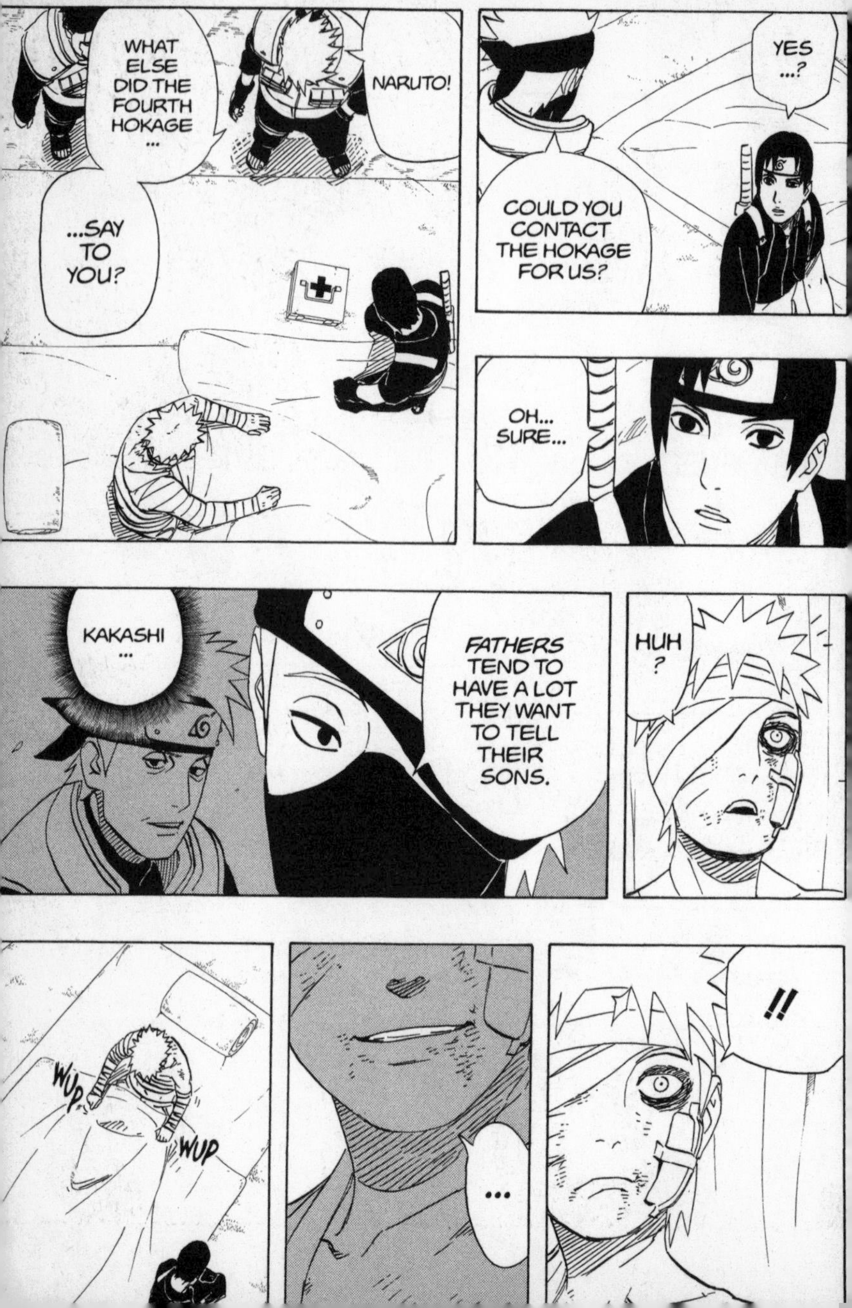
YES ...?
COULD YOU CONTACT THE HOKAGE FOR US?
OH... SURE...
NARUTO!
WHAT ELSE DID THE FOURTH HOKAGE ...
...SAY TO YOU?
HUH ?
FATHERS TEND TO HAVE A LOT THEY WANT TO TELL THEIR SONS.
KAKASHI ...
!!
...
WUP
WUP

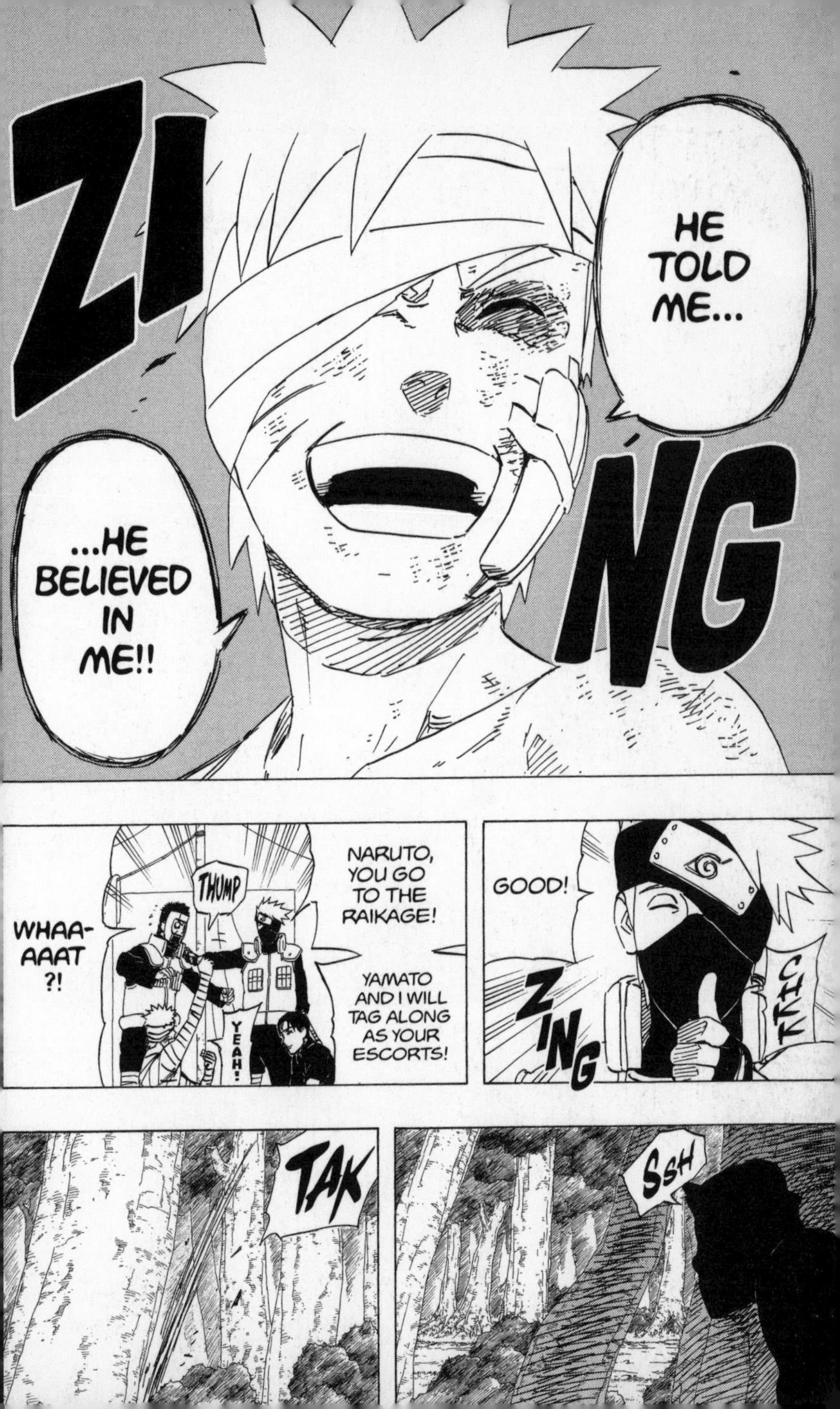

HE TOLD ME...
ZING
...HE BELIEVED IN ME!!
GOOD!
ZING
CHK
NARUTO, YOU GO TO THE RAIKAGE!
YAMATO AND I WILL TAG ALONG AS YOUR ESCORTS!
THUMP
YEAH!
WHAA-AAAT?!
SSH
TAK

READ THIS WAY

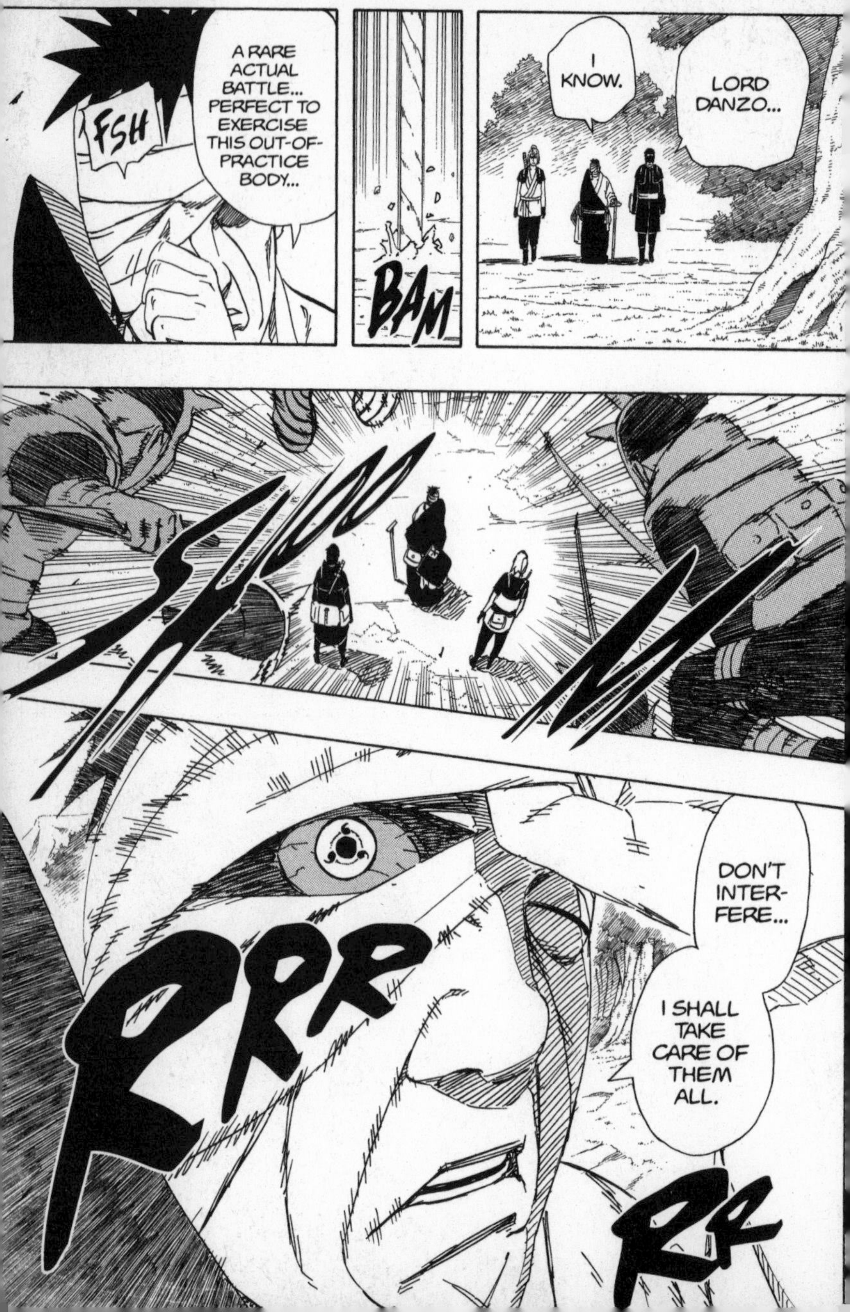
LORD DANZO...
I KNOW.
BAM
A RARE ACTUAL BATTLE... PERFECT TO EXERCISE THIS OUT-OF-PRACTICE BODY...
FSH
SHUNN
DON'T INTER-FERE...
I SHALL TAKE CARE OF THEM ALL.
RPPP
RR

Number 456: Naruto Heads Out...!!

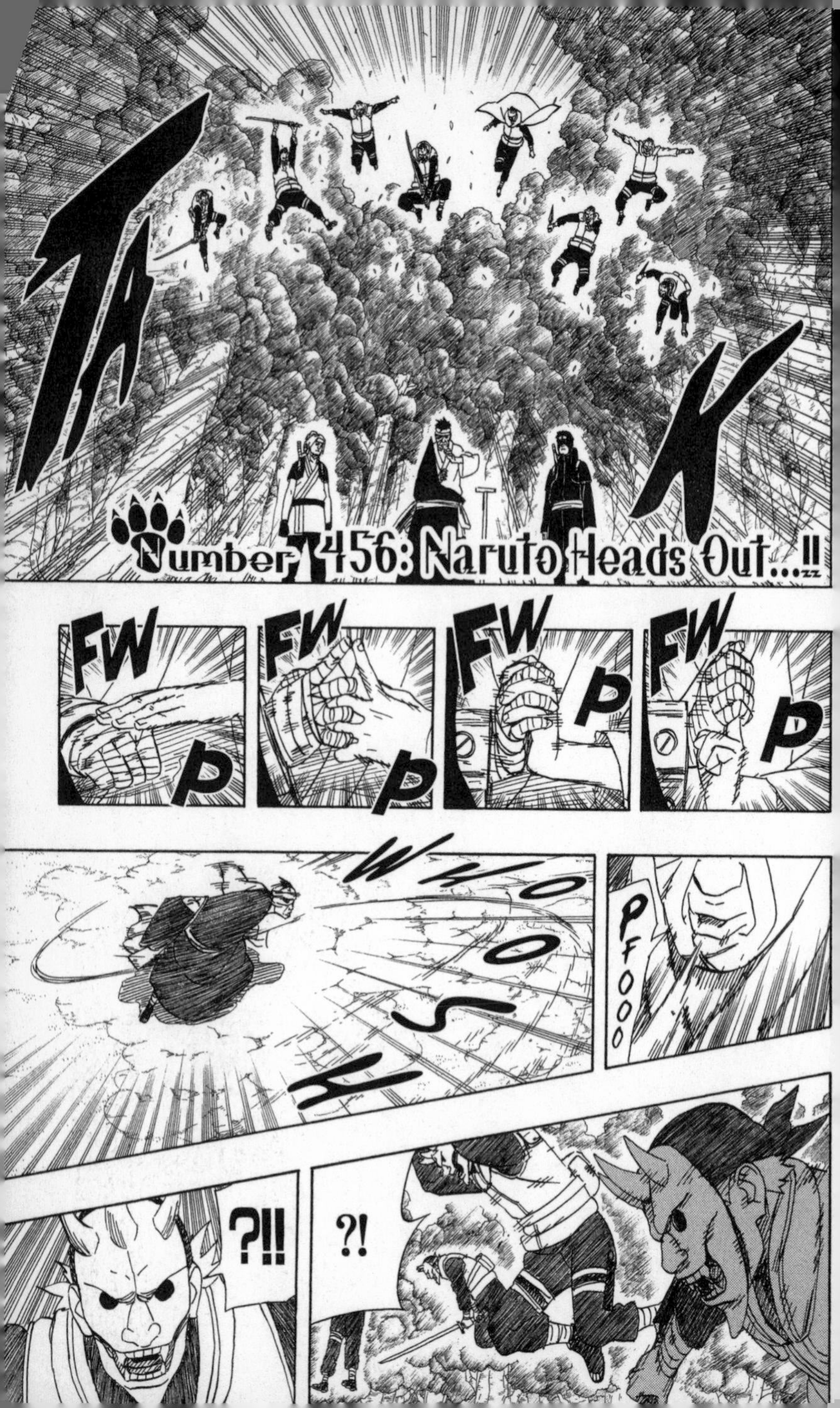
TAK
FWP
FWP
FWP
FWP
PFOOO
WHOOSH
?!
?!!

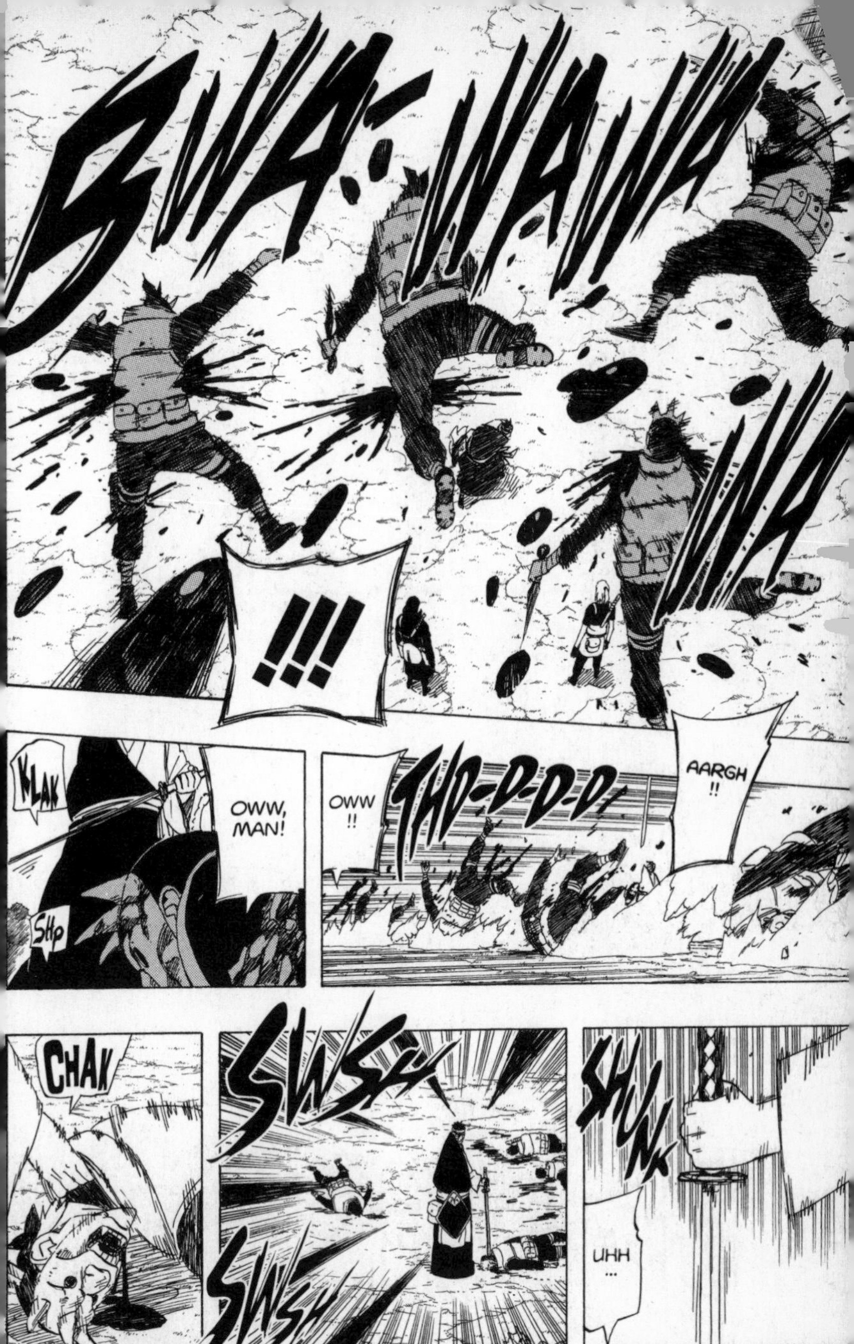
SWA-WAWAWA
!!!
AARGH !!
THD-D-D-D
OWW !!
OWW, MAN!
KLAK
SHP
SHUNK
UHH ...
SWSH
SWSH
CHAK

READ THIS WAY

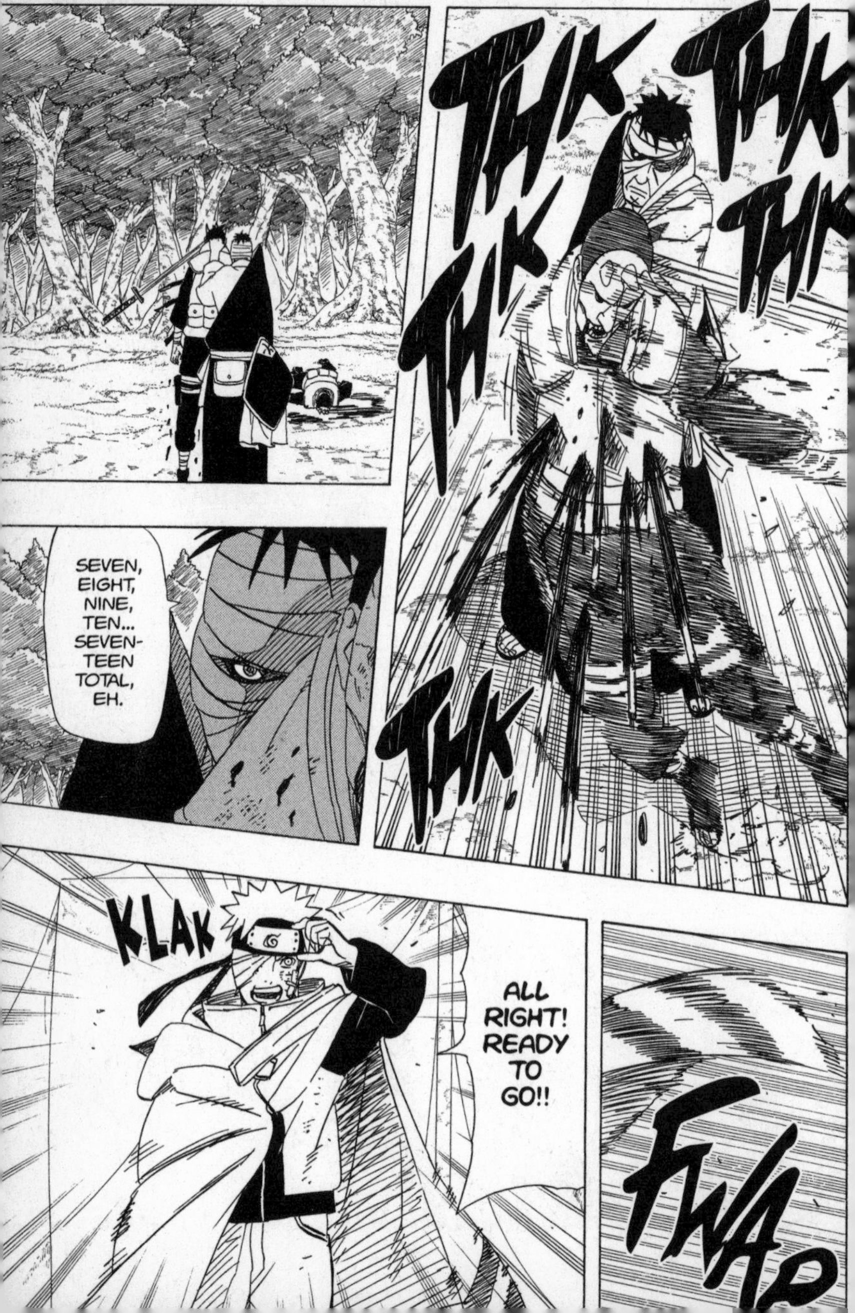
THK THK THK THK THK THK
THK
SEVEN, EIGHT, NINE, TEN... SEVENTEEN TOTAL, EH.
FWAP
KLAK
ALL RIGHT! READY TO GO!!

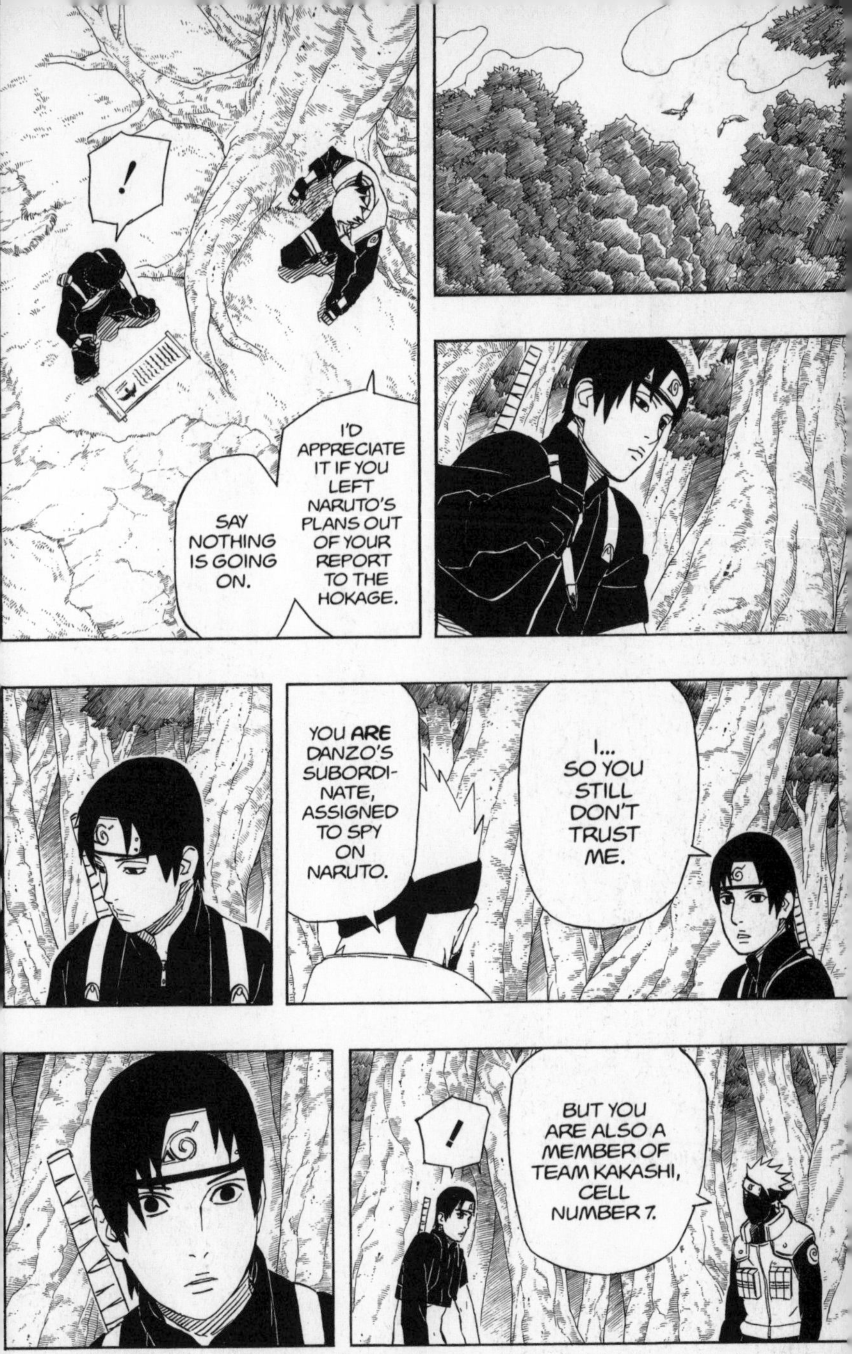
!
I'D APPRECIATE IT IF YOU LEFT NARUTO'S PLANS OUT OF YOUR REPORT TO THE HOKAGE.
SAY NOTHING IS GOING ON.
I... SO YOU STILL DON'T TRUST ME.
YOU **ARE** DANZO'S SUBORDI-NATE, ASSIGNED TO SPY ON NARUTO.
BUT YOU ARE ALSO A MEMBER OF TEAM KAKASHI, CELL NUMBER 7.
!

READ THIS WAY

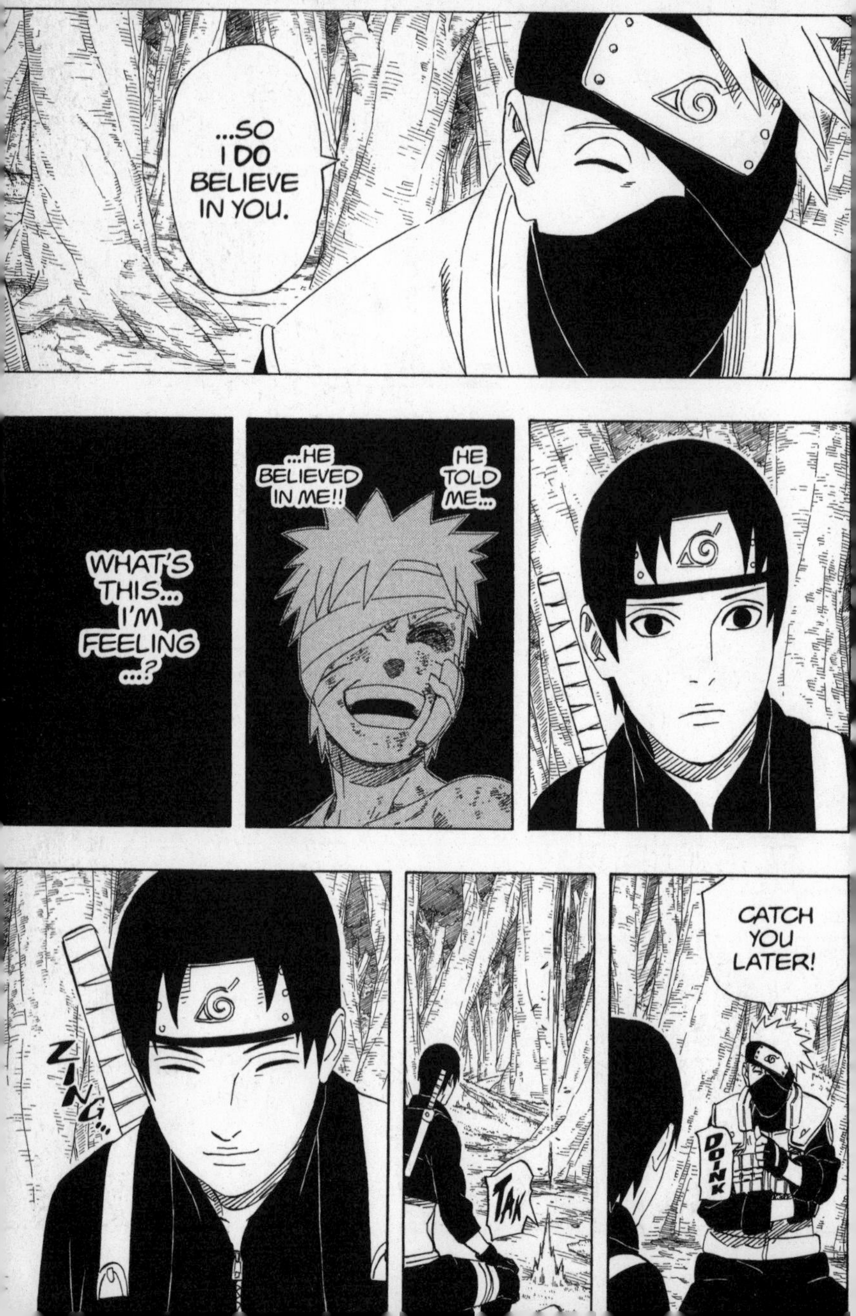
...SO I DO BELIEVE IN YOU.
HE TOLD ME...
...HE BELIEVED IN ME!!
WHAT'S THIS... I'M FEELING ...?
CATCH YOU LATER!
DOINK
TAK
ZING...

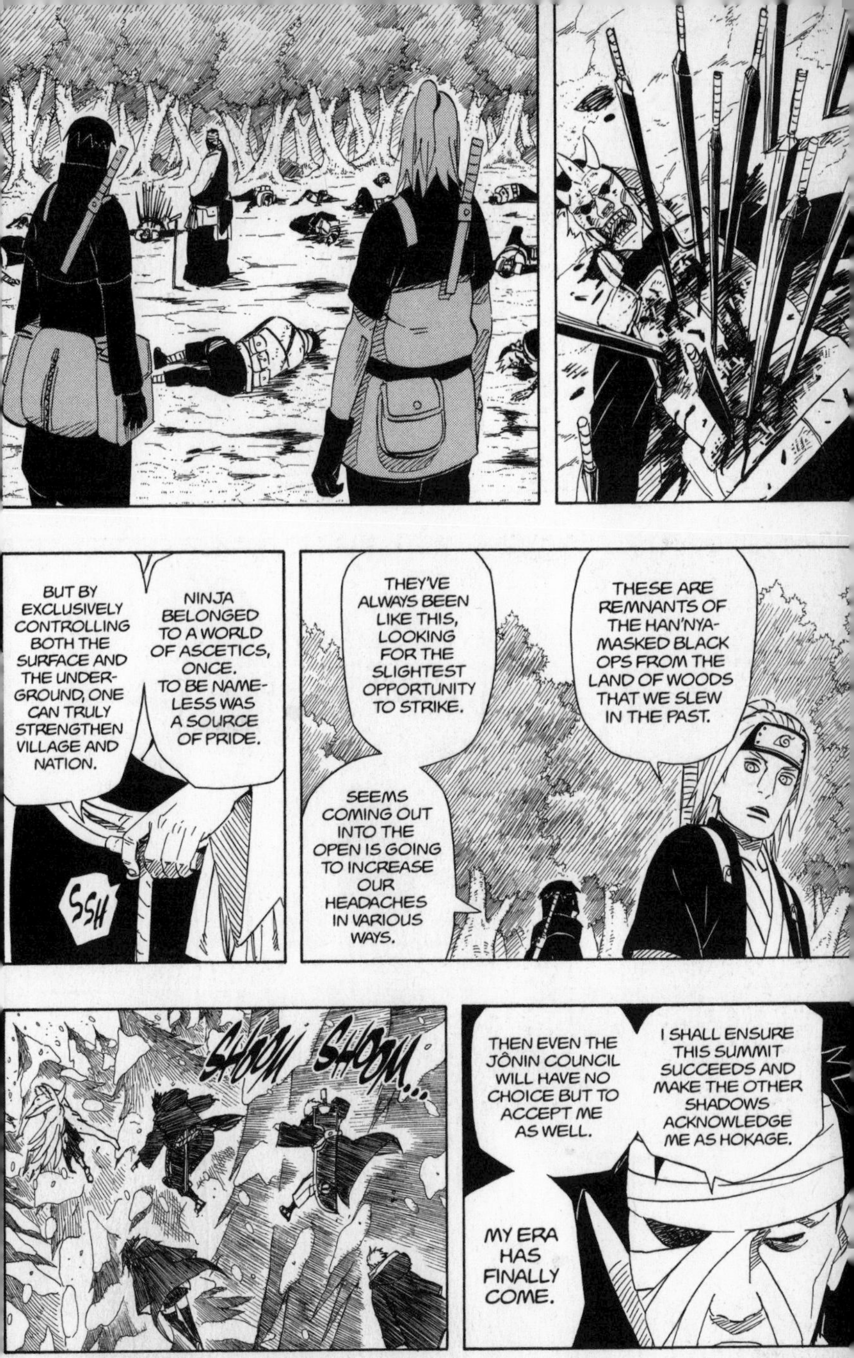

THESE ARE REMNANTS OF THE HAN'NYA-MASKED BLACK OPS FROM THE LAND OF WOODS THAT WE SLEW IN THE PAST.
THEY'VE ALWAYS BEEN LIKE THIS, LOOKING FOR THE SLIGHTEST OPPORTUNITY TO STRIKE.
SEEMS COMING OUT INTO THE OPEN IS GOING TO INCREASE OUR HEADACHES IN VARIOUS WAYS.
NINJA BELONGED TO A WORLD OF ASCETICS, ONCE. TO BE NAMELESS WAS A SOURCE OF PRIDE.
BUT BY EXCLUSIVELY CONTROLLING BOTH THE SURFACE AND THE UNDERGROUND, ONE CAN TRULY STRENGTHEN VILLAGE AND NATION.
SSH
I SHALL ENSURE THIS SUMMIT SUCCEEDS AND MAKE THE OTHER SHADOWS ACKNOWLEDGE ME AS HOKAGE.
THEN EVEN THE JÔNIN COUNCIL WILL HAVE NO CHOICE BUT TO ACCEPT ME AS WELL.
MY ERA HAS FINALLY COME.
SHOOM SHOOM...

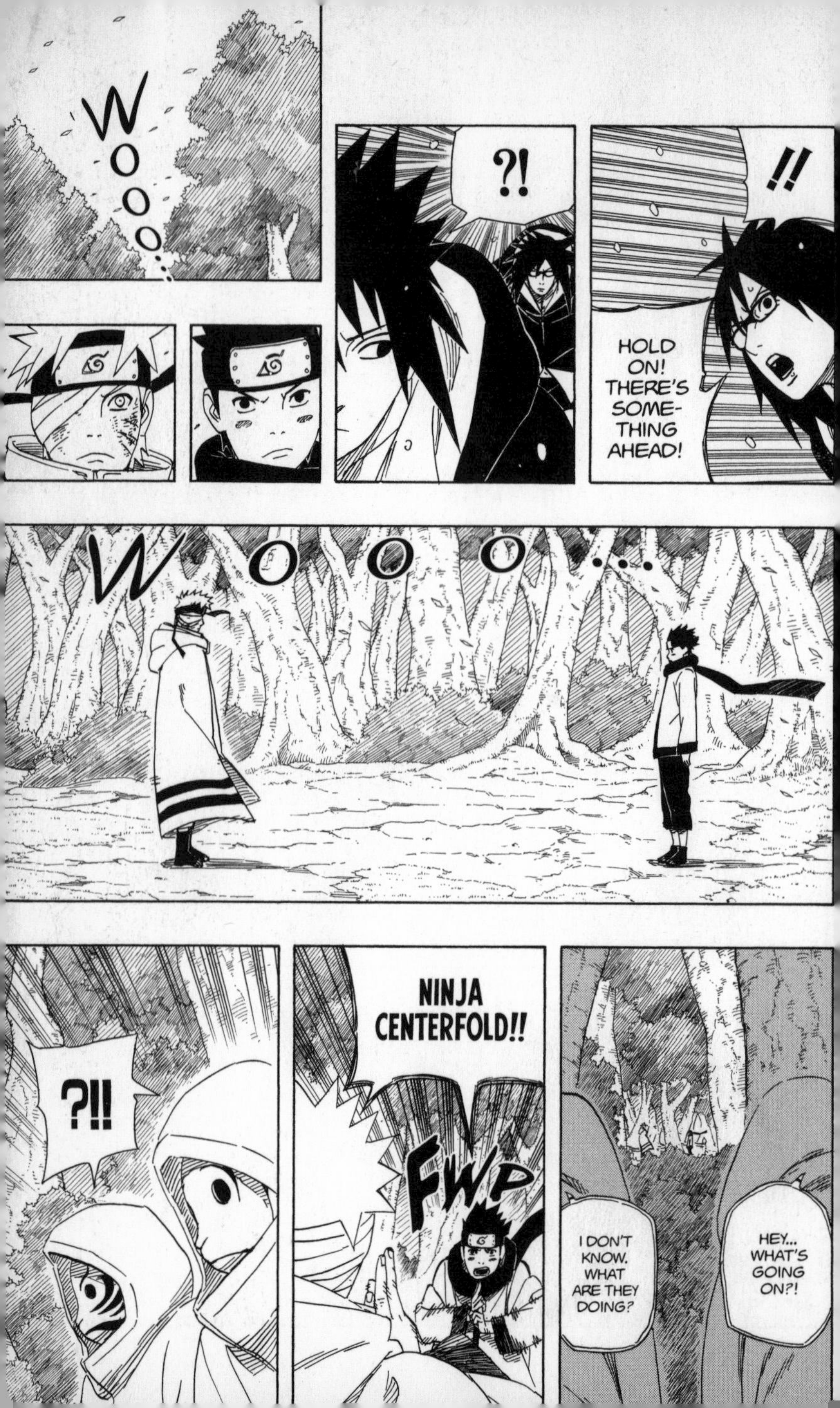
!!
HOLD ON! THERE'S SOME-THING AHEAD!
?!
WOOO...
WOOOO...
HEY... WHAT'S GOING ON?!
I DON'T KNOW. WHAT ARE THEY DOING?
NINJA CENTERFOLD!!
FWP
?!!

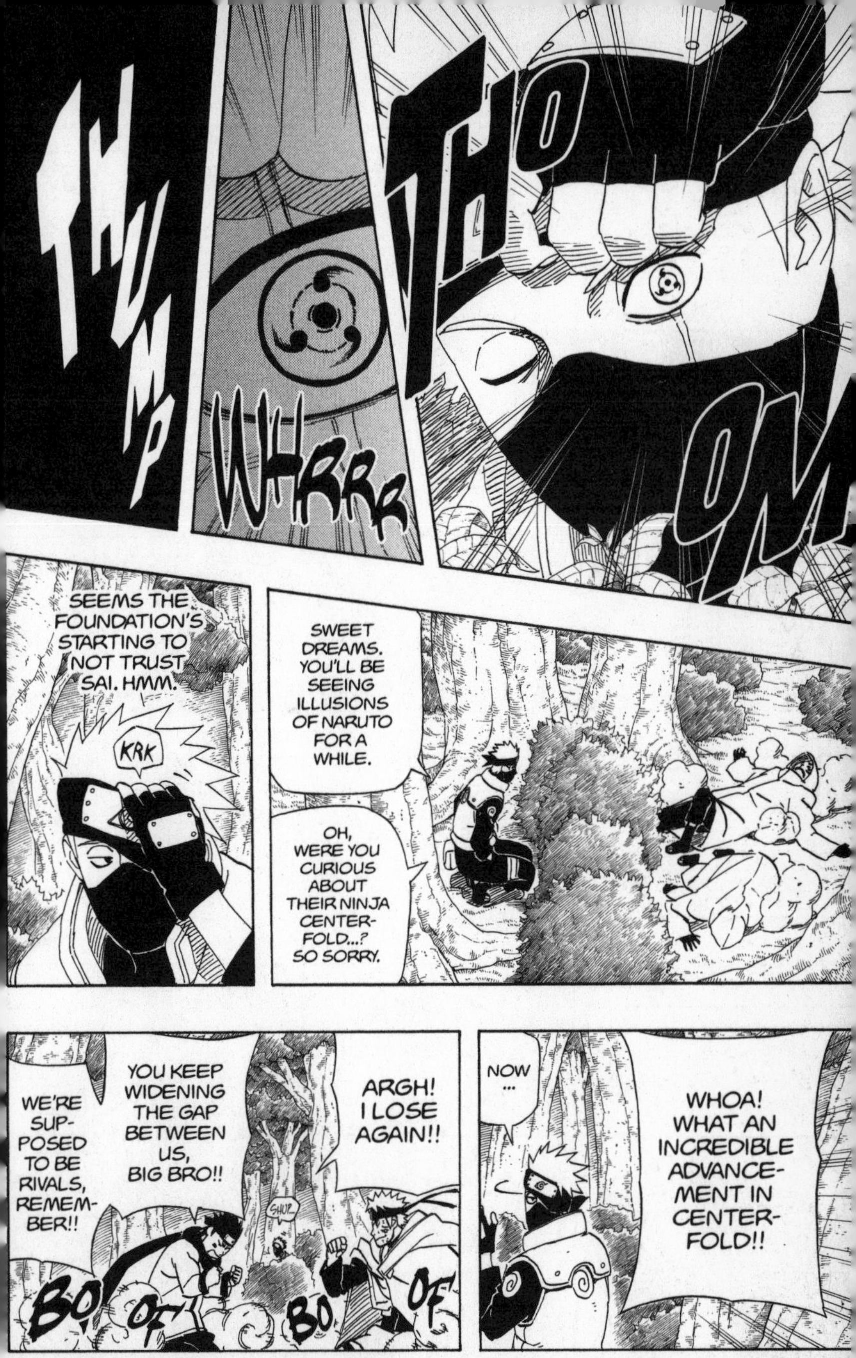
THOOM
WHRRR
THUMP
SWEET DREAMS. YOU'LL BE SEEING ILLUSIONS OF NARUTO FOR A WHILE.
OH, WERE YOU CURIOUS ABOUT THEIR NINJA CENTER-FOLD...? SO SORRY.
SEEMS THE FOUNDATION'S STARTING TO NOT TRUST SAI. HMM.
KRK
WHOA! WHAT AN INCREDIBLE ADVANCE-MENT IN CENTER-FOLD!!
NOW ...
ARGH! I LOSE AGAIN!!
YOU KEEP WIDENING THE GAP BETWEEN US, BIG BRO!!
WE'RE SUP-POSED TO BE RIVALS, REMEM-BER!!
BOOF
BOOF

READ THIS WAY

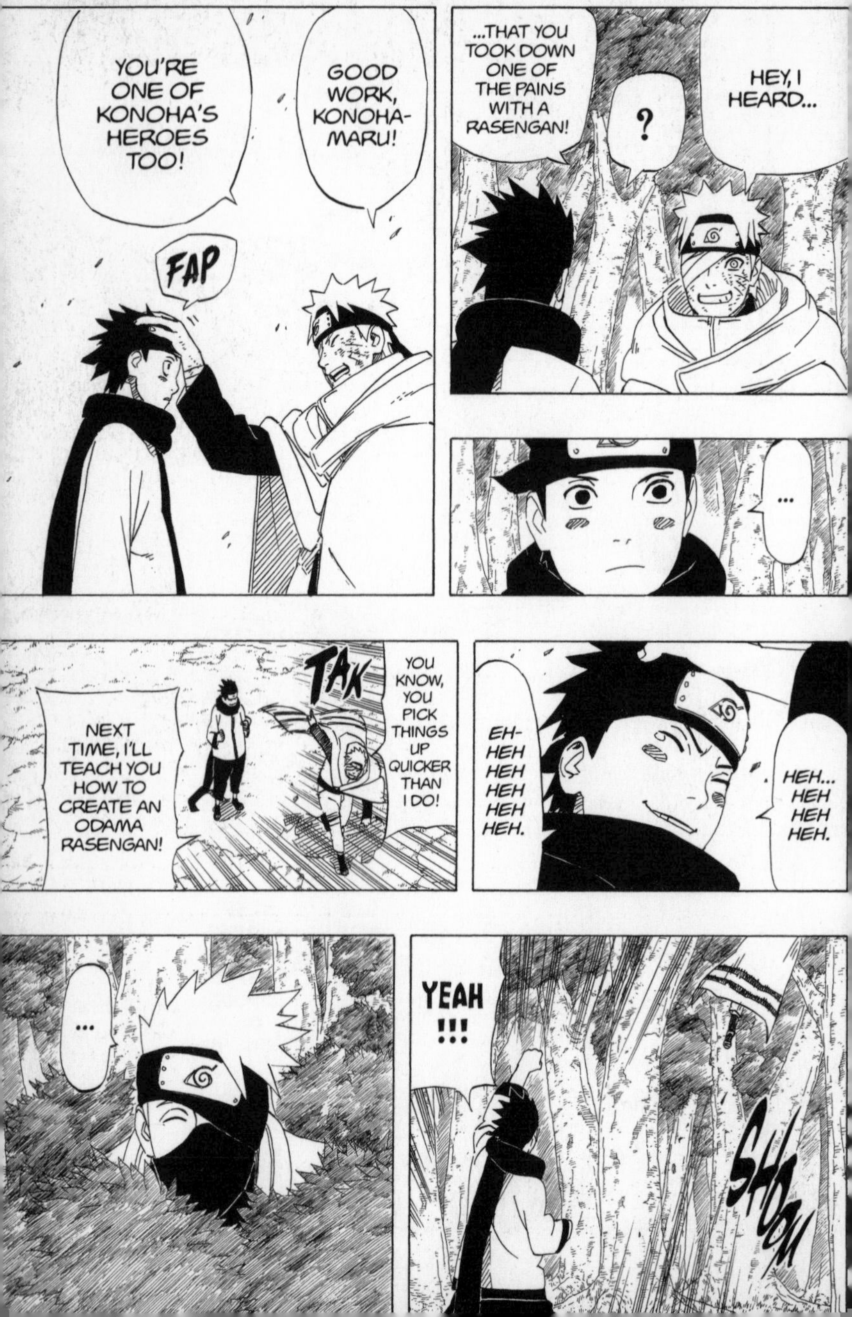
HEY, I HEARD...
?
...THAT YOU TOOK DOWN ONE OF THE PAINS WITH A RASENGAN!
...
GOOD WORK, KONOHAMARU!
YOU'RE ONE OF KONOHA'S HEROES TOO!
FAP
HEH... HEH HEH HEH.
EH-HEH HEH HEH HEH HEH.
TAK
YOU KNOW, YOU PICK THINGS UP QUICKER THAN I DO!
NEXT TIME, I'LL TEACH YOU HOW TO CREATE AN ODAMA RASENGAN!
YEAH !!!
SHOOM
...

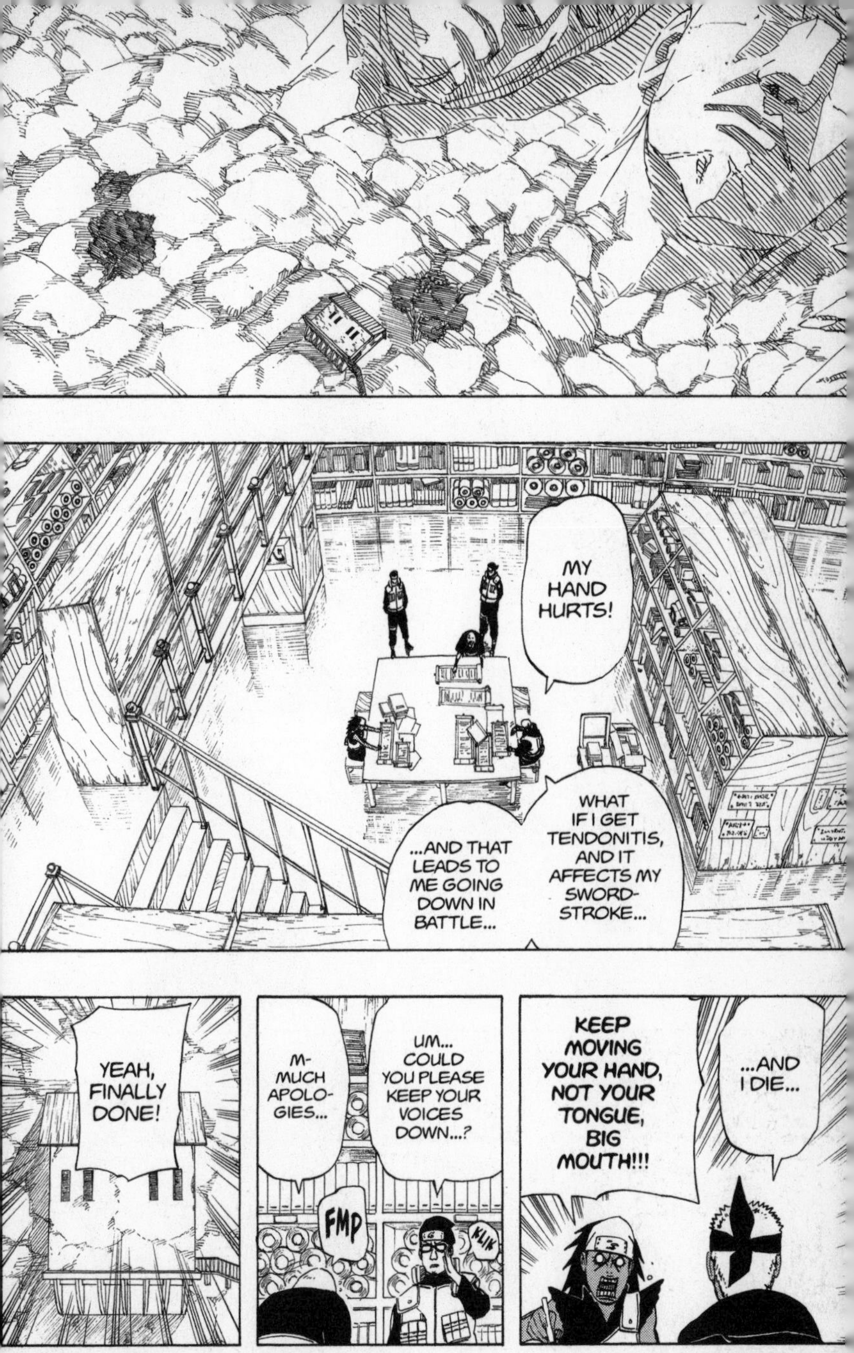
MY HAND HURTS!
WHAT IF I GET TENDONITIS, AND IT AFFECTS MY SWORD-STROKE...
...AND THAT LEADS TO ME GOING DOWN IN BATTLE...
...AND I DIE...
KEEP MOVING YOUR HAND, NOT YOUR TONGUE, BIG MOUTH!!!
UM... COULD YOU PLEASE KEEP YOUR VOICES DOWN...?
KLIK
FMP
M-MUCH APOLOGIES...
YEAH, FINALLY DONE!

READ THIS WAY

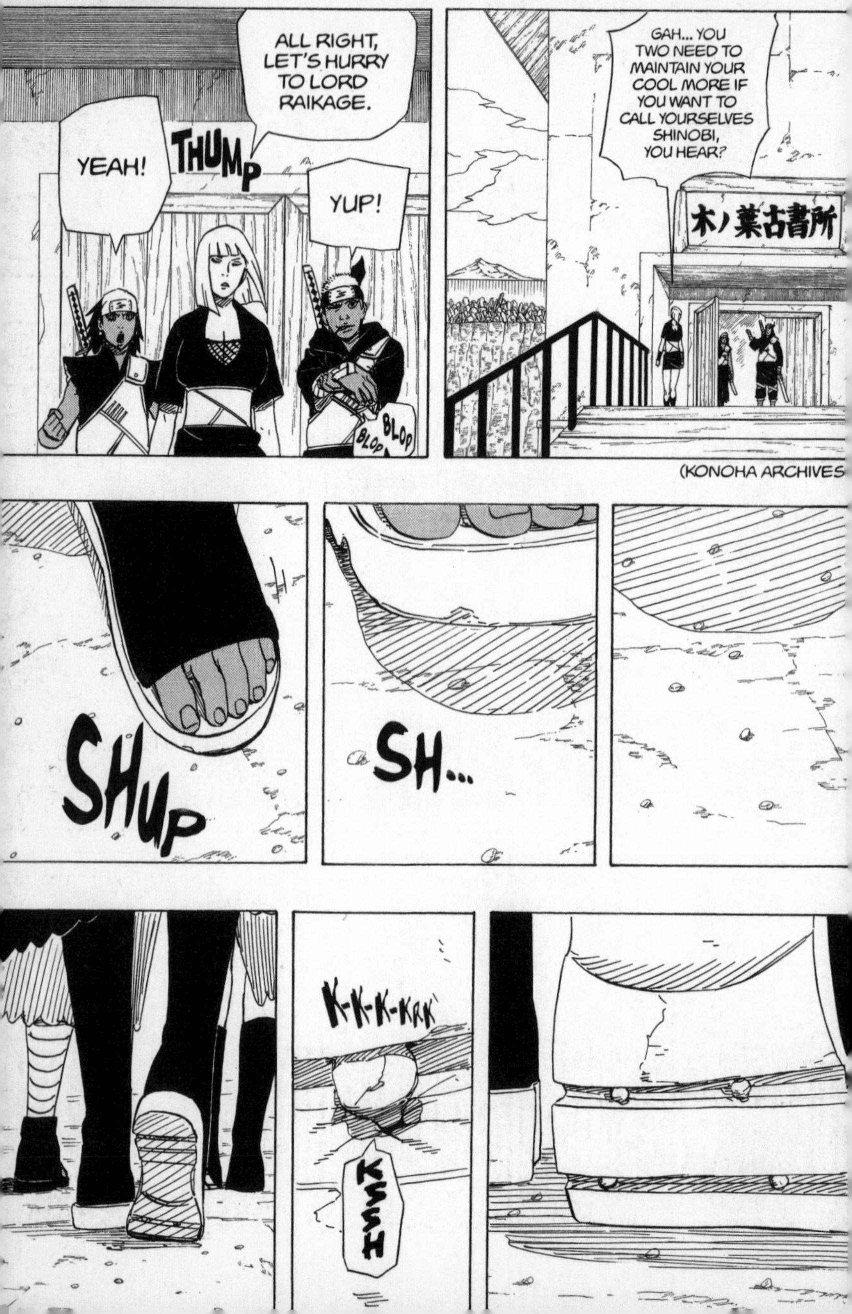
GAH... YOU TWO NEED TO MAINTAIN YOUR COOL MORE IF YOU WANT TO CALL YOURSELVES SHINOBI, YOU HEAR?
木ノ葉古書所
(KONOHA ARCHIVES
ALL RIGHT, LET'S HURRY TO LORD RAIKAGE.
YEAH!
THUMP
YUP!
BLOP
BLOP
SH...
SHUP
K-K-K-KRK
KSSH

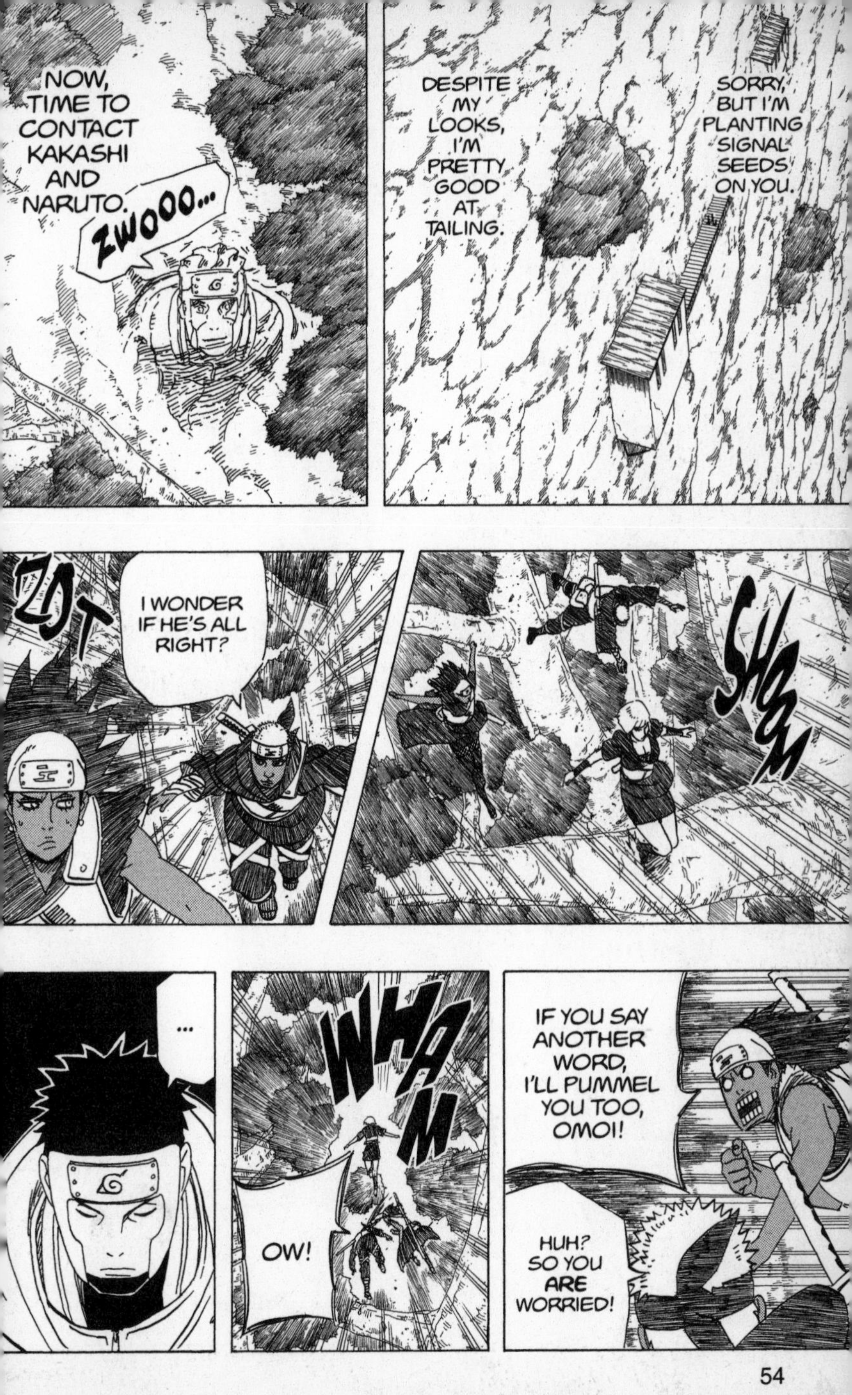

SORRY, BUT I'M PLANTING SIGNAL SEEDS ON YOU.
DESPITE MY LOOKS, I'M PRETTY GOOD AT TAILING.
NOW, TIME TO CONTACT KAKASHI AND NARUTO.
ZWOOO...
SHOOM
ZOT
I WONDER IF HE'S ALL RIGHT?
IF YOU SAY ANOTHER WORD, I'LL PUMMEL YOU TOO, OMOI!
HUH? SO YOU **ARE** WORRIED!
WHAM
OW!
...

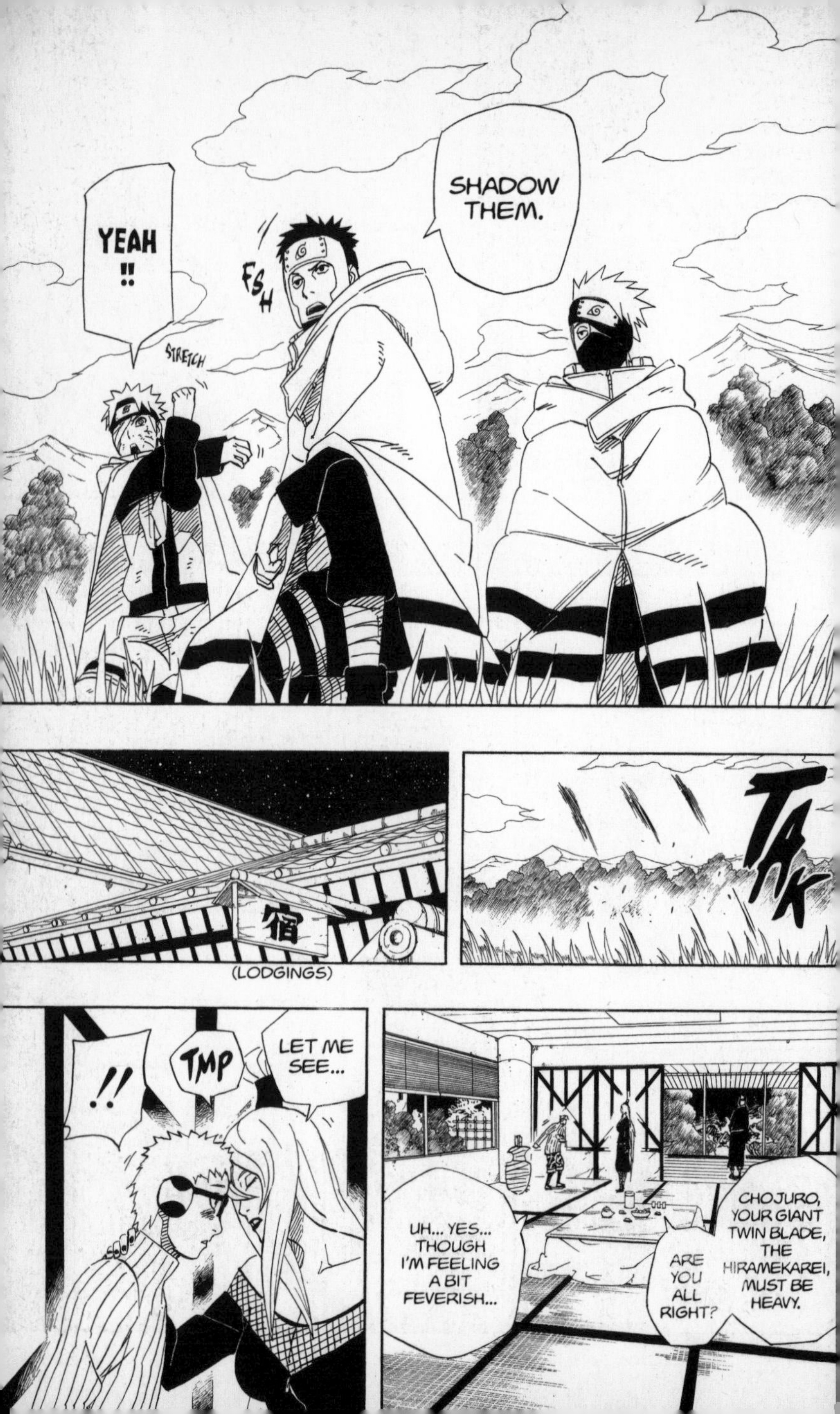
SHADOW THEM.
FSH
YEAH!!
STRETCH
TAK
(LODGINGS)
CHOJURO, YOUR GIANT TWIN BLADE, THE HIRAMEKAREI, MUST BE HEAVY.
ARE YOU ALL RIGHT?
UH... YES... THOUGH I'M FEELING A BIT FEVERISH...
LET ME SEE...
TMP
!!

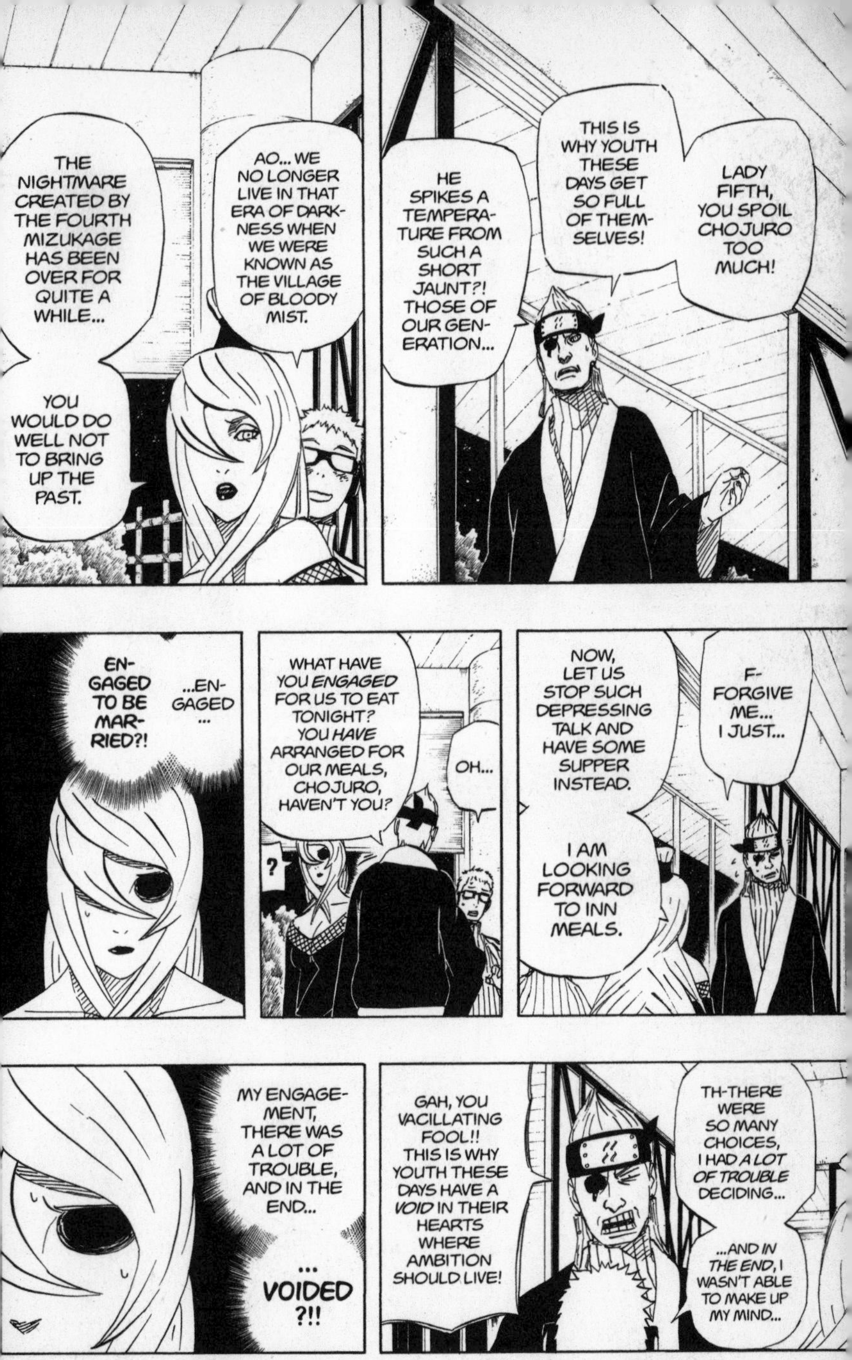
LADY FIFTH, YOU SPOIL CHOJURO TOO MUCH!
THIS IS WHY YOUTH THESE DAYS GET SO FULL OF THEMSELVES!
HE SPIKES A TEMPERATURE FROM SUCH A SHORT JAUNT?! THOSE OF OUR GENERATION...
AO... WE NO LONGER LIVE IN THAT ERA OF DARKNESS WHEN WE WERE KNOWN AS THE VILLAGE OF BLOODY MIST.
THE NIGHTMARE CREATED BY THE FOURTH MIZUKAGE HAS BEEN OVER FOR QUITE A WHILE...
YOU WOULD DO WELL NOT TO BRING UP THE PAST.
F-FORGIVE ME... I JUST...
NOW, LET US STOP SUCH DEPRESSING TALK AND HAVE SOME SUPPER INSTEAD.
I AM LOOKING FORWARD TO INN MEALS.
OH...
WHAT HAVE YOU *ENGAGED* FOR US TO EAT TONIGHT? YOU *HAVE* ARRANGED FOR OUR MEALS, CHOJURO, HAVEN'T YOU?
?
...ENGAGED...
ENGAGED TO BE MARRIED?!
TH-THERE WERE SO MANY CHOICES, I HAD *A LOT OF TROUBLE* DECIDING...
...AND *IN THE END*, I WASN'T ABLE TO MAKE UP MY MIND...
GAH, YOU VACILLATING FOOL!! THIS IS WHY YOUTH THESE DAYS HAVE A *VOID* IN THEIR HEARTS WHERE AMBITION SHOULD LIVE!
MY ENGAGEMENT, THERE WAS A LOT OF TROUBLE, AND IN THE END...
...VOIDED?!!

READ THIS WAY

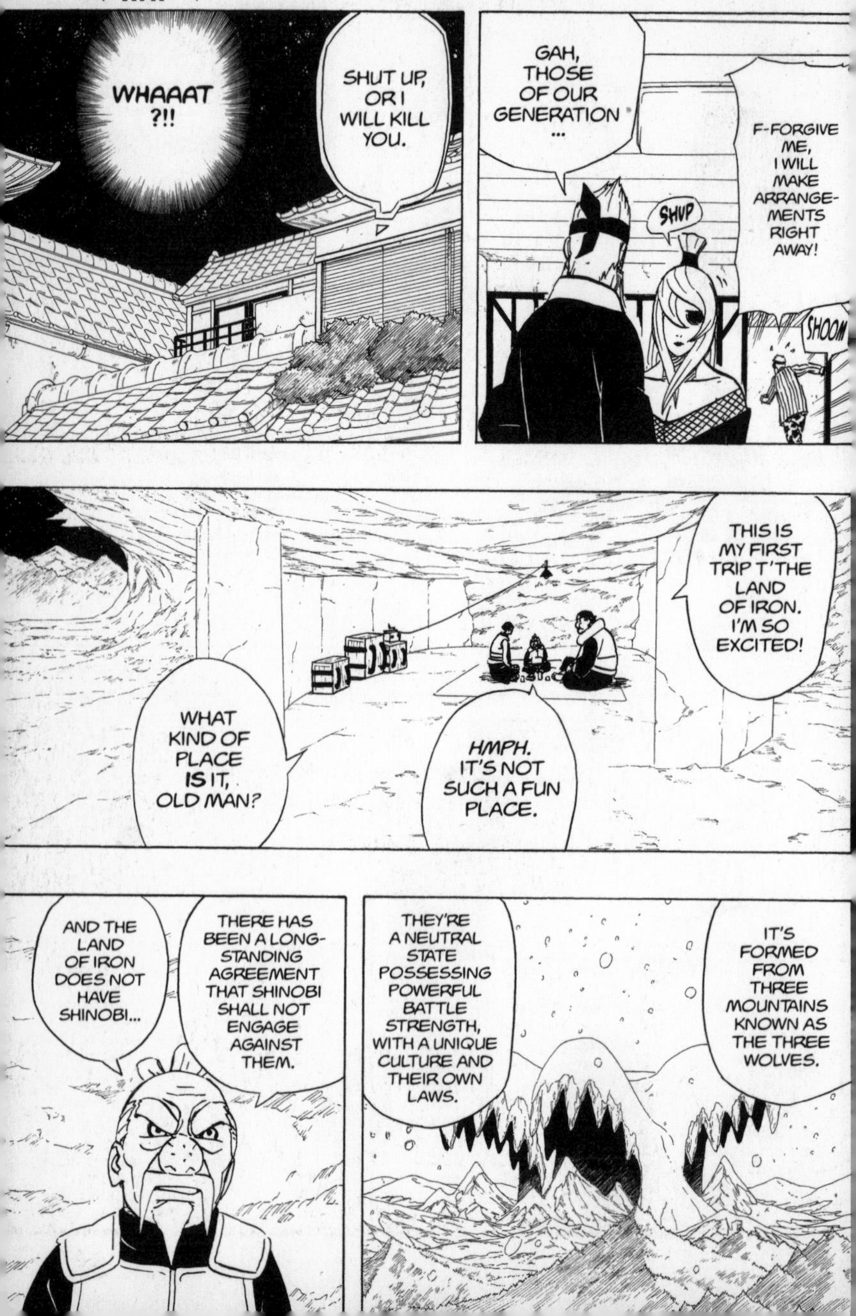

F-FORGIVE ME, I WILL MAKE ARRANGEMENTS RIGHT AWAY!
SHOOM
SHUP
GAH, THOSE OF OUR GENERATION ...
SHUT UP, OR I WILL KILL YOU.
WHAAAT ?!!
THIS IS MY FIRST TRIP T'THE LAND OF IRON. I'M SO EXCITED!
WHAT KIND OF PLACE IS IT, OLD MAN?
HMPH. IT'S NOT SUCH A FUN PLACE.
IT'S FORMED FROM THREE MOUNTAINS KNOWN AS THE THREE WOLVES.
THEY'RE A NEUTRAL STATE POSSESSING POWERFUL BATTLE STRENGTH, WITH A UNIQUE CULTURE AND THEIR OWN LAWS.
THERE HAS BEEN A LONG-STANDING AGREEMENT THAT SHINOBI SHALL NOT ENGAGE AGAINST THEM.
AND THE LAND OF IRON DOES NOT HAVE SHINOBI...

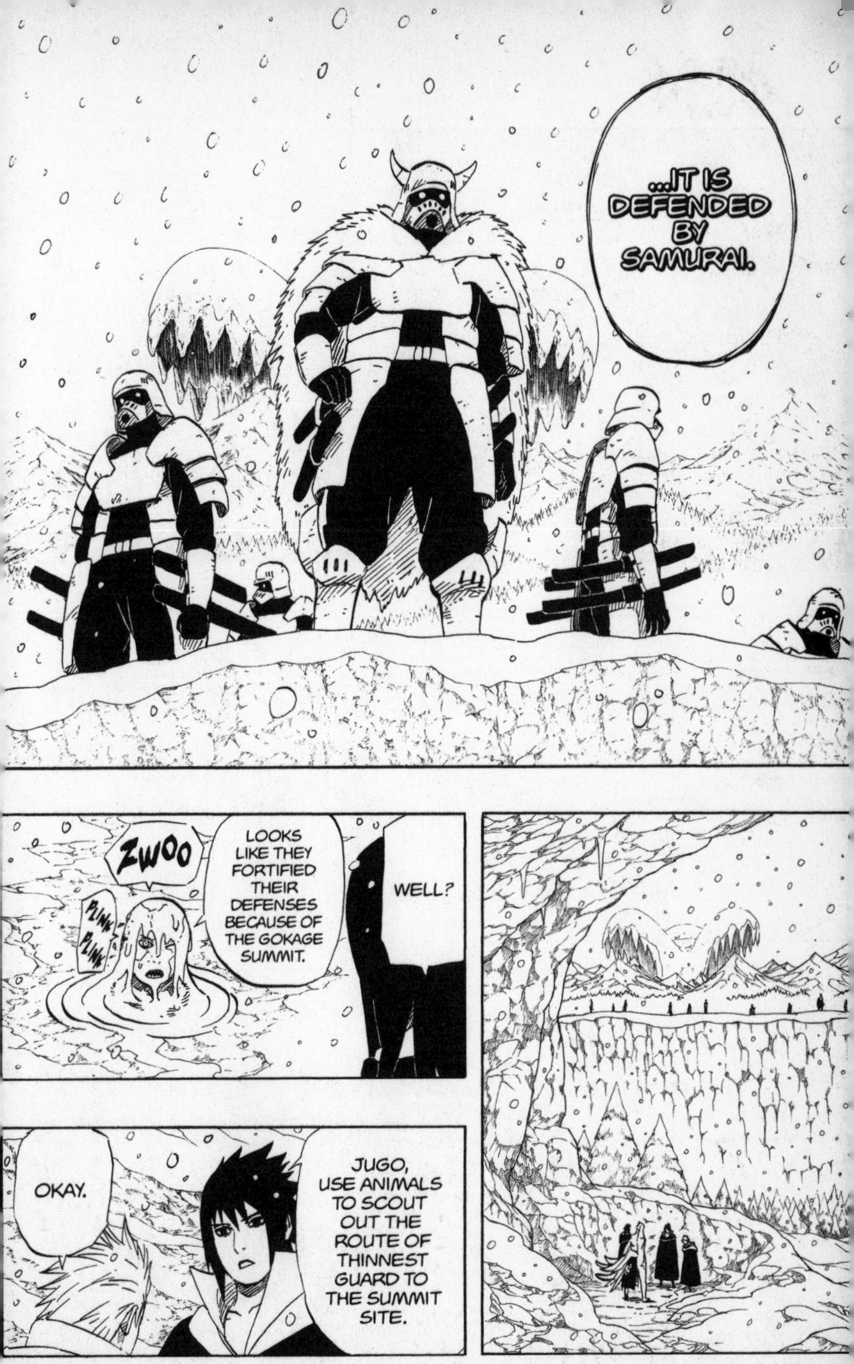

...IT IS DEFENDED BY SAMURAI.
WELL?
LOOKS LIKE THEY FORTIFIED THEIR DEFENSES BECAUSE OF THE GOKAGE SUMMIT.
ZWOO
PLINK PLINK
JUGO, USE ANIMALS TO SCOUT OUT THE ROUTE OF THINNEST GUARD TO THE SUMMIT SITE.
OKAY.

READ THIS WAY

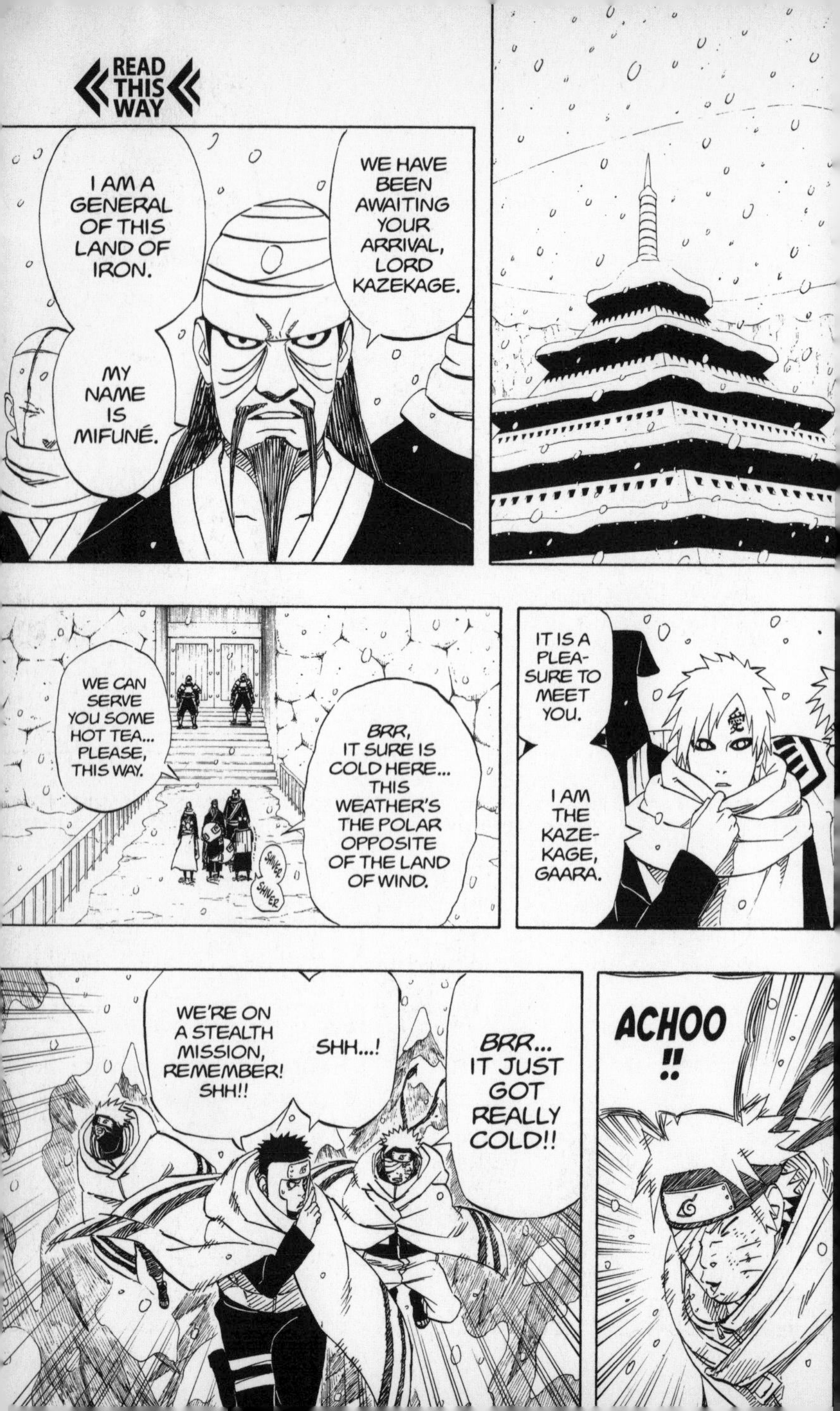

WE HAVE BEEN AWAITING YOUR ARRIVAL, LORD KAZEKAGE.
I AM A GENERAL OF THIS LAND OF IRON.
MY NAME IS MIFUNÉ.
IT IS A PLEASURE TO MEET YOU.
I AM THE KAZEKAGE, GAARA.
WE CAN SERVE YOU SOME HOT TEA... PLEASE, THIS WAY.
BRR, IT SURE IS COLD HERE... THIS WEATHER'S THE POLAR OPPOSITE OF THE LAND OF WIND.
SHIVER
SHIVER
ACHOO!!
BRR... IT JUST GOT REALLY COLD!!
SHH...!
WE'RE ON A STEALTH MISSION, REMEMBER! SHH!!

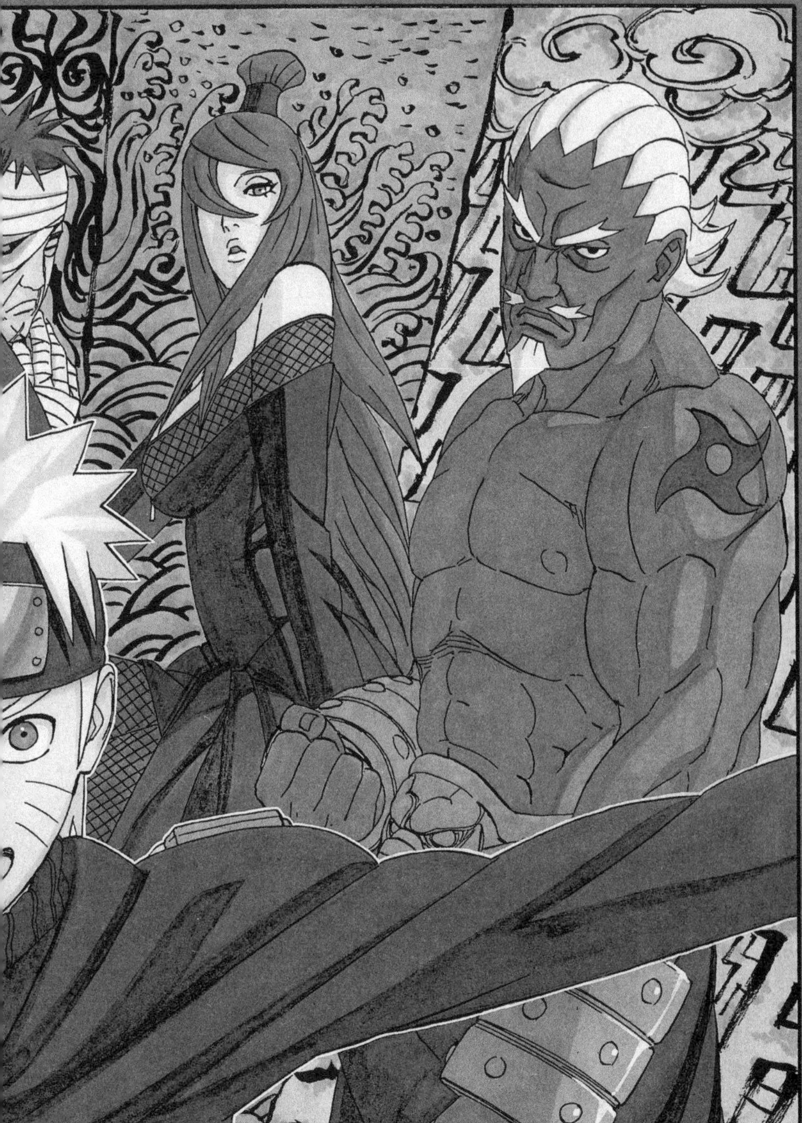

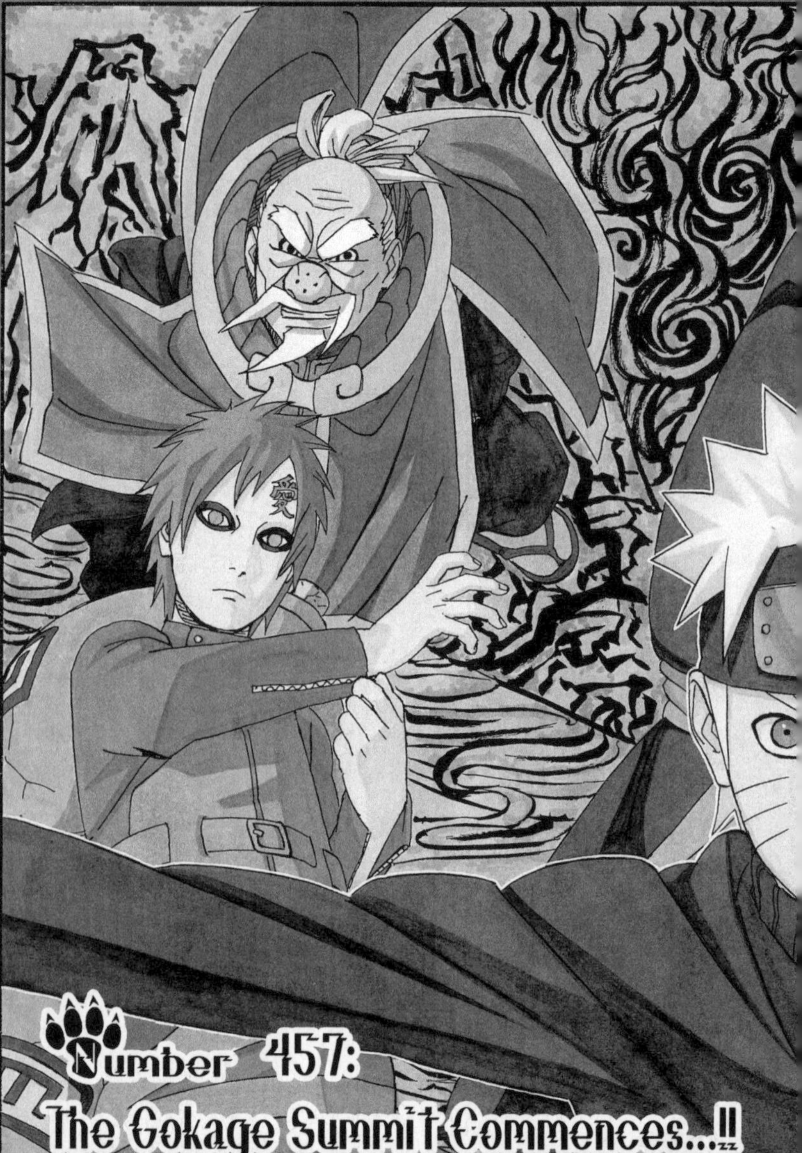
Number 457:
The Gokage Summit Commences...!!

NARUTO

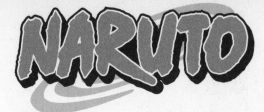

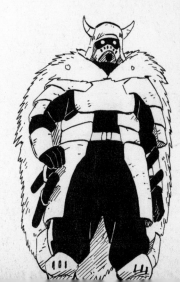

READ THIS WAY

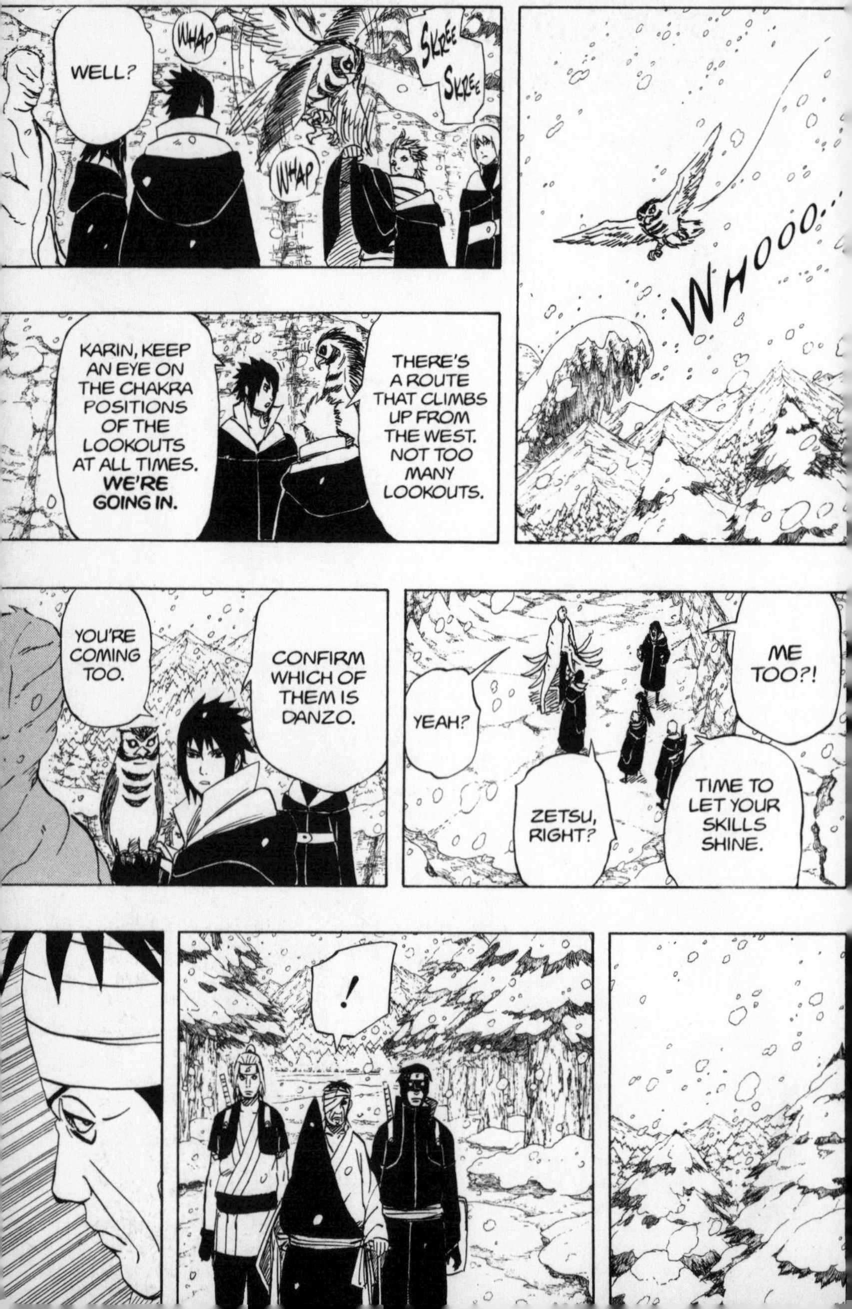
WHOOO...
SKREE
SKREE
WHAP
WELL?
WHAP
THERE'S A ROUTE THAT CLIMBS UP FROM THE WEST. NOT TOO MANY LOOKOUTS.
KARIN, KEEP AN EYE ON THE CHAKRA POSITIONS OF THE LOOKOUTS AT ALL TIMES. **WE'RE GOING IN.**
ME TOO?!
YEAH?
TIME TO LET YOUR SKILLS SHINE.
ZETSU, RIGHT?
CONFIRM WHICH OF THEM IS DANZO.
YOU'RE COMING TOO.
!

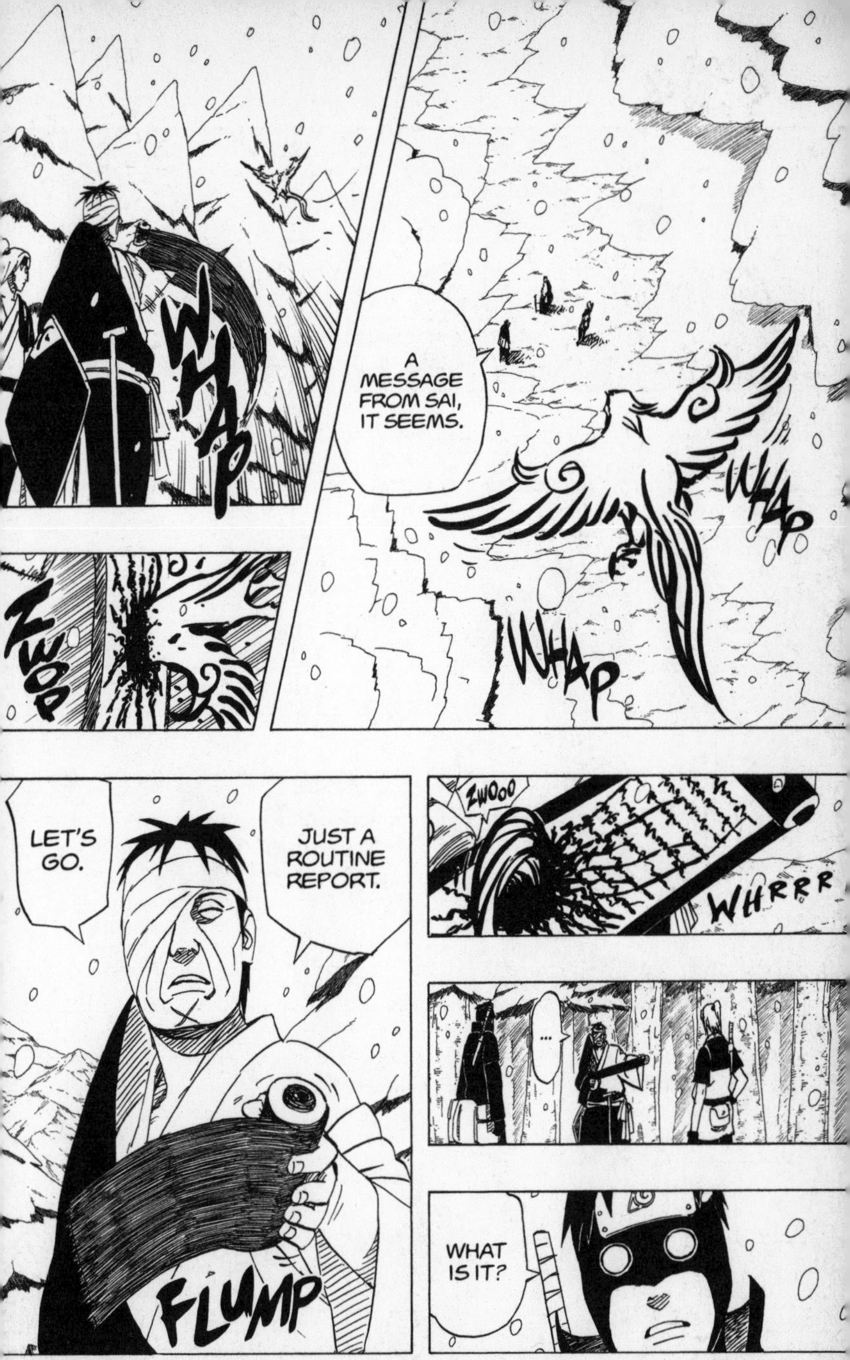
A MESSAGE FROM SAI, IT SEEMS.
WHAP
WHAP
WHAP
ZWOO
ZWOOO
WHRRR
...
WHAT IS IT?
JUST A ROUTINE REPORT.
LET'S GO.
FLUMP

READ THIS WAY

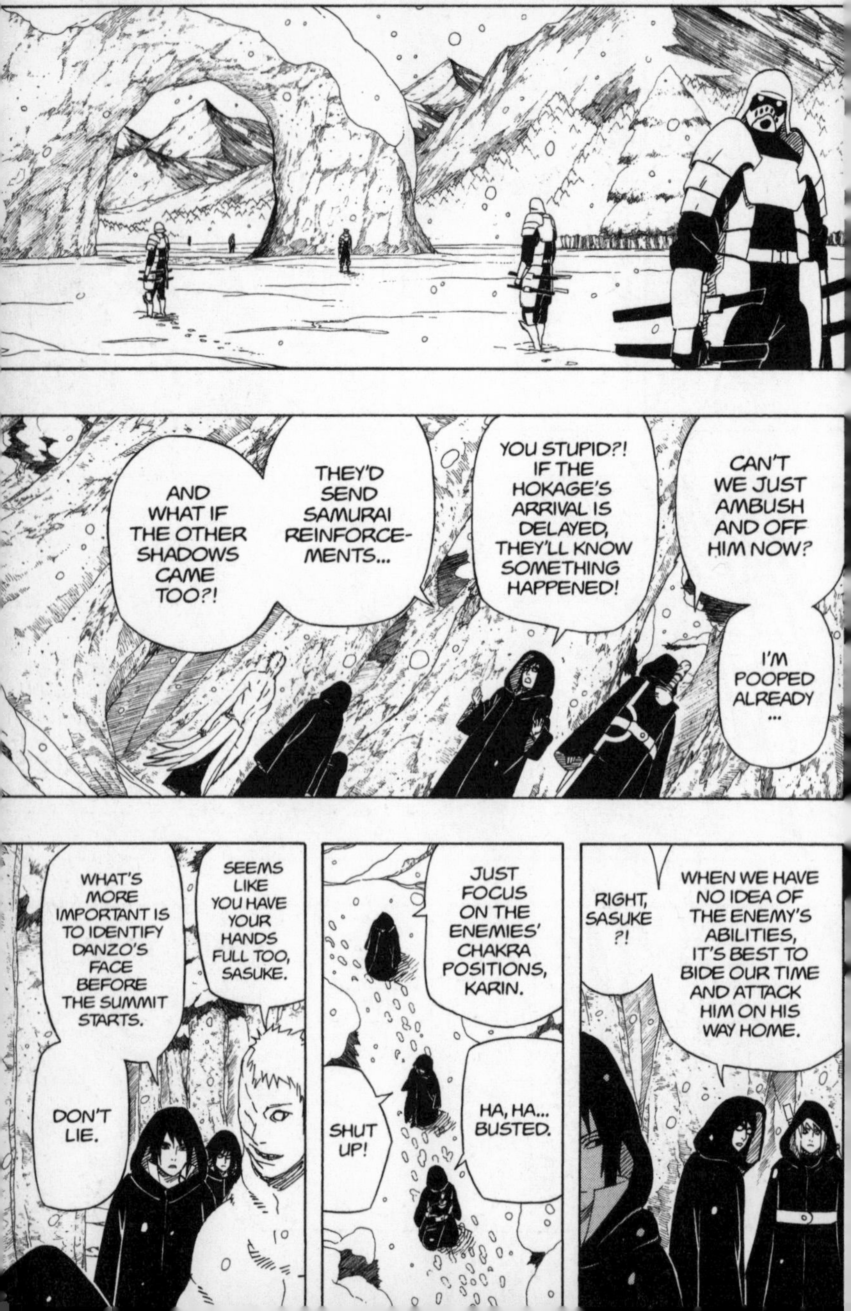
CAN'T WE JUST AMBUSH AND OFF HIM NOW?
I'M POOPED ALREADY ...
YOU STUPID?! IF THE HOKAGE'S ARRIVAL IS DELAYED, THEY'LL KNOW SOMETHING HAPPENED!
THEY'D SEND SAMURAI REINFORCE-MENTS...
AND WHAT IF THE OTHER SHADOWS CAME TOO?!
WHEN WE HAVE NO IDEA OF THE ENEMY'S ABILITIES, IT'S BEST TO BIDE OUR TIME AND ATTACK HIM ON HIS WAY HOME.
RIGHT, SASUKE ?!
JUST FOCUS ON THE ENEMIES' CHAKRA POSITIONS, KARIN.
HA, HA... BUSTED.
SHUT UP!
SEEMS LIKE YOU HAVE YOUR HANDS FULL TOO, SASUKE.
WHAT'S MORE IMPORTANT IS TO IDENTIFY DANZO'S FACE BEFORE THE SUMMIT STARTS.
DON'T LIE.

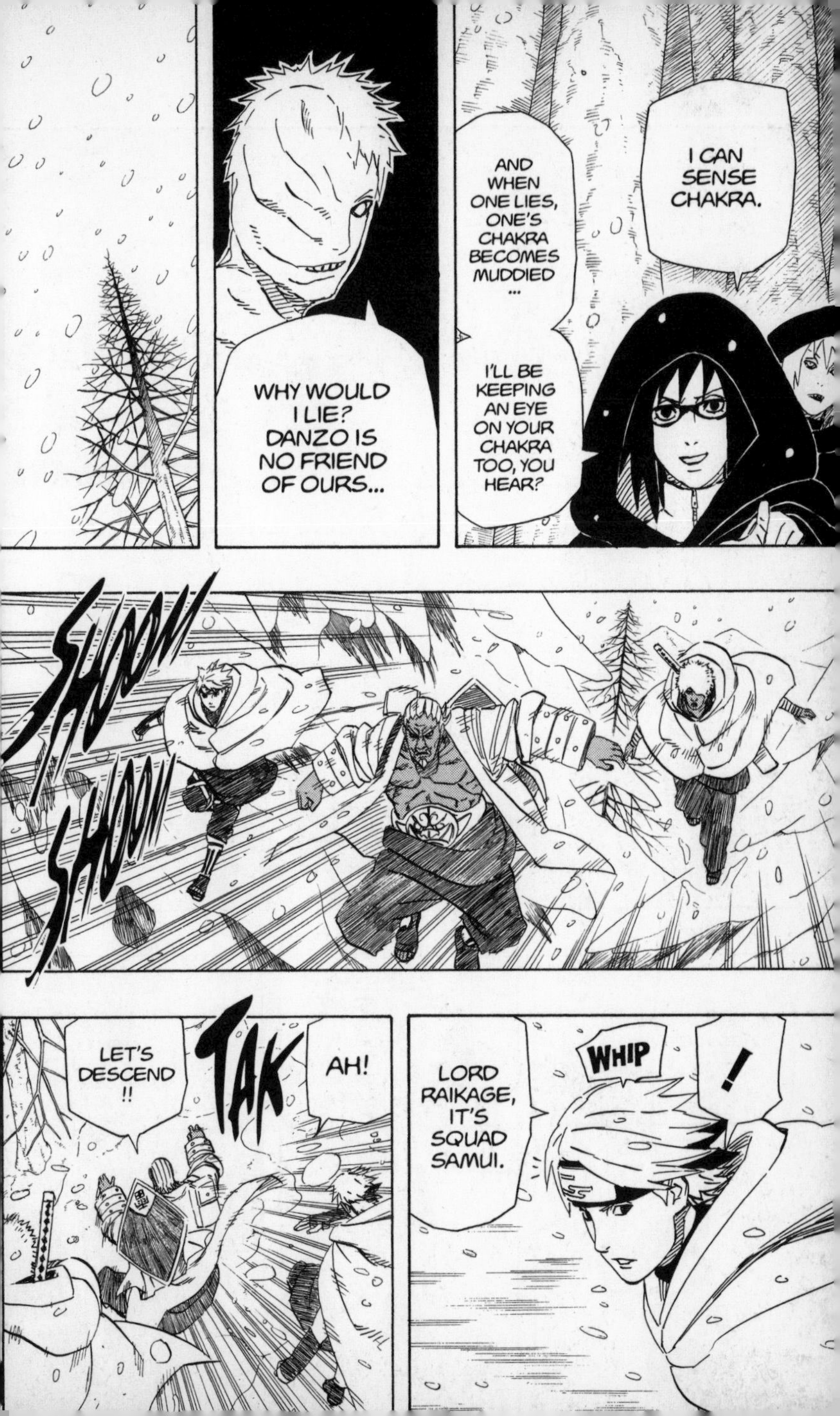
I CAN SENSE CHAKRA.
AND WHEN ONE LIES, ONE'S CHAKRA BECOMES MUDDIED ...
I'LL BE KEEPING AN EYE ON YOUR CHAKRA TOO, YOU HEAR?
WHY WOULD I LIE? DANZO IS NO FRIEND OF OURS...
SHOOM
SHOOM
WHIP
!
LORD RAIKAGE, IT'S SQUAD SAMUI.
AH!
TAK
LET'S DESCEND !!

READ THIS WAY

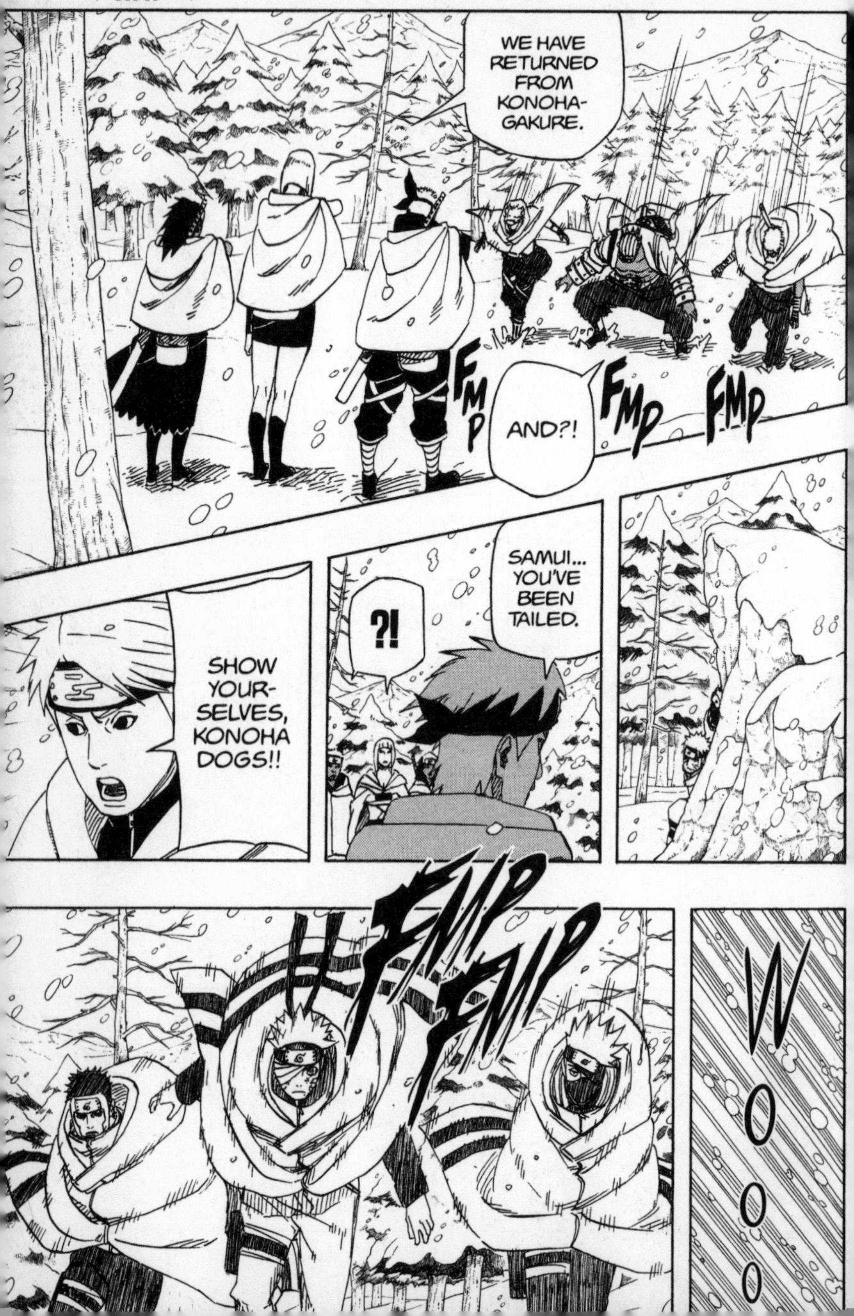

WE HAVE RETURNED FROM KONOHA-GAKURE.
FMP
FMP
AND?!
FMP
SAMUI... YOU'VE BEEN TAILED.
?!
SHOW YOURSELVES, KONOHA DOGS!!
WOOO
FMP
FMP
FMP

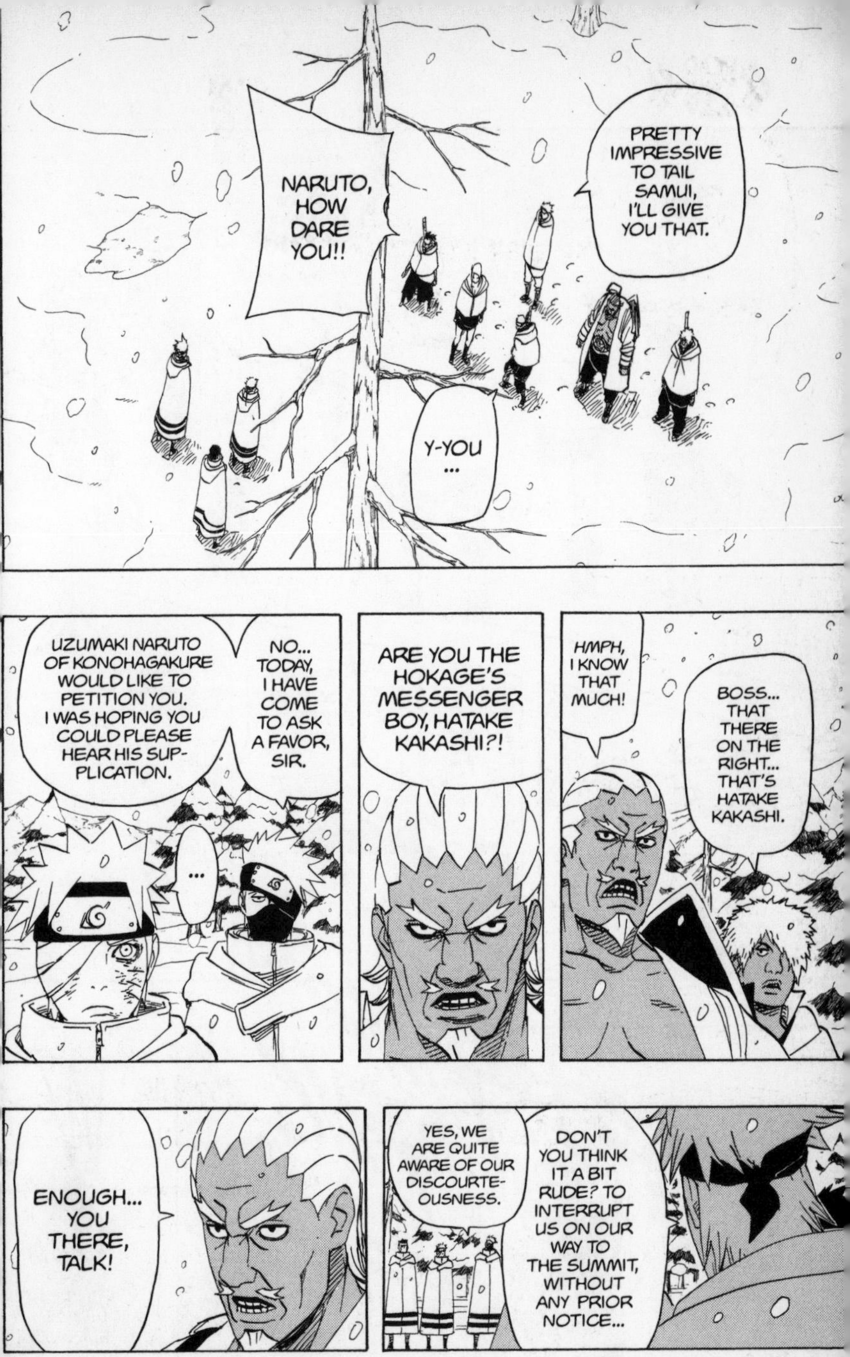
PRETTY IMPRESSIVE TO TAIL SAMUI, I'LL GIVE YOU THAT.
NARUTO, HOW DARE YOU!!
Y-YOU ...
BOSS... THAT THERE ON THE RIGHT... THAT'S HATAKE KAKASHI.
HMPH, I KNOW THAT MUCH!
ARE YOU THE HOKAGE'S MESSENGER BOY, HATAKE KAKASHI?!
NO... TODAY, I HAVE COME TO ASK A FAVOR, SIR.
UZUMAKI NARUTO OF KONOHAGAKURE WOULD LIKE TO PETITION YOU. I WAS HOPING YOU COULD PLEASE HEAR HIS SUPPLICATION.
...
DON'T YOU THINK IT A BIT RUDE? TO INTERRUPT US ON OUR WAY TO THE SUMMIT, WITHOUT ANY PRIOR NOTICE...
YES, WE ARE QUITE AWARE OF OUR DISCOURTEOUSNESS.
ENOUGH... YOU THERE, TALK!

READ THIS WAY

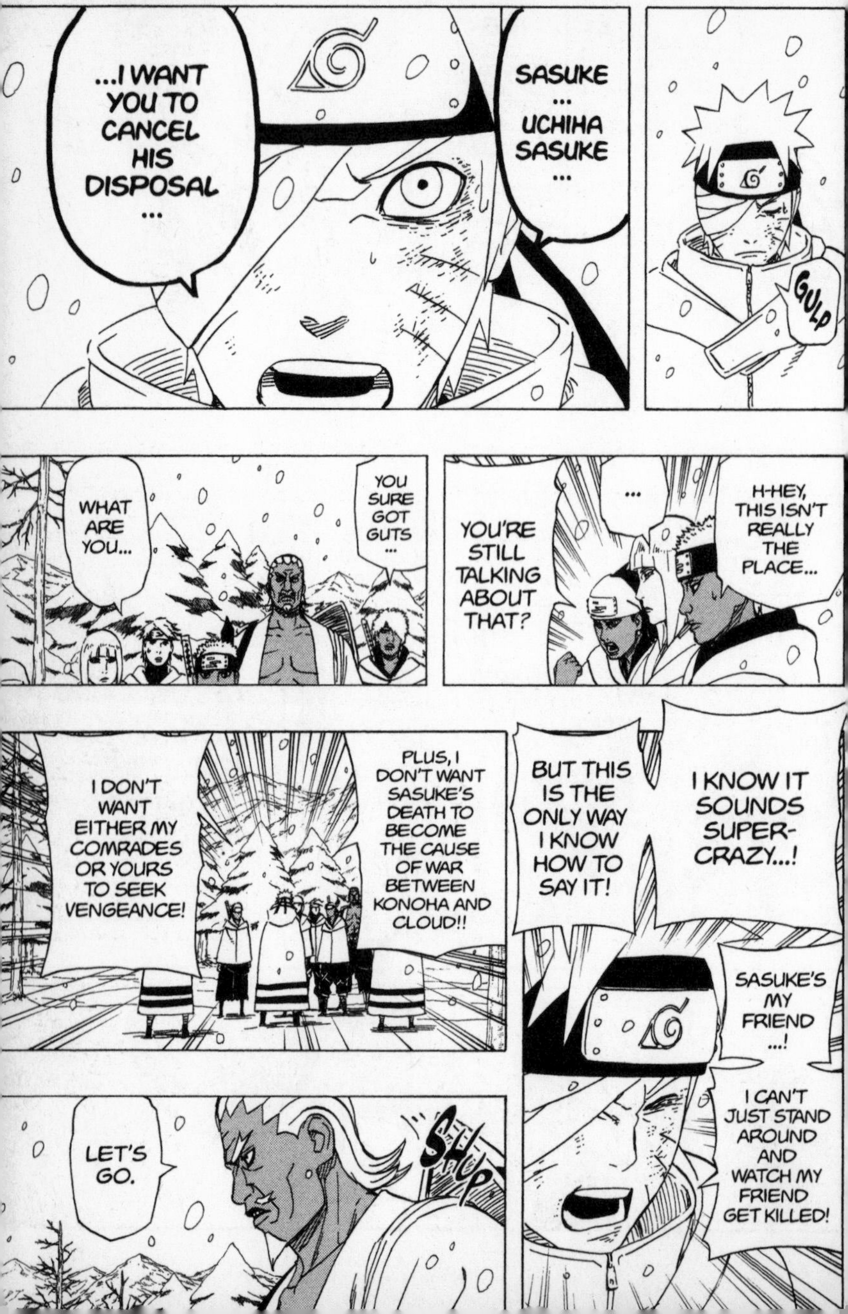
GULP
SASUKE ... UCHIHA SASUKE ...
...I WANT YOU TO CANCEL HIS DISPOSAL ...
H-HEY, THIS ISN'T REALLY THE PLACE...
...
YOU'RE STILL TALKING ABOUT THAT?
YOU SURE GOT GUTS ...
WHAT ARE YOU...
I KNOW IT SOUNDS SUPER-CRAZY...!
BUT THIS IS THE ONLY WAY I KNOW HOW TO SAY IT!
SASUKE'S MY FRIEND ...!
I CAN'T JUST STAND AROUND AND WATCH MY FRIEND GET KILLED!
PLUS, I DON'T WANT SASUKE'S DEATH TO BECOME THE CAUSE OF WAR BETWEEN KONOHA AND CLOUD!!
I DON'T WANT EITHER MY COMRADES OR YOURS TO SEEK VENGEANCE!
SHUP
LET'S GO.

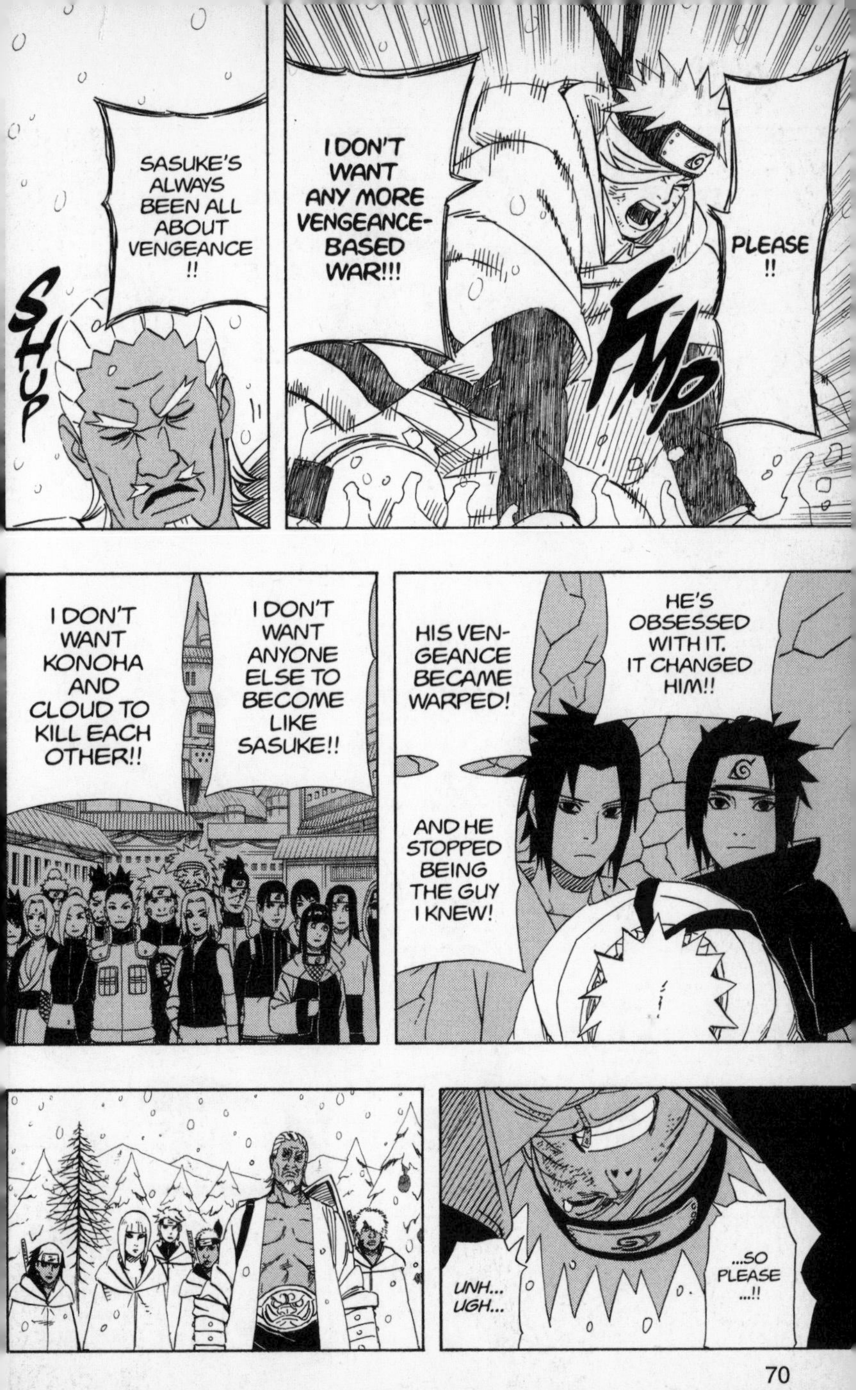
I DON'T WANT ANY MORE VENGEANCE-BASED WAR!!!
PLEASE !!
FMP
SASUKE'S ALWAYS BEEN ALL ABOUT VENGEANCE !!
SHUP
HE'S OBSESSED WITH IT. IT CHANGED HIM!!
HIS VEN-GEANCE BECAME WARPED!
AND HE STOPPED BEING THE GUY I KNEW!
I DON'T WANT ANYONE ELSE TO BECOME LIKE SASUKE!!
I DON'T WANT KONOHA AND CLOUD TO KILL EACH OTHER!!
...SO PLEASE ...!!
UNH... UGH...

READ THIS WAY

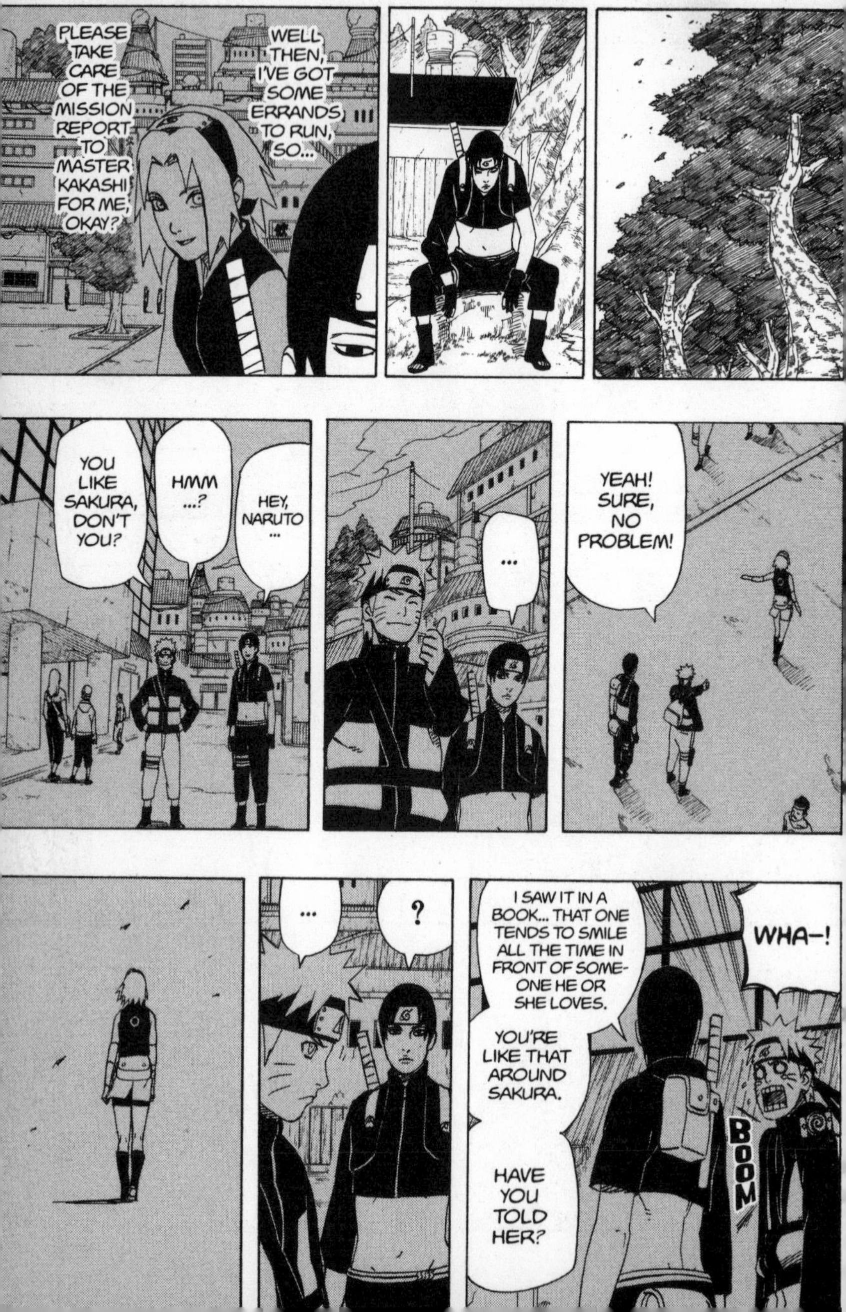
WELL THEN, I'VE GOT SOME ERRANDS TO RUN, SO...
PLEASE TAKE CARE OF THE MISSION REPORT TO MASTER KAKASHI FOR ME, OKAY?
YEAH! SURE, NO PROBLEM!
...
HEY, NARUTO ...
HMM ...?
YOU LIKE SAKURA, DON'T YOU?
WHA–!
BOOM
I SAW IT IN A BOOK... THAT ONE TENDS TO SMILE ALL THE TIME IN FRONT OF SOMEONE HE OR SHE LOVES.
YOU'RE LIKE THAT AROUND SAKURA.
HAVE YOU TOLD HER?
?
...

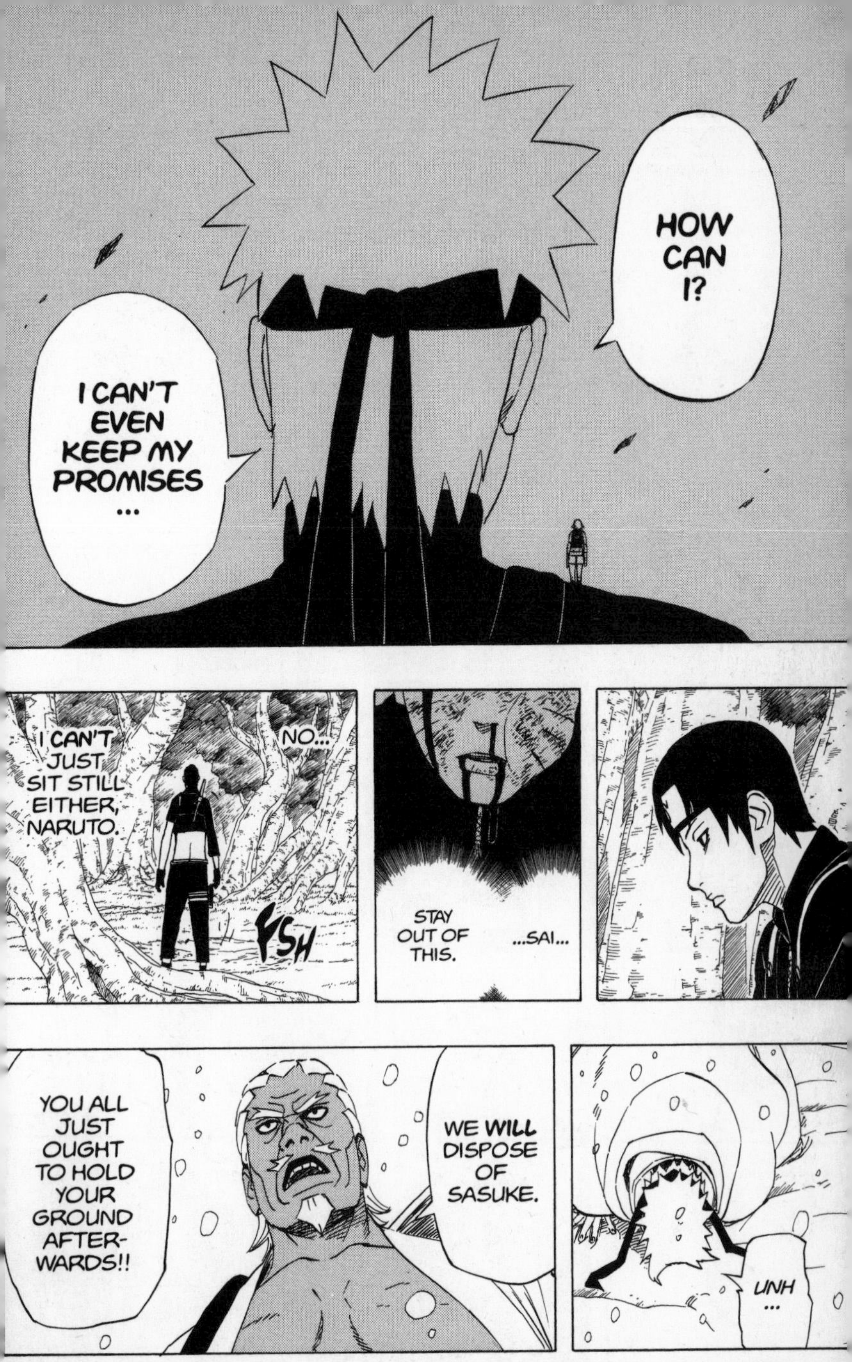
HOW CAN I?
I CAN'T EVEN KEEP MY PROMISES ...
...SAI...
STAY OUT OF THIS.
NO...
I CAN'T JUST SIT STILL EITHER, NARUTO.
FSH
UNH ...
WE **WILL** DISPOSE OF SASUKE.
YOU ALL JUST OUGHT TO HOLD YOUR GROUND AFTER-WARDS!!

READ THIS WAY

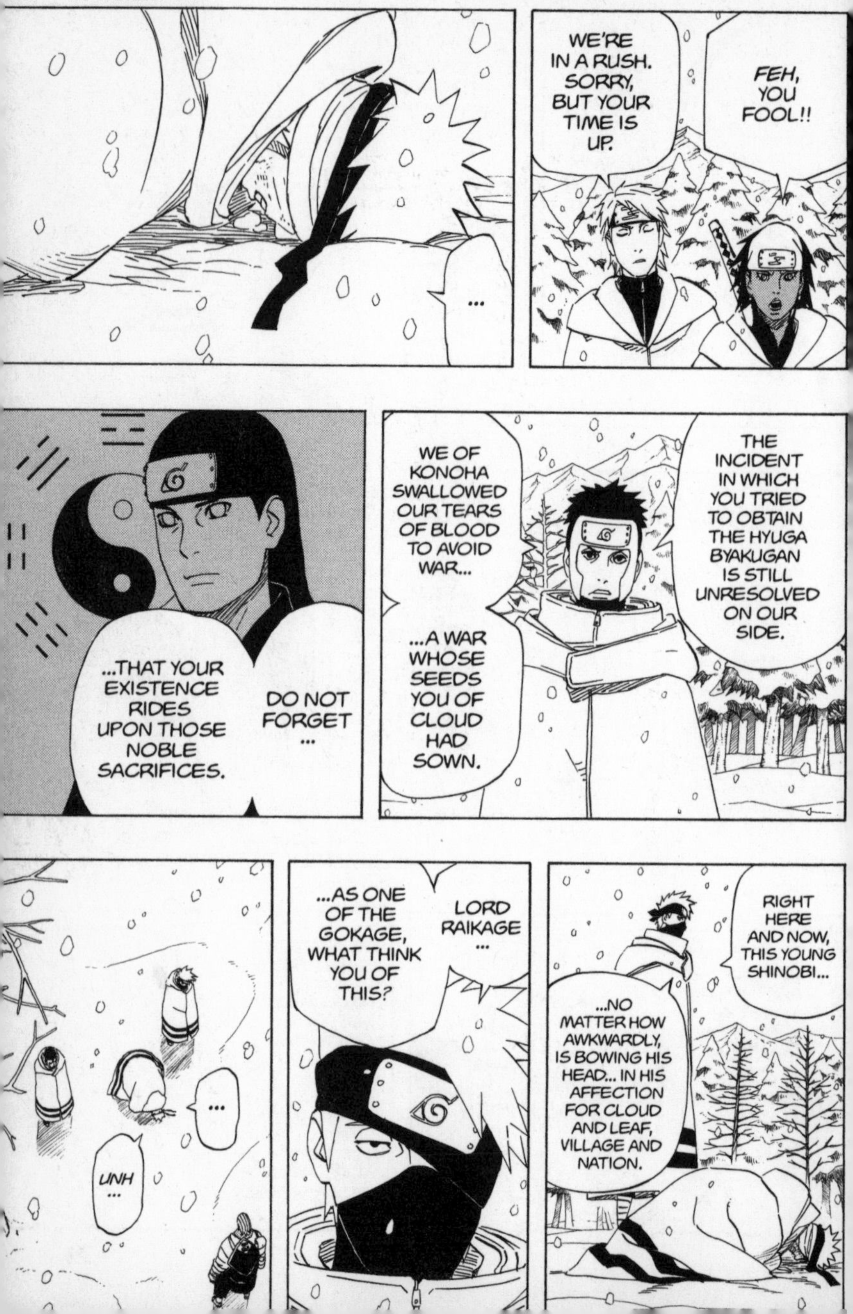

FEH, YOU FOOL!!
WE'RE IN A RUSH. SORRY, BUT YOUR TIME IS UP.
...
THE INCIDENT IN WHICH YOU TRIED TO OBTAIN THE HYUGA BYAKUGAN IS STILL UNRESOLVED ON OUR SIDE.
WE OF KONOHA SWALLOWED OUR TEARS OF BLOOD TO AVOID WAR...
...A WAR WHOSE SEEDS YOU OF CLOUD HAD SOWN.
DO NOT FORGET ...
...THAT YOUR EXISTENCE RIDES UPON THOSE NOBLE SACRIFICES.
RIGHT HERE AND NOW, THIS YOUNG SHINOBI...
...NO MATTER HOW AWKWARDLY, IS BOWING HIS HEAD... IN HIS AFFECTION FOR CLOUD AND LEAF, VILLAGE AND NATION.
LORD RAIKAGE ...
...AS ONE OF THE GOKAGE, WHAT THINK YOU OF THIS?
...
UNH ...

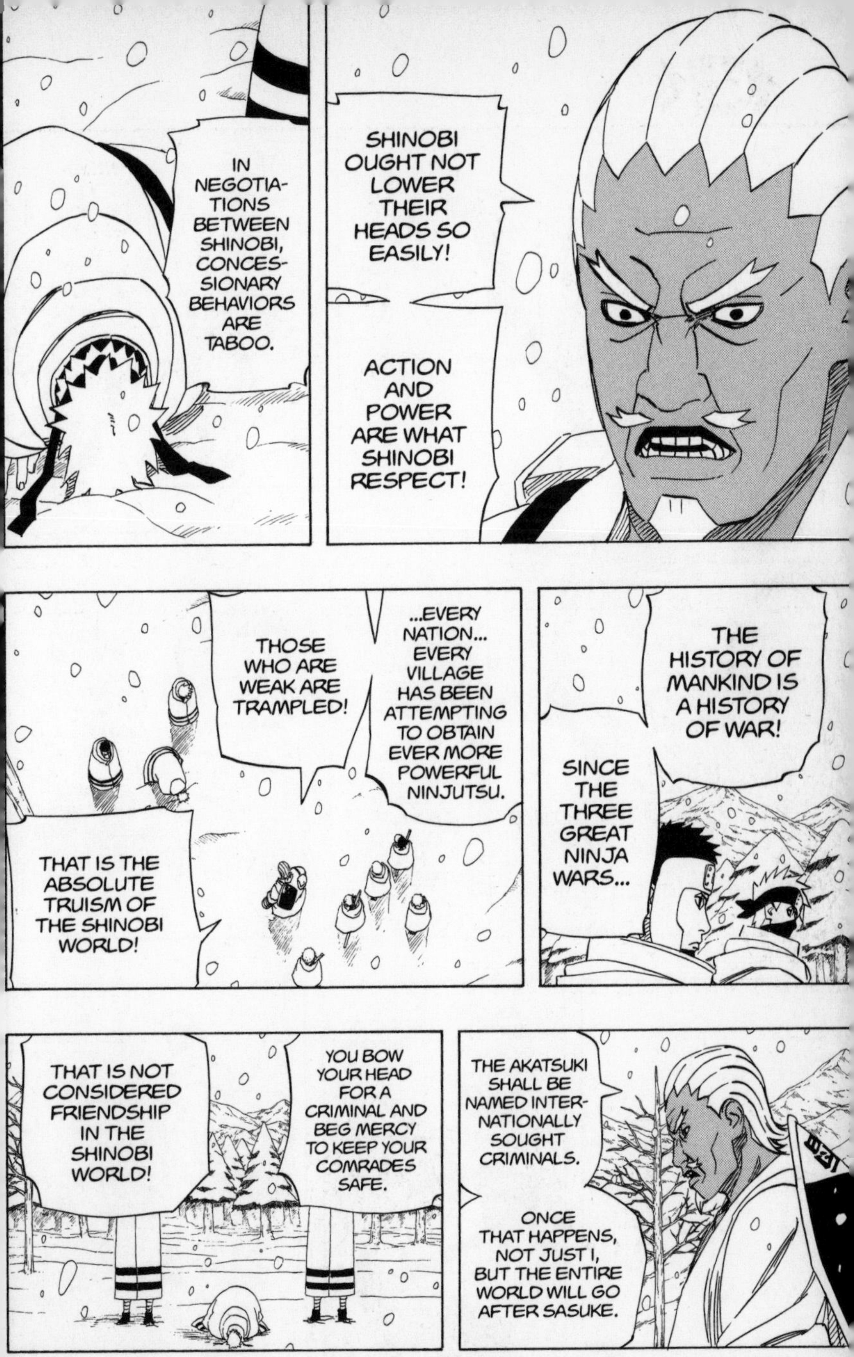

SHINOBI OUGHT NOT LOWER THEIR HEADS SO EASILY!
ACTION AND POWER ARE WHAT SHINOBI RESPECT!
IN NEGOTIATIONS BETWEEN SHINOBI, CONCESSIONARY BEHAVIORS ARE TABOO.
THE HISTORY OF MANKIND IS A HISTORY OF WAR!
SINCE THE THREE GREAT NINJA WARS...
...EVERY NATION... EVERY VILLAGE HAS BEEN ATTEMPTING TO OBTAIN EVER MORE POWERFUL NINJUTSU.
THOSE WHO ARE WEAK ARE TRAMPLED!
THAT IS THE ABSOLUTE TRUISM OF THE SHINOBI WORLD!
THE AKATSUKI SHALL BE NAMED INTERNATIONALLY SOUGHT CRIMINALS.
ONCE THAT HAPPENS, NOT JUST I, BUT THE ENTIRE WORLD WILL GO AFTER SASUKE.
YOU BOW YOUR HEAD FOR A CRIMINAL AND BEG MERCY TO KEEP YOUR COMRADES SAFE.
THAT IS NOT CONSIDERED FRIENDSHIP IN THE SHINOBI WORLD!

READ THIS WAY

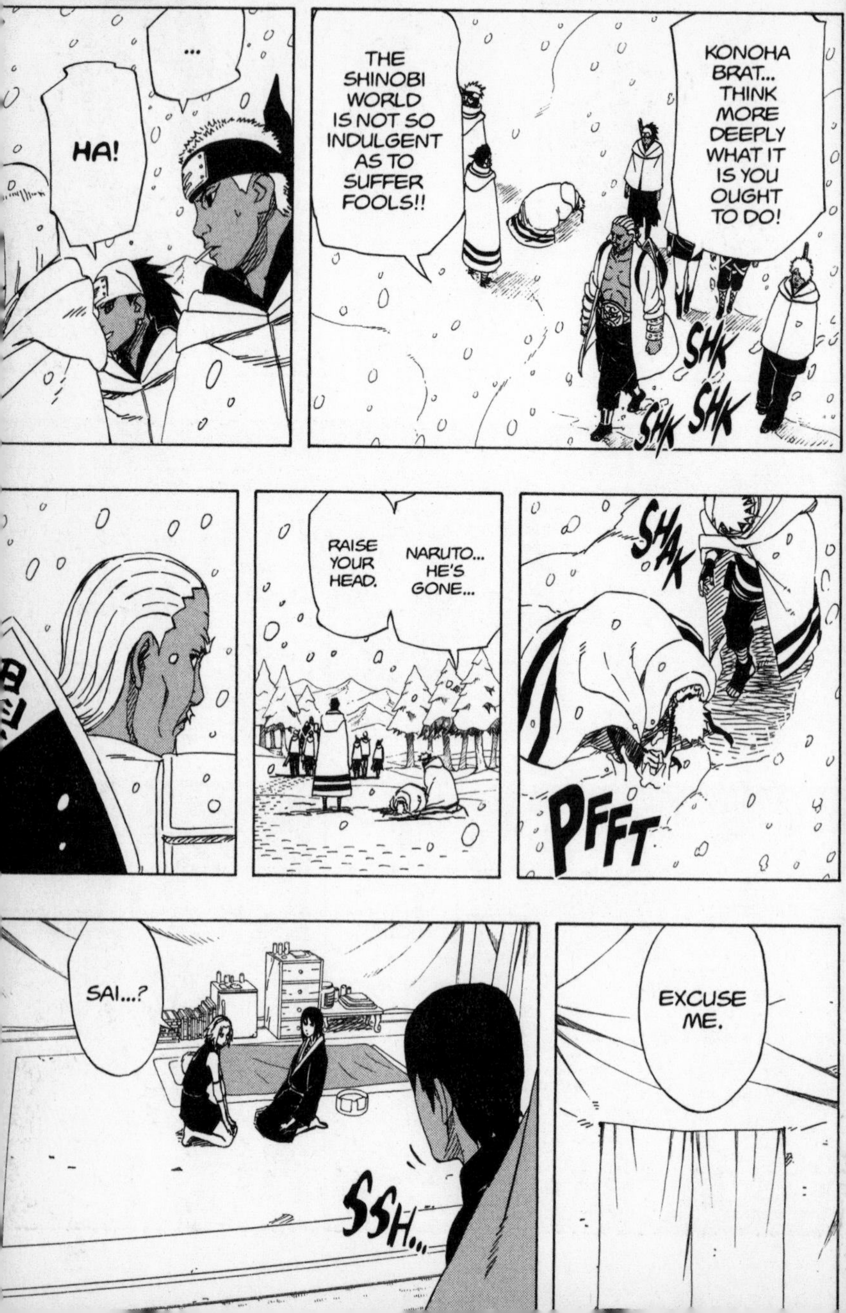
KONOHA BRAT... THINK MORE DEEPLY WHAT IT IS YOU OUGHT TO DO!
THE SHINOBI WORLD IS NOT SO INDULGENT AS TO SUFFER FOOLS!!
SHK
SHK
SHK
...
HA!
SHAK
PFFT
NARUTO... HE'S GONE...
RAISE YOUR HEAD.
EXCUSE ME.
SAI...?
SSH...

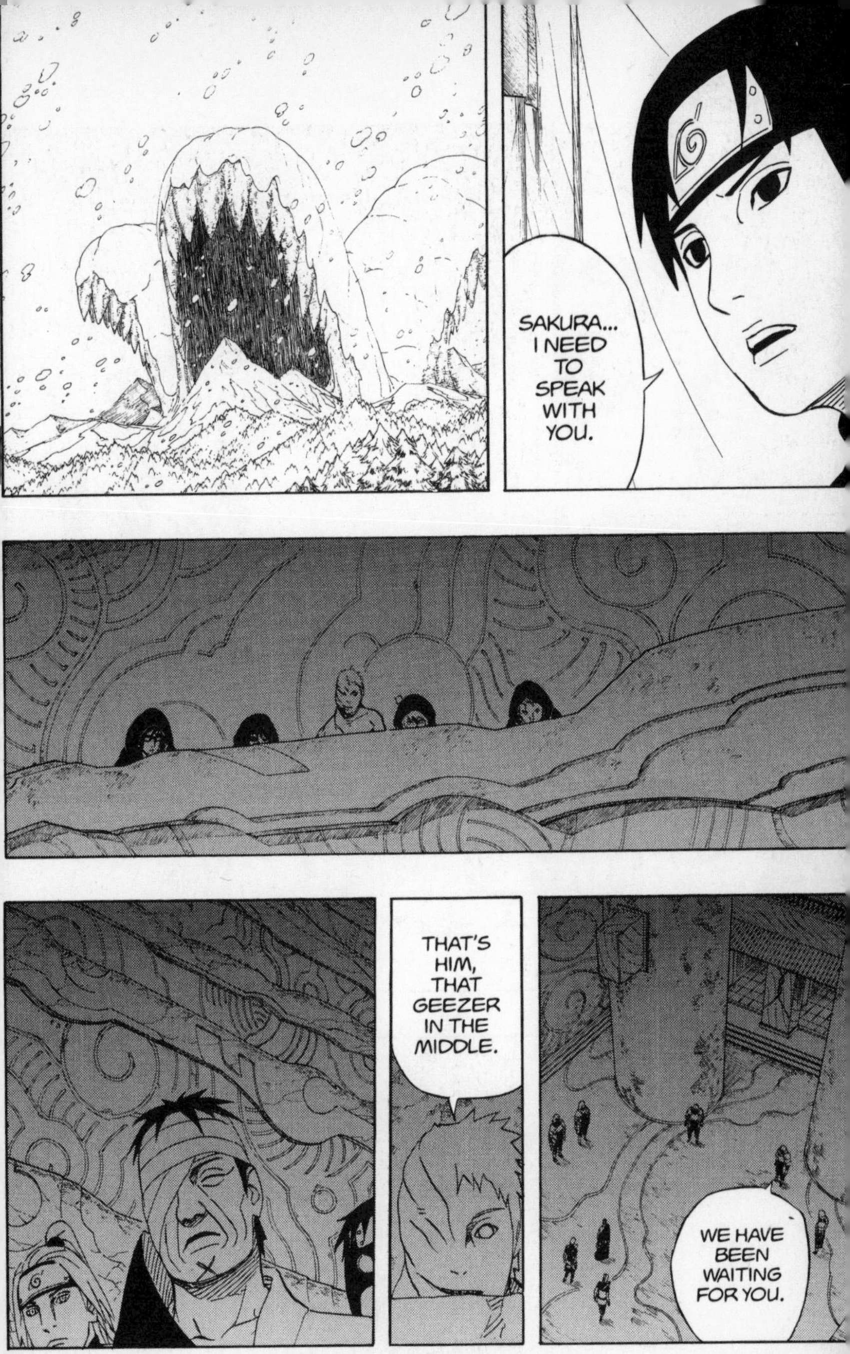
SAKURA... I NEED TO SPEAK WITH YOU.
WE HAVE BEEN WAITING FOR YOU.
THAT'S HIM, THAT GEEZER IN THE MIDDLE.

SO
THAT'S...
DANZO.

(SAMURAI)

FSH...

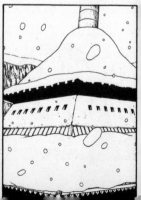

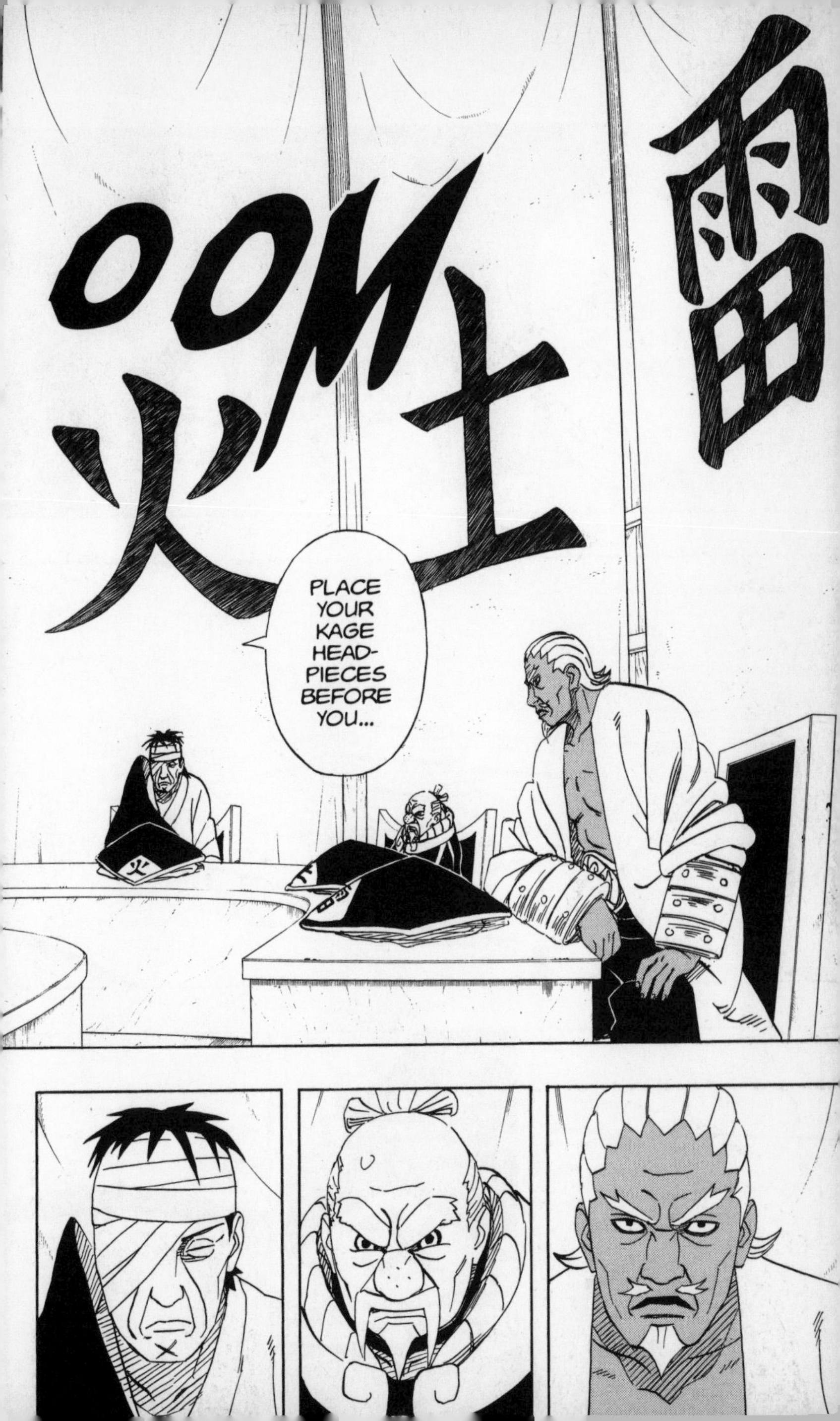
雷
土
火
PLACE YOUR KAGE HEAD-PIECES BEFORE YOU...

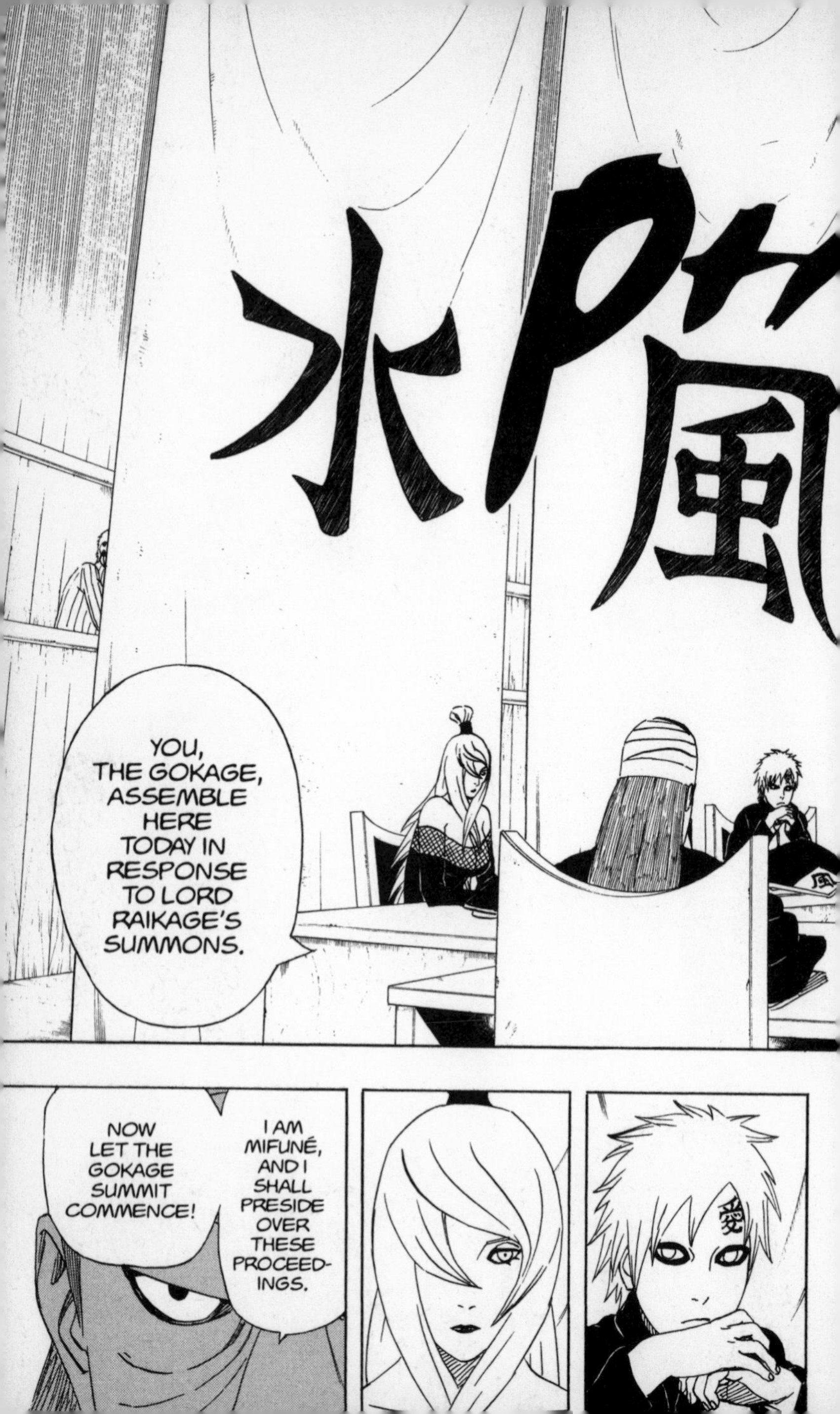
YOU, THE GOKAGE, ASSEMBLE HERE TODAY IN RESPONSE TO LORD RAIKAGE'S SUMMONS.
I AM MIFUNÉ, AND I SHALL PRESIDE OVER THESE PROCEED-INGS.
NOW LET THE GOKAGE SUMMIT COMMENCE!

NARUTO

Number 458: The Great Gokage Debate...!!

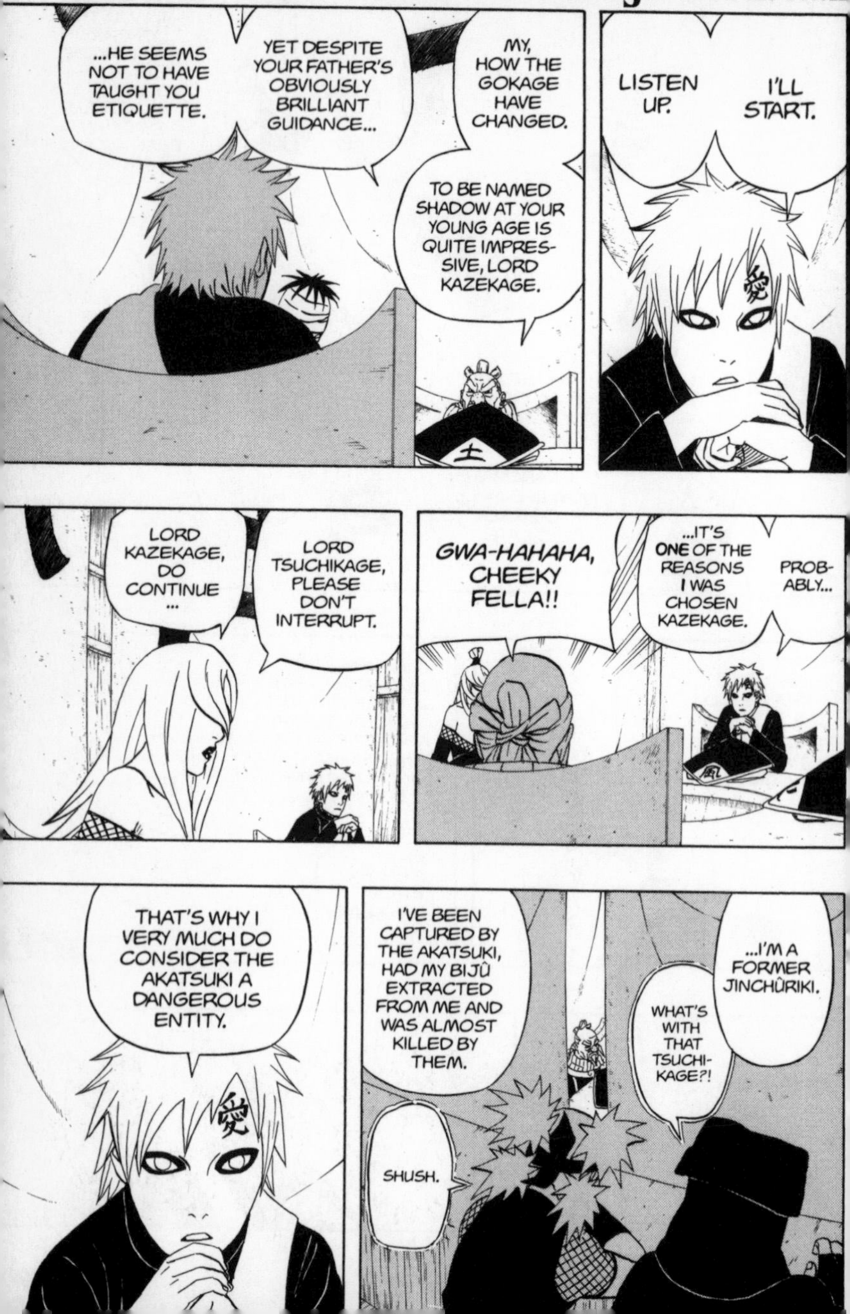
I'LL START.
LISTEN UP.
MY, HOW THE GOKAGE HAVE CHANGED.
TO BE NAMED SHADOW AT YOUR YOUNG AGE IS QUITE IMPRESSIVE, LORD KAZEKAGE.
YET DESPITE YOUR FATHER'S OBVIOUSLY BRILLIANT GUIDANCE...
...HE SEEMS NOT TO HAVE TAUGHT YOU ETIQUETTE.
PROBABLY...
...IT'S ONE OF THE REASONS I WAS CHOSEN KAZEKAGE.
GWA-HAHAHA, CHEEKY FELLA!!
LORD TSUCHIKAGE, PLEASE DON'T INTERRUPT.
LORD KAZEKAGE, DO CONTINUE...
...I'M A FORMER JINCHÛRIKI.
WHAT'S WITH THAT TSUCHIKAGE?!
I'VE BEEN CAPTURED BY THE AKATSUKI, HAD MY BIJÛ EXTRACTED FROM ME AND WAS ALMOST KILLED BY THEM.
SHUSH.
THAT'S WHY I VERY MUCH DO CONSIDER THE AKATSUKI A DANGEROUS ENTITY.

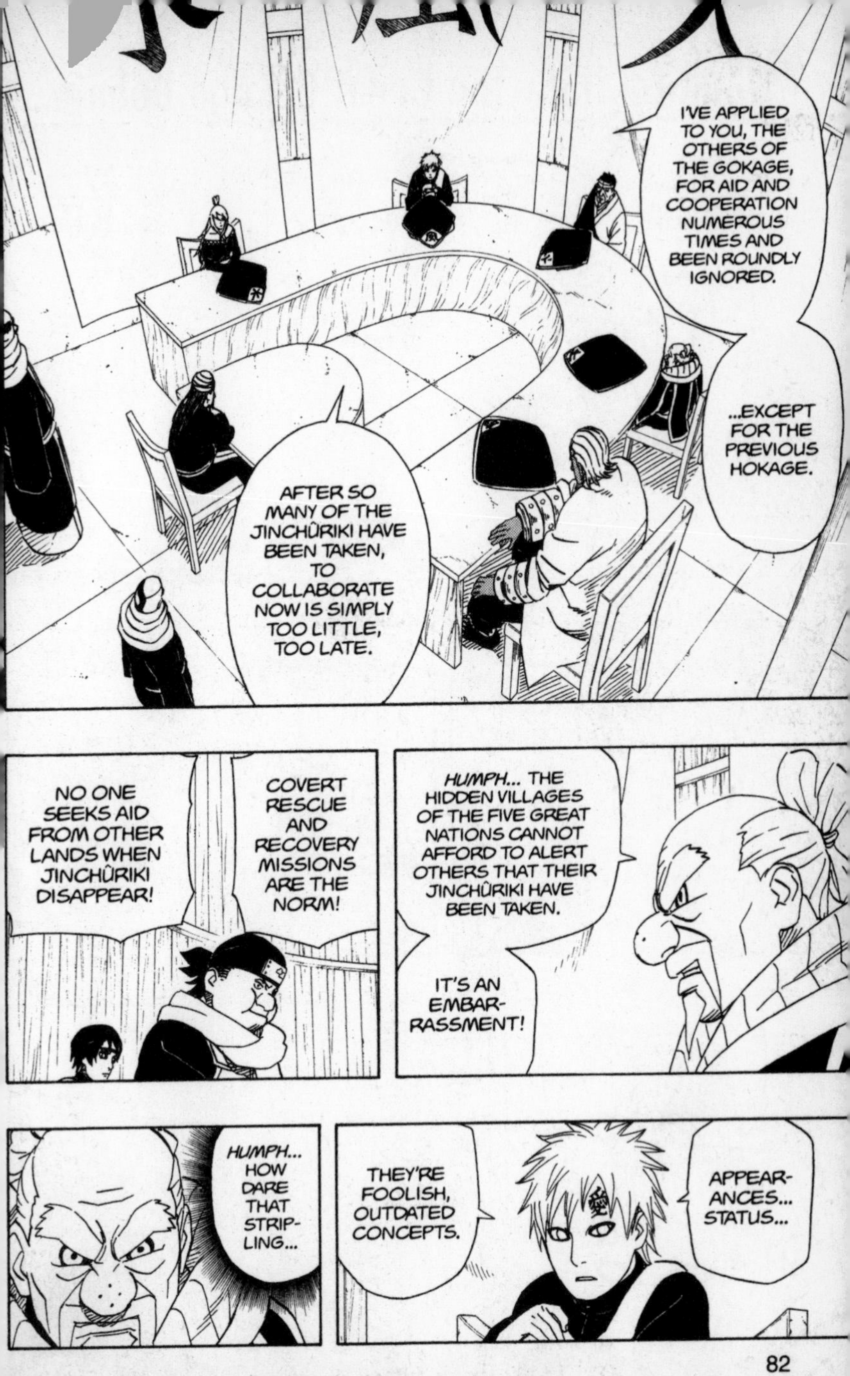
I'VE APPLIED TO YOU, THE OTHERS OF THE GOKAGE, FOR AID AND COOPERATION NUMEROUS TIMES AND BEEN ROUNDLY IGNORED.
...EXCEPT FOR THE PREVIOUS HOKAGE.
AFTER SO MANY OF THE JINCHÛRIKI HAVE BEEN TAKEN, TO COLLABORATE NOW IS SIMPLY TOO LITTLE, TOO LATE.
HUMPH... THE HIDDEN VILLAGES OF THE FIVE GREAT NATIONS CANNOT AFFORD TO ALERT OTHERS THAT THEIR JINCHÛRIKI HAVE BEEN TAKEN.
IT'S AN EMBARRASSMENT!
COVERT RESCUE AND RECOVERY MISSIONS ARE THE NORM!
NO ONE SEEKS AID FROM OTHER LANDS WHEN JINCHÛRIKI DISAPPEAR!
APPEARANCES... STATUS...
THEY'RE FOOLISH, OUTDATED CONCEPTS.
HUMPH... HOW DARE THAT STRIPLING...

READ THIS WAY

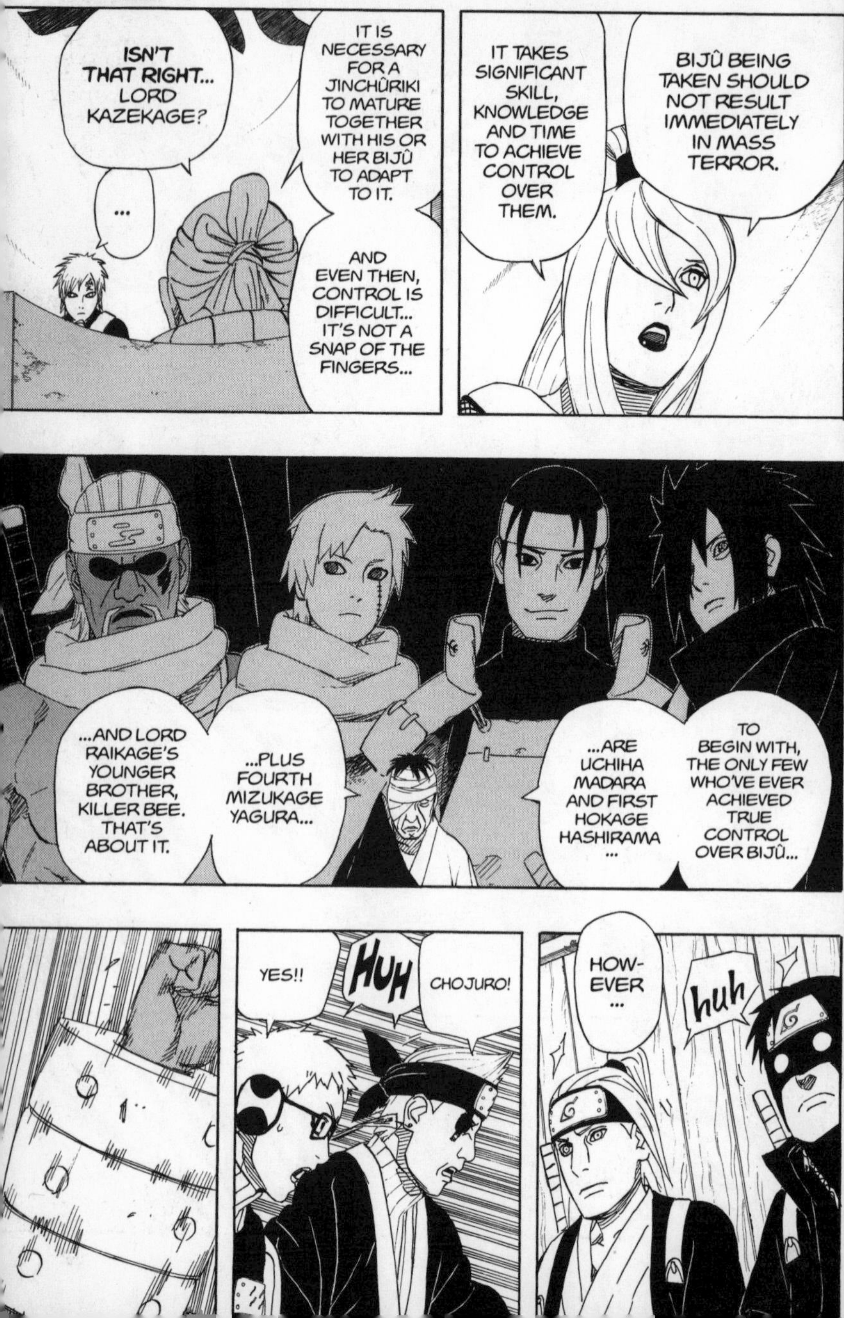
BIJÛ BEING TAKEN SHOULD NOT RESULT IMMEDIATELY IN MASS TERROR.
IT TAKES SIGNIFICANT SKILL, KNOWLEDGE AND TIME TO ACHIEVE CONTROL OVER THEM.
IT IS NECESSARY FOR A JINCHÛRIKI TO MATURE TOGETHER WITH HIS OR HER BIJÛ TO ADAPT TO IT.
AND EVEN THEN, CONTROL IS DIFFICULT... IT'S NOT A SNAP OF THE FINGERS...
ISN'T THAT RIGHT... LORD KAZEKAGE?
...
TO BEGIN WITH, THE ONLY FEW WHO'VE EVER ACHIEVED TRUE CONTROL OVER BIJÛ...
...ARE UCHIHA MADARA AND FIRST HOKAGE HASHIRAMA ...
...PLUS FOURTH MIZUKAGE YAGURA...
...AND LORD RAIKAGE'S YOUNGER BROTHER, KILLER BEE. THAT'S ABOUT IT.
huh
HOW-EVER ...
CHOJURO!
HUH
YES!!

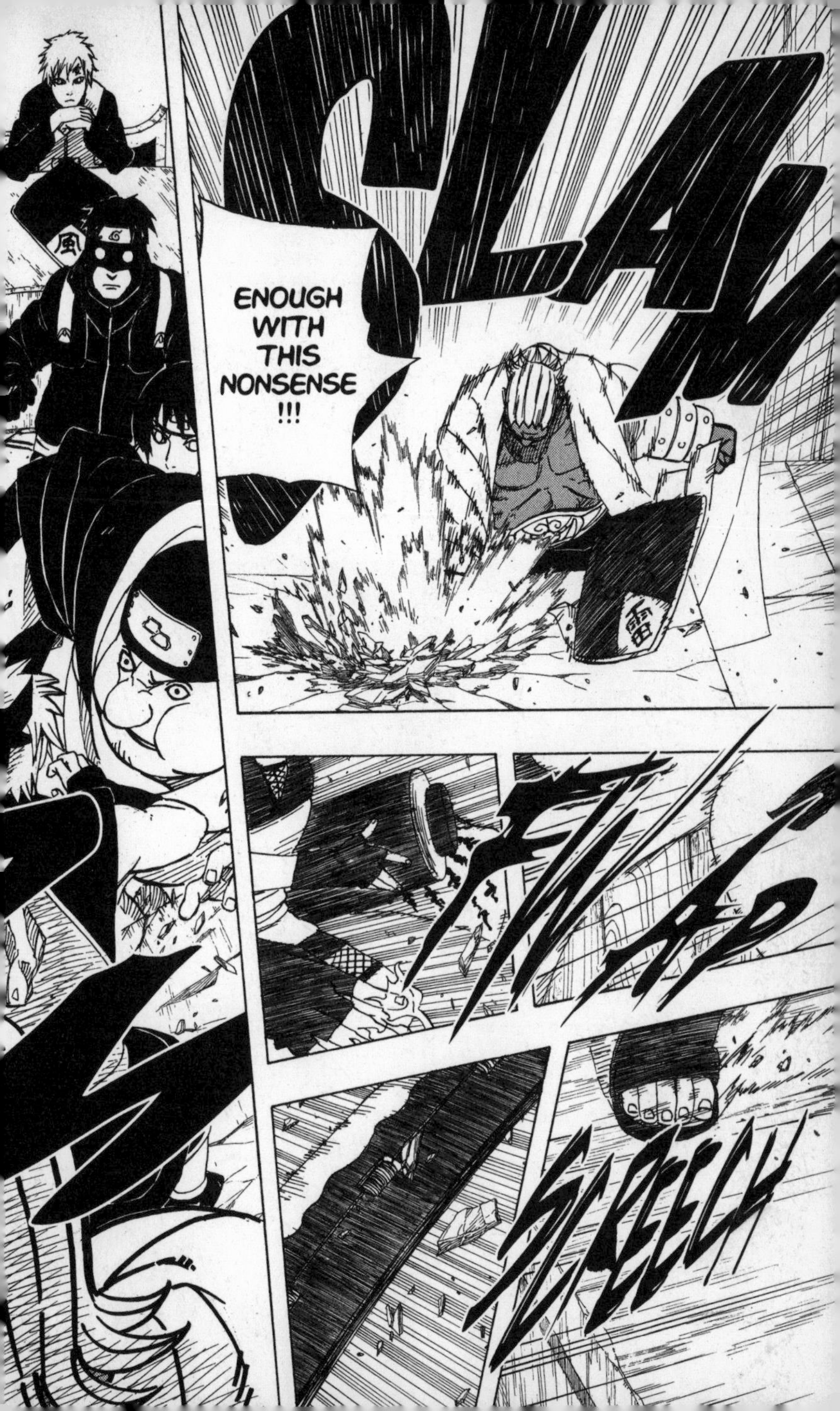
SLAM
ENOUGH WITH THIS NONSENSE!!!
SMAP
SKREECH

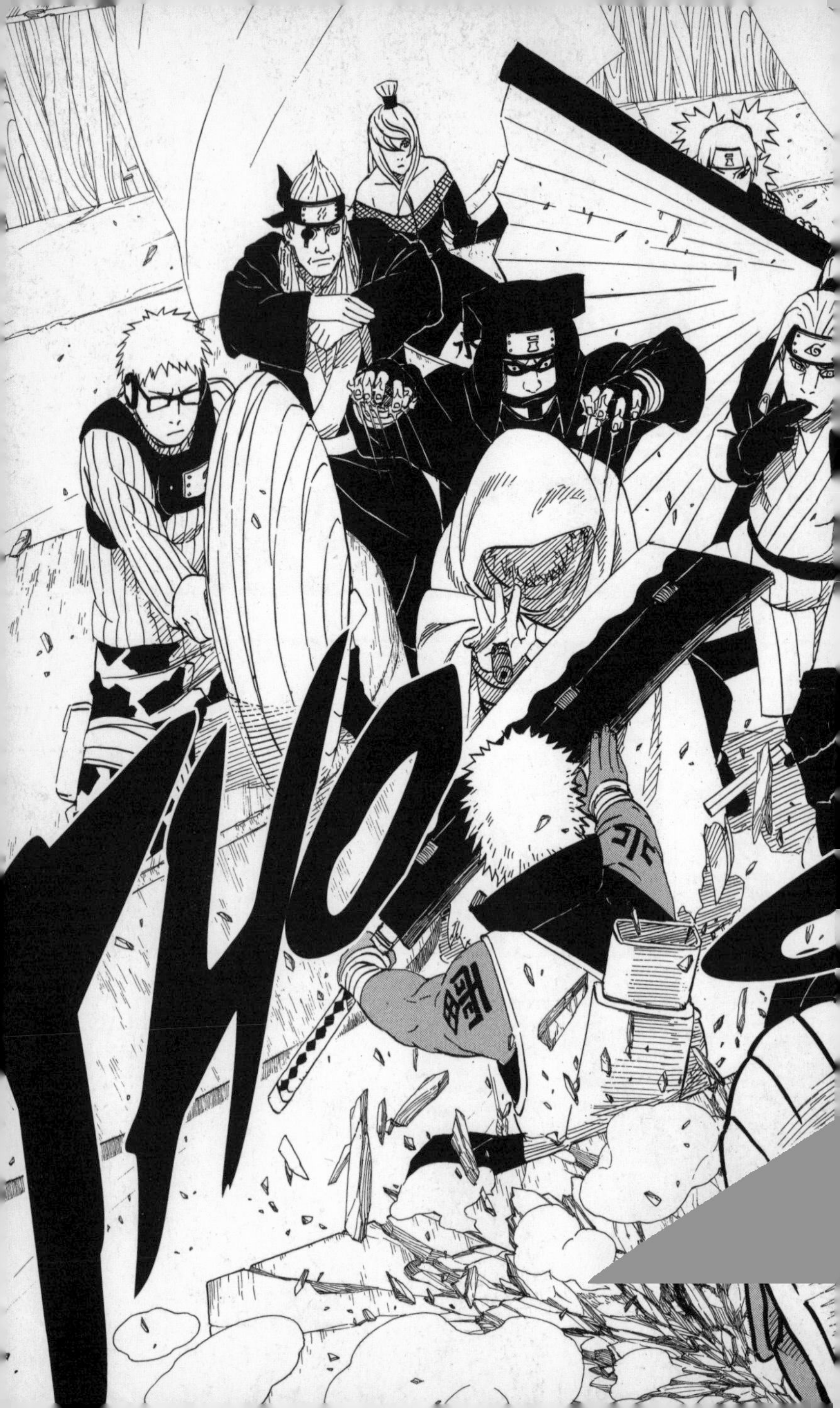

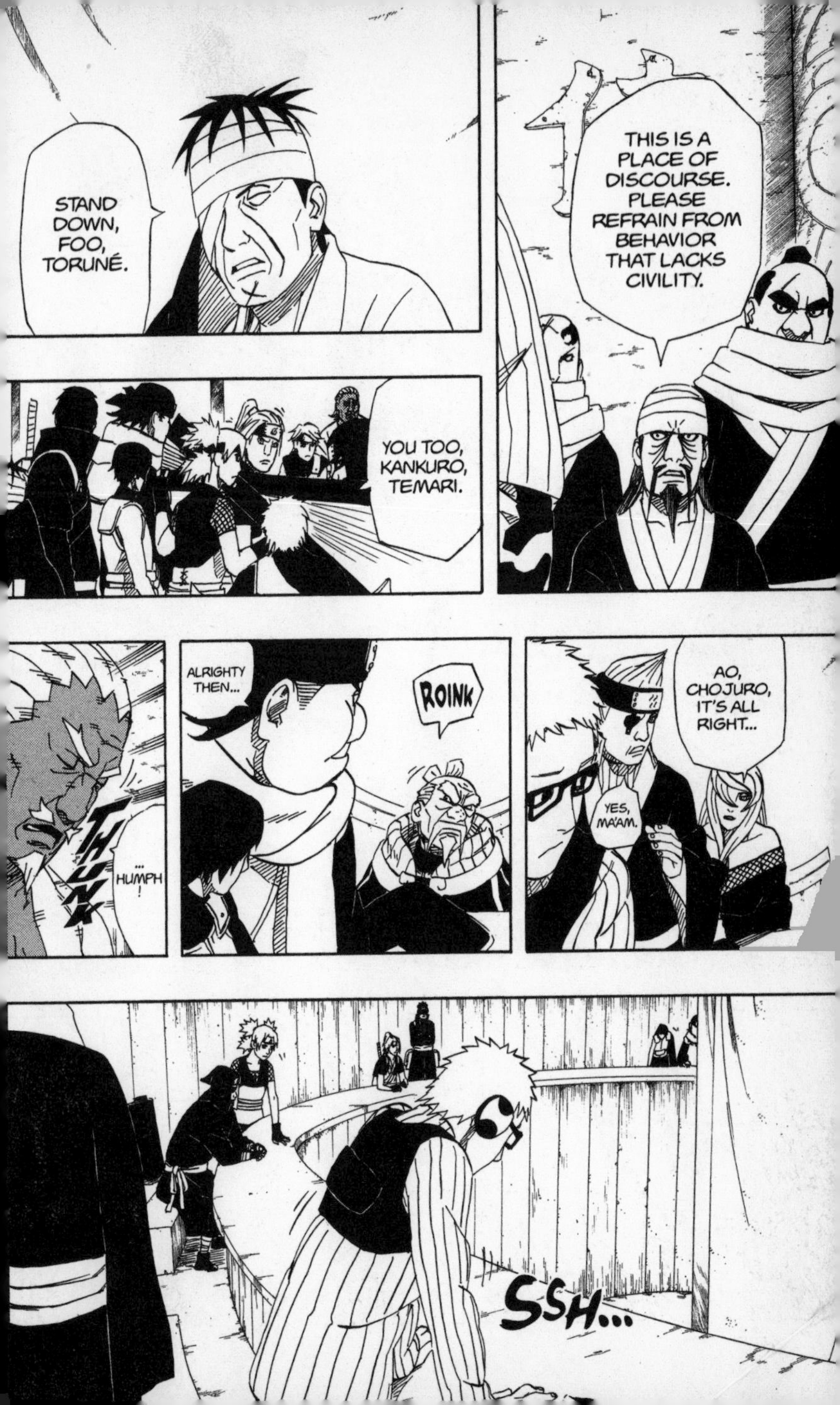
THIS IS A PLACE OF DISCOURSE. PLEASE REFRAIN FROM BEHAVIOR THAT LACKS CIVILITY.
STAND DOWN, FOO, TORUNÉ.
YOU TOO, KANKURO, TEMARI.
AO, CHOJURO, IT'S ALL RIGHT...
YES, MA'AM.
ROINK
ALRIGHTY THEN...
...HUMPH!
THUNK
SSH...

READ THIS WAY

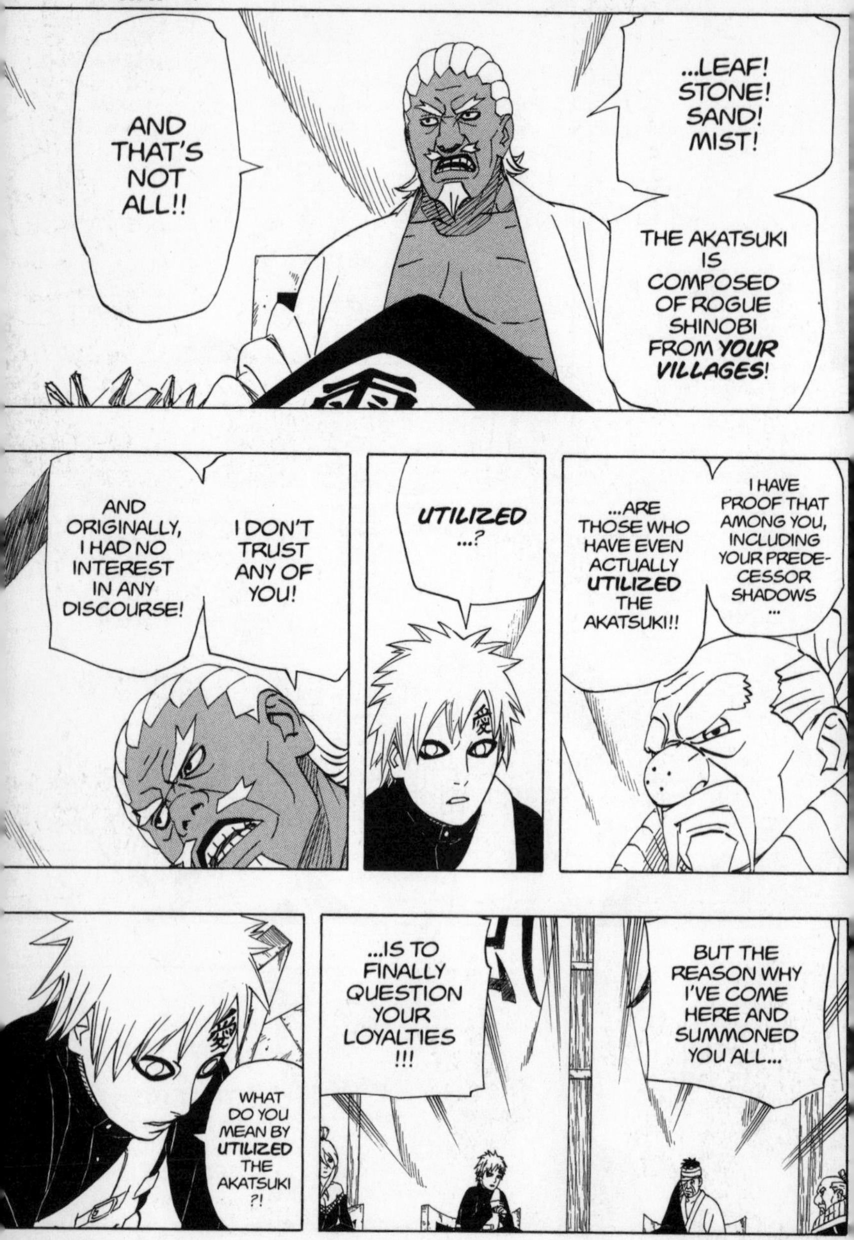
...LEAF! STONE! SAND! MIST!
THE AKATSUKI IS COMPOSED OF ROGUE SHINOBI FROM YOUR VILLAGES!
AND THAT'S NOT ALL!!
I HAVE PROOF THAT AMONG YOU, INCLUDING YOUR PREDECESSOR SHADOWS ...
...ARE THOSE WHO HAVE EVEN ACTUALLY UTILIZED THE AKATSUKI!!
UTILIZED ...?
I DON'T TRUST ANY OF YOU!
AND ORIGINALLY, I HAD NO INTEREST IN ANY DISCOURSE!
BUT THE REASON WHY I'VE COME HERE AND SUMMONED YOU ALL...
...IS TO FINALLY QUESTION YOUR LOYALTIES !!!
WHAT DO YOU MEAN BY UTILIZED THE AKATSUKI ?!

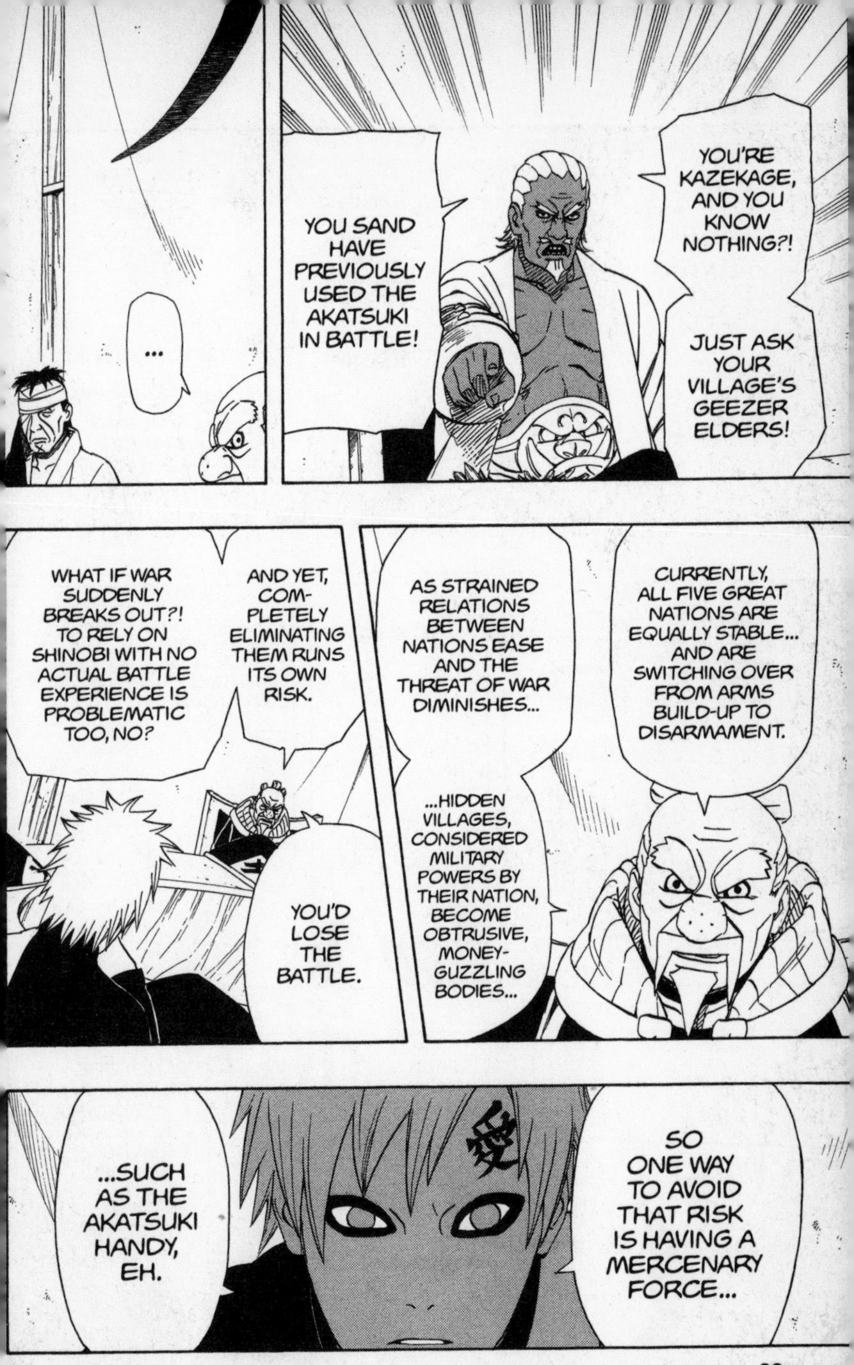
YOU'RE KAZEKAGE, AND YOU KNOW NOTHING?!
JUST ASK YOUR VILLAGE'S GEEZER ELDERS!
YOU SAND HAVE PREVIOUSLY USED THE AKATSUKI IN BATTLE!
...
CURRENTLY, ALL FIVE GREAT NATIONS ARE EQUALLY STABLE... AND ARE SWITCHING OVER FROM ARMS BUILD-UP TO DISARMAMENT.
AS STRAINED RELATIONS BETWEEN NATIONS EASE AND THE THREAT OF WAR DIMINISHES...
...HIDDEN VILLAGES, CONSIDERED MILITARY POWERS BY THEIR NATION, BECOME OBTRUSIVE, MONEY-GUZZLING BODIES...
AND YET, COM-PLETELY ELIMINATING THEM RUNS ITS OWN RISK.
WHAT IF WAR SUDDENLY BREAKS OUT?! TO RELY ON SHINOBI WITH NO ACTUAL BATTLE EXPERIENCE IS PROBLEMATIC TOO, NO?
YOU'D LOSE THE BATTLE.
SO ONE WAY TO AVOID THAT RISK IS HAVING A MERCENARY FORCE...
...SUCH AS THE AKATSUKI HANDY, EH.

READ THIS WAY

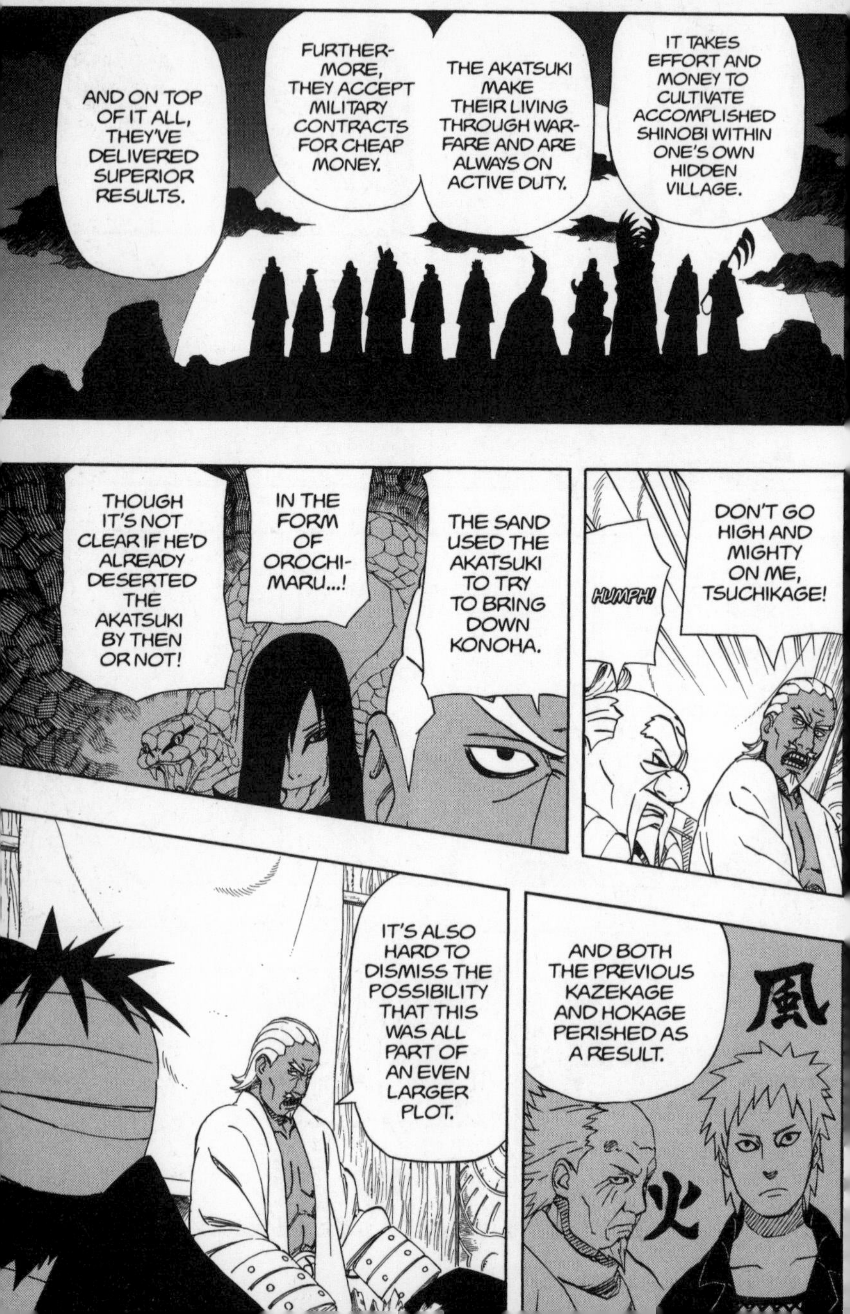
IT TAKES EFFORT AND MONEY TO CULTIVATE ACCOMPLISHED SHINOBI WITHIN ONE'S OWN HIDDEN VILLAGE.
THE AKATSUKI MAKE THEIR LIVING THROUGH WAR-FARE AND ARE ALWAYS ON ACTIVE DUTY.
FURTHER-MORE, THEY ACCEPT MILITARY CONTRACTS FOR CHEAP MONEY.
AND ON TOP OF IT ALL, THEY'VE DELIVERED SUPERIOR RESULTS.
DON'T GO HIGH AND MIGHTY ON ME, TSUCHIKAGE!
HUMPH!
THE SAND USED THE AKATSUKI TO TRY TO BRING DOWN KONOHA.
IN THE FORM OF OROCHI-MARU...!
THOUGH IT'S NOT CLEAR IF HE'D ALREADY DESERTED THE AKATSUKI BY THEN OR NOT!
AND BOTH THE PREVIOUS KAZEKAGE AND HOKAGE PERISHED AS A RESULT.
IT'S ALSO HARD TO DISMISS THE POSSIBILITY THAT THIS WAS ALL PART OF AN EVEN LARGER PLOT.

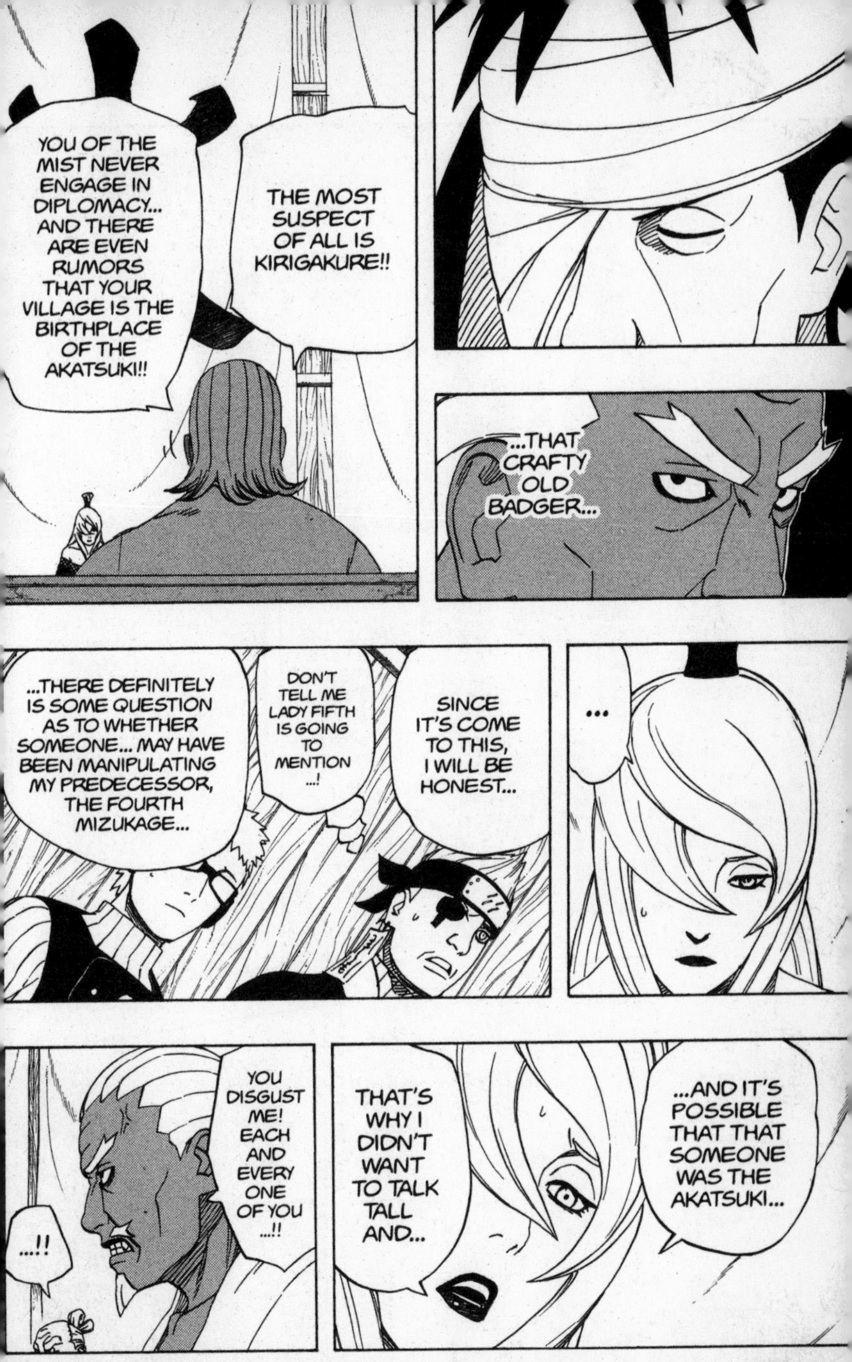
...THAT CRAFTY OLD BADGER...
THE MOST SUSPECT OF ALL IS KIRIGAKURE!!
YOU OF THE MIST NEVER ENGAGE IN DIPLOMACY... AND THERE ARE EVEN RUMORS THAT YOUR VILLAGE IS THE BIRTHPLACE OF THE AKATSUKI!!
...
SINCE IT'S COME TO THIS, I WILL BE HONEST...
DON'T TELL ME LADY FIFTH IS GOING TO MENTION ...!
...THERE DEFINITELY IS SOME QUESTION AS TO WHETHER SOMEONE... MAY HAVE BEEN MANIPULATING MY PREDECESSOR, THE FOURTH MIZUKAGE...
...AND IT'S POSSIBLE THAT THAT SOMEONE WAS THE AKATSUKI...
THAT'S WHY I DIDN'T WANT TO TALK TALL AND...
YOU DISGUST ME! EACH AND EVERY ONE OF YOU ...!!
...!!

READ THIS WAY

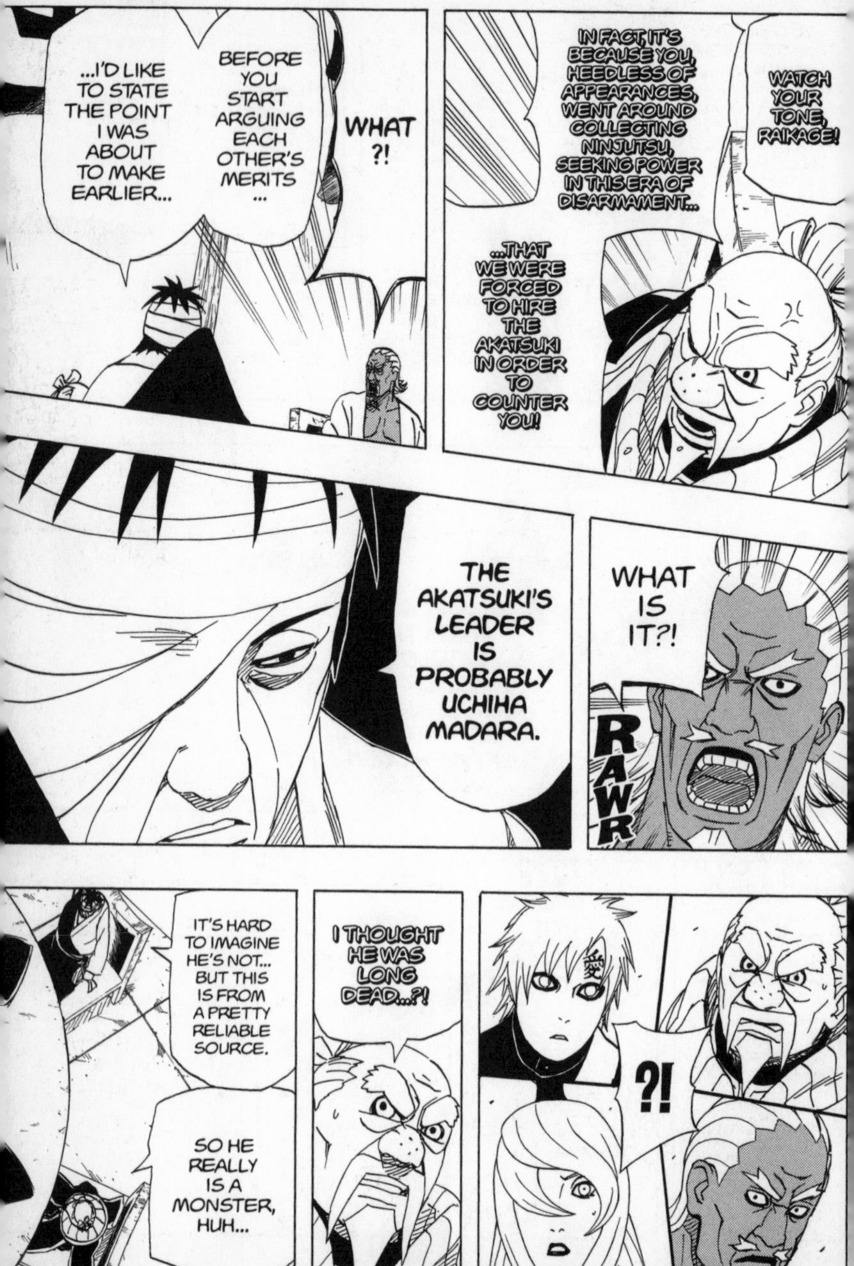

WATCH YOUR TONE, RAIKAGE!
IN FACT, IT'S BECAUSE YOU, HEEDLESS OF APPEARANCES, WENT AROUND COLLECTING NINJUTSU, SEEKING POWER IN THIS ERA OF DISARMAMENT...
...THAT WE WERE FORCED TO HIRE THE AKATSUKI IN ORDER TO COUNTER YOU!
WHAT ?!
BEFORE YOU START ARGUING EACH OTHER'S MERITS ...
...I'D LIKE TO STATE THE POINT I WAS ABOUT TO MAKE EARLIER...
WHAT IS IT?!
RAWR
THE AKATSUKI'S LEADER IS PROBABLY UCHIHA MADARA.
?!
I THOUGHT HE WAS LONG DEAD...?!
IT'S HARD TO IMAGINE HE'S NOT... BUT THIS IS FROM A PRETTY RELIABLE SOURCE.
SO HE REALLY IS A MONSTER, HUH...

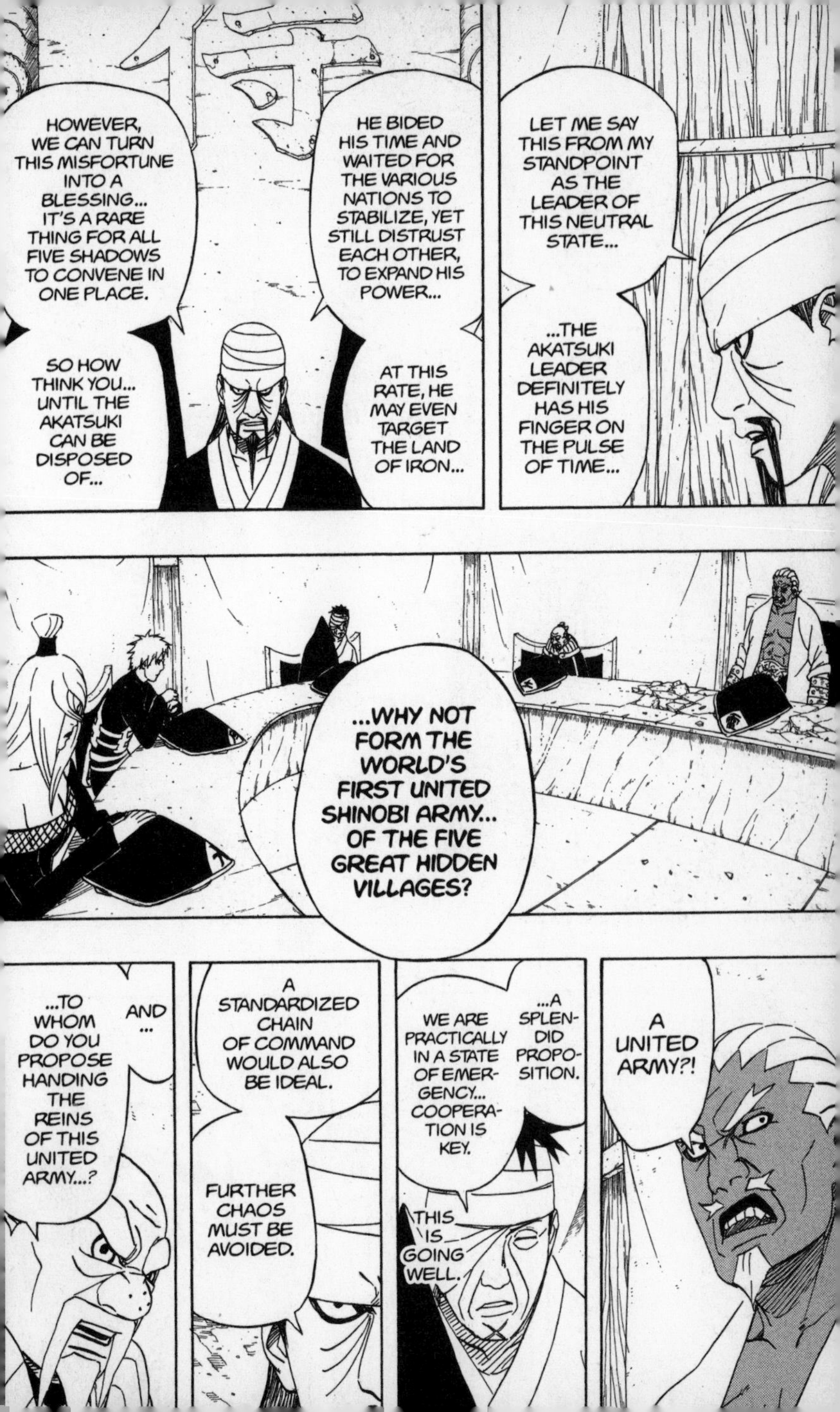
LET ME SAY THIS FROM MY STANDPOINT AS THE LEADER OF THIS NEUTRAL STATE...
...THE AKATSUKI LEADER DEFINITELY HAS HIS FINGER ON THE PULSE OF TIME...
HE BIDED HIS TIME AND WAITED FOR THE VARIOUS NATIONS TO STABILIZE, YET STILL DISTRUST EACH OTHER, TO EXPAND HIS POWER...
AT THIS RATE, HE MAY EVEN TARGET THE LAND OF IRON...
HOWEVER, WE CAN TURN THIS MISFORTUNE INTO A BLESSING... IT'S A RARE THING FOR ALL FIVE SHADOWS TO CONVENE IN ONE PLACE.
SO HOW THINK YOU... UNTIL THE AKATSUKI CAN BE DISPOSED OF...
...WHY NOT FORM THE WORLD'S FIRST UNITED SHINOBI ARMY... OF THE FIVE GREAT HIDDEN VILLAGES?
A UNITED ARMY?!
...A SPLEN-DID PROPO-SITION.
WE ARE PRACTICALLY IN A STATE OF EMER-GENCY... COOPERA-TION IS KEY.
THIS IS GOING WELL.
A STANDARDIZED CHAIN OF COMMAND WOULD ALSO BE IDEAL.
FURTHER CHAOS MUST BE AVOIDED.
AND...
...TO WHOM DO YOU PROPOSE HANDING THE REINS OF THIS UNITED ARMY...?

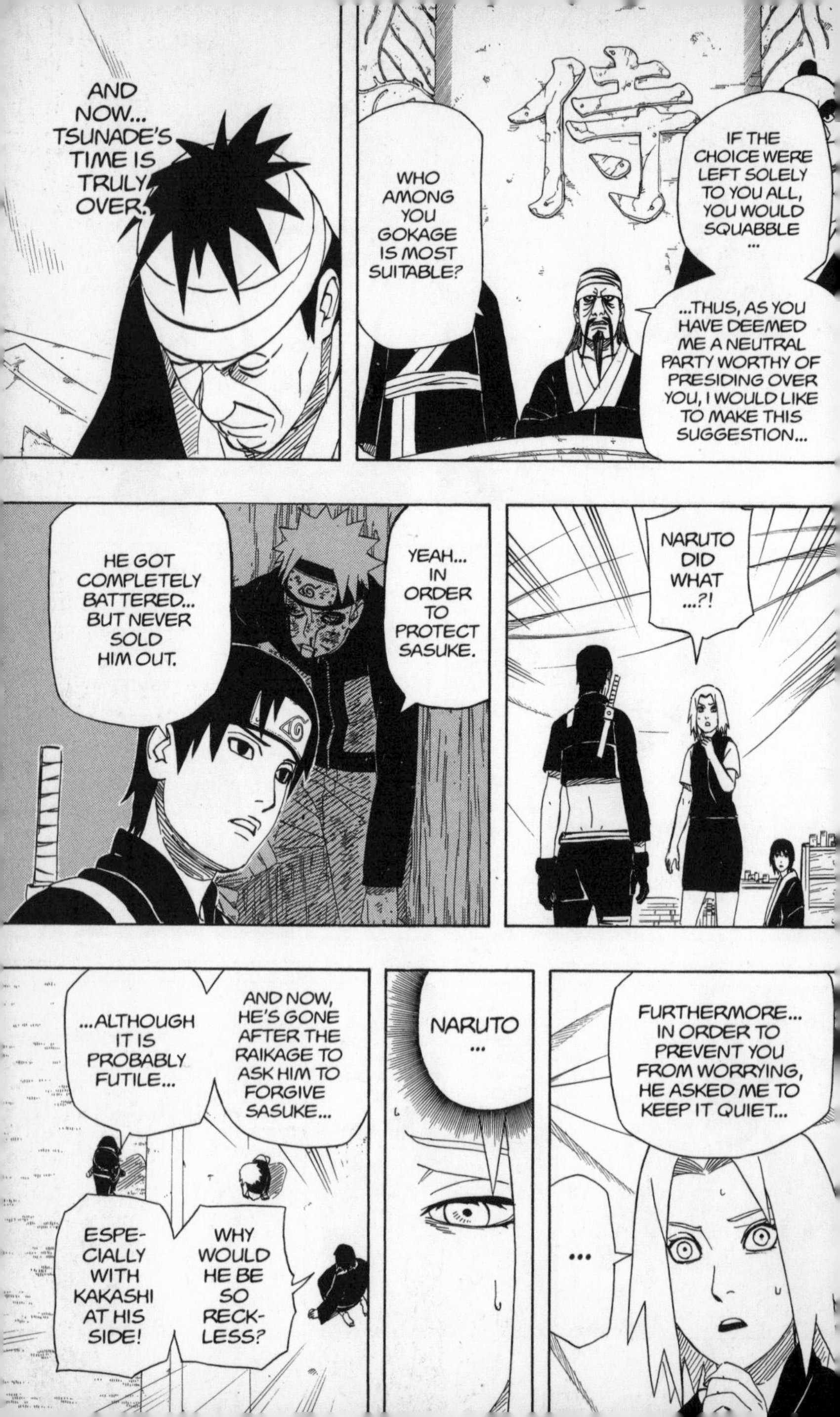
WHO AMONG YOU GOKAGE IS MOST SUITABLE?
IF THE CHOICE WERE LEFT SOLELY TO YOU ALL, YOU WOULD SQUABBLE ...
...THUS, AS YOU HAVE DEEMED ME A NEUTRAL PARTY WORTHY OF PRESIDING OVER YOU, I WOULD LIKE TO MAKE THIS SUGGESTION...
AND NOW... TSUNADE'S TIME IS TRULY OVER.
NARUTO DID WHAT ...?!
YEAH... IN ORDER TO PROTECT SASUKE.
HE GOT COMPLETELY BATTERED... BUT NEVER SOLD HIM OUT.
FURTHERMORE... IN ORDER TO PREVENT YOU FROM WORRYING, HE ASKED ME TO KEEP IT QUIET...
...
NARUTO ...
AND NOW, HE'S GONE AFTER THE RAIKAGE TO ASK HIM TO FORGIVE SASUKE...
...ALTHOUGH IT IS PROBABLY FUTILE...
WHY WOULD HE BE SO RECK-LESS?
ESPE-CIALLY WITH KAKASHI AT HIS SIDE!

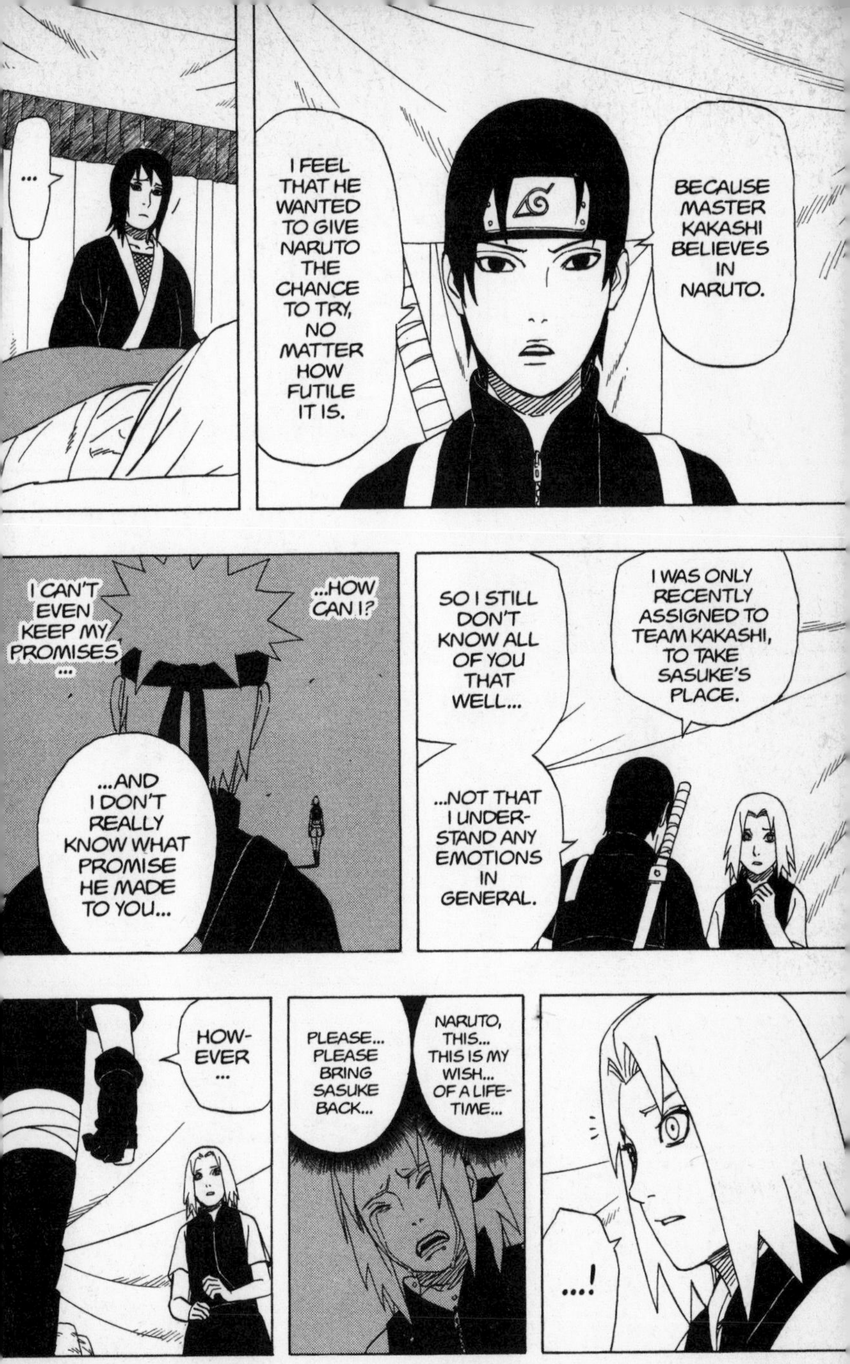
BECAUSE MASTER KAKASHI BELIEVES IN NARUTO.
I FEEL THAT HE WANTED TO GIVE NARUTO THE CHANCE TO TRY, NO MATTER HOW FUTILE IT IS.
...
I WAS ONLY RECENTLY ASSIGNED TO TEAM KAKASHI, TO TAKE SASUKE'S PLACE.
SO I STILL DON'T KNOW ALL OF YOU THAT WELL...
...NOT THAT I UNDER-STAND ANY EMOTIONS IN GENERAL.
...HOW CAN I?
I CAN'T EVEN KEEP MY PROMISES...
...AND I DON'T REALLY KNOW WHAT PROMISE HE MADE TO YOU...
...!
NARUTO, THIS... THIS IS MY WISH... OF A LIFE-TIME...
PLEASE... PLEASE BRING SASUKE BACK...
HOW-EVER...

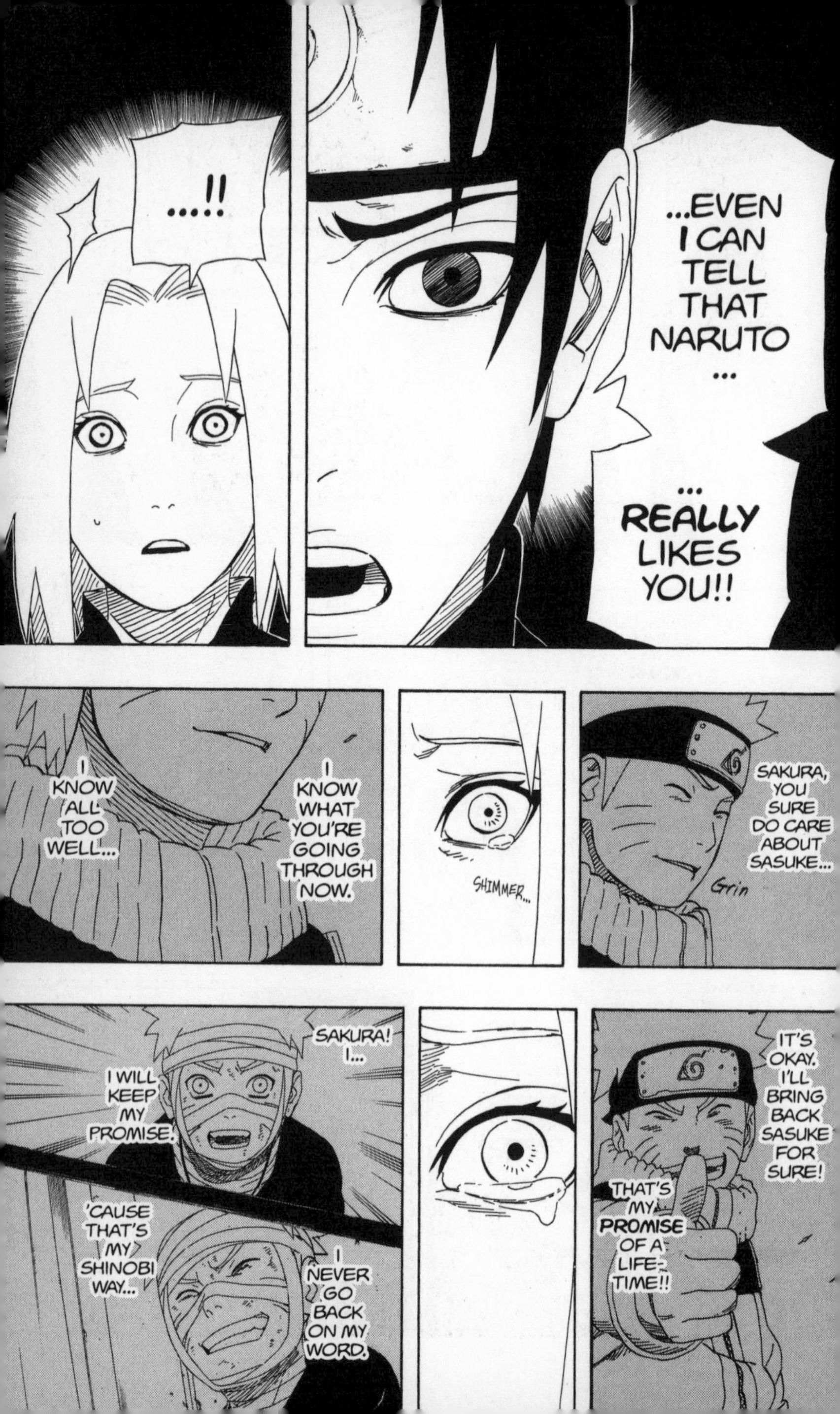
...EVEN I CAN TELL THAT NARUTO ...
... REALLY LIKES YOU!!
...!!
SAKURA, YOU SURE DO CARE ABOUT SASUKE...
Grin
SHIMMER...
I KNOW WHAT YOU'RE GOING THROUGH NOW.
I KNOW ALL TOO WELL...
IT'S OKAY. I'LL BRING BACK SASUKE FOR SURE!
THAT'S MY PROMISE OF A LIFE-TIME!!
SAKURA! I...
I WILL KEEP MY PROMISE.
I NEVER GO BACK ON MY WORD.
'CAUSE THAT'S MY SHINOBI WAY...

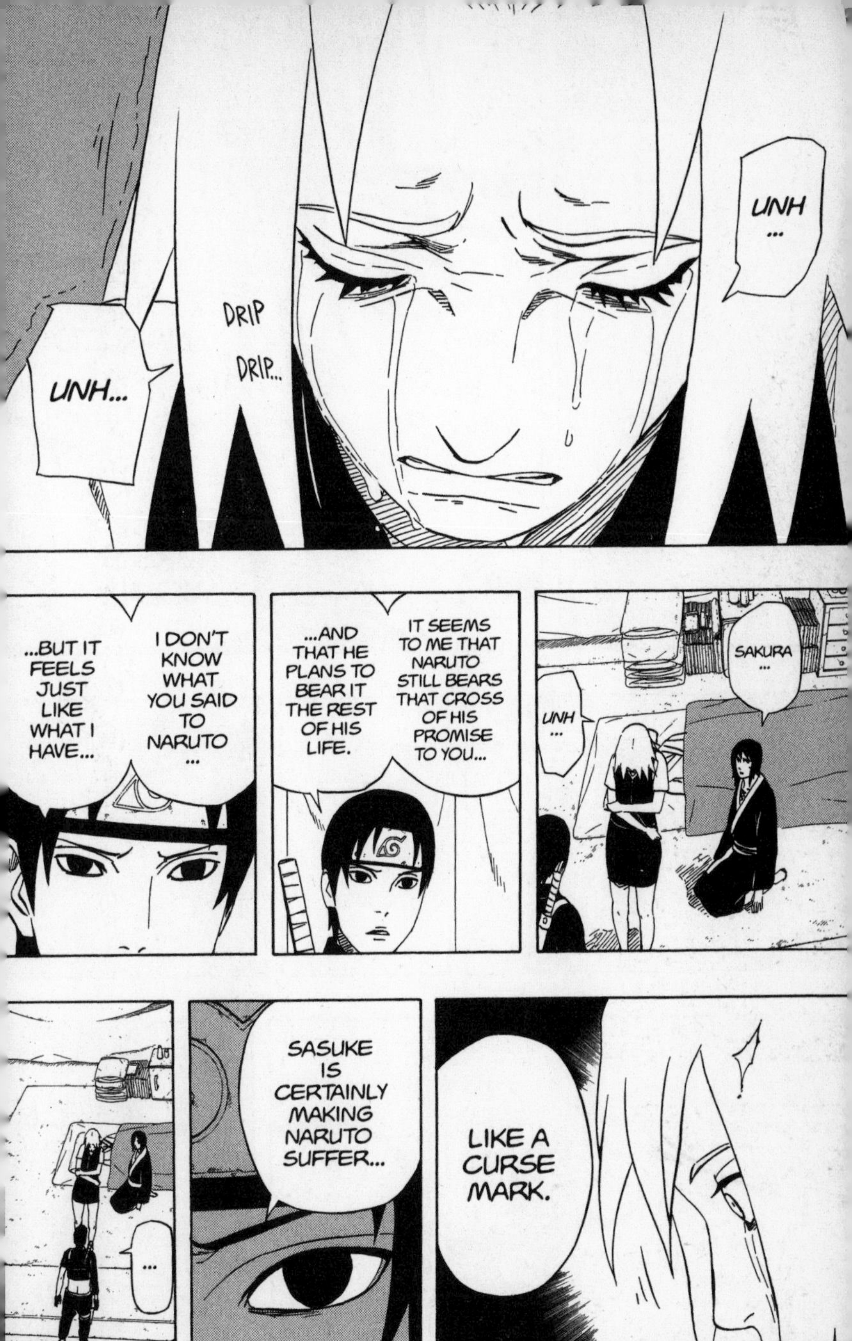
UNH ...
DRIP
DRIP...
UNH...
SAKURA ...
UNH ...
IT SEEMS TO ME THAT NARUTO STILL BEARS THAT CROSS OF HIS PROMISE TO YOU...
...AND THAT HE PLANS TO BEAR IT THE REST OF HIS LIFE.
I DON'T KNOW WHAT YOU SAID TO NARUTO ...
...BUT IT FEELS JUST LIKE WHAT I HAVE...
LIKE A CURSE MARK.
SASUKE IS CERTAINLY MAKING NARUTO SUFFER...
...

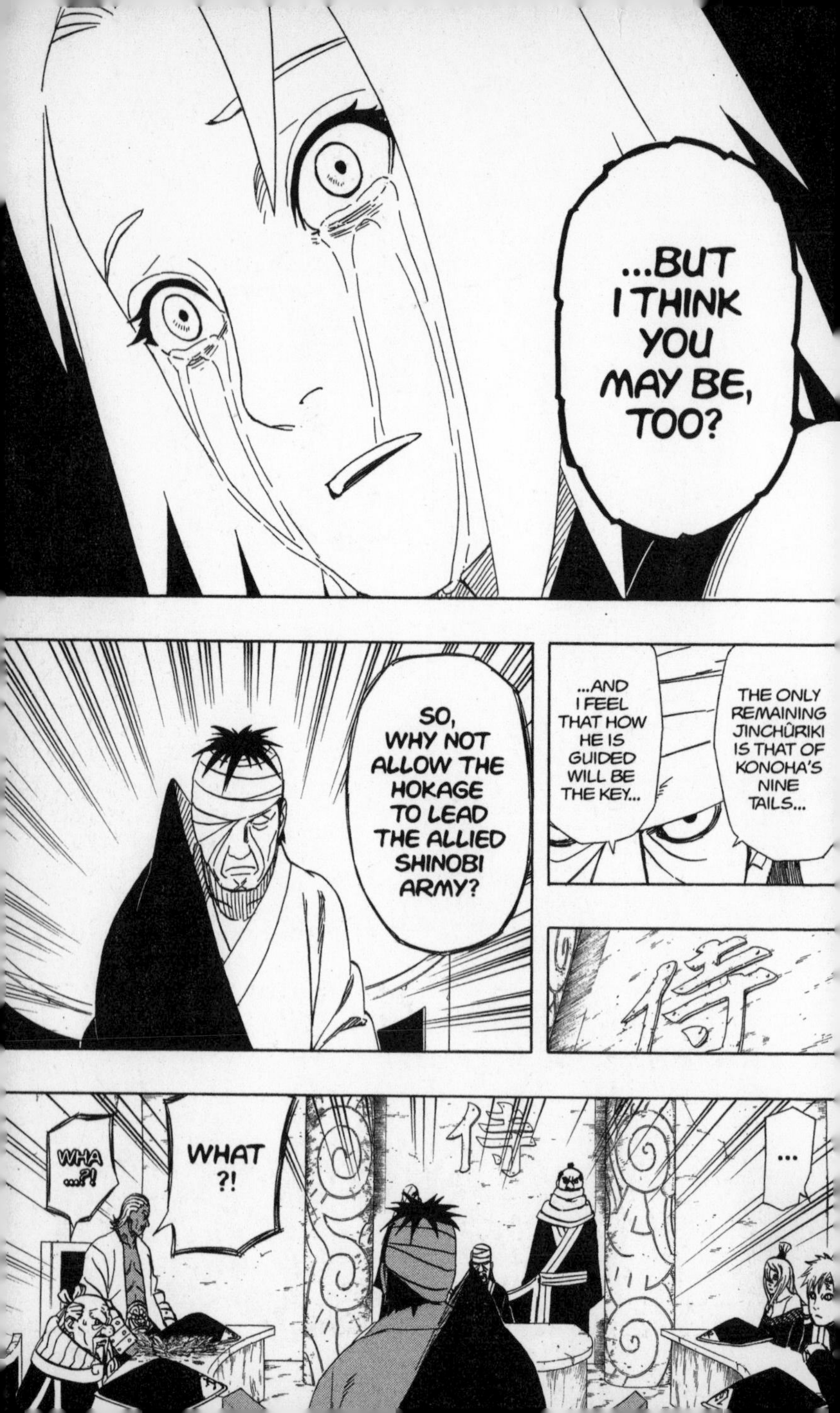
...BUT I THINK YOU MAY BE, TOO?
THE ONLY REMAINING JINCHŪRIKI IS THAT OF KONOHA'S NINE TAILS...
...AND I FEEL THAT HOW HE IS GUIDED WILL BE THE KEY...
SO, WHY NOT ALLOW THE HOKAGE TO LEAD THE ALLIED SHINOBI ARMY?
...
WHAT ?!
WHA ...?!

NARUTO

Number 459: Sakura's Resolve!

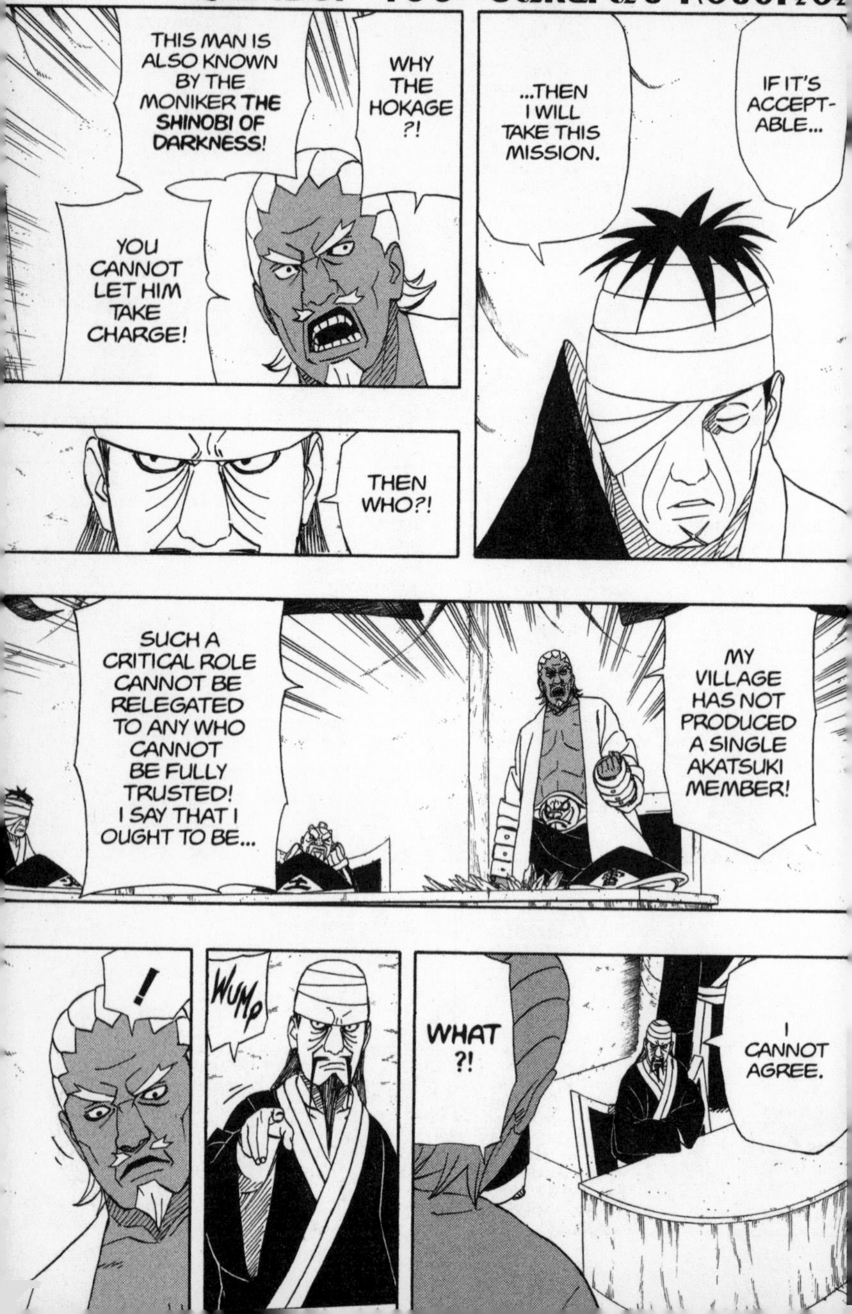
IF IT'S ACCEPTABLE...
...THEN I WILL TAKE THIS MISSION.
WHY THE HOKAGE ?!
THIS MAN IS ALSO KNOWN BY THE MONIKER THE SHINOBI OF DARKNESS!
YOU CANNOT LET HIM TAKE CHARGE!
THEN WHO?!
MY VILLAGE HAS NOT PRODUCED A SINGLE AKATSUKI MEMBER!
SUCH A CRITICAL ROLE CANNOT BE RELEGATED TO ANY WHO CANNOT BE FULLY TRUSTED! I SAY THAT I OUGHT TO BE...
I CANNOT AGREE.
WHAT ?!
WUMP
!

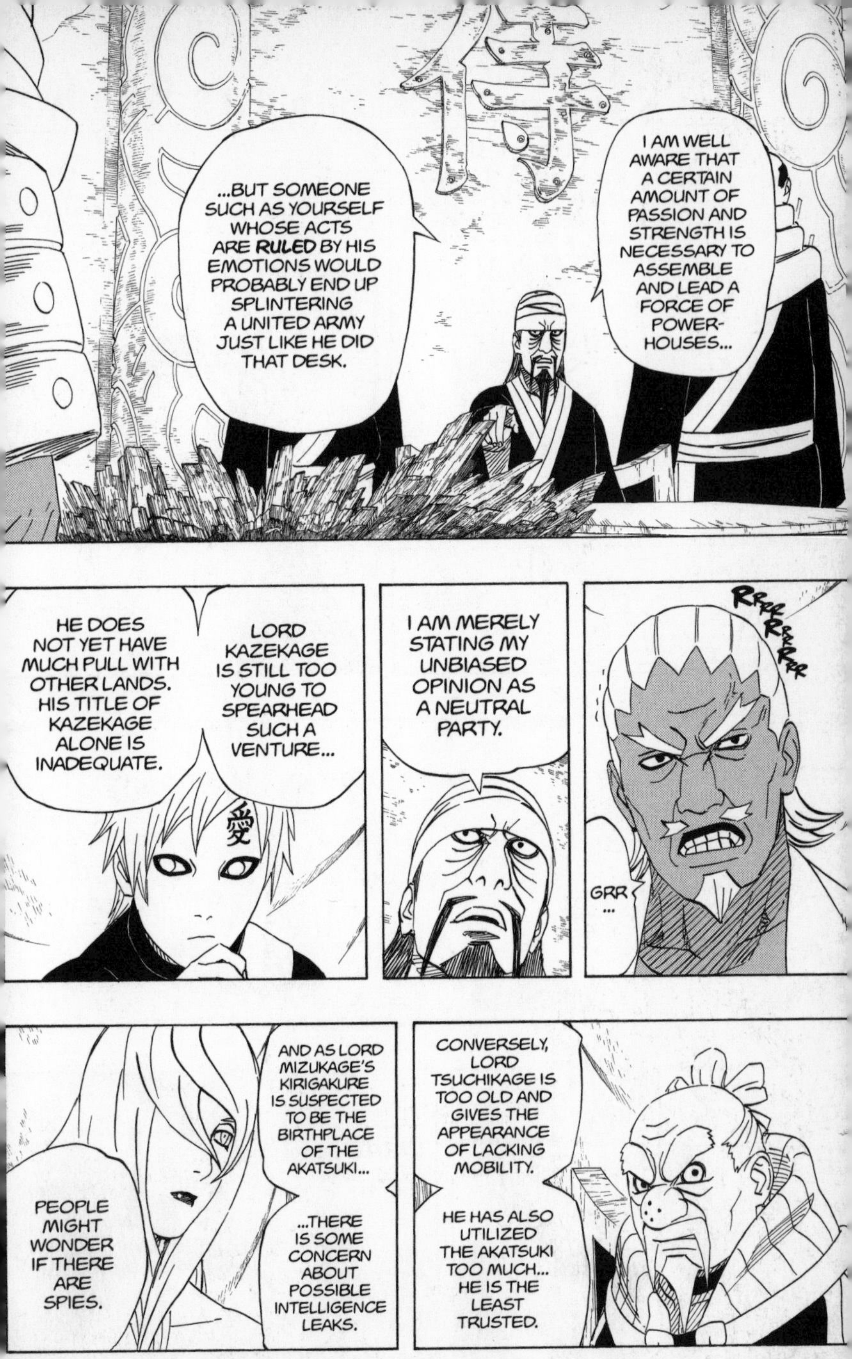
I AM WELL AWARE THAT A CERTAIN AMOUNT OF PASSION AND STRENGTH IS NECESSARY TO ASSEMBLE AND LEAD A FORCE OF POWER-HOUSES...
...BUT SOMEONE SUCH AS YOURSELF WHOSE ACTS ARE **RULED** BY HIS EMOTIONS WOULD PROBABLY END UP SPLINTERING A UNITED ARMY JUST LIKE HE DID THAT DESK.
RRRRRRRRRR
GRR...
I AM MERELY STATING MY UNBIASED OPINION AS A NEUTRAL PARTY.
LORD KAZEKAGE IS STILL TOO YOUNG TO SPEARHEAD SUCH A VENTURE...
HE DOES NOT YET HAVE MUCH PULL WITH OTHER LANDS. HIS TITLE OF KAZEKAGE ALONE IS INADEQUATE.
CONVERSELY, LORD TSUCHIKAGE IS TOO OLD AND GIVES THE APPEARANCE OF LACKING MOBILITY.
HE HAS ALSO UTILIZED THE AKATSUKI TOO MUCH... HE IS THE LEAST TRUSTED.
AND AS LORD MIZUKAGE'S KIRIGAKURE IS SUSPECTED TO BE THE BIRTHPLACE OF THE AKATSUKI...
...THERE IS SOME CONCERN ABOUT POSSIBLE INTELLIGENCE LEAKS.
PEOPLE MIGHT WONDER IF THERE ARE SPIES.

READ THIS WAY

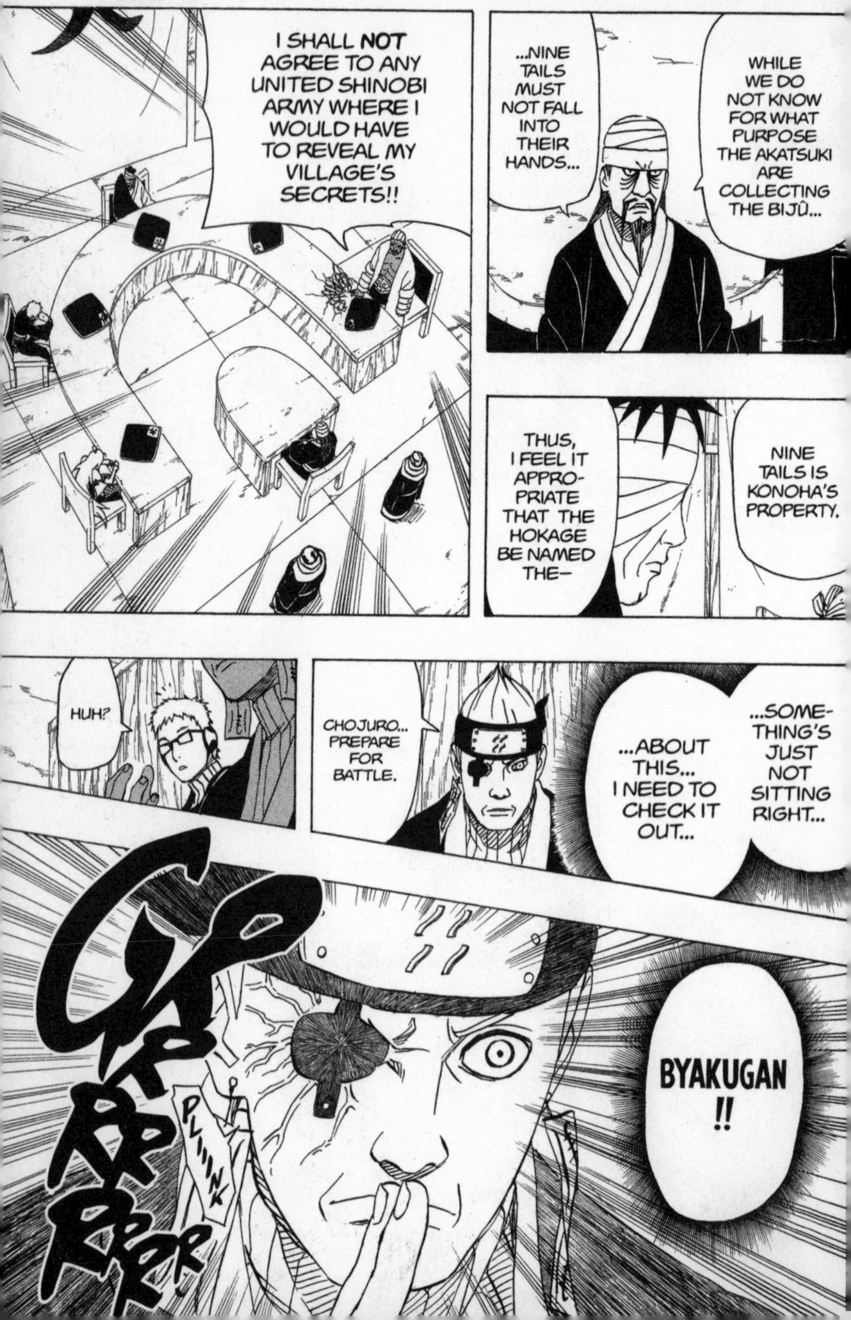
WHILE WE DO NOT KNOW FOR WHAT PURPOSE THE AKATSUKI ARE COLLECTING THE BIJÛ...
...NINE TAILS MUST NOT FALL INTO THEIR HANDS...
NINE TAILS IS KONOHA'S PROPERTY.
THUS, I FEEL IT APPROPRIATE THAT THE HOKAGE BE NAMED THE–
I SHALL **NOT** AGREE TO ANY UNITED SHINOBI ARMY WHERE I WOULD HAVE TO REVEAL MY VILLAGE'S SECRETS!!
...SOMETHING'S JUST NOT SITTING RIGHT...
...ABOUT THIS... I NEED TO CHECK IT OUT...
CHOJURO... PREPARE FOR BATTLE.
HUH?
BYAKUGAN!!
PLIIIINK

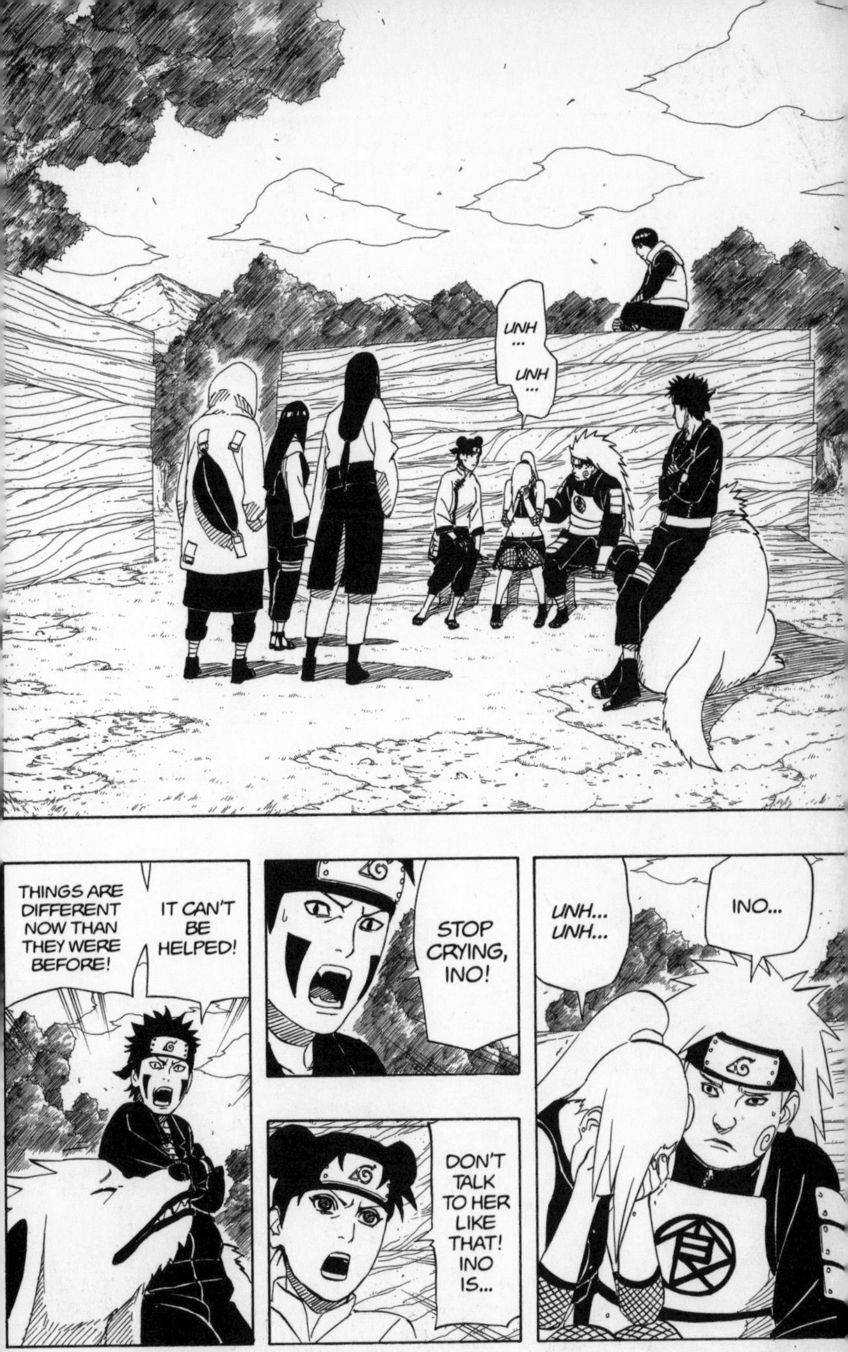
UNH ... UNH ...
INO...
UNH... UNH...
STOP CRYING, INO!
DON'T TALK TO HER LIKE THAT! INO IS...
IT CAN'T BE HELPED!
THINGS ARE DIFFERENT NOW THAN THEY WERE BEFORE!

READ THIS WAY

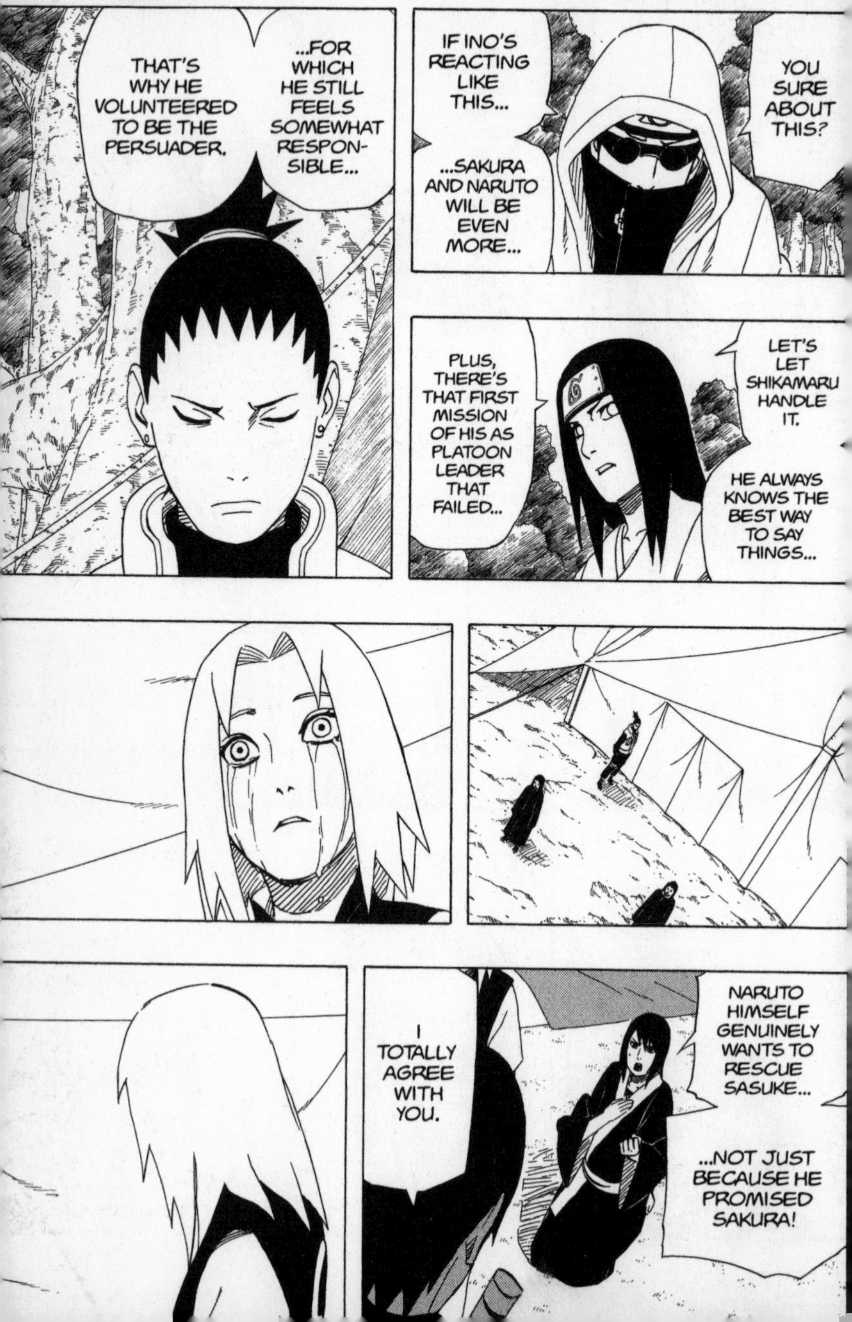
YOU SURE ABOUT THIS?
IF INO'S REACTING LIKE THIS...
...SAKURA AND NARUTO WILL BE EVEN MORE...
LET'S LET SHIKAMARU HANDLE IT.
HE ALWAYS KNOWS THE BEST WAY TO SAY THINGS...
PLUS, THERE'S THAT FIRST MISSION OF HIS AS PLATOON LEADER THAT FAILED...
...FOR WHICH HE STILL FEELS SOMEWHAT RESPONSIBLE...
THAT'S WHY HE VOLUNTEERED TO BE THE PERSUADER.
NARUTO HIMSELF GENUINELY WANTS TO RESCUE SASUKE...
...NOT JUST BECAUSE HE PROMISED SAKURA!
I TOTALLY AGREE WITH YOU.

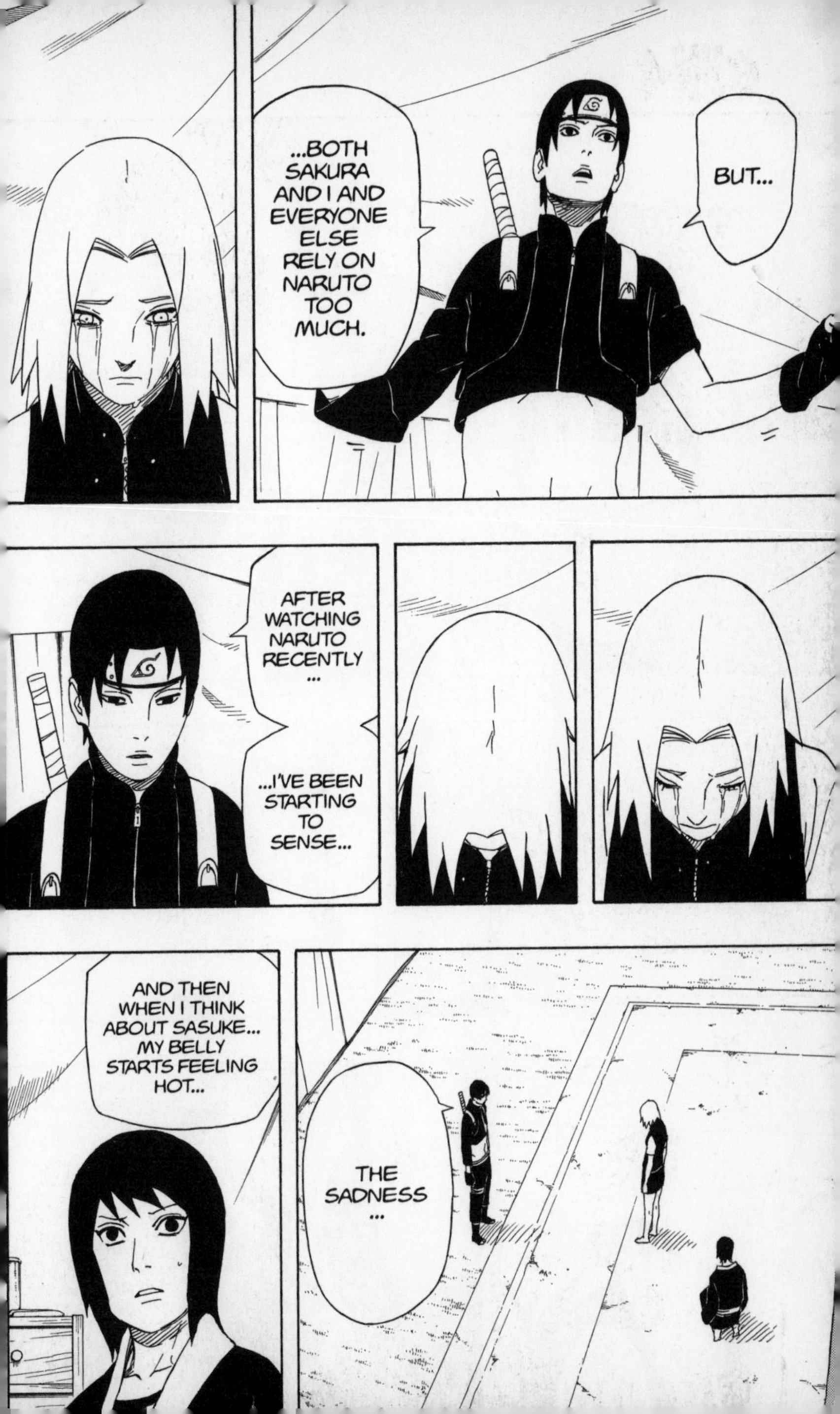
BUT...
...BOTH SAKURA AND I AND EVERYONE ELSE RELY ON NARUTO TOO MUCH.
AFTER WATCHING NARUTO RECENTLY ...
...I'VE BEEN STARTING TO SENSE...
THE SADNESS ...
AND THEN WHEN I THINK ABOUT SASUKE... MY BELLY STARTS FEELING HOT...

READ THIS WAY

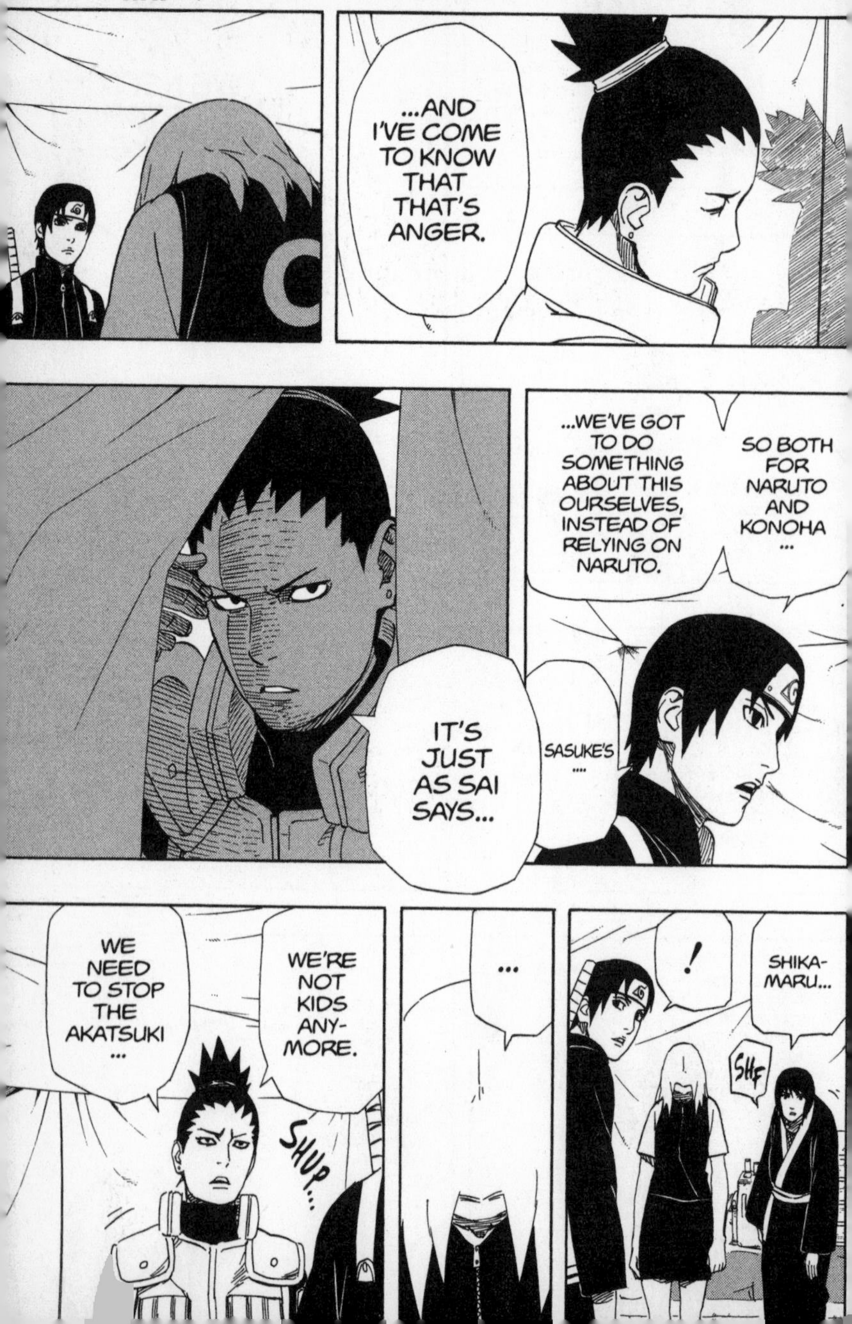
...AND I'VE COME TO KNOW THAT THAT'S ANGER.
SO BOTH FOR NARUTO AND KONOHA...
...WE'VE GOT TO DO SOMETHING ABOUT THIS OURSELVES, INSTEAD OF RELYING ON NARUTO.
SASUKE'S ....
IT'S JUST AS SAI SAYS...
SHIKA-MARU...
!
SHF
...
WE'RE NOT KIDS ANYMORE.
WE NEED TO STOP THE AKATSUKI...
SHUP...

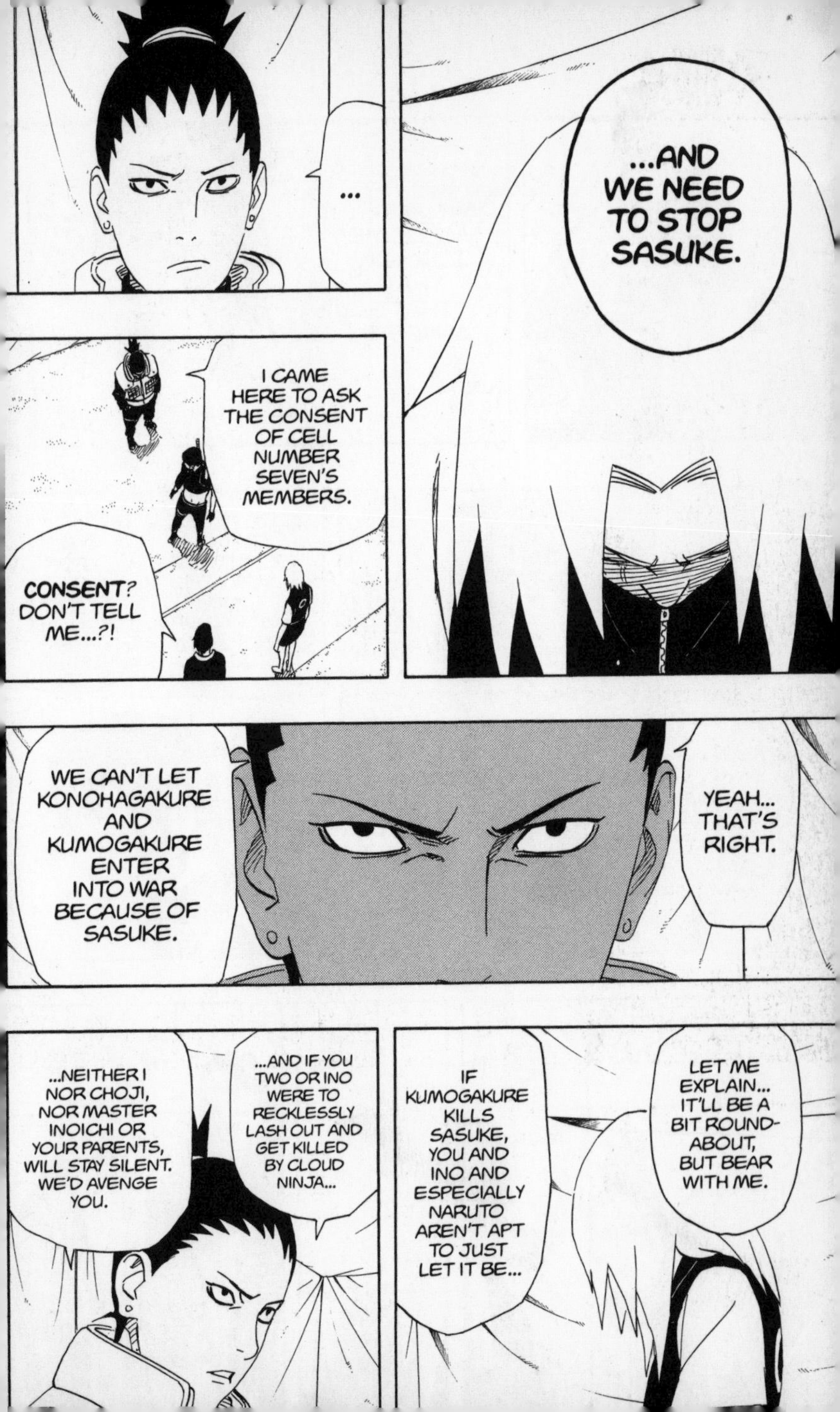
...AND WE NEED TO STOP SASUKE.
...
I CAME HERE TO ASK THE CONSENT OF CELL NUMBER SEVEN'S MEMBERS.
CONSENT? DON'T TELL ME...?!
YEAH... THAT'S RIGHT.
WE CAN'T LET KONOHAGAKURE AND KUMOGAKURE ENTER INTO WAR BECAUSE OF SASUKE.
LET ME EXPLAIN... IT'LL BE A BIT ROUND-ABOUT, BUT BEAR WITH ME.
IF KUMOGAKURE KILLS SASUKE, YOU AND INO AND ESPECIALLY NARUTO AREN'T APT TO JUST LET IT BE...
...AND IF YOU TWO OR INO WERE TO RECKLESSLY LASH OUT AND GET KILLED BY CLOUD NINJA...
...NEITHER I NOR CHOJI, NOR MASTER INOICHI OR YOUR PARENTS, WILL STAY SILENT. WE'D AVENGE YOU.

READ THIS WAY

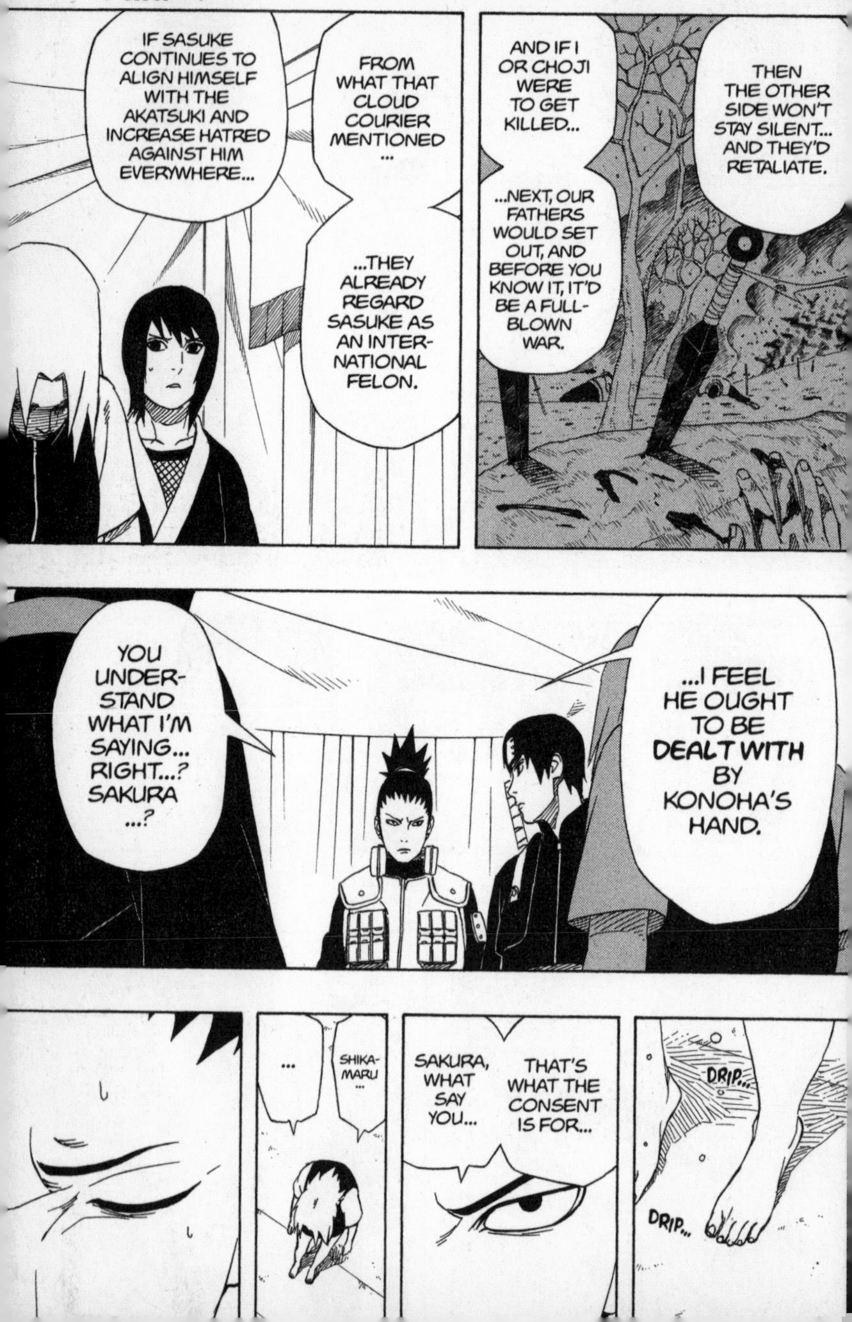
THEN THE OTHER SIDE WON'T STAY SILENT... AND THEY'D RETALIATE.
AND IF I OR CHOJI WERE TO GET KILLED...
...NEXT, OUR FATHERS WOULD SET OUT, AND BEFORE YOU KNOW IT, IT'D BE A FULL-BLOWN WAR.
FROM WHAT THAT CLOUD COURIER MENTIONED...
...THEY ALREADY REGARD SASUKE AS AN INTERNATIONAL FELON.
IF SASUKE CONTINUES TO ALIGN HIMSELF WITH THE AKATSUKI AND INCREASE HATRED AGAINST HIM EVERYWHERE...
...I FEEL HE OUGHT TO BE **DEALT WITH** BY KONOHA'S HAND.
YOU UNDERSTAND WHAT I'M SAYING... RIGHT...? SAKURA...?
DRIP...
DRIP...
THAT'S WHAT THE CONSENT IS FOR...
SAKURA, WHAT SAY YOU...
SHIKAMARU...
...

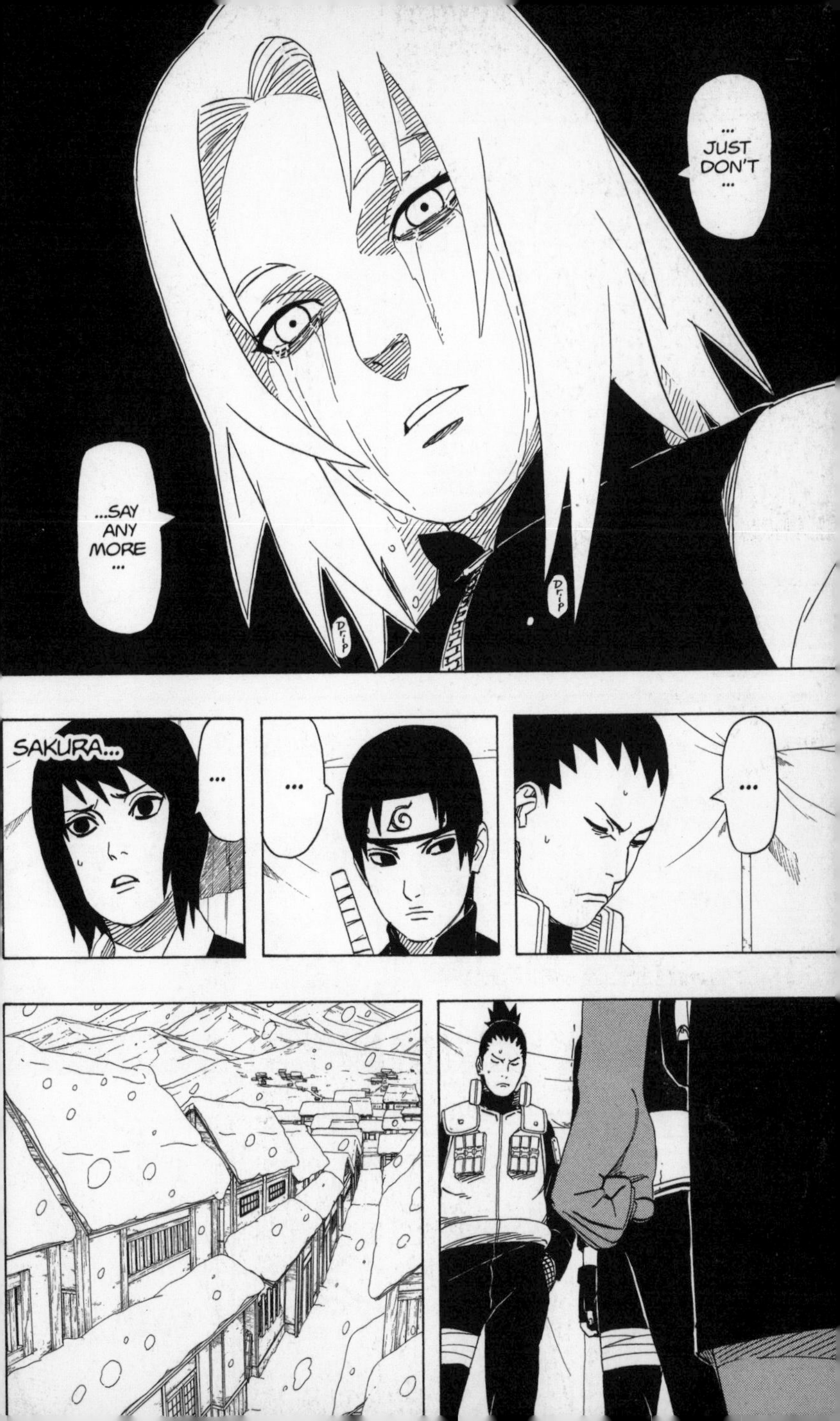
...
JUST
DON'T
...
...SAY
ANY
MORE
...
Drip
Drip
...
...
...
SAKURA...

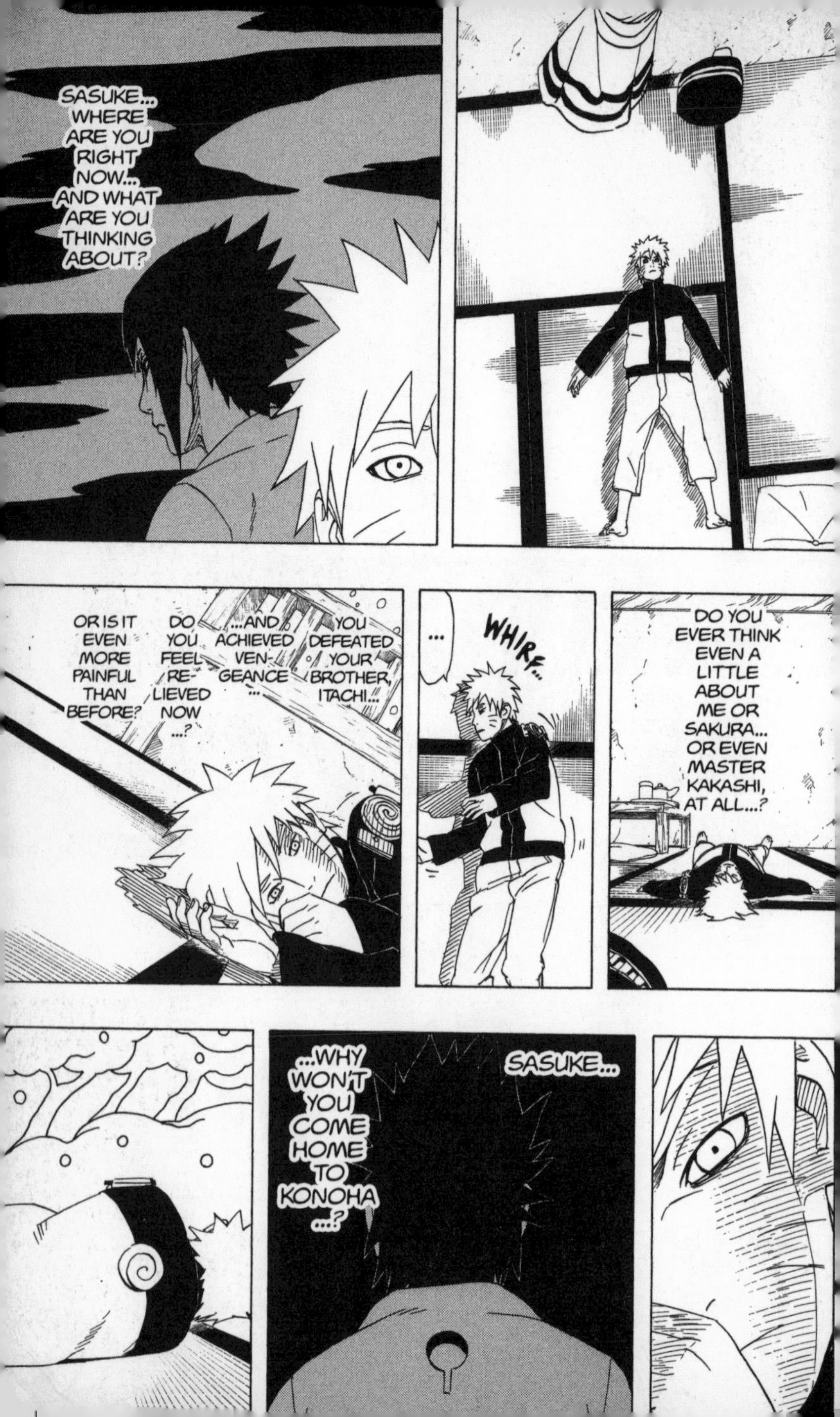
SASUKE... WHERE ARE YOU RIGHT NOW... AND WHAT ARE YOU THINKING ABOUT?
DO YOU EVER THINK EVEN A LITTLE ABOUT ME OR SAKURA... OR EVEN MASTER KAKASHI, AT ALL...?
...
WHIRF...
YOU DEFEATED YOUR BROTHER, ITACHI...
...AND ACHIEVED VENGEANCE...
DO YOU FEEL RELIEVED NOW...?
OR IS IT EVEN MORE PAINFUL THAN BEFORE?
SASUKE...
...WHY WON'T YOU COME HOME TO KONOHA...?

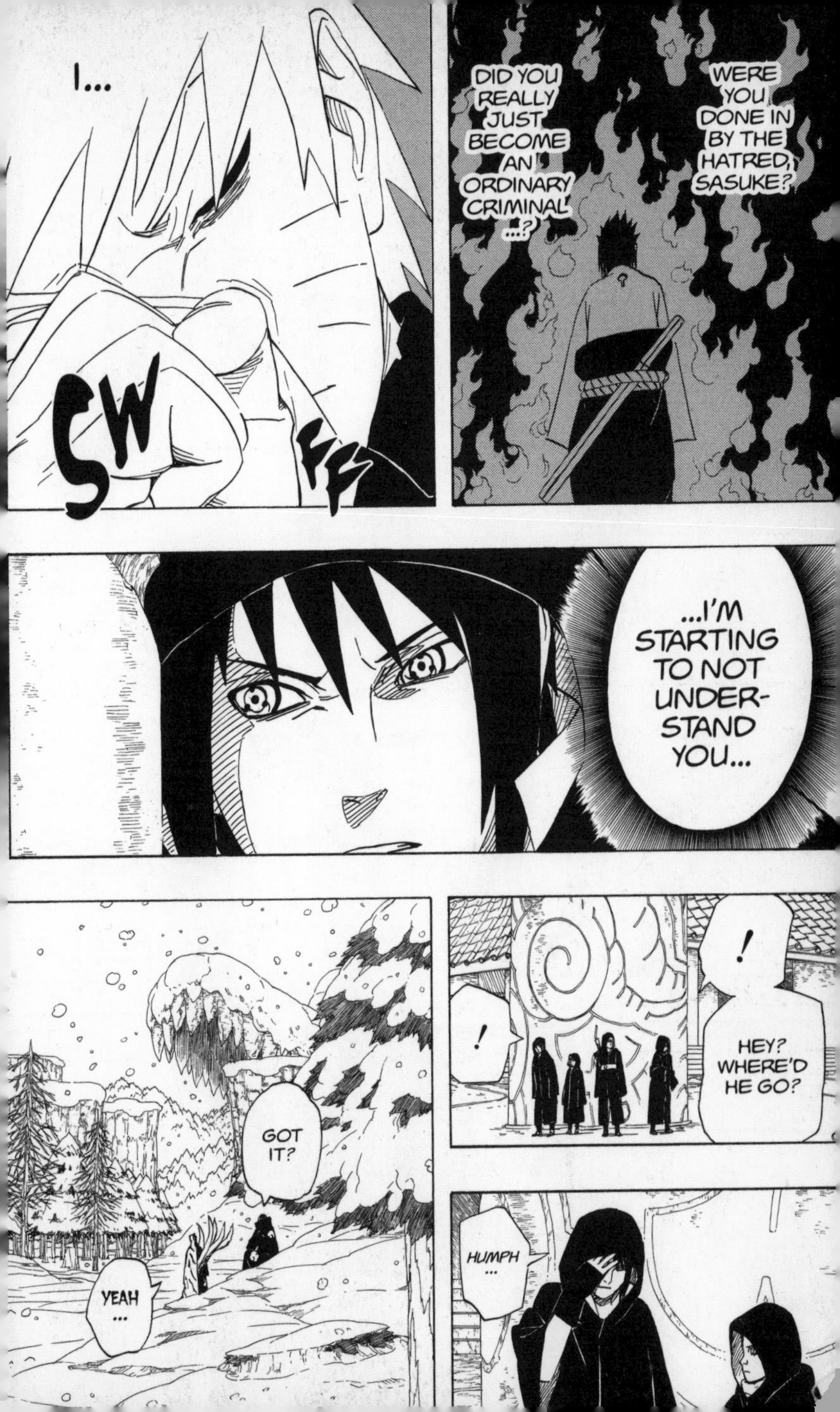
WERE YOU DONE IN BY THE HATRED, SASUKE?
DID YOU REALLY JUST BECOME AN ORDINARY CRIMINAL ...?
I...
SWFF
...I'M STARTING TO NOT UNDER-STAND YOU...
!
HEY? WHERE'D HE GO?
!
HUMPH ...
GOT IT?
YEAH ...

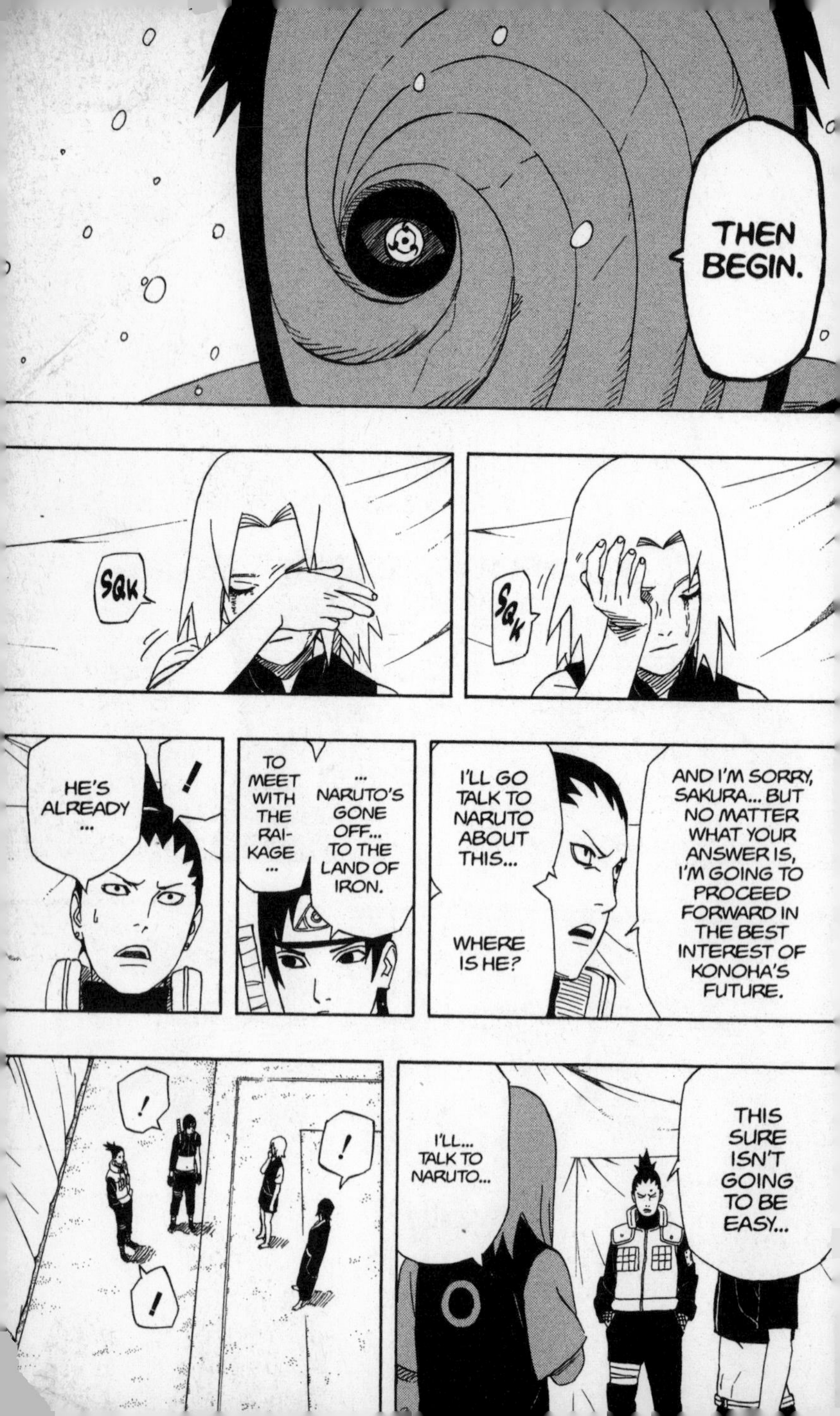
THEN BEGIN.
SQK
SQK
AND I'M SORRY, SAKURA... BUT NO MATTER WHAT YOUR ANSWER IS, I'M GOING TO PROCEED FORWARD IN THE BEST INTEREST OF KONOHA'S FUTURE.
I'LL GO TALK TO NARUTO ABOUT THIS...
WHERE IS HE?
... NARUTO'S GONE OFF... TO THE LAND OF IRON.
TO MEET WITH THE RAI-KAGE ...
!
HE'S ALREADY ...
THIS SURE ISN'T GOING TO BE EASY...
I'LL... TALK TO NARUTO...
!
!
!

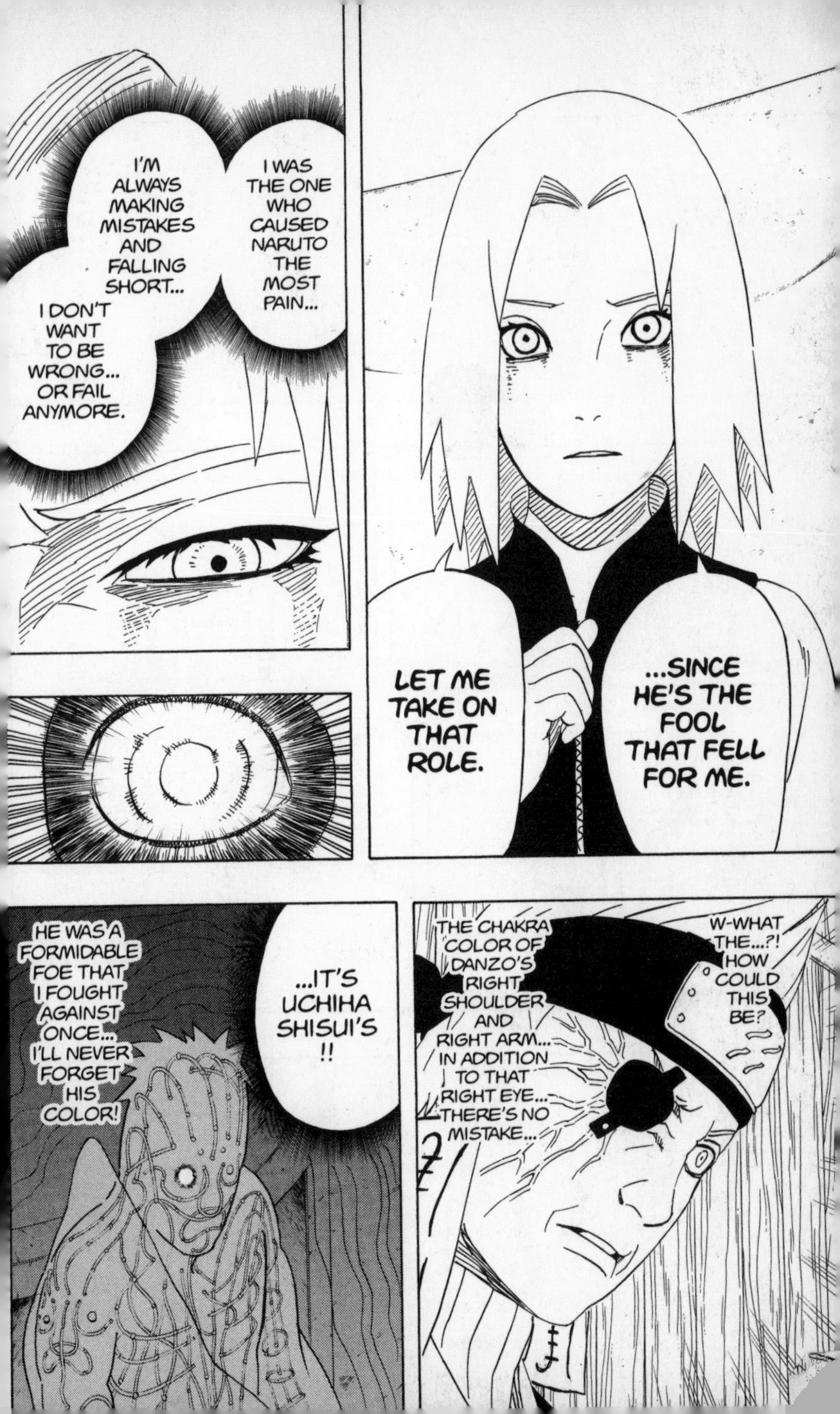
...SINCE HE'S THE FOOL THAT FELL FOR ME.
LET ME TAKE ON THAT ROLE.
I WAS THE ONE WHO CAUSED NARUTO THE MOST PAIN...
I'M ALWAYS MAKING MISTAKES AND FALLING SHORT...
I DON'T WANT TO BE WRONG... OR FAIL ANYMORE.
W-WHAT THE...?! HOW COULD THIS BE?
THE CHAKRA COLOR OF DANZO'S RIGHT SHOULDER AND RIGHT ARM... IN ADDITION TO THAT RIGHT EYE... THERE'S NO MISTAKE...
...IT'S UCHIHA SHISUI'S!!
HE WAS A FORMIDABLE FOE THAT I FOUGHT AGAINST ONCE... I'LL NEVER FORGET HIS COLOR!

READ THIS WAY

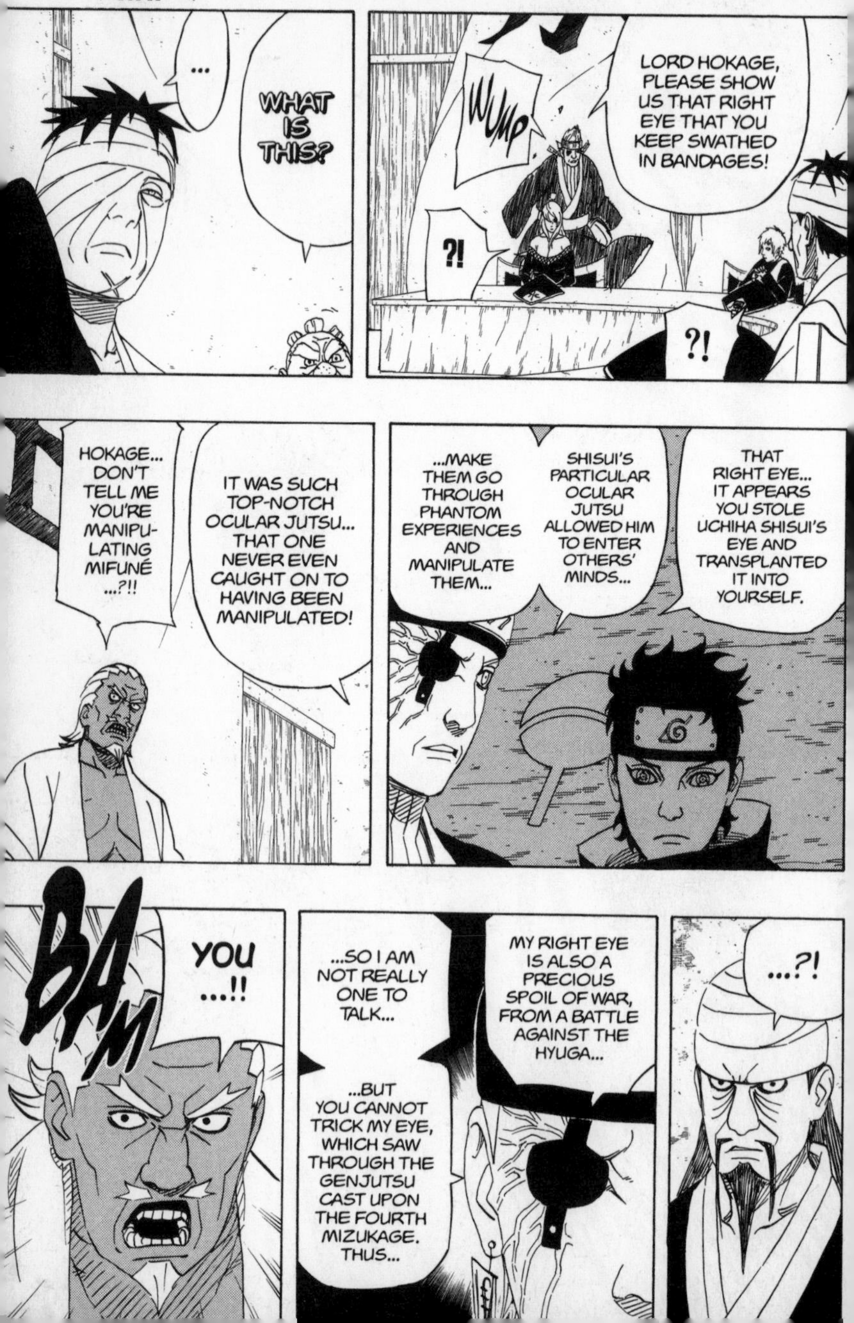
LORD HOKAGE, PLEASE SHOW US THAT RIGHT EYE THAT YOU KEEP SWATHED IN BANDAGES!
WUMP
?!
?!
...
WHAT IS THIS?
THAT RIGHT EYE... IT APPEARS YOU STOLE UCHIHA SHISUI'S EYE AND TRANSPLANTED IT INTO YOURSELF.
SHISUI'S PARTICULAR OCULAR JUTSU ALLOWED HIM TO ENTER OTHERS' MINDS...
...MAKE THEM GO THROUGH PHANTOM EXPERIENCES AND MANIPULATE THEM...
IT WAS SUCH TOP-NOTCH OCULAR JUTSU... THAT ONE NEVER EVEN CAUGHT ON TO HAVING BEEN MANIPULATED!
HOKAGE... DON'T TELL ME YOU'RE MANIPU-LATING MIFUNÉ ...?!!
...?!
MY RIGHT EYE IS ALSO A PRECIOUS SPOIL OF WAR, FROM A BATTLE AGAINST THE HYUGA...
...SO I AM NOT REALLY ONE TO TALK...
...BUT YOU CANNOT TRICK MY EYE, WHICH SAW THROUGH THE GENJUTSU CAST UPON THE FOURTH MIZUKAGE. THUS...
YOU ...!!
BAM

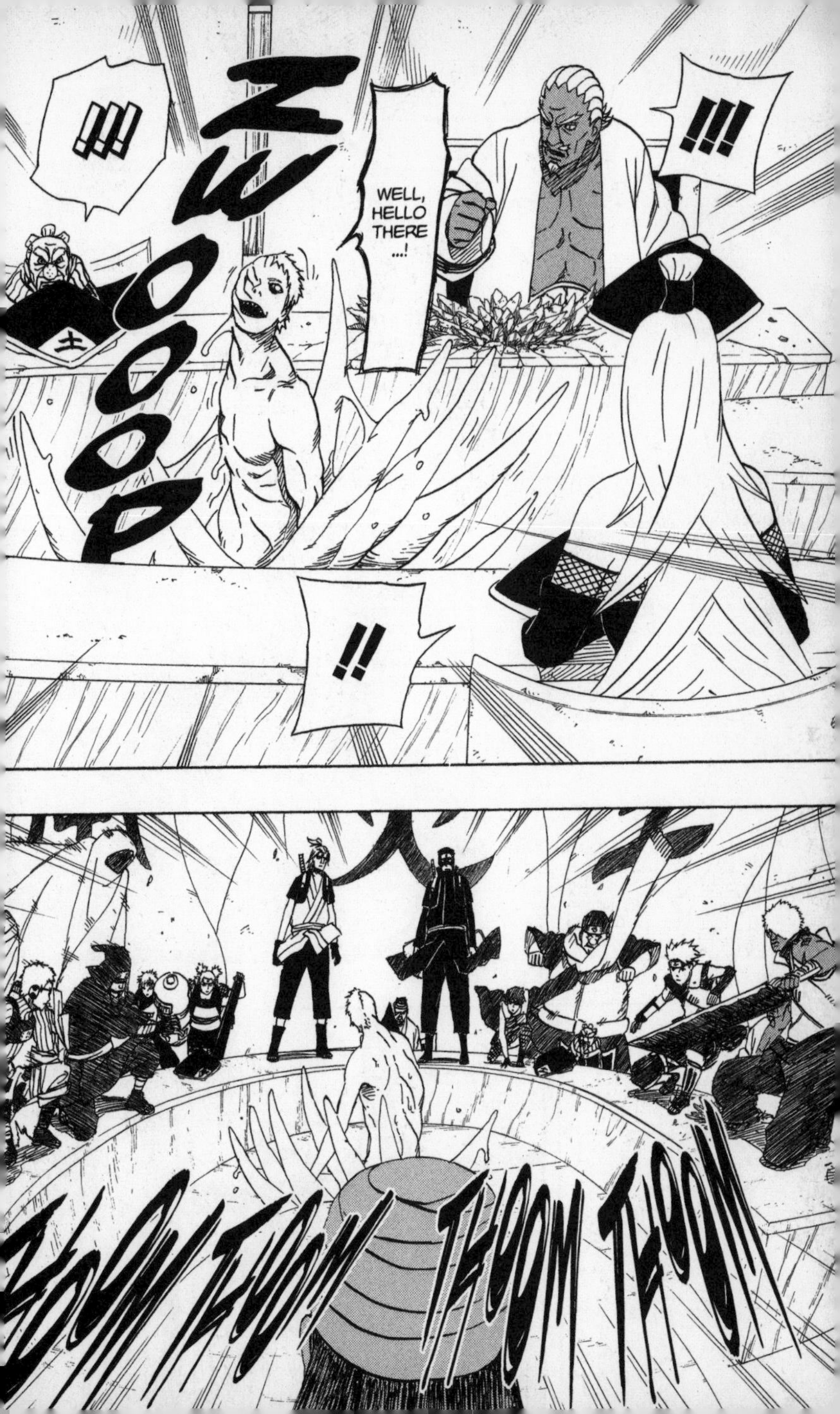
!!!
WELL, HELLO THERE ...!
ZWOOOP
!!!
!!
THOOM THOOM THOOM THOOM

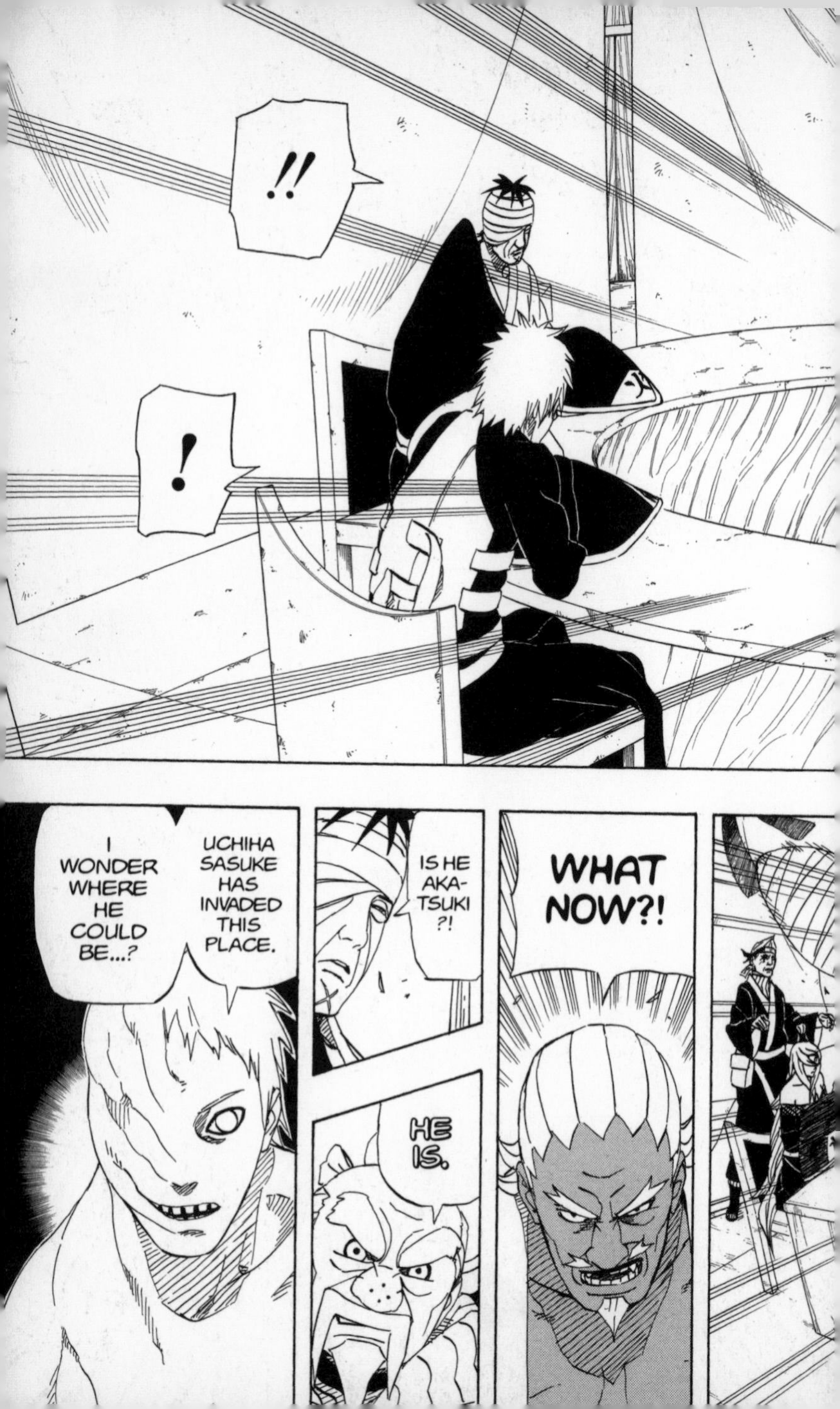
!!
!
WHAT NOW?!
IS HE AKATSUKI?!
HE IS.
UCHIHA SASUKE HAS INVADED THIS PLACE.
I WONDER WHERE HE COULD BE...?

NARUTO

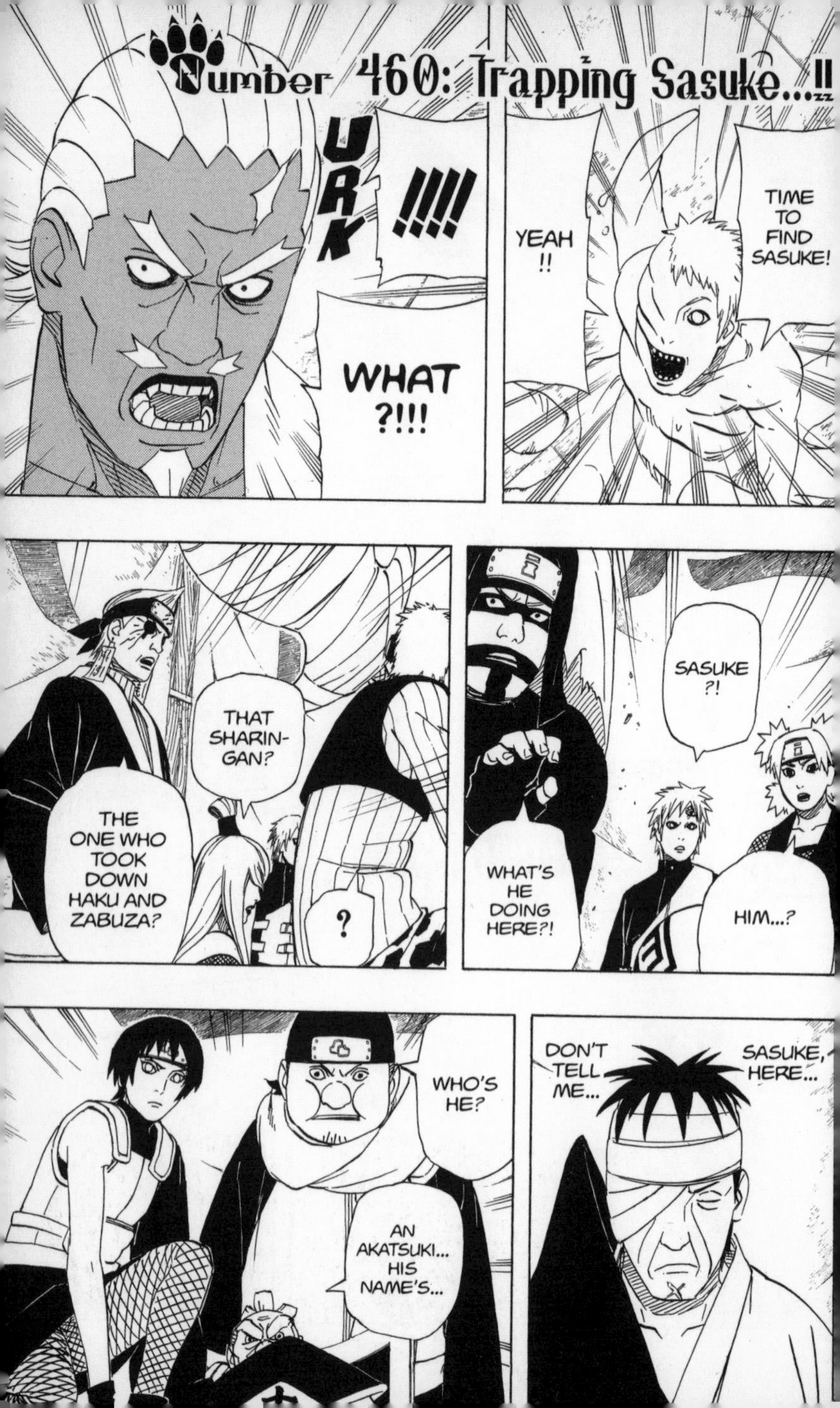
Number 460: Trapping Sasuke...!!
TIME TO FIND SASUKE!
YEAH !!
URK !!!!
WHAT ?!!!
SASUKE ?!
HIM...?
WHAT'S HE DOING HERE?!
THAT SHARIN-GAN?
THE ONE WHO TOOK DOWN HAKU AND ZABUZA?
?
SASUKE, HERE...
DON'T TELL ME...
WHO'S HE?
AN AKATSUKI... HIS NAME'S...

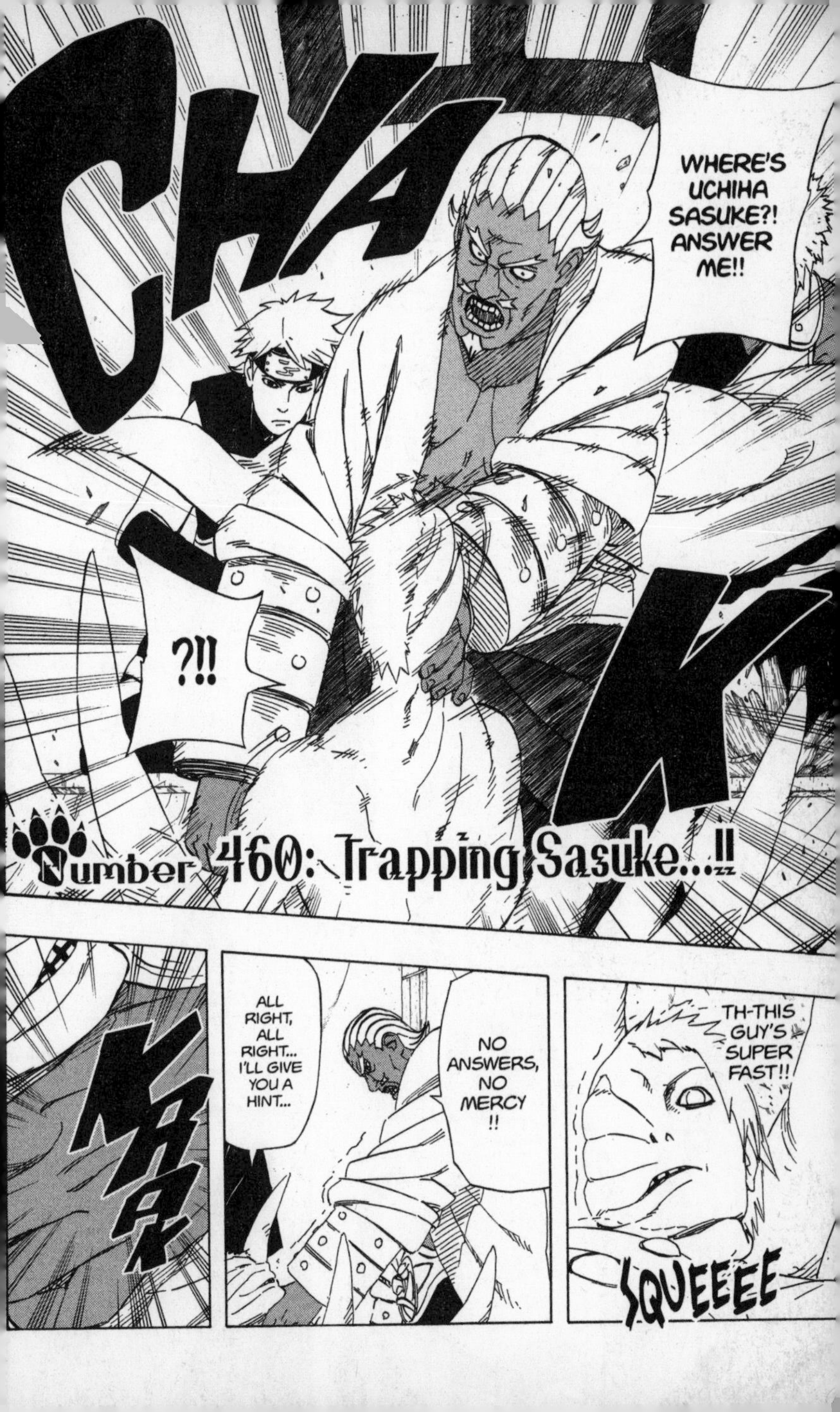
CHAK
WHERE'S UCHIHA SASUKE?! ANSWER ME!!
?!!
Number 460: Trapping Sasuke...!!
TH-THIS GUY'S SUPER FAST!!
SQUEEEE
NO ANSWERS, NO MERCY !!
ALL RIGHT, ALL RIGHT... I'LL GIVE YOU A HINT...

READ THIS WAY

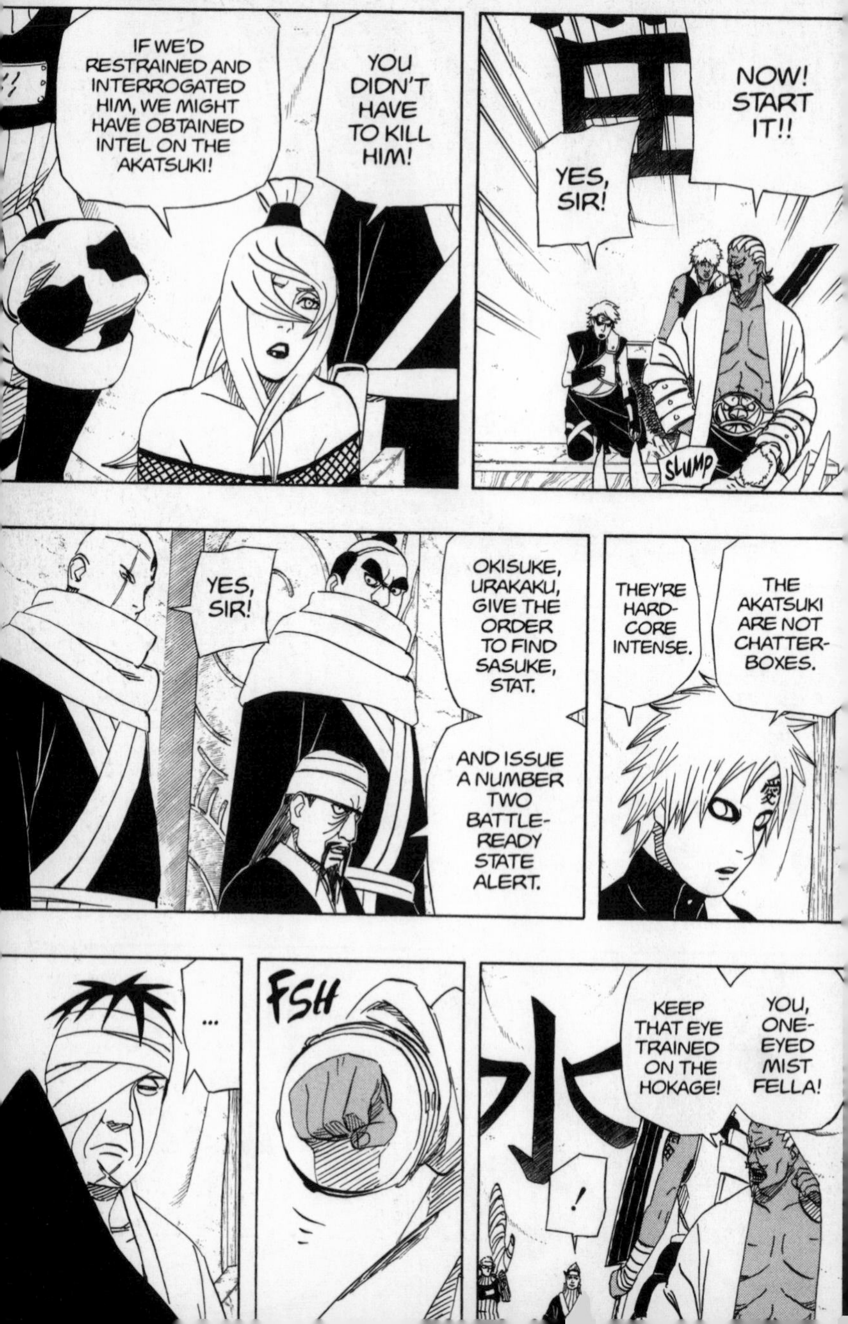
NOW! START IT!!
YES, SIR!
SLUMP
YOU DIDN'T HAVE TO KILL HIM!
IF WE'D RESTRAINED AND INTERROGATED HIM, WE MIGHT HAVE OBTAINED INTEL ON THE AKATSUKI!
THE AKATSUKI ARE NOT CHATTER-BOXES.
THEY'RE HARD-CORE INTENSE.
OKISUKE, URAKAKU, GIVE THE ORDER TO FIND SASUKE, STAT.
AND ISSUE A NUMBER TWO BATTLE-READY STATE ALERT.
YES, SIR!
YOU, ONE-EYED MIST FELLA!
KEEP THAT EYE TRAINED ON THE HOKAGE!
!
FSH
...

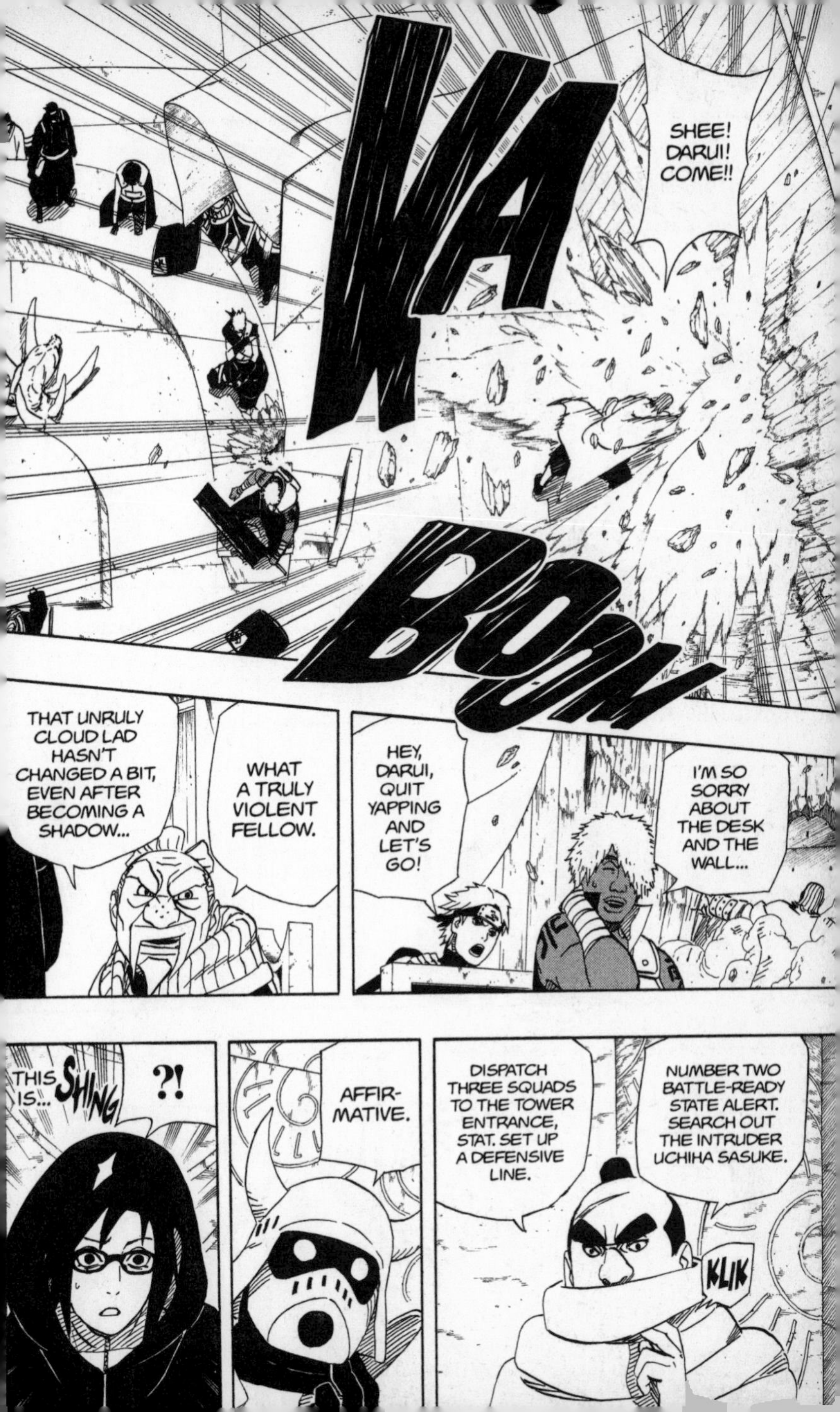
SHEE! DARUI! COME!!
KA
BOOM
I'M SO SORRY ABOUT THE DESK AND THE WALL...
HEY, DARUI, QUIT YAPPING AND LET'S GO!
WHAT A TRULY VIOLENT FELLOW.
THAT UNRULY CLOUD LAD HASN'T CHANGED A BIT, EVEN AFTER BECOMING A SHADOW...
NUMBER TWO BATTLE-READY STATE ALERT. SEARCH OUT THE INTRUDER UCHIHA SASUKE.
DISPATCH THREE SQUADS TO THE TOWER ENTRANCE, STAT. SET UP A DEFENSIVE LINE.
KLIK
AFFIR-MATIVE.
?!
THIS IS...
SHING

READ THIS WAY

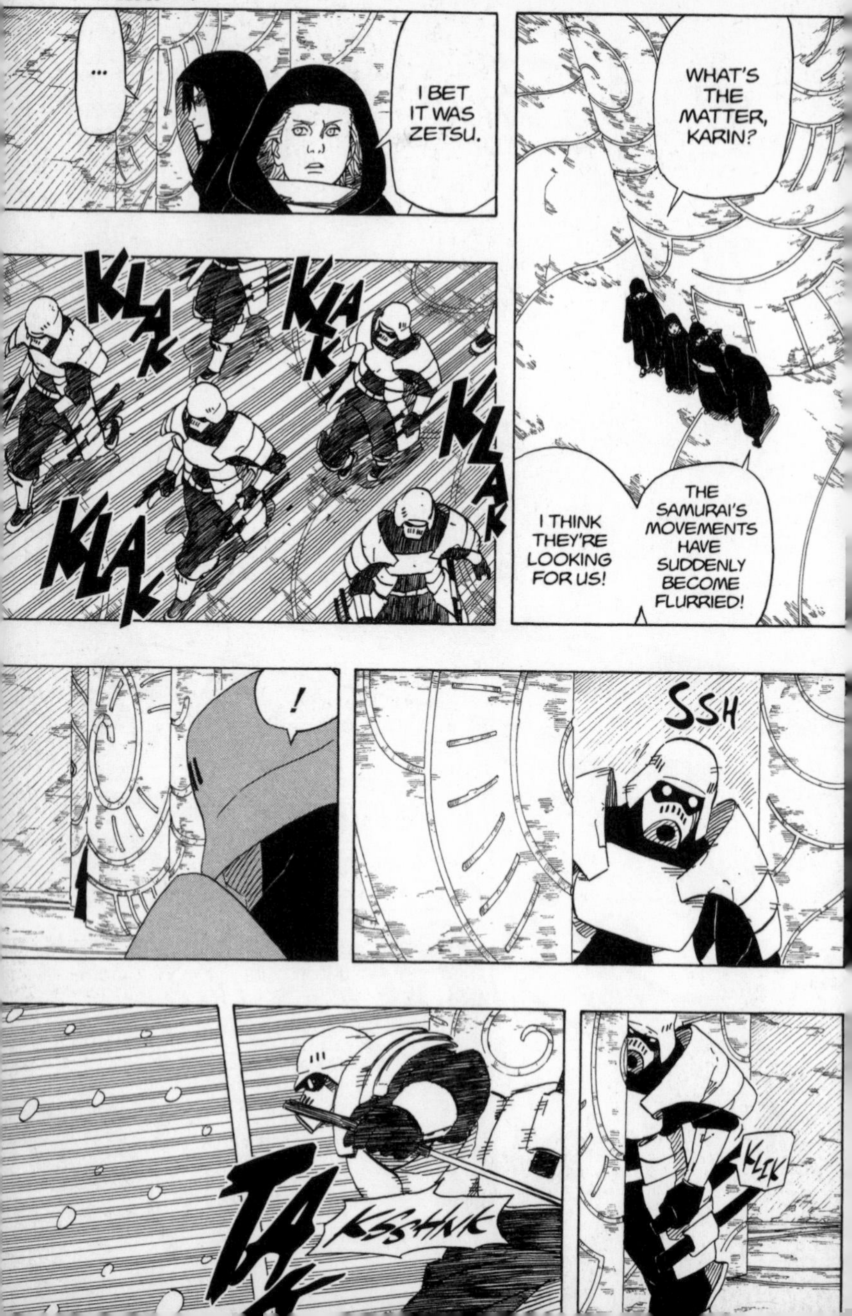

WHAT'S THE MATTER, KARIN?
THE SAMURAI'S MOVEMENTS HAVE SUDDENLY BECOME FLURRIED!
I THINK THEY'RE LOOKING FOR US!
I BET IT WAS ZETSU.
...
KLAK
KLAK
KLAK
KLAK
SSH
!
KLIK
KSSHNK
TA

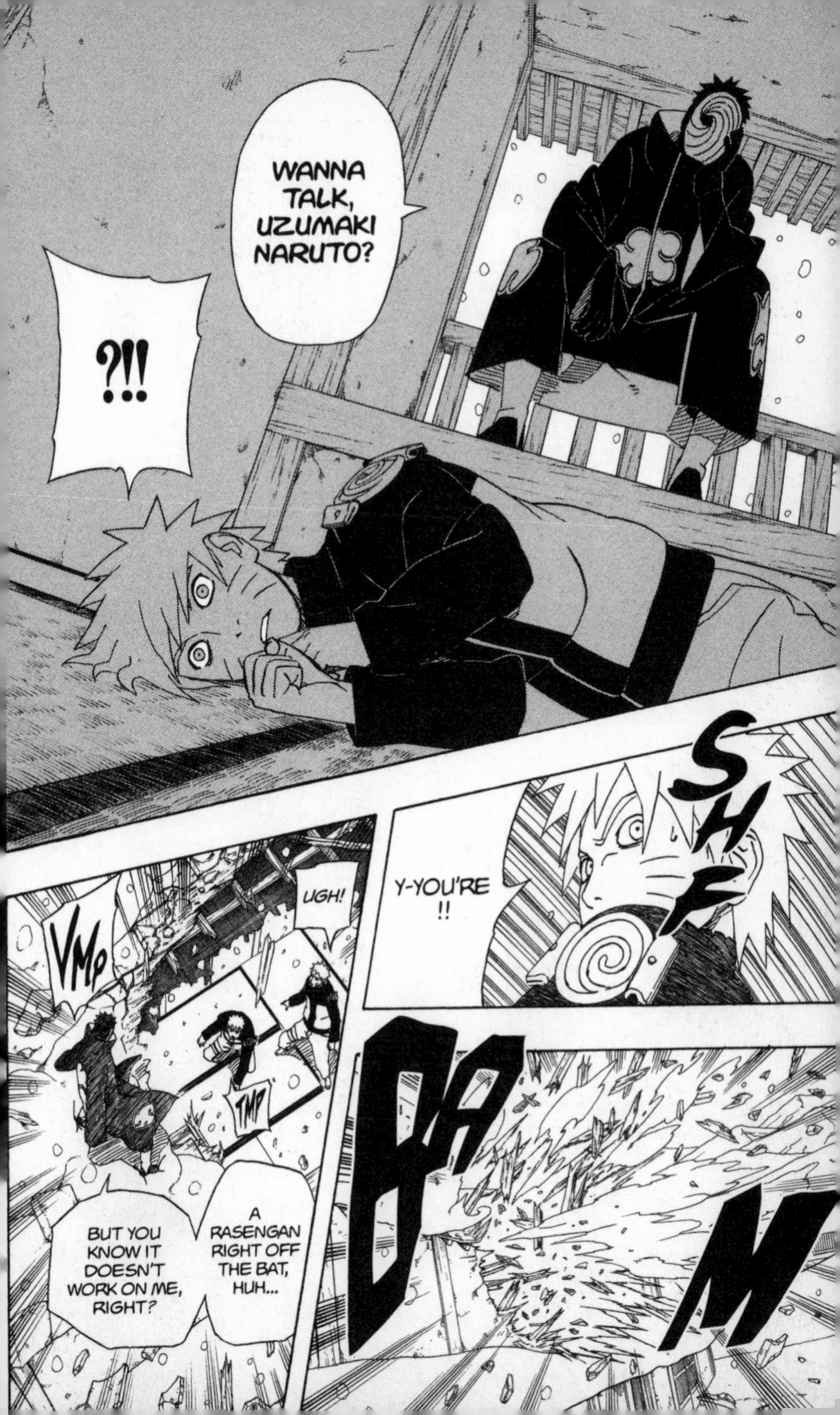
WANNA TALK, UZUMAKI NARUTO?
?!!
SHF
Y-YOU'RE !!
BAM
UGH!
VMP
TMP
A RASENGAN RIGHT OFF THE BAT, HUH...
BUT YOU KNOW IT DOESN'T WORK ON ME, RIGHT?

READ THIS WAY

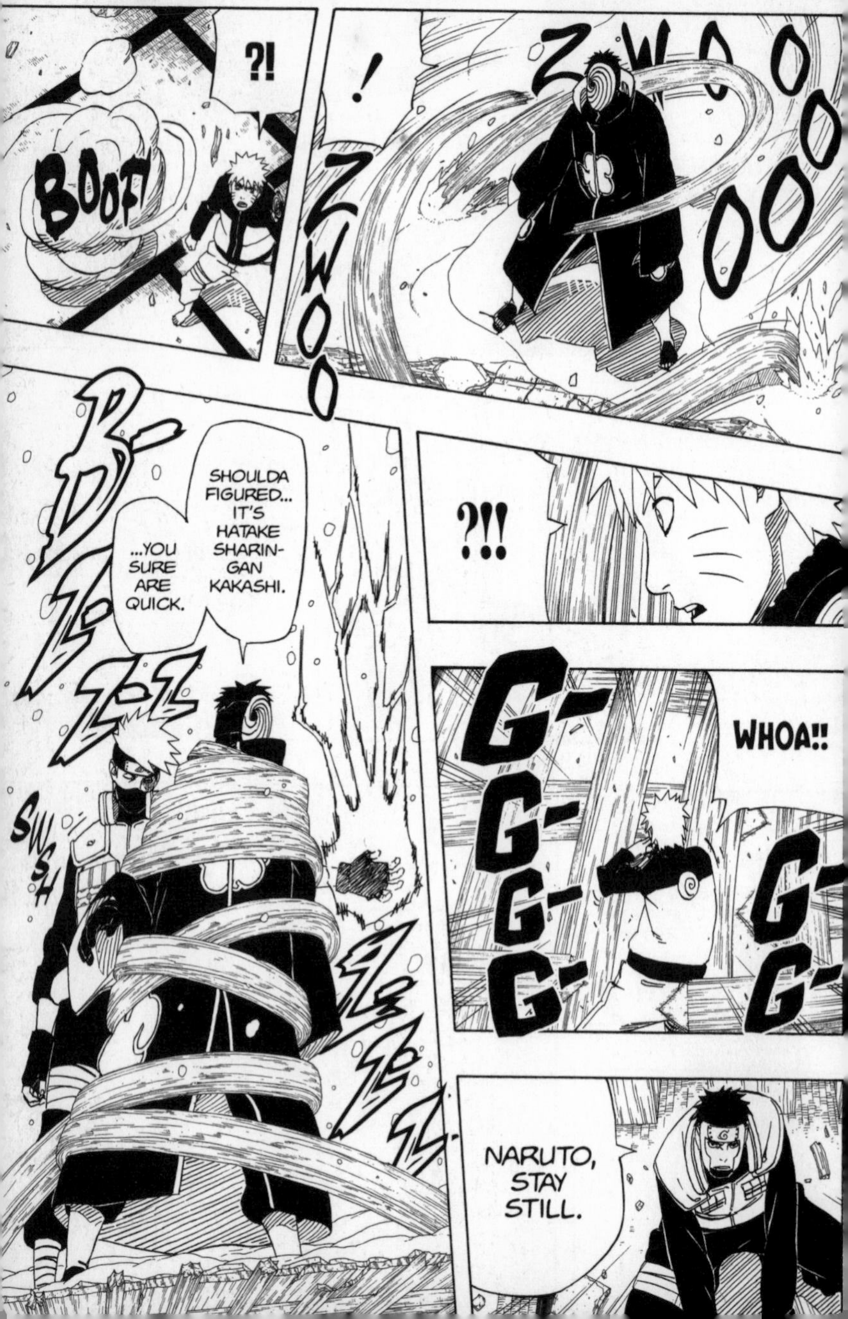

ZWOOOOOOO
!
ZWOOO
?!
BOOF!
?!!
G-G-G-G-
WHOA!!
G-G-
NARUTO, STAY STILL.
SHOULDA FIGURED... IT'S HATAKE SHARINGAN KAKASHI.
...YOU SURE ARE QUICK.
SWSH

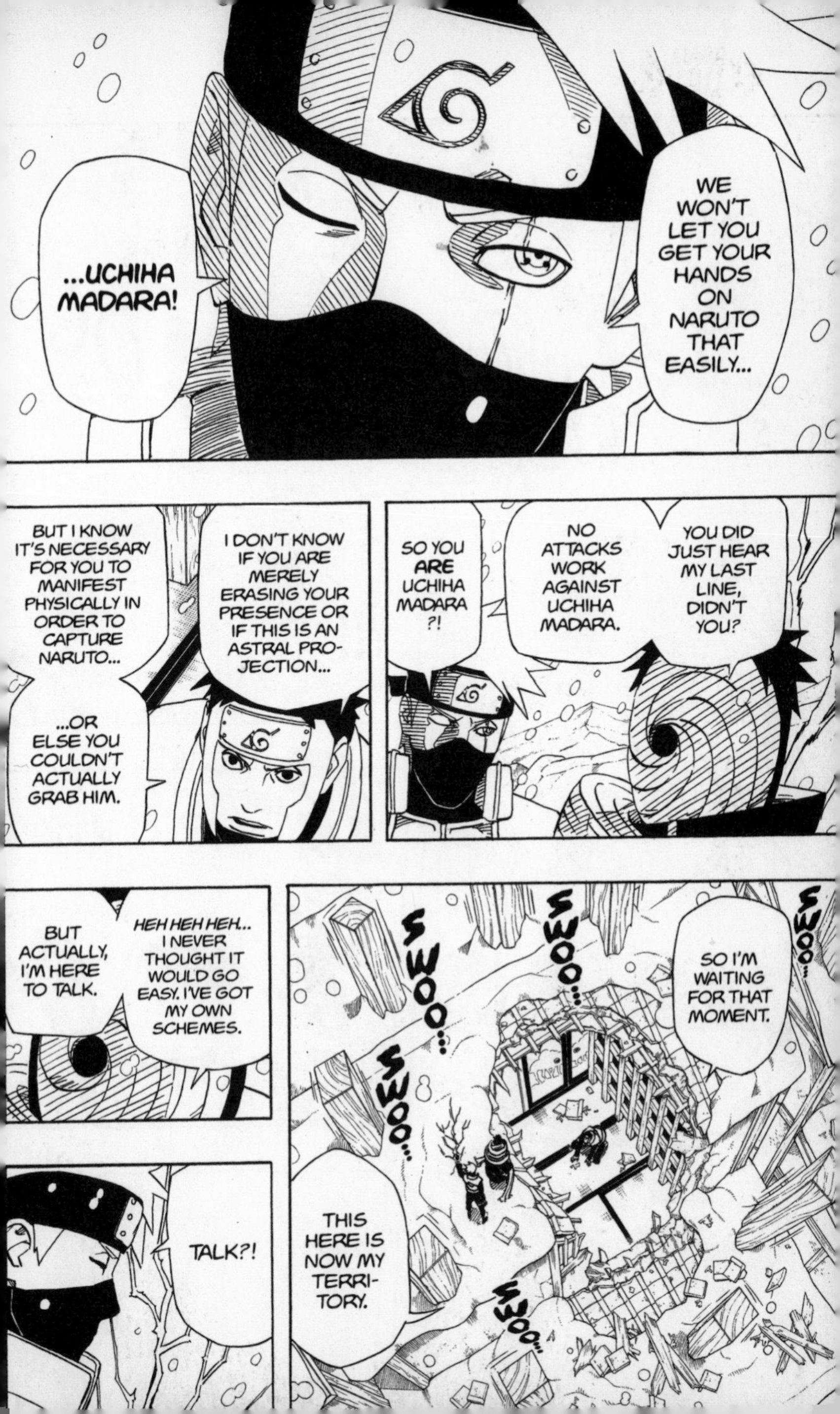
WE WON'T LET YOU GET YOUR HANDS ON NARUTO THAT EASILY...
...UCHIHA MADARA!
YOU DID JUST HEAR MY LAST LINE, DIDN'T YOU?
NO ATTACKS WORK AGAINST UCHIHA MADARA.
SO YOU ARE UCHIHA MADARA?!
I DON'T KNOW IF YOU ARE MERELY ERASING YOUR PRESENCE OR IF THIS IS AN ASTRAL PROJECTION...
BUT I KNOW IT'S NECESSARY FOR YOU TO MANIFEST PHYSICALLY IN ORDER TO CAPTURE NARUTO...
...OR ELSE YOU COULDN'T ACTUALLY GRAB HIM.
SWOO...
SO I'M WAITING FOR THAT MOMENT.
SWOO...
SWOO...
SWOO...
THIS HERE IS NOW MY TERRITORY.
SWOO...
HEH HEH HEH... I NEVER THOUGHT IT WOULD GO EASY. I'VE GOT MY OWN SCHEMES.
BUT ACTUALLY, I'M HERE TO TALK.
TALK?!

READ THIS WAY

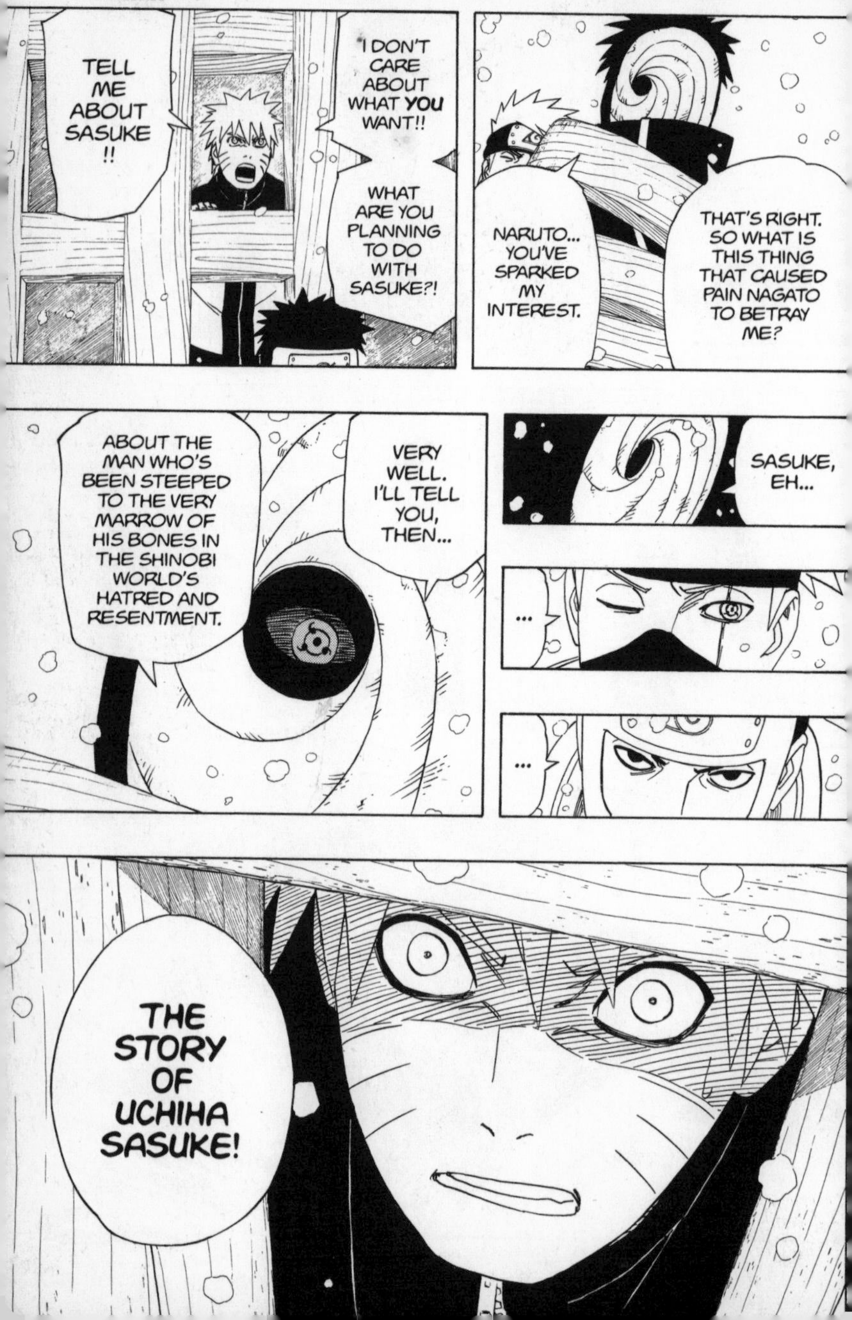

THAT'S RIGHT. SO WHAT IS THIS THING THAT CAUSED PAIN NAGATO TO BETRAY ME?
NARUTO... YOU'VE SPARKED MY INTEREST.
I DON'T CARE ABOUT WHAT **YOU** WANT!!
WHAT ARE YOU PLANNING TO DO WITH SASUKE?!
TELL ME ABOUT SASUKE!!
SASUKE, EH...
...
...
VERY WELL. I'LL TELL YOU, THEN...
ABOUT THE MAN WHO'S BEEN STEEPED TO THE VERY MARROW OF HIS BONES IN THE SHINOBI WORLD'S HATRED AND RESENTMENT.
THE STORY OF UCHIHA SASUKE!

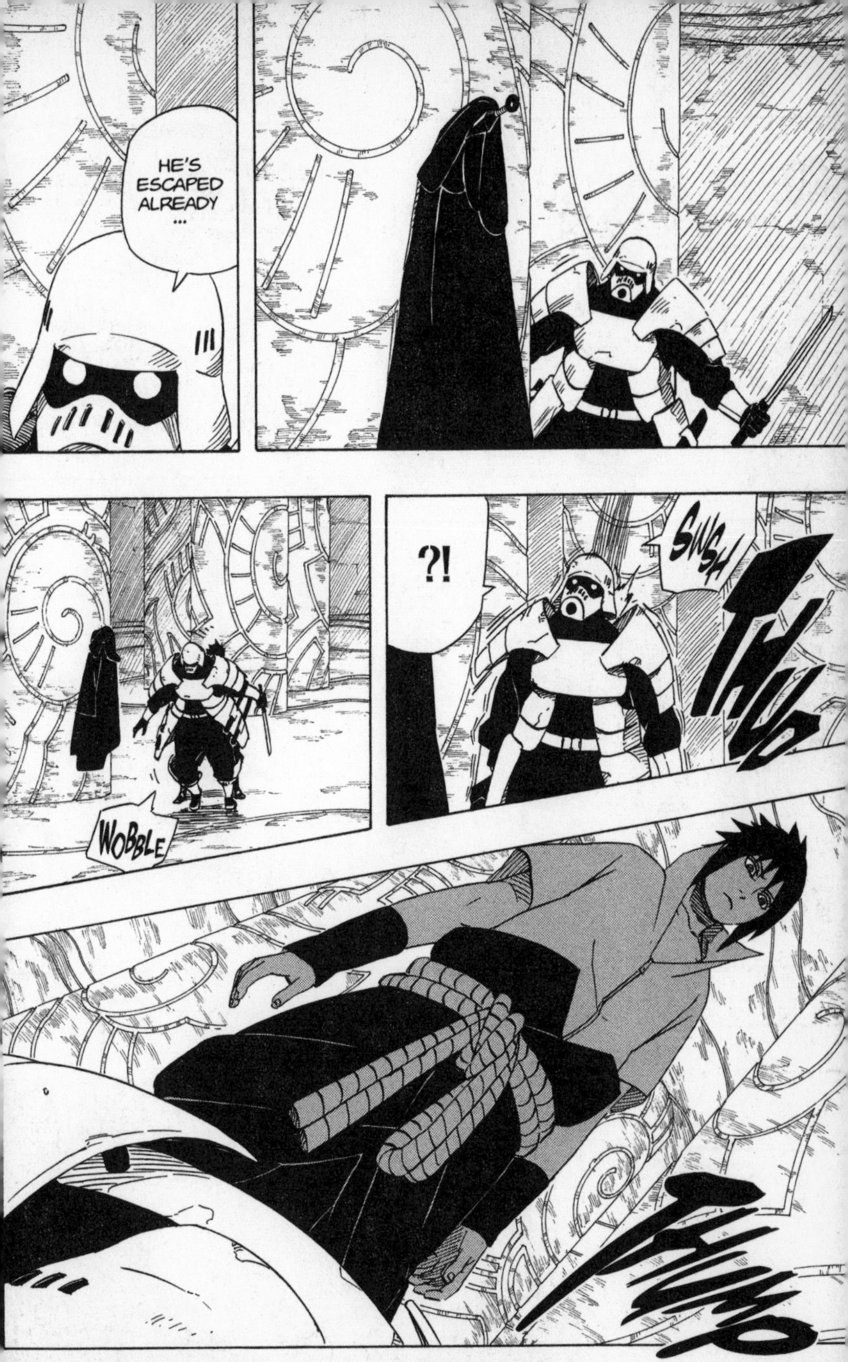
HE'S ESCAPED ALREADY ...
SWSH
?!
THUD
WOBBLE
THUMP

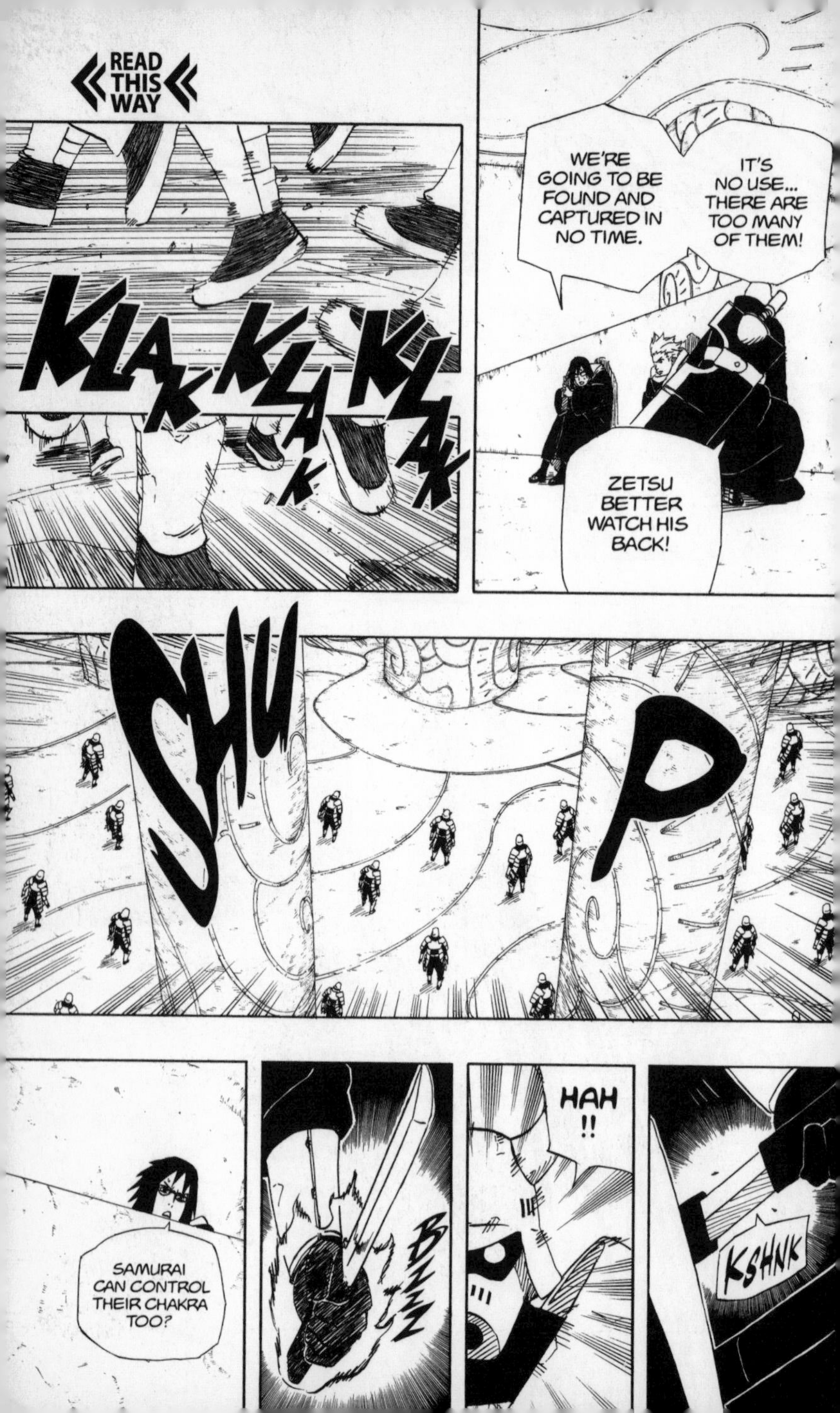

READ THIS WAY
IT'S NO USE... THERE ARE TOO MANY OF THEM!
WE'RE GOING TO BE FOUND AND CAPTURED IN NO TIME.
ZETSU BETTER WATCH HIS BACK!
KLAK KLAK KLAK KLAK KLAK KLAK
SHUP
KSHNK
HAH!!
BZWMM
SAMURAI CAN CONTROL THEIR CHAKRA TOO?

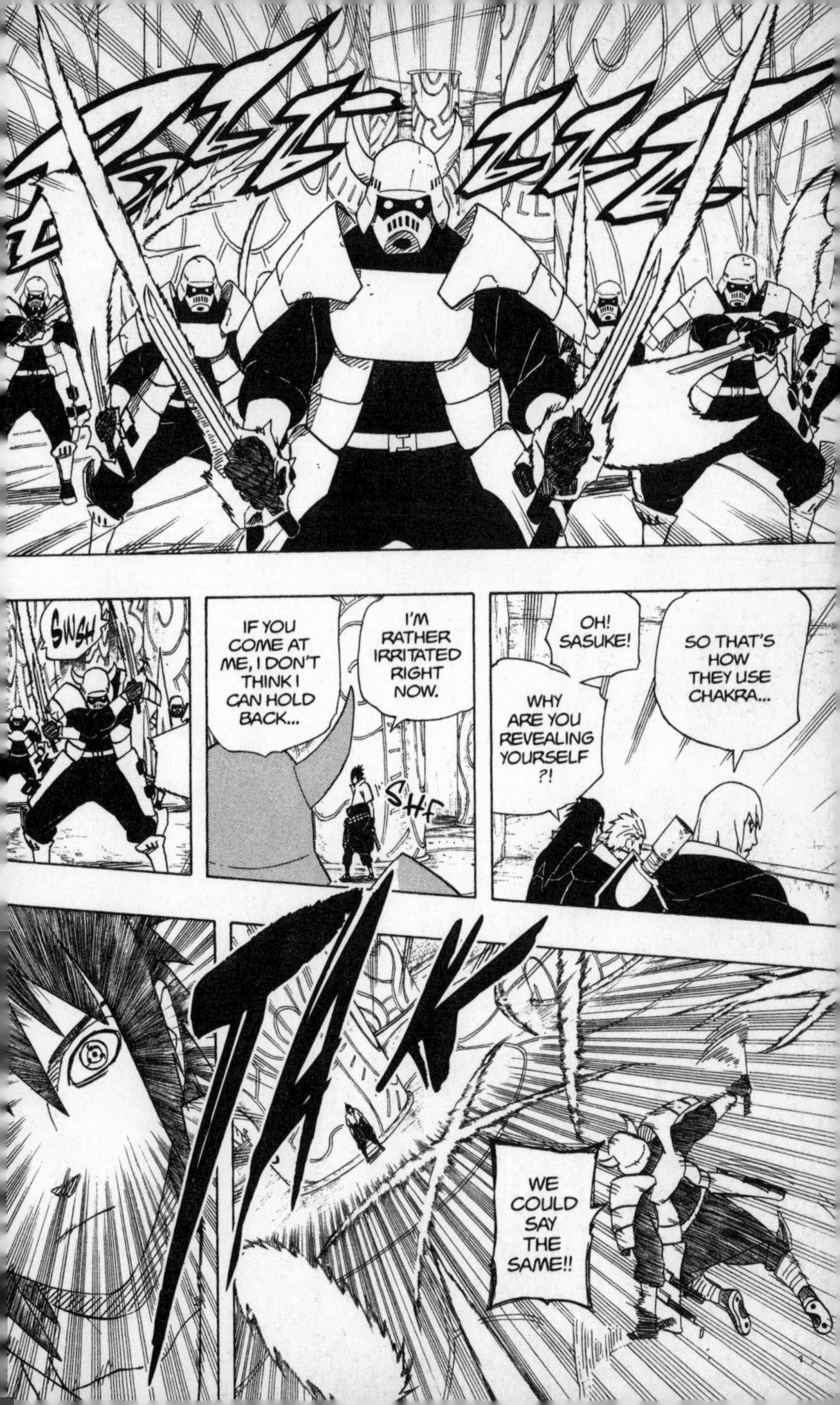
SO THAT'S HOW THEY USE CHAKRA...
OH! SASUKE!
WHY ARE YOU REVEALING YOURSELF?!
I'M RATHER IRRITATED RIGHT NOW.
IF YOU COME AT ME, I DON'T THINK I CAN HOLD BACK...
SHF
SWSH
WE COULD SAY THE SAME!!

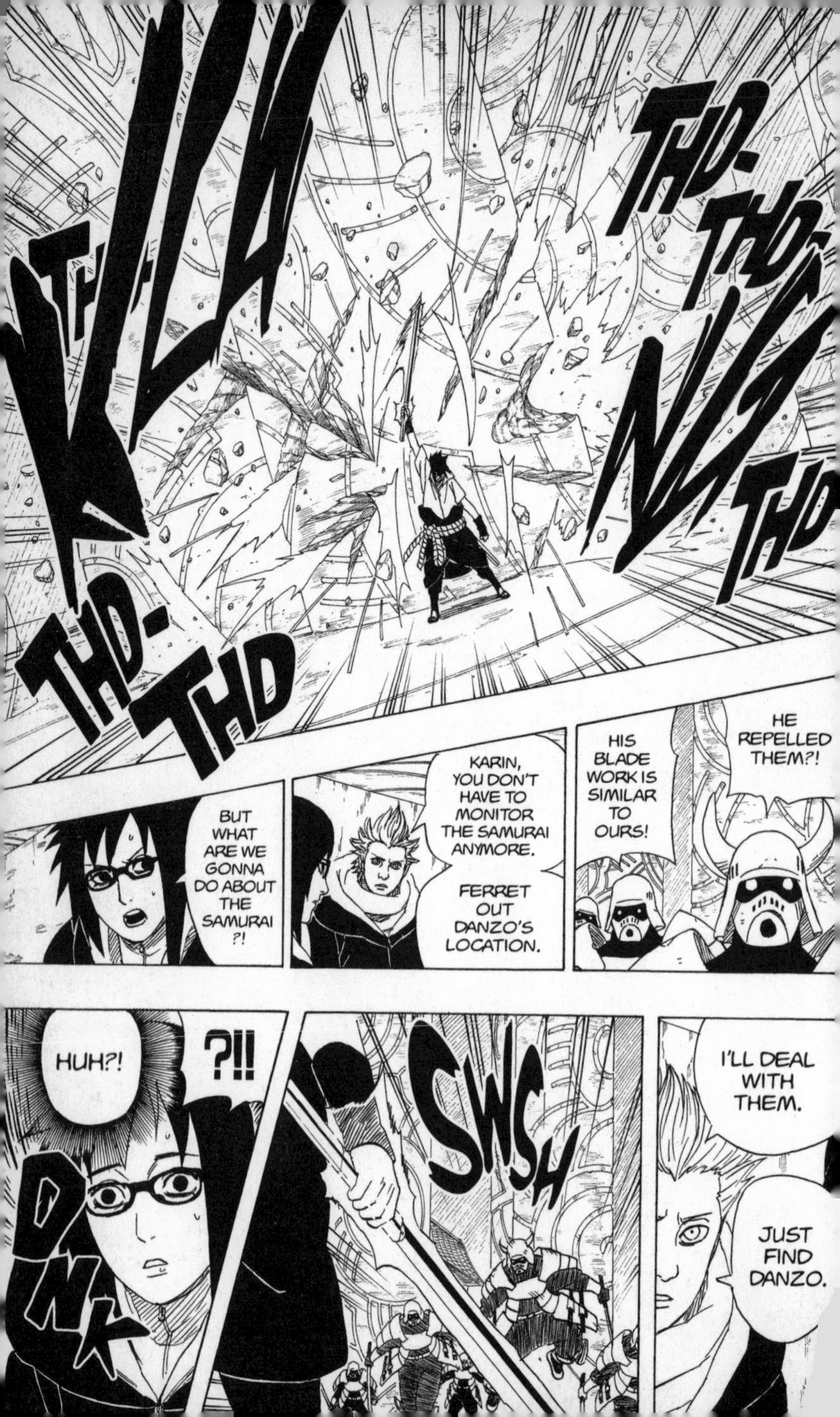
THD-THD-
THD
THD-THD
HE REPELLED THEM?!
HIS BLADE WORK IS SIMILAR TO OURS!
KARIN, YOU DON'T HAVE TO MONITOR THE SAMURAI ANYMORE.
FERRET OUT DANZO'S LOCATION.
BUT WHAT ARE WE GONNA DO ABOUT THE SAMURAI ?!
I'LL DEAL WITH THEM.
JUST FIND DANZO.
SWSH
?!!
HUH?!

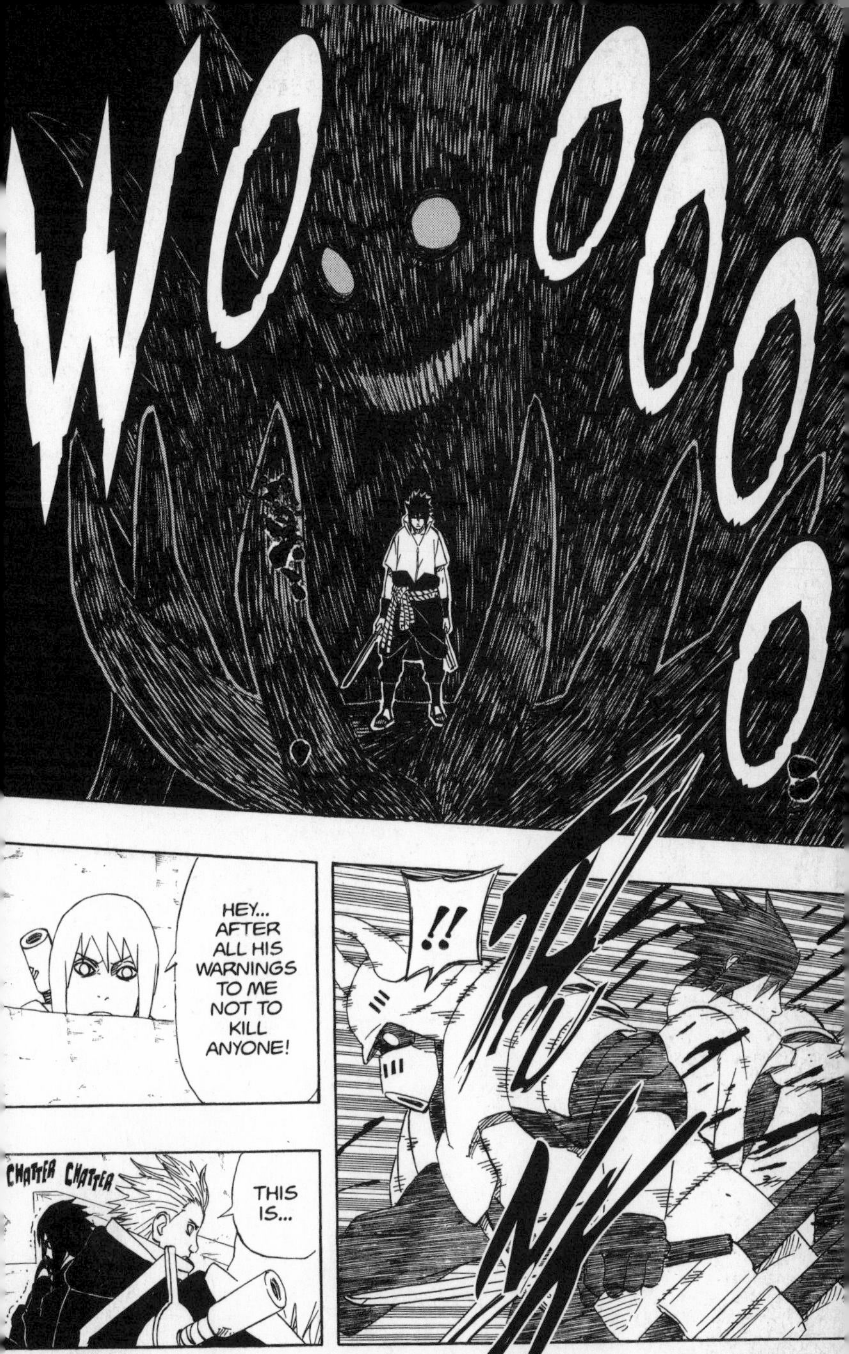
WO...OOOO
!!
HEY... AFTER ALL HIS WARNINGS TO ME NOT TO KILL ANYONE!
CHATTER CHATTER
THIS IS...

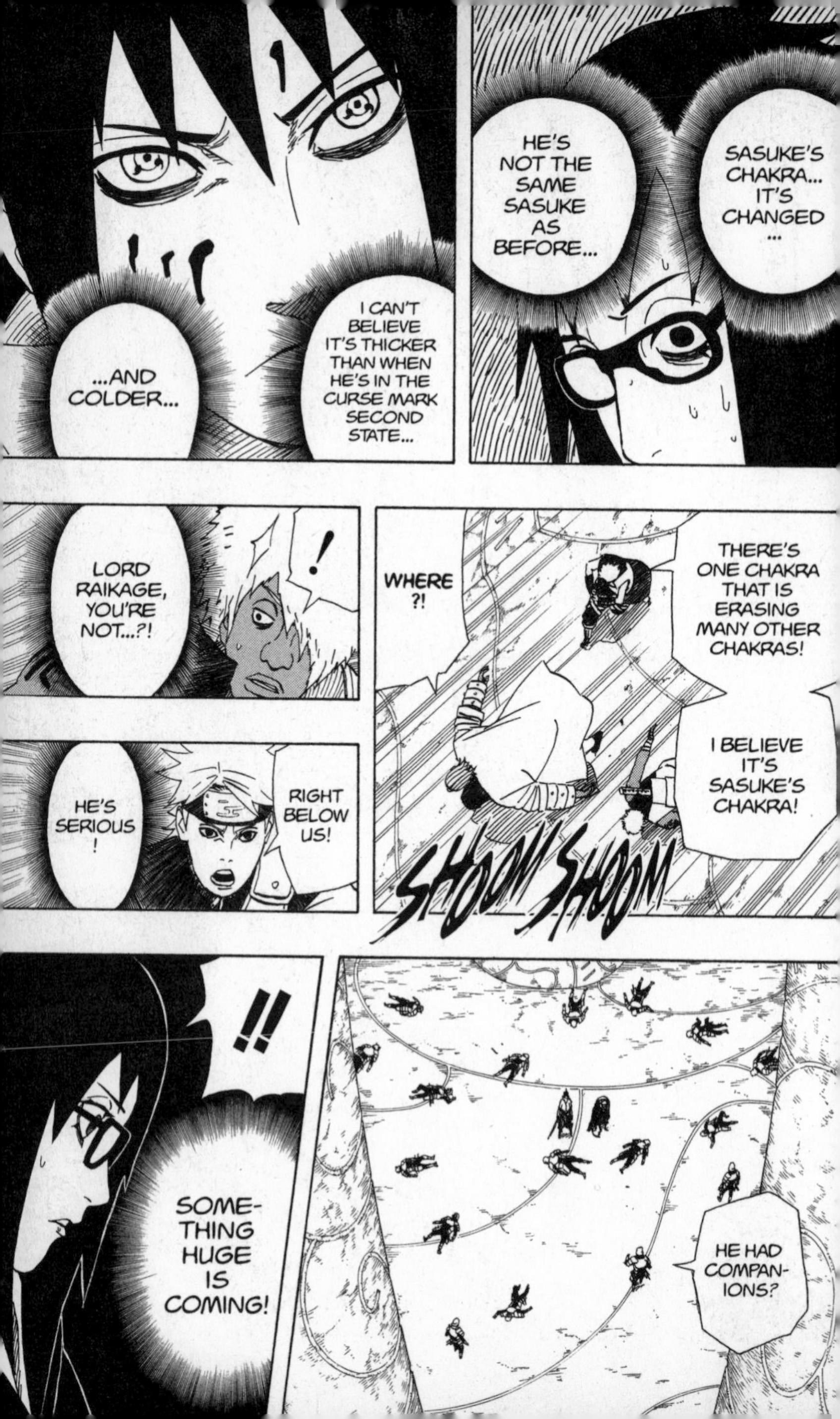
SASUKE'S CHAKRA... IT'S CHANGED ...
HE'S NOT THE SAME SASUKE AS BEFORE...
I CAN'T BELIEVE IT'S THICKER THAN WHEN HE'S IN THE CURSE MARK SECOND STATE...
...AND COLDER...
THERE'S ONE CHAKRA THAT IS ERASING MANY OTHER CHAKRAS!
WHERE ?!
I BELIEVE IT'S SASUKE'S CHAKRA!
SHOOM SHOOM
!
LORD RAIKAGE, YOU'RE NOT...?!
RIGHT BELOW US!
HE'S SERIOUS !
HE HAD COMPAN-IONS?
!!
SOME-THING HUGE IS COMING!

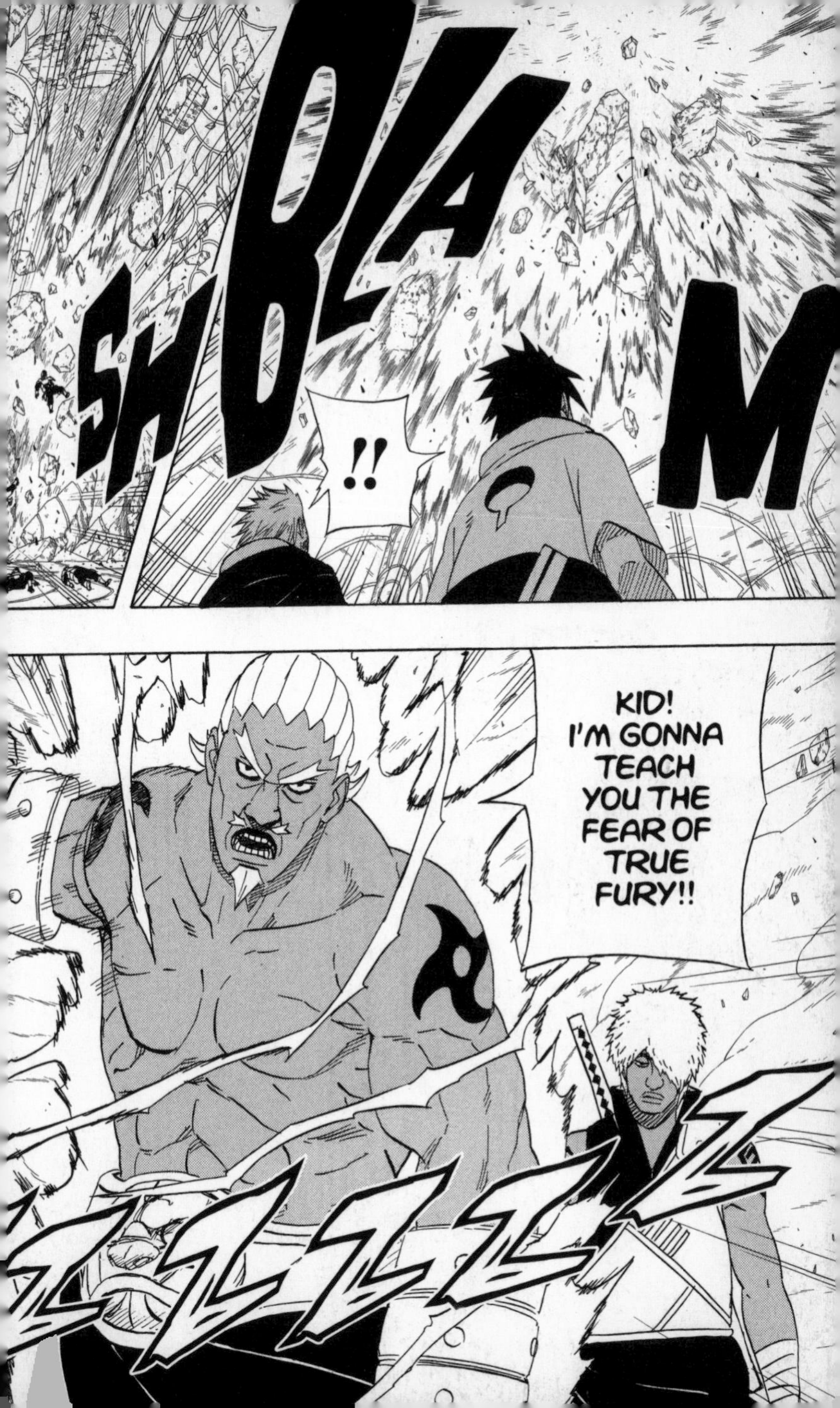
SHBLAM
!!
KID! I'M GONNA TEACH YOU THE FEAR OF TRUE FURY!!
ZZZZZZK

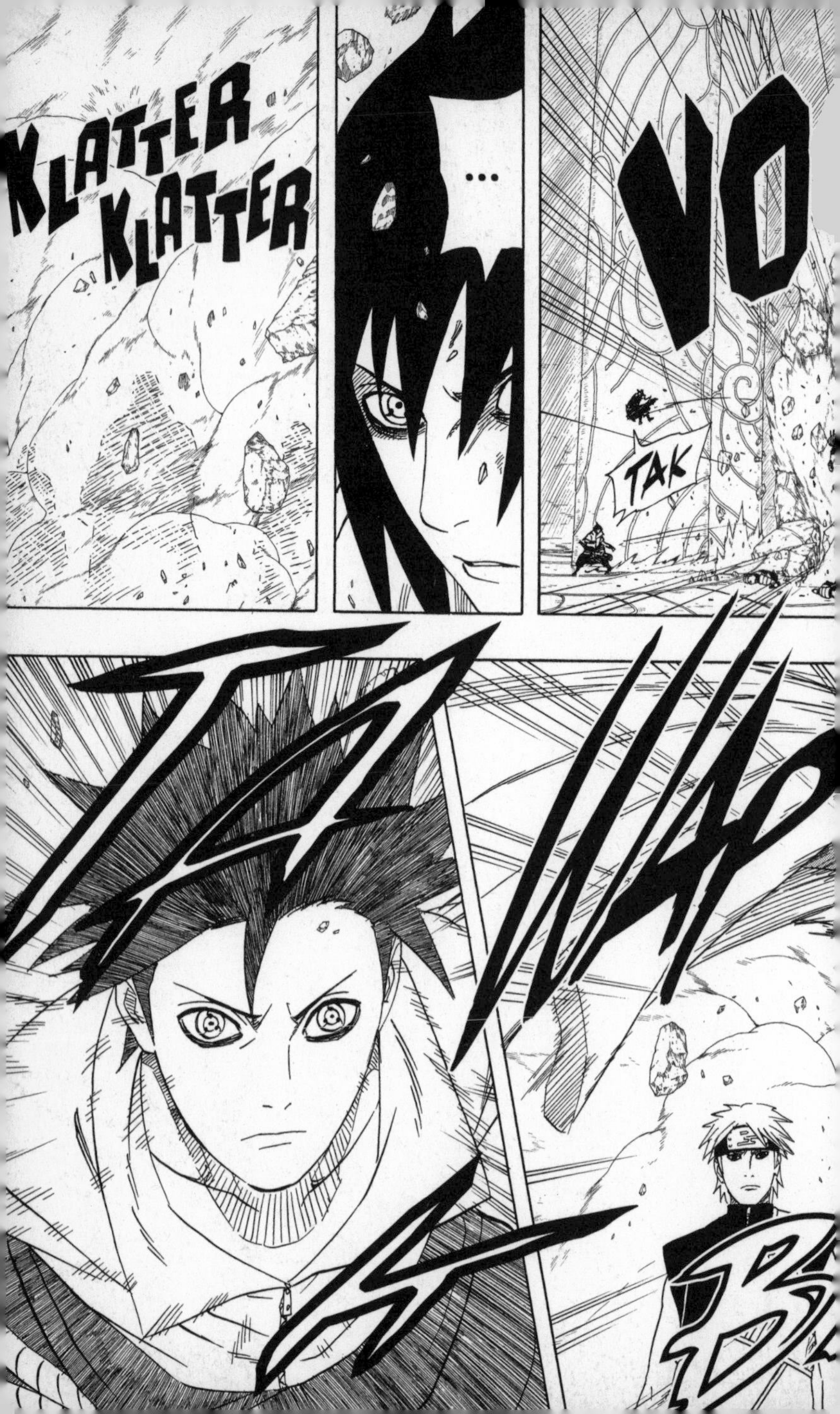
VO
TAK
...
KLATTER KLATTER

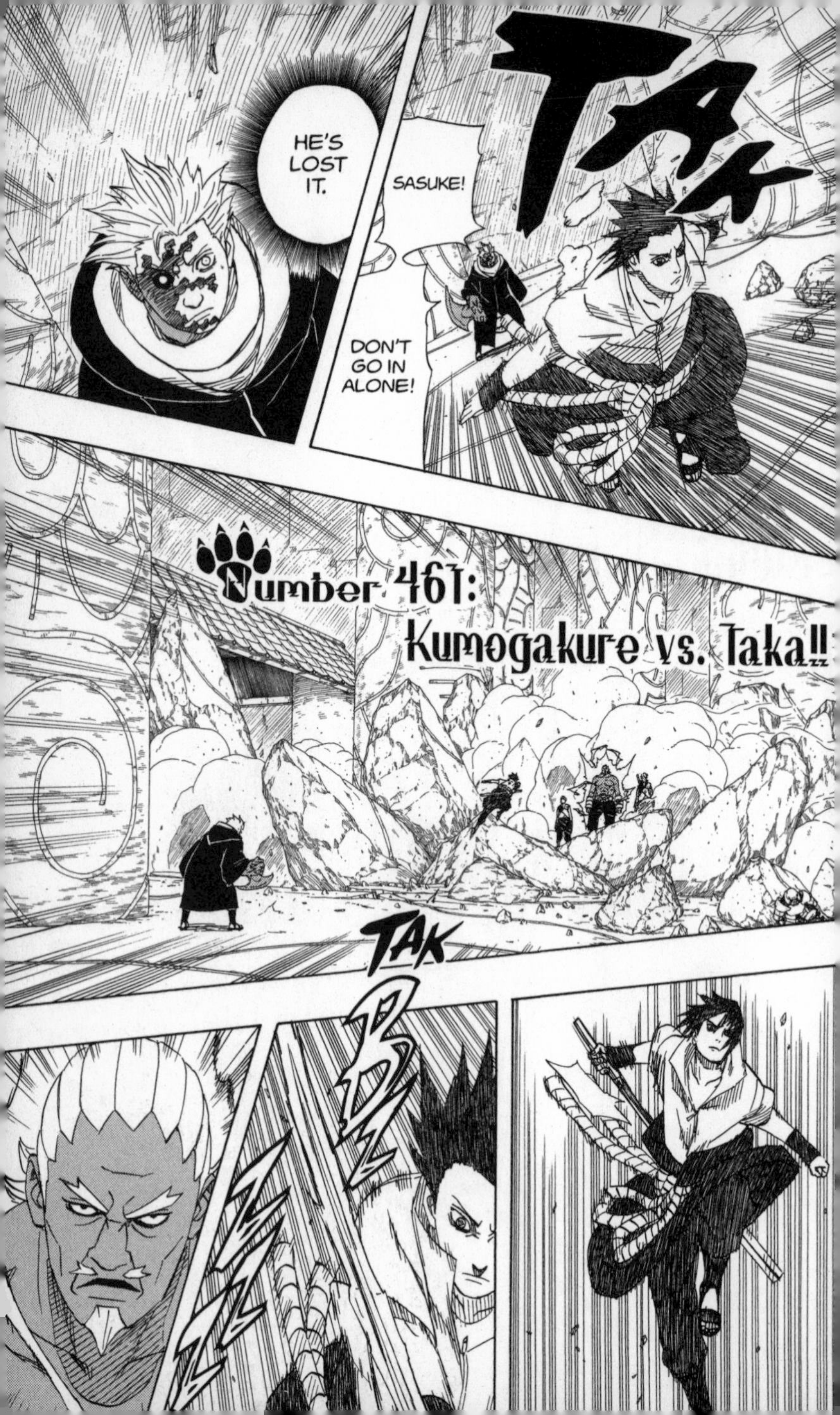
TAK
SASUKE!
DON'T GO IN ALONE!
HE'S LOST IT.
Number 461: Kumogakure vs. Taka!!
TAK

Number 461: Kumogakure vs. Taka!!

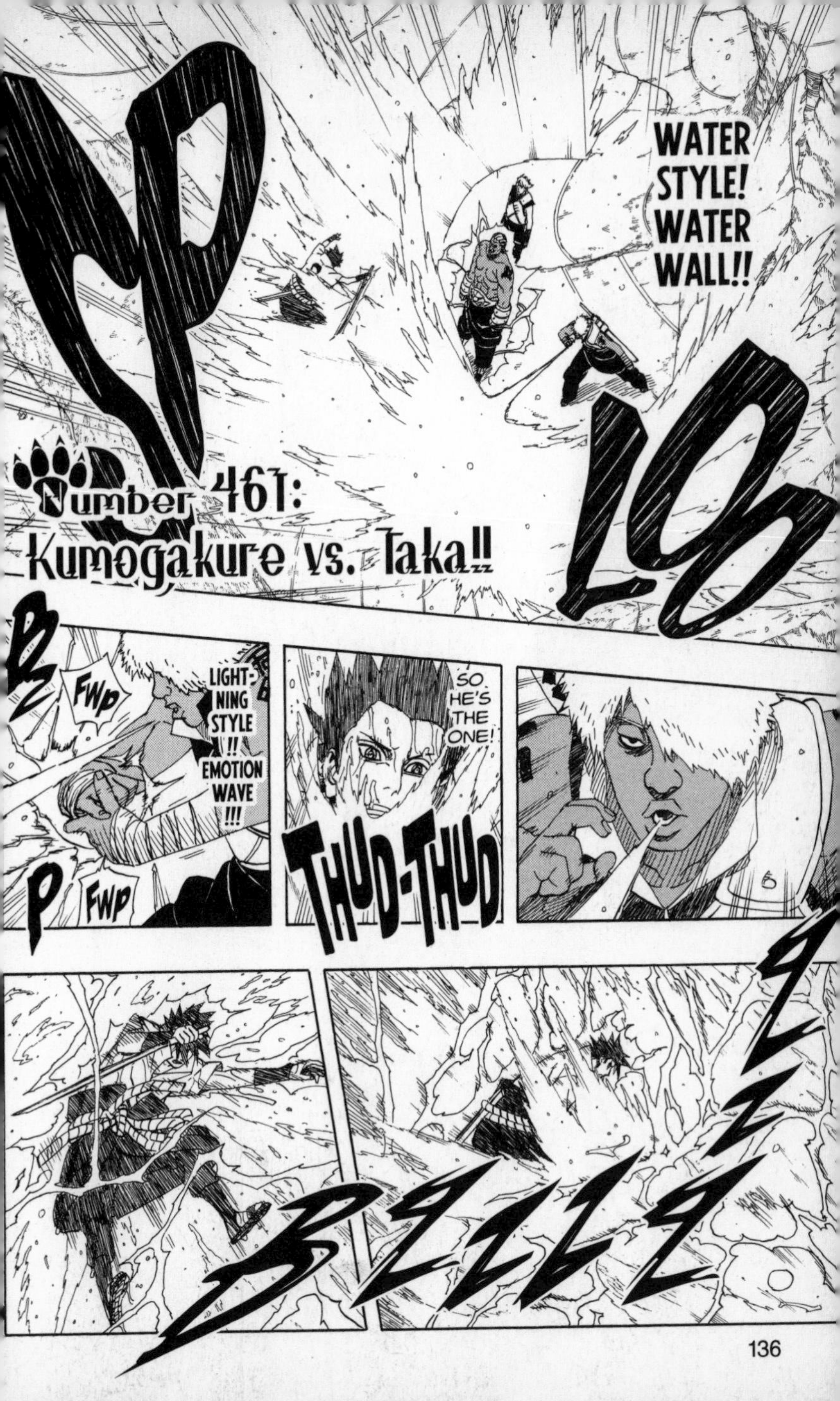
WATER STYLE! WATER WALL!!
SO HE'S THE ONE!
THUD-THUD
LIGHTNING STYLE!! EMOTION WAVE!!!
FWP
FWP

READ THIS WAY

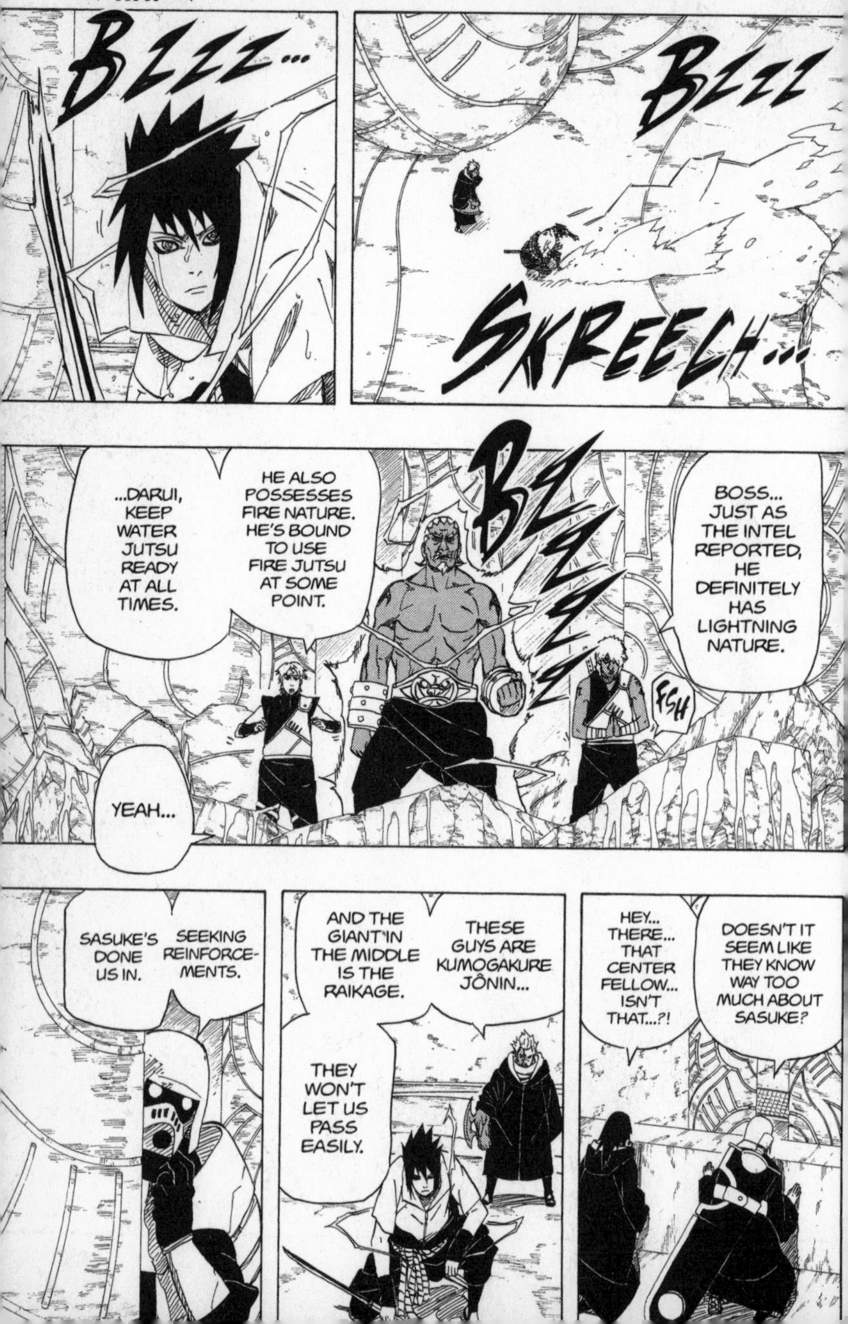
BZZZ
SKREECH...
BZZZ...
BOSS... JUST AS THE INTEL REPORTED, HE DEFINITELY HAS LIGHTNING NATURE.
FSH
BZZZZZ
HE ALSO POSSESSES FIRE NATURE. HE'S BOUND TO USE FIRE JUTSU AT SOME POINT.
...DARUI, KEEP WATER JUTSU READY AT ALL TIMES.
YEAH...
DOESN'T IT SEEM LIKE THEY KNOW WAY TOO MUCH ABOUT SASUKE?
HEY... THERE... THAT CENTER FELLOW... ISN'T THAT...?!
THESE GUYS ARE KUMOGAKURE JÔNIN...
AND THE GIANT IN THE MIDDLE IS THE RAIKAGE.
THEY WON'T LET US PASS EASILY.
SEEKING REINFORCEMENTS.
SASUKE'S DONE US IN.

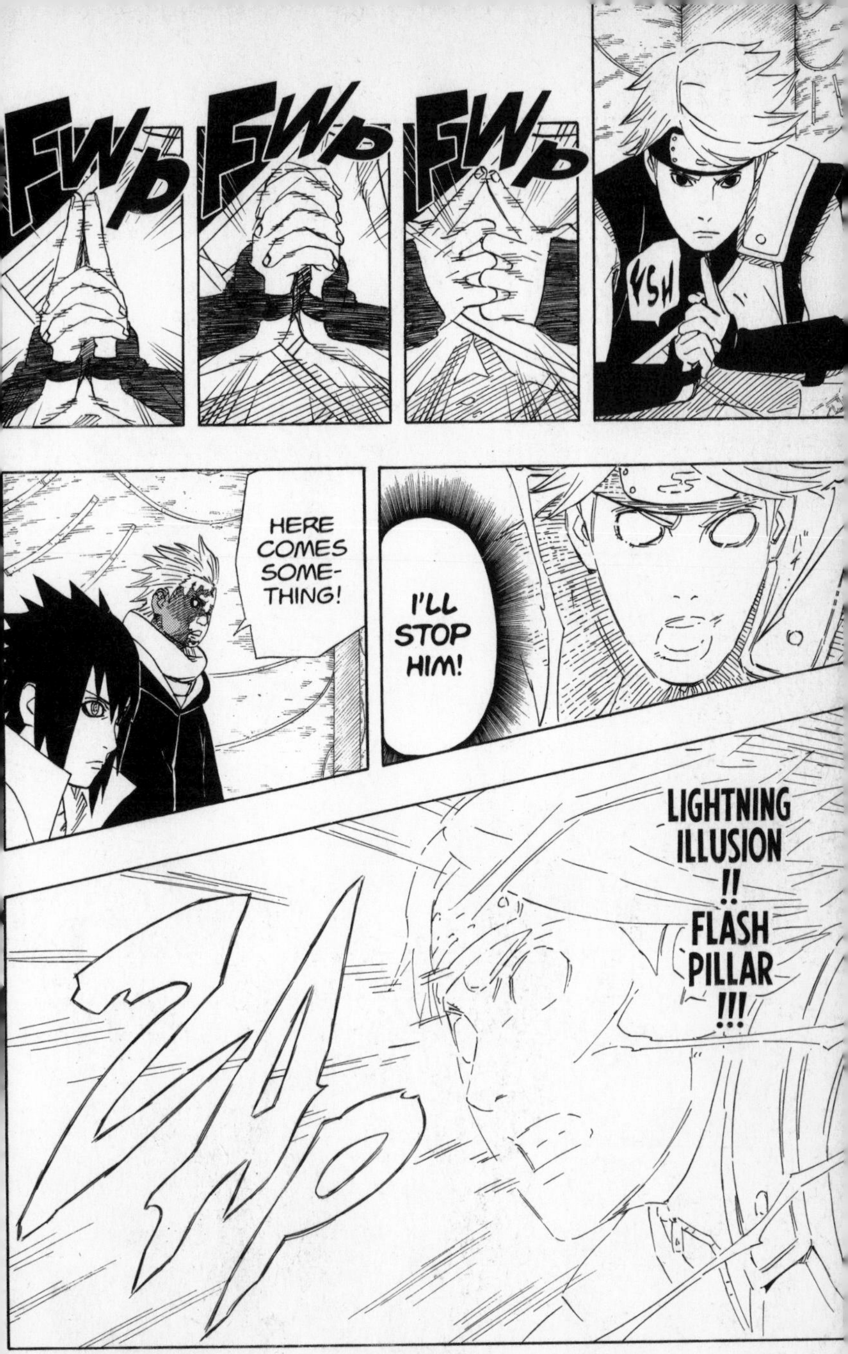
YSH
FWP
FWP
FWP
I'LL STOP HIM!
HERE COMES SOME-THING!
LIGHTNING ILLUSION!! FLASH PILLAR!!!

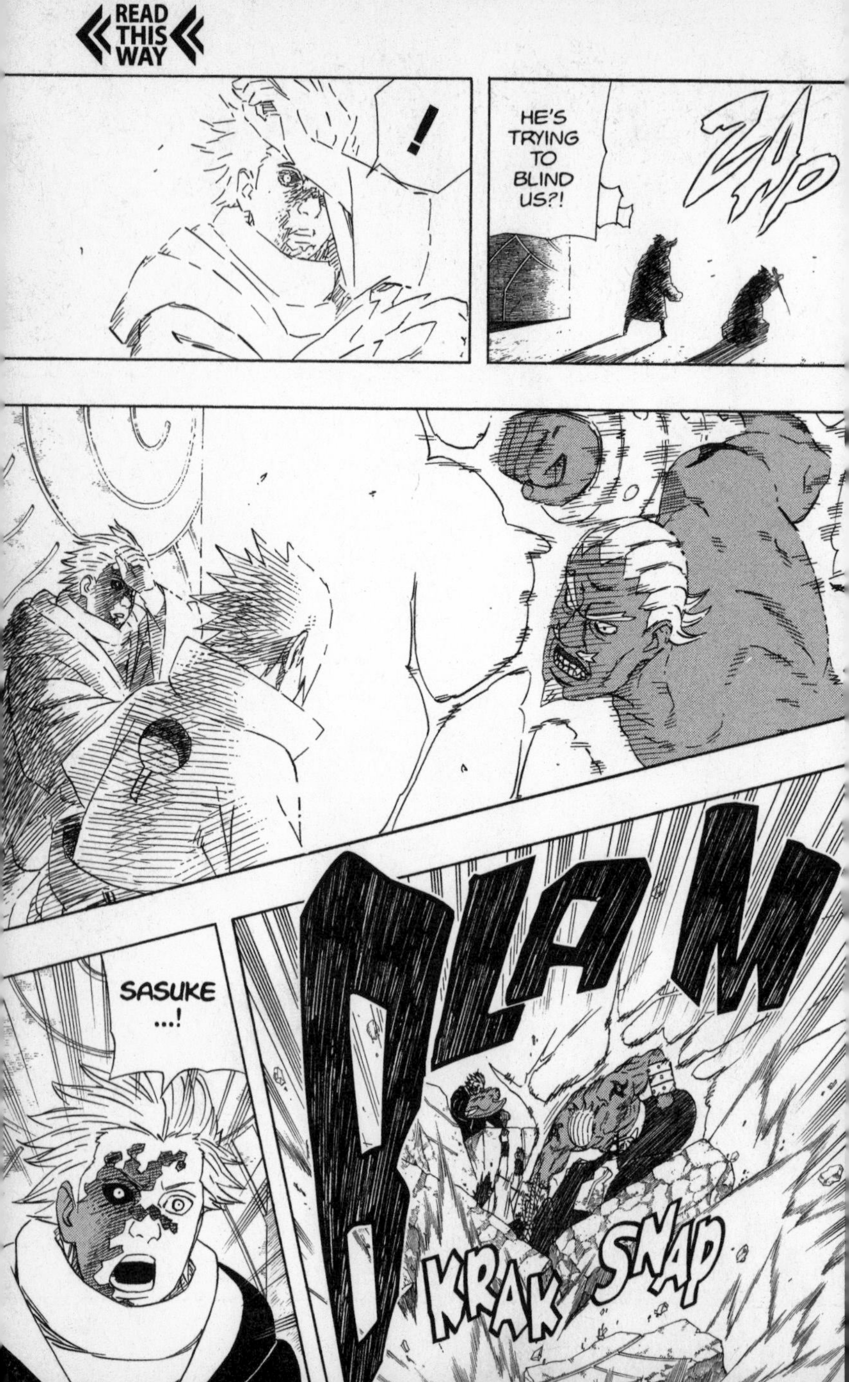
READ THIS WAY
HE'S TRYING TO BLIND US?!
ZAP
!
BLAM
KRAK SNAP
SASUKE ...!

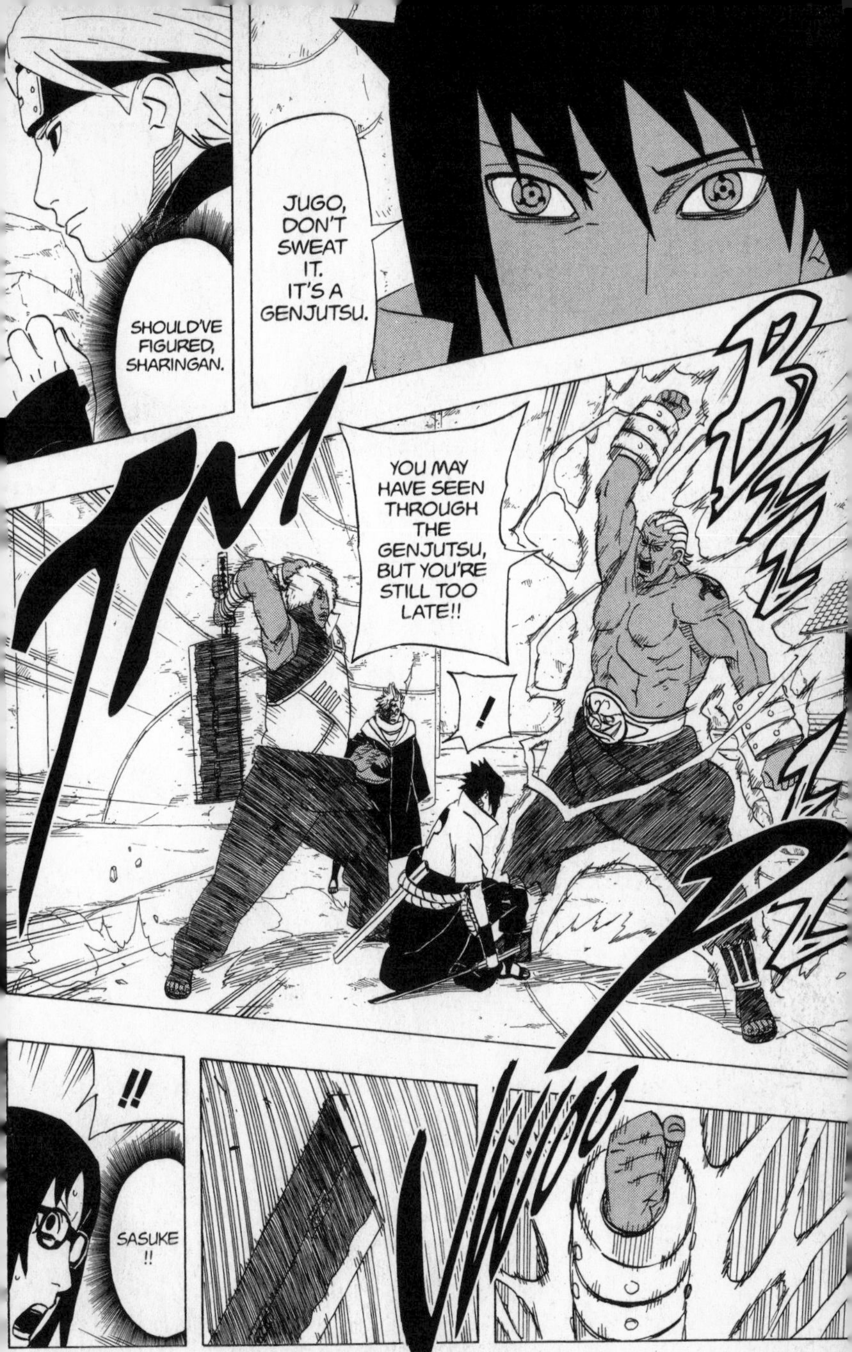
JUGO, DON'T SWEAT IT. IT'S A GENJUTSU.
SHOULD'VE FIGURED, SHARINGAN.
YOU MAY HAVE SEEN THROUGH THE GENJUTSU, BUT YOU'RE STILL TOO LATE!!
!
!!
SASUKE !!

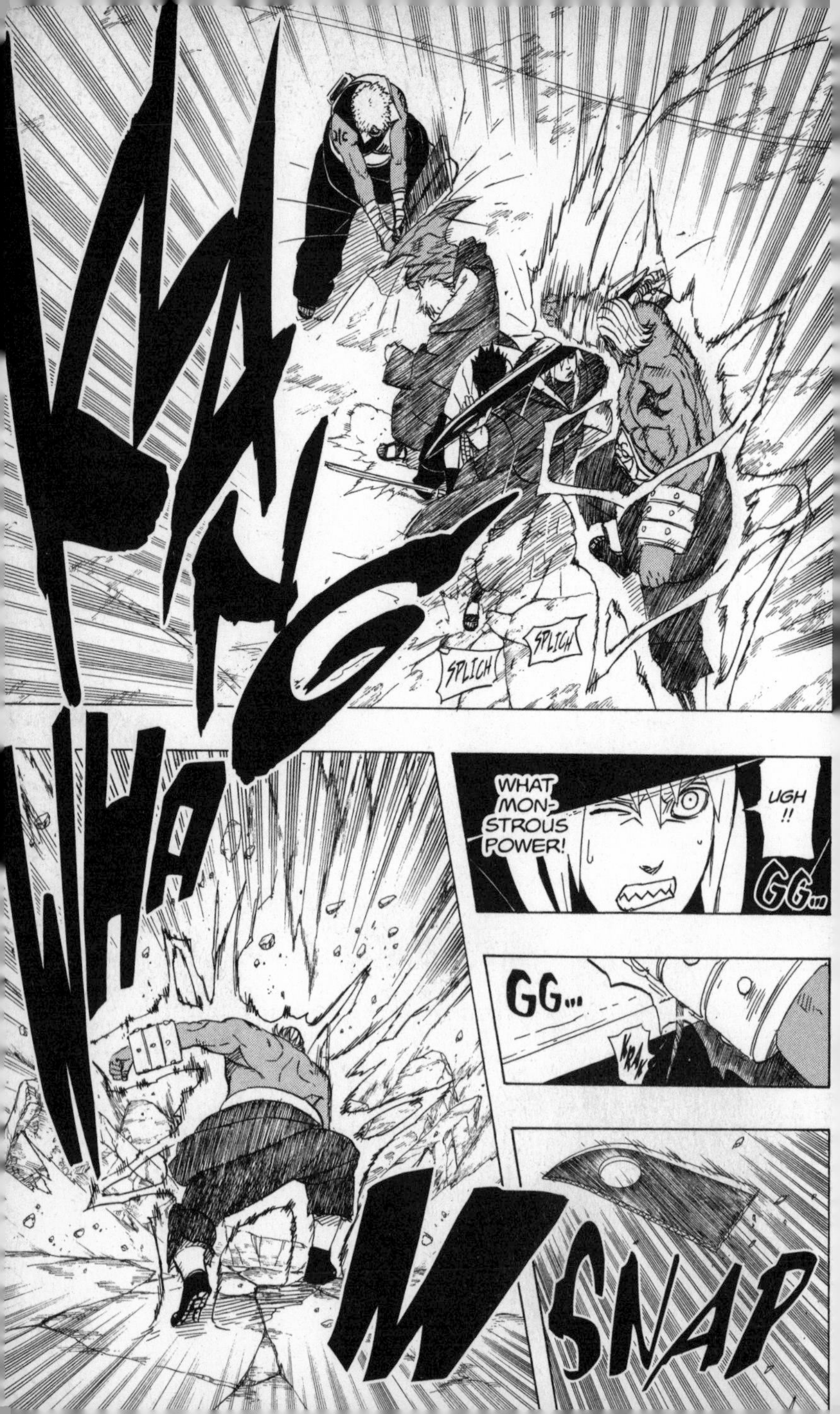
SPLICH
SPLICH
UGH !!
WHAT MON-STROUS POWER!
GG...
GG...
KRAK
SNAP
WHAM

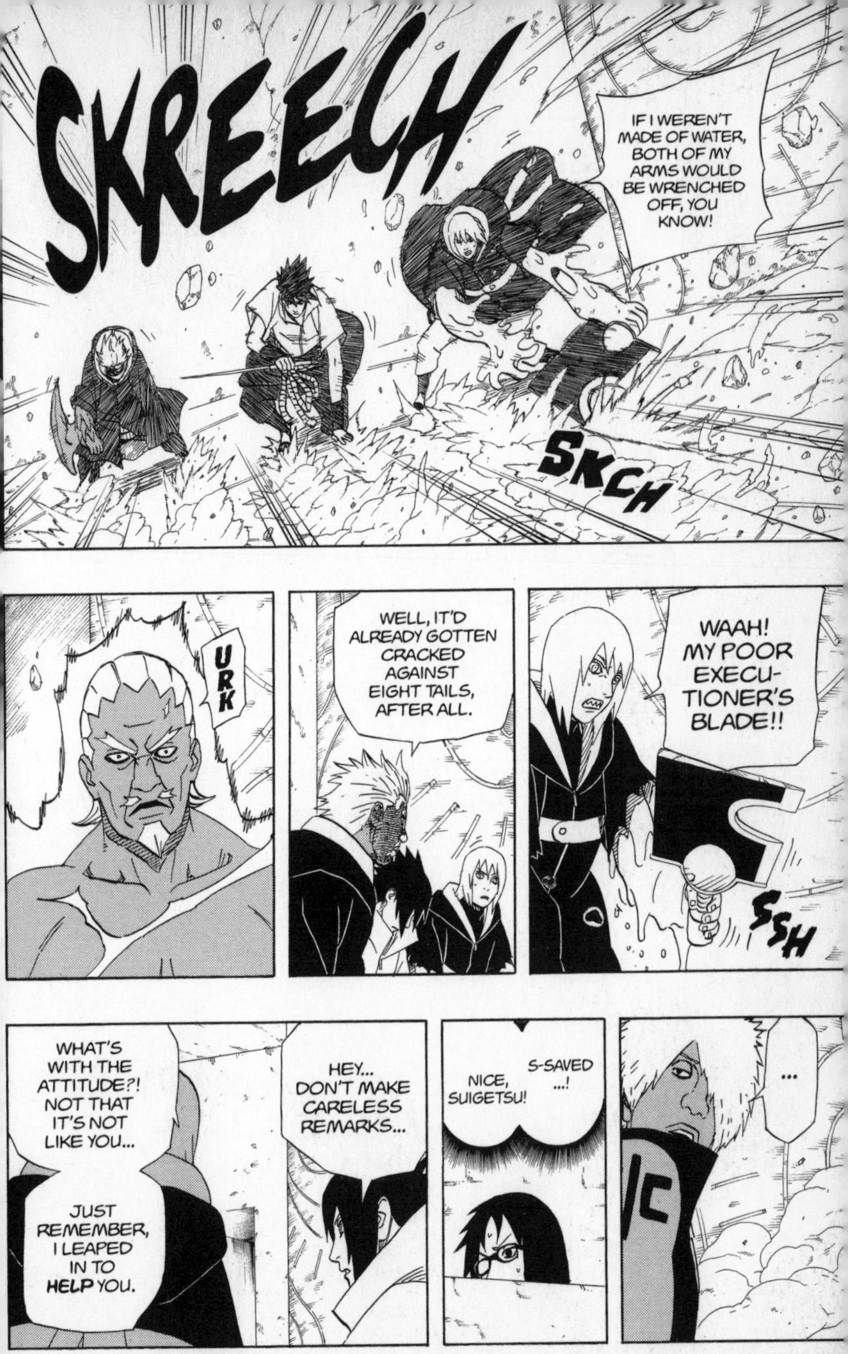
SKREECH
IF I WEREN'T MADE OF WATER, BOTH OF MY ARMS WOULD BE WRENCHED OFF, YOU KNOW!
SKCH
WAAH! MY POOR EXECU-TIONER'S BLADE!!
SSH
WELL, IT'D ALREADY GOTTEN CRACKED AGAINST EIGHT TAILS, AFTER ALL.
URK
...
S-SAVED ...!
NICE, SUIGETSU!
HEY... DON'T MAKE CARELESS REMARKS...
WHAT'S WITH THE ATTITUDE?! NOT THAT IT'S NOT LIKE YOU...
JUST REMEMBER, I LEAPED IN TO HELP YOU.

READ THIS WAY

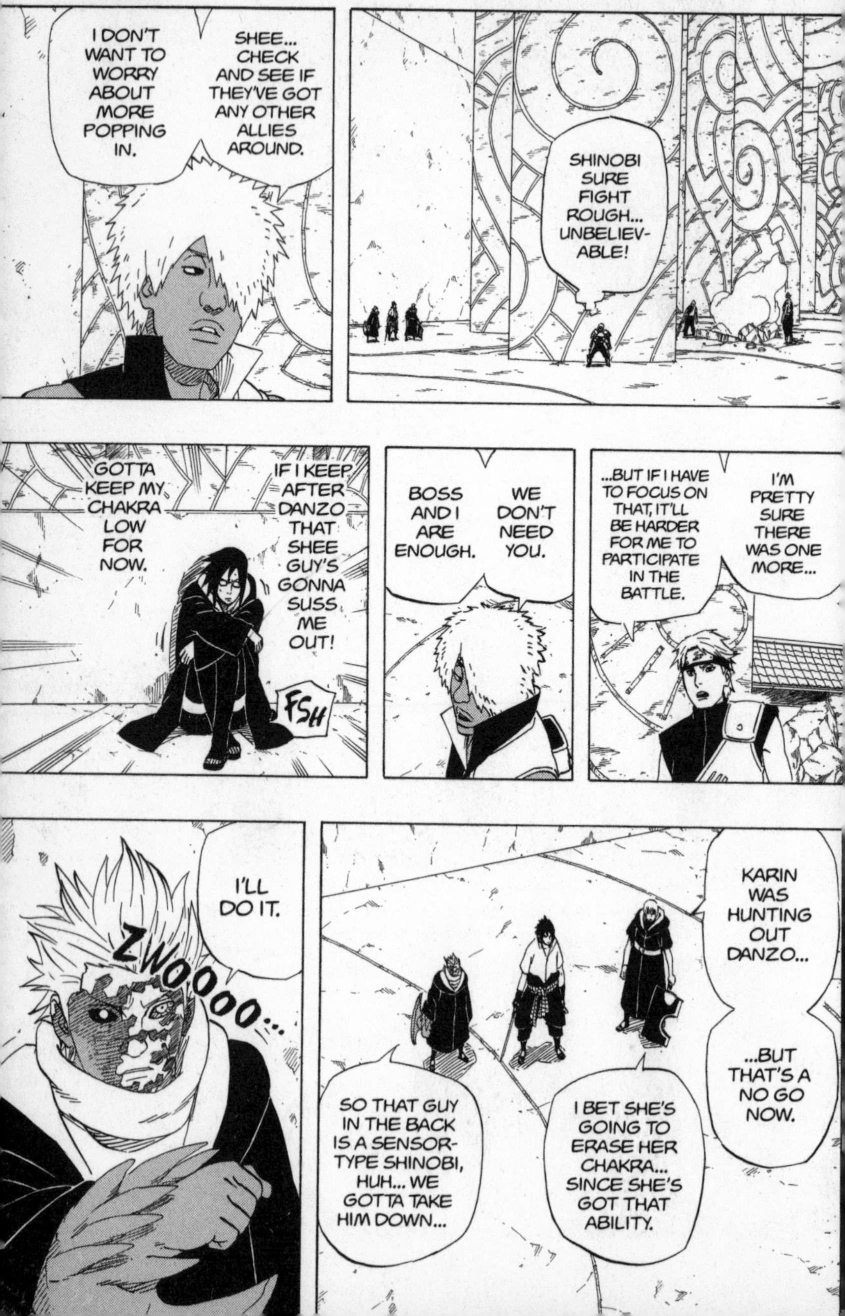
SHINOBI SURE FIGHT ROUGH... UNBELIEV-ABLE!
SHEE... CHECK AND SEE IF THEY'VE GOT ANY OTHER ALLIES AROUND.
I DON'T WANT TO WORRY ABOUT MORE POPPING IN.
I'M PRETTY SURE THERE WAS ONE MORE...
...BUT IF I HAVE TO FOCUS ON THAT, IT'LL BE HARDER FOR ME TO PARTICIPATE IN THE BATTLE.
WE DON'T NEED YOU.
BOSS AND I ARE ENOUGH.
IF I KEEP AFTER DANZO THAT SHEE GUY'S GONNA SUSS ME OUT!
GOTTA KEEP MY CHAKRA LOW FOR NOW.
FSH
KARIN WAS HUNTING OUT DANZO...
...BUT THAT'S A NO GO NOW.
I BET SHE'S GOING TO ERASE HER CHAKRA... SINCE SHE'S GOT THAT ABILITY.
SO THAT GUY IN THE BACK IS A SENSOR-TYPE SHINOBI, HUH... WE GOTTA TAKE HIM DOWN...
I'LL DO IT.
ZWOOOO...

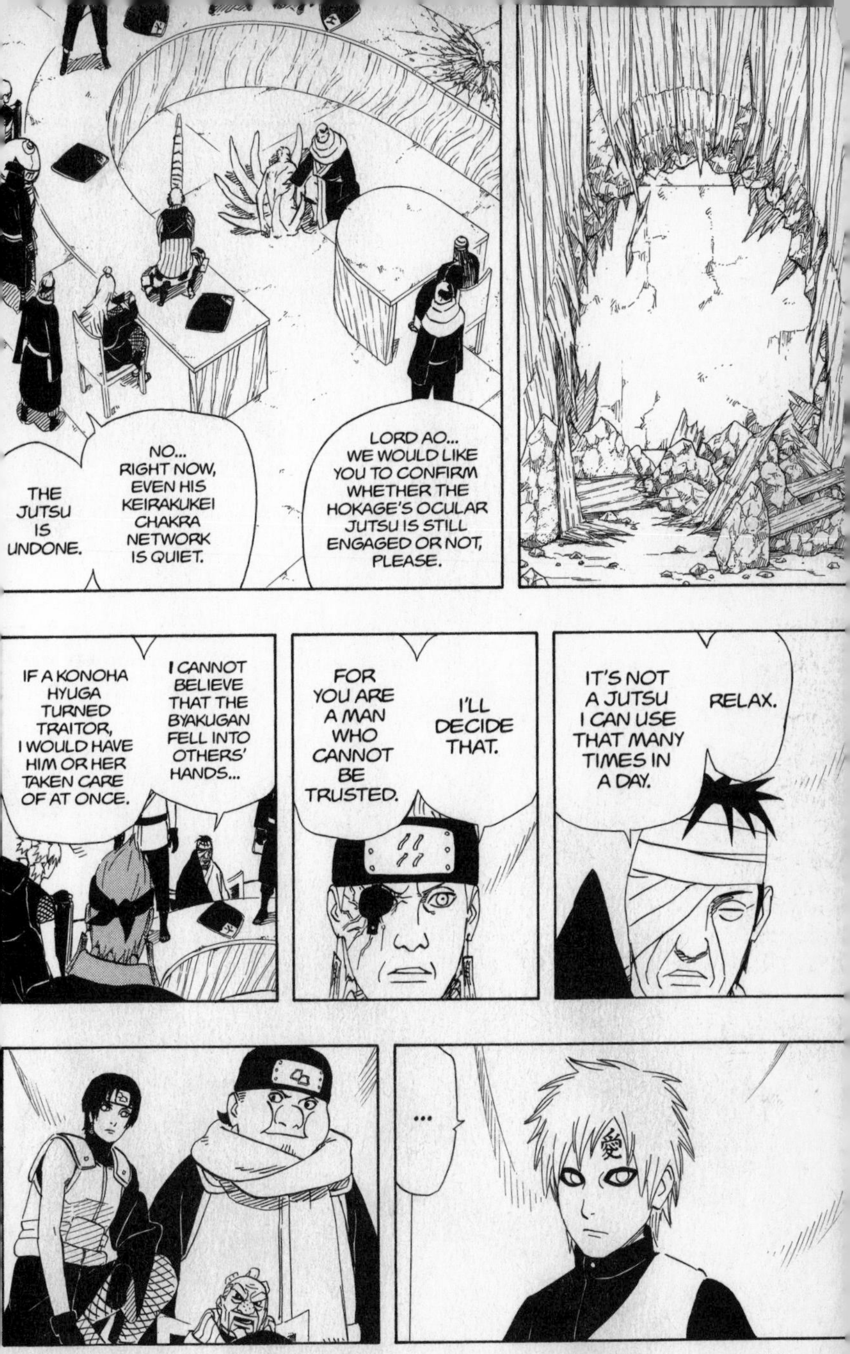
LORD AO... WE WOULD LIKE YOU TO CONFIRM WHETHER THE HOKAGE'S OCULAR JUTSU IS STILL ENGAGED OR NOT, PLEASE.
NO... RIGHT NOW, EVEN HIS KEIRAKUKEI CHAKRA NETWORK IS QUIET.
THE JUTSU IS UNDONE.
RELAX.
IT'S NOT A JUTSU I CAN USE THAT MANY TIMES IN A DAY.
I'LL DECIDE THAT.
FOR YOU ARE A MAN WHO CANNOT BE TRUSTED.
I CANNOT BELIEVE THAT THE BYAKUGAN FELL INTO OTHERS' HANDS...
IF A KONOHA HYUGA TURNED TRAITOR, I WOULD HAVE HIM OR HER TAKEN CARE OF AT ONCE.
...

READ THIS WAY

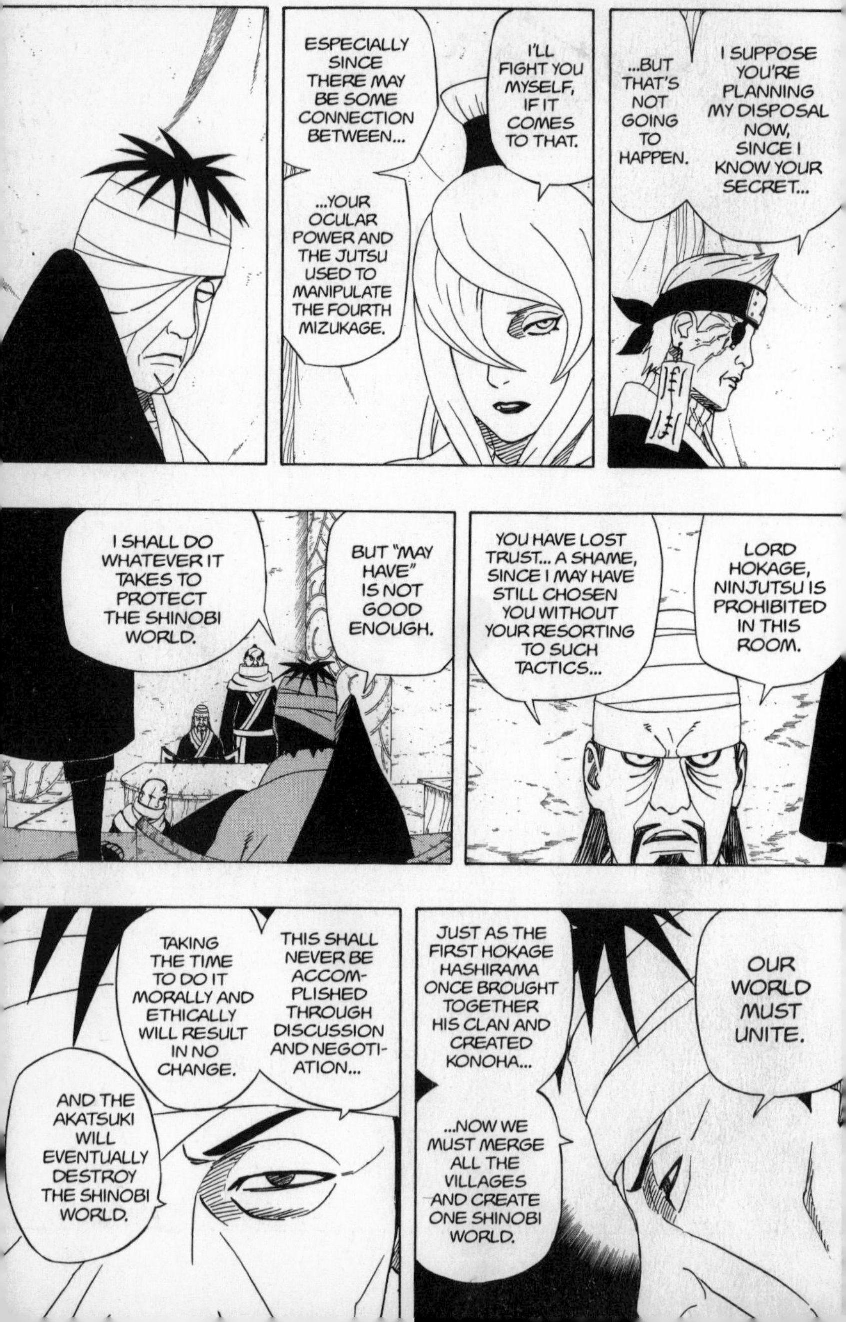
I SUPPOSE YOU'RE PLANNING MY DISPOSAL NOW, SINCE I KNOW YOUR SECRET...
...BUT THAT'S NOT GOING TO HAPPEN.
I'LL FIGHT YOU MYSELF, IF IT COMES TO THAT.
ESPECIALLY SINCE THERE MAY BE SOME CONNECTION BETWEEN...
...YOUR OCULAR POWER AND THE JUTSU USED TO MANIPULATE THE FOURTH MIZUKAGE.
LORD HOKAGE, NINJUTSU IS PROHIBITED IN THIS ROOM.
YOU HAVE LOST TRUST... A SHAME, SINCE I MAY HAVE STILL CHOSEN YOU WITHOUT YOUR RESORTING TO SUCH TACTICS...
BUT "MAY HAVE" IS NOT GOOD ENOUGH.
I SHALL DO WHATEVER IT TAKES TO PROTECT THE SHINOBI WORLD.
OUR WORLD MUST UNITE.
JUST AS THE FIRST HOKAGE HASHIRAMA ONCE BROUGHT TOGETHER HIS CLAN AND CREATED KONOHA...
...NOW WE MUST MERGE ALL THE VILLAGES AND CREATE ONE SHINOBI WORLD.
THIS SHALL NEVER BE ACCOM-PLISHED THROUGH DISCUSSION AND NEGOTI-ATION...
TAKING THE TIME TO DO IT MORALLY AND ETHICALLY WILL RESULT IN NO CHANGE.
AND THE AKATSUKI WILL EVENTUALLY DESTROY THE SHINOBI WORLD.

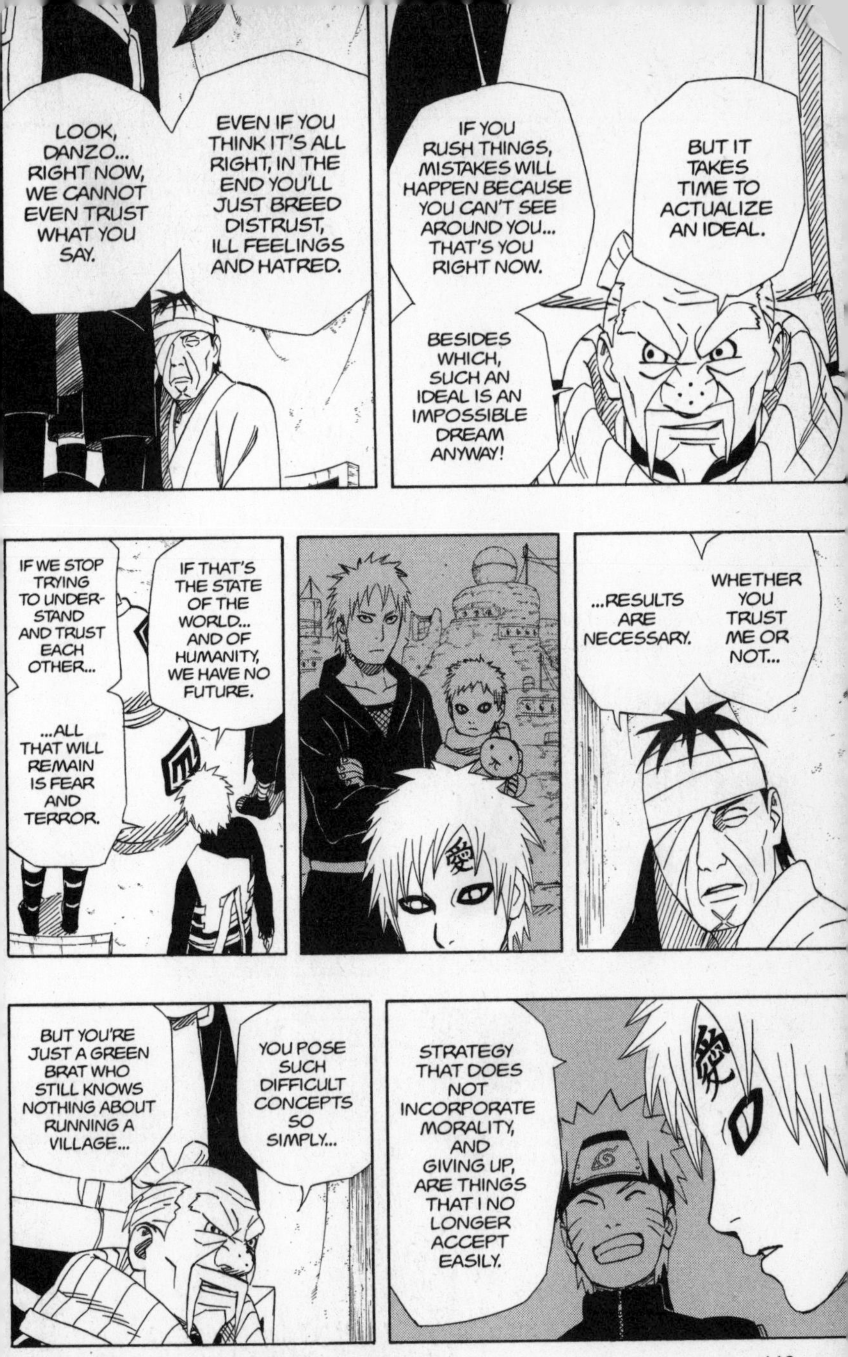
BUT IT TAKES TIME TO ACTUALIZE AN IDEAL.
IF YOU RUSH THINGS, MISTAKES WILL HAPPEN BECAUSE YOU CAN'T SEE AROUND YOU... THAT'S YOU RIGHT NOW.
BESIDES WHICH, SUCH AN IDEAL IS AN IMPOSSIBLE DREAM ANYWAY!
EVEN IF YOU THINK IT'S ALL RIGHT, IN THE END YOU'LL JUST BREED DISTRUST, ILL FEELINGS AND HATRED.
LOOK, DANZO... RIGHT NOW, WE CANNOT EVEN TRUST WHAT YOU SAY.
WHETHER YOU TRUST ME OR NOT...
...RESULTS ARE NECESSARY.
IF THAT'S THE STATE OF THE WORLD... AND OF HUMANITY, WE HAVE NO FUTURE.
IF WE STOP TRYING TO UNDER-STAND AND TRUST EACH OTHER...
...ALL THAT WILL REMAIN IS FEAR AND TERROR.
STRATEGY THAT DOES NOT INCORPORATE MORALITY, AND GIVING UP, ARE THINGS THAT I NO LONGER ACCEPT EASILY.
YOU POSE SUCH DIFFICULT CONCEPTS SO SIMPLY...
BUT YOU'RE JUST A GREEN BRAT WHO STILL KNOWS NOTHING ABOUT RUNNING A VILLAGE...

READ THIS WAY

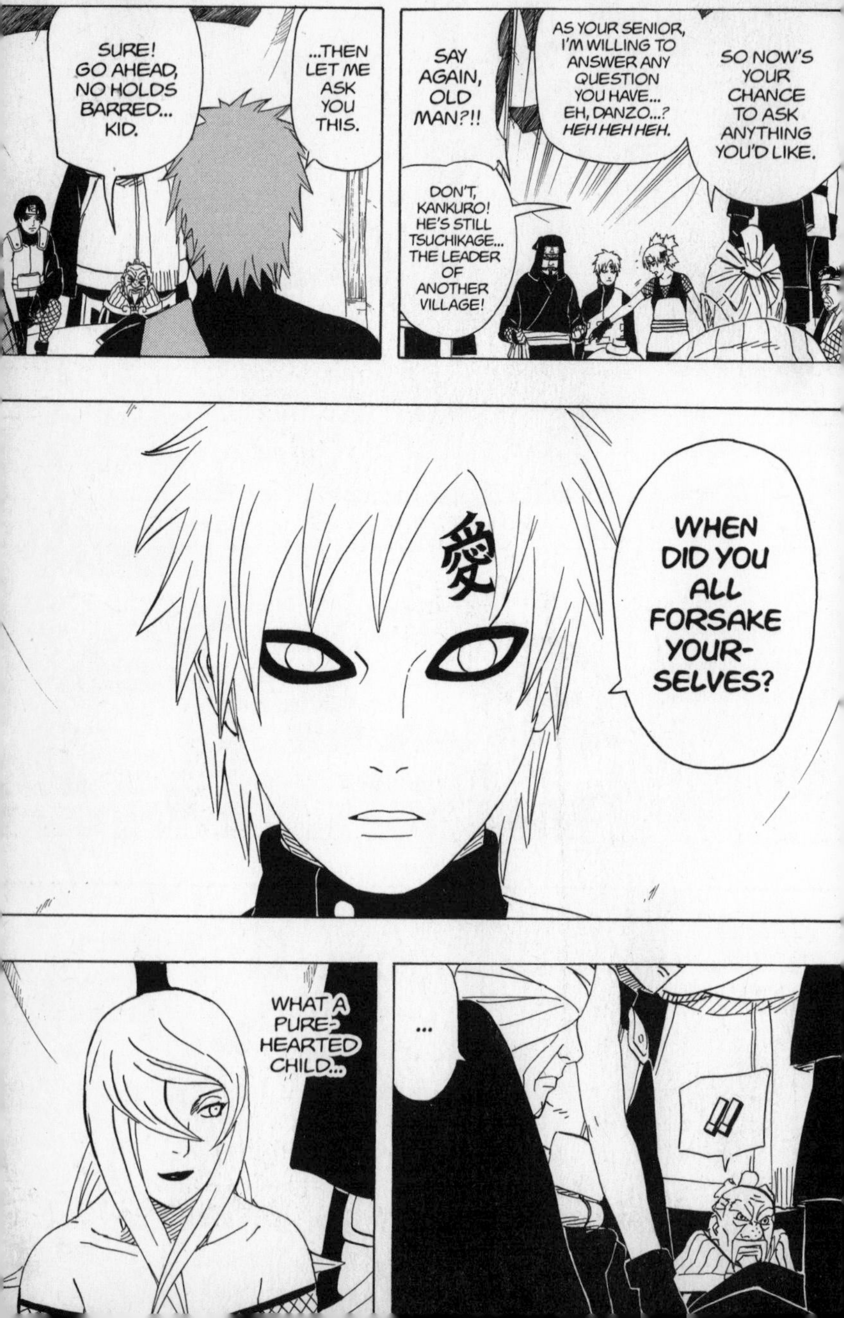
SO NOW'S YOUR CHANCE TO ASK ANYTHING YOU'D LIKE.
AS YOUR SENIOR, I'M WILLING TO ANSWER ANY QUESTION YOU HAVE... EH, DANZO...? HEH HEH HEH.
SAY AGAIN, OLD MAN?!!
DON'T, KANKURO! HE'S STILL TSUCHIKAGE... THE LEADER OF ANOTHER VILLAGE!
...THEN LET ME ASK YOU THIS.
SURE! GO AHEAD, NO HOLDS BARRED... KID.
WHEN DID YOU ALL FORSAKE YOUR-SELVES?
...
!!
WHAT A PURE-HEARTED CHILD...

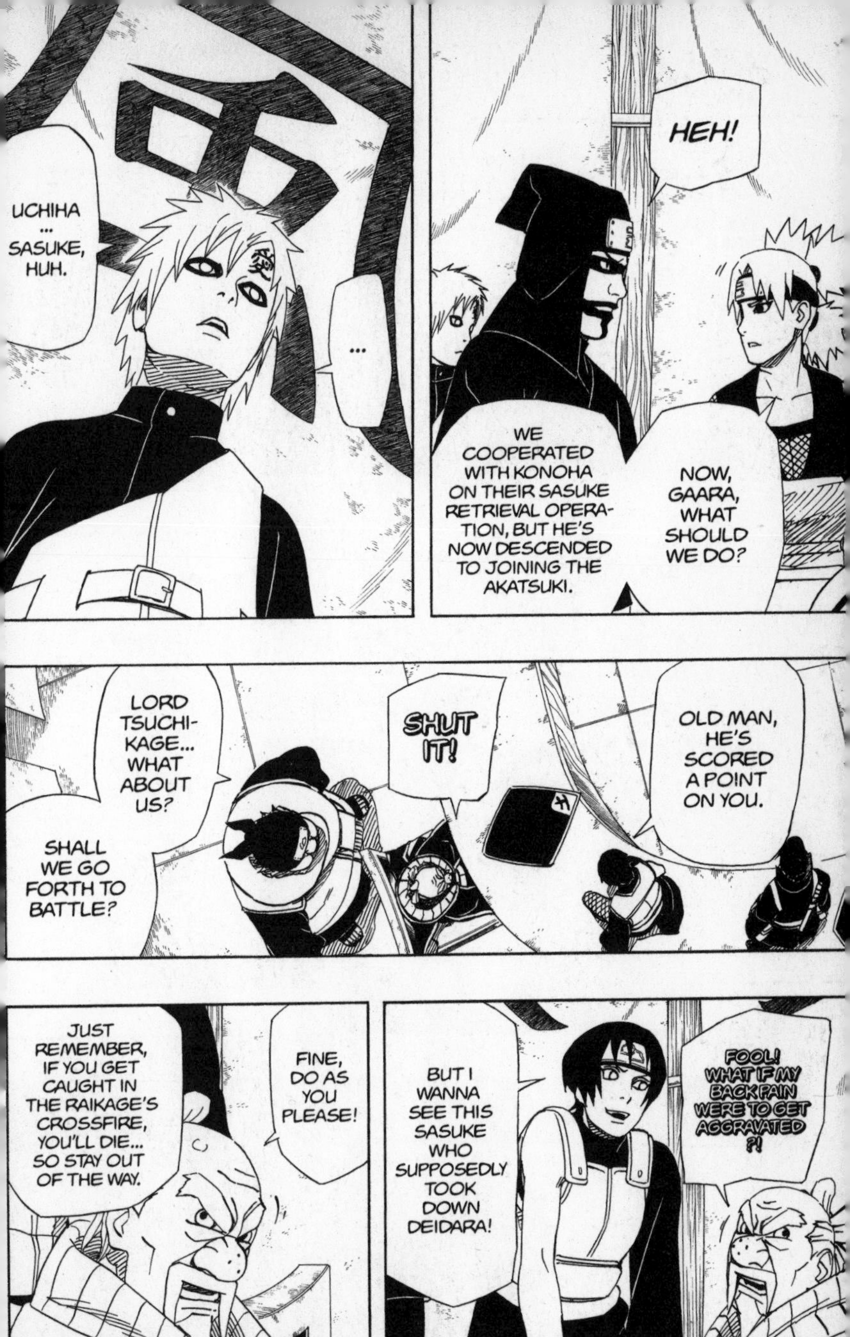
HEH!
WE COOPERATED WITH KONOHA ON THEIR SASUKE RETRIEVAL OPERATION, BUT HE'S NOW DESCENDED TO JOINING THE AKATSUKI.
NOW, GAARA, WHAT SHOULD WE DO?
...
UCHIHA ... SASUKE, HUH.
OLD MAN, HE'S SCORED A POINT ON YOU.
SHUT IT!
LORD TSUCHIKAGE... WHAT ABOUT US?
SHALL WE GO FORTH TO BATTLE?
FOOL! WHAT IF MY BACK PAIN WERE TO GET AGGRAVATED ?!
BUT I WANNA SEE THIS SASUKE WHO SUPPOSEDLY TOOK DOWN DEIDARA!
FINE, DO AS YOU PLEASE!
JUST REMEMBER, IF YOU GET CAUGHT IN THE RAIKAGE'S CROSSFIRE, YOU'LL DIE... SO STAY OUT OF THE WAY.

READ THIS WAY

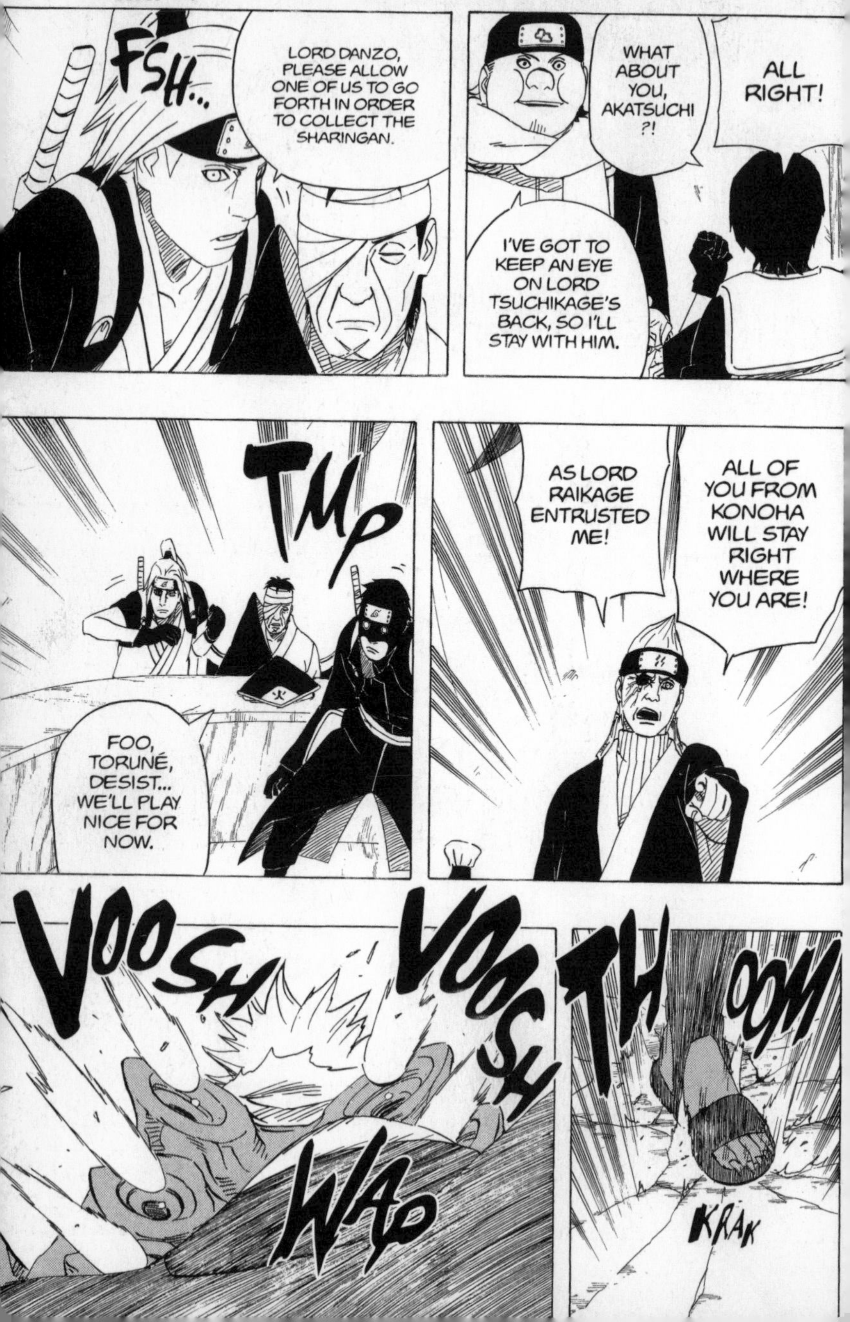

ALL RIGHT!
WHAT ABOUT YOU, AKATSUCHI ?!
I'VE GOT TO KEEP AN EYE ON LORD TSUCHIKAGE'S BACK, SO I'LL STAY WITH HIM.
LORD DANZO, PLEASE ALLOW ONE OF US TO GO FORTH IN ORDER TO COLLECT THE SHARINGAN.
FSH...
ALL OF YOU FROM KONOHA WILL STAY RIGHT WHERE YOU ARE!
AS LORD RAIKAGE ENTRUSTED ME!
TMP
FOO, TORUNÉ, DESIST... WE'LL PLAY NICE FOR NOW.
THOOM
KRAK
VOOSH
VOOSH
WAP

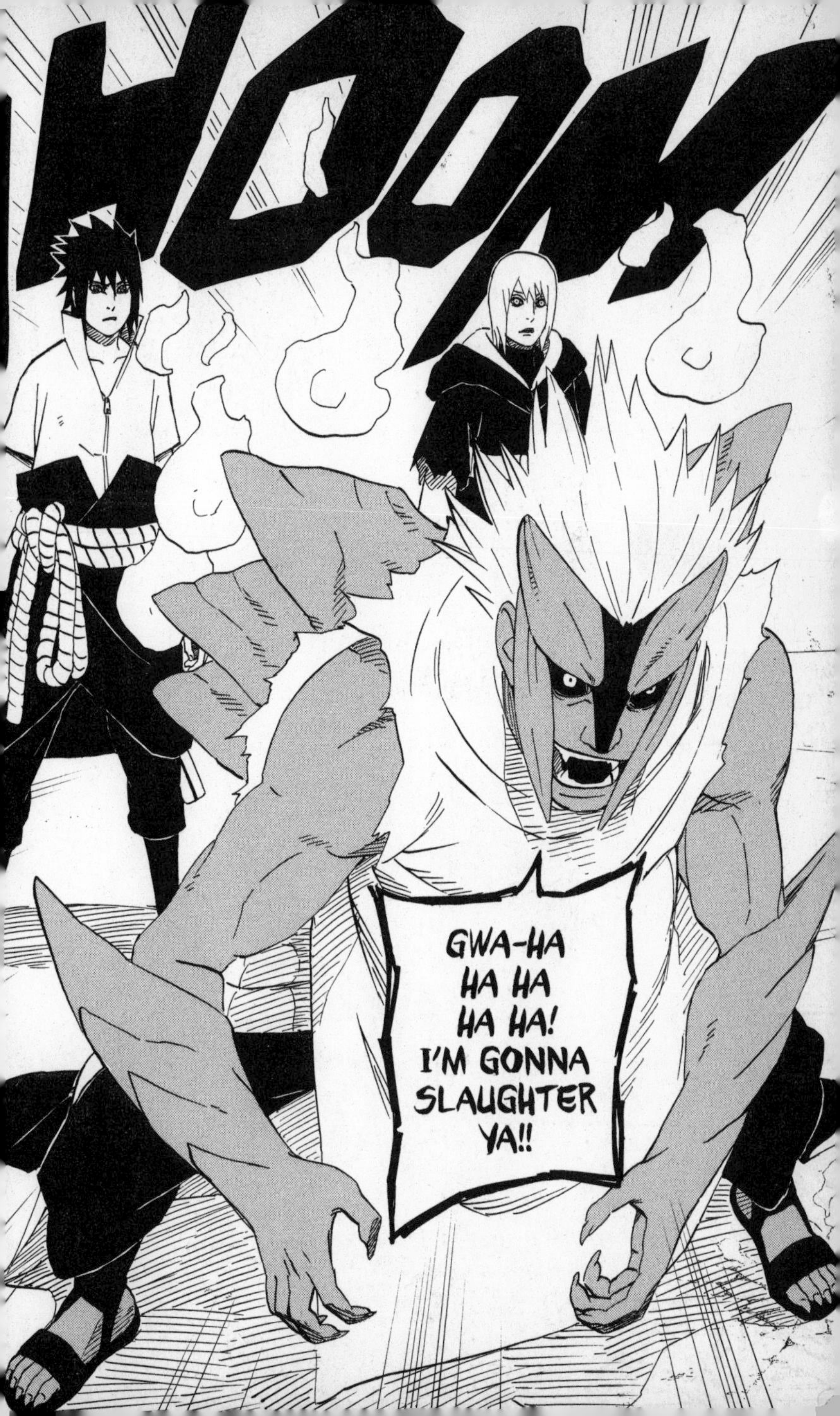

WOOM
GWA-HA HA HA HA HA! I'M GONNA SLAUGHTER YA!!

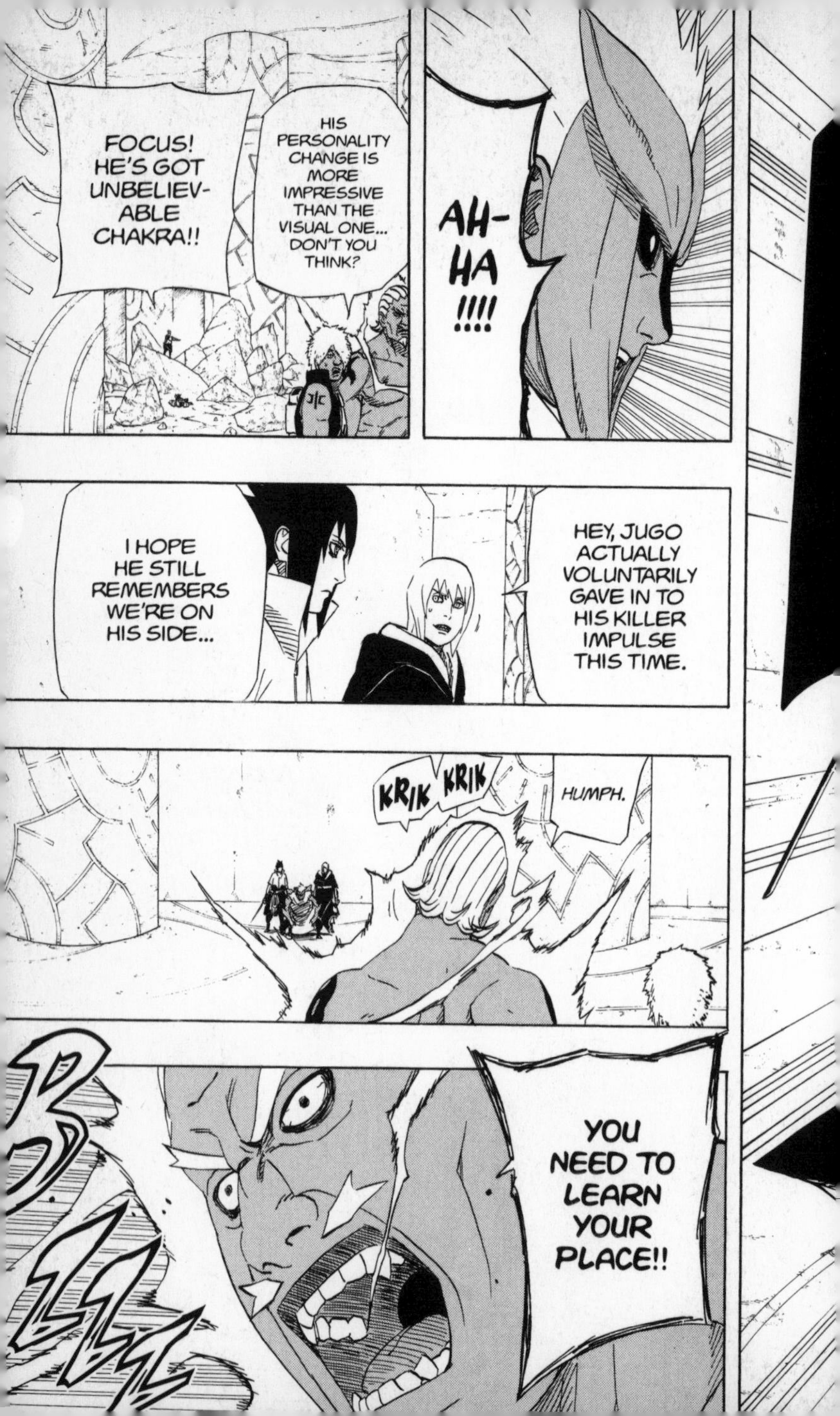
AH-HA!!!!
HIS PERSONALITY CHANGE IS MORE IMPRESSIVE THAN THE VISUAL ONE... DON'T YOU THINK?
FOCUS! HE'S GOT UNBELIEVABLE CHAKRA!!
HEY, JUGO ACTUALLY VOLUNTARILY GAVE IN TO HIS KILLER IMPULSE THIS TIME.
I HOPE HE STILL REMEMBERS WE'RE ON HIS SIDE...
HUMPH.
KRIK KRIK
YOU NEED TO LEARN YOUR PLACE!!

NARUTO

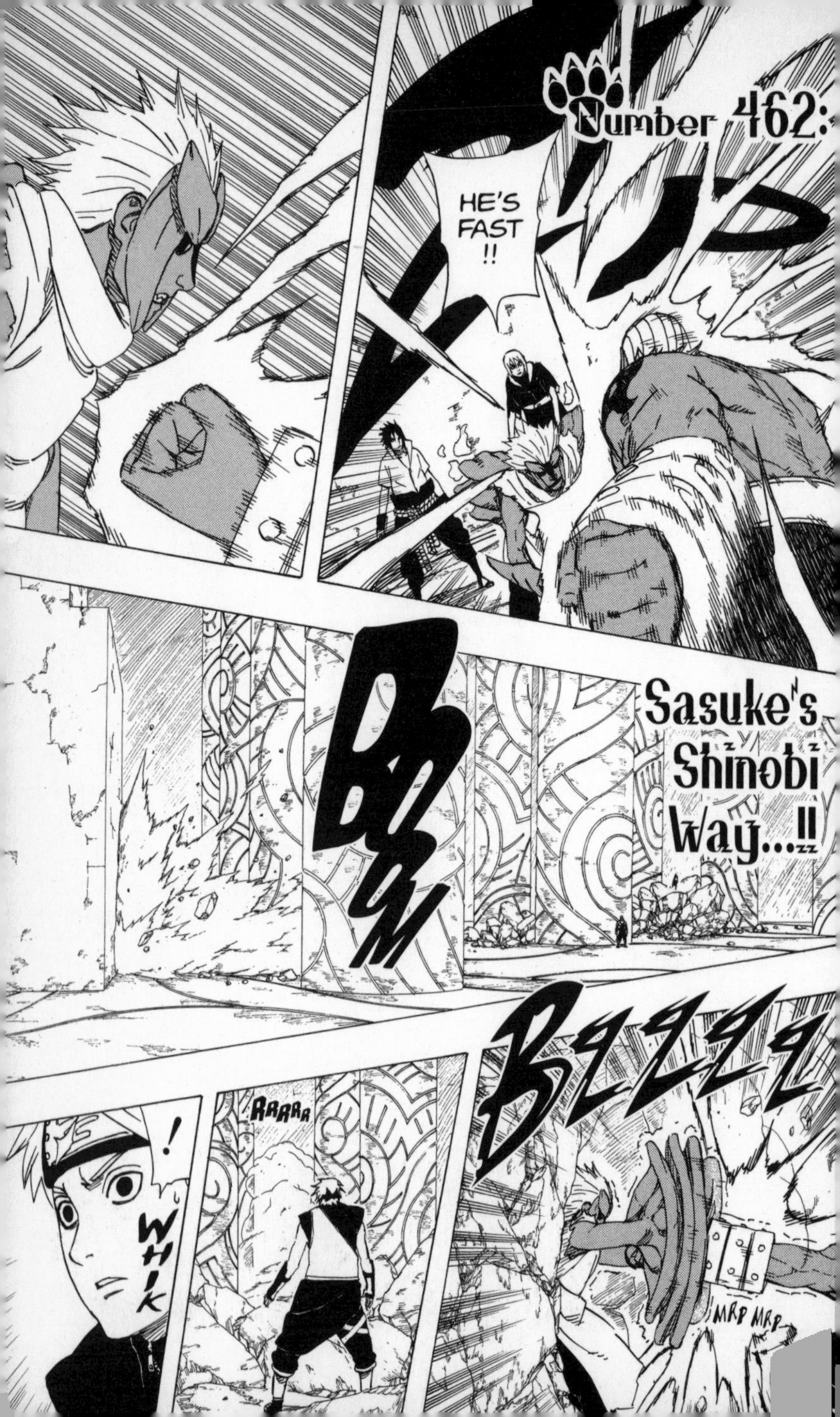
Number 462: Sasuke's Shinobi Way...!!
HE'S FAST !!
BOOM
BZZZZ
MRP MRP
RRRRR
!
WHIK

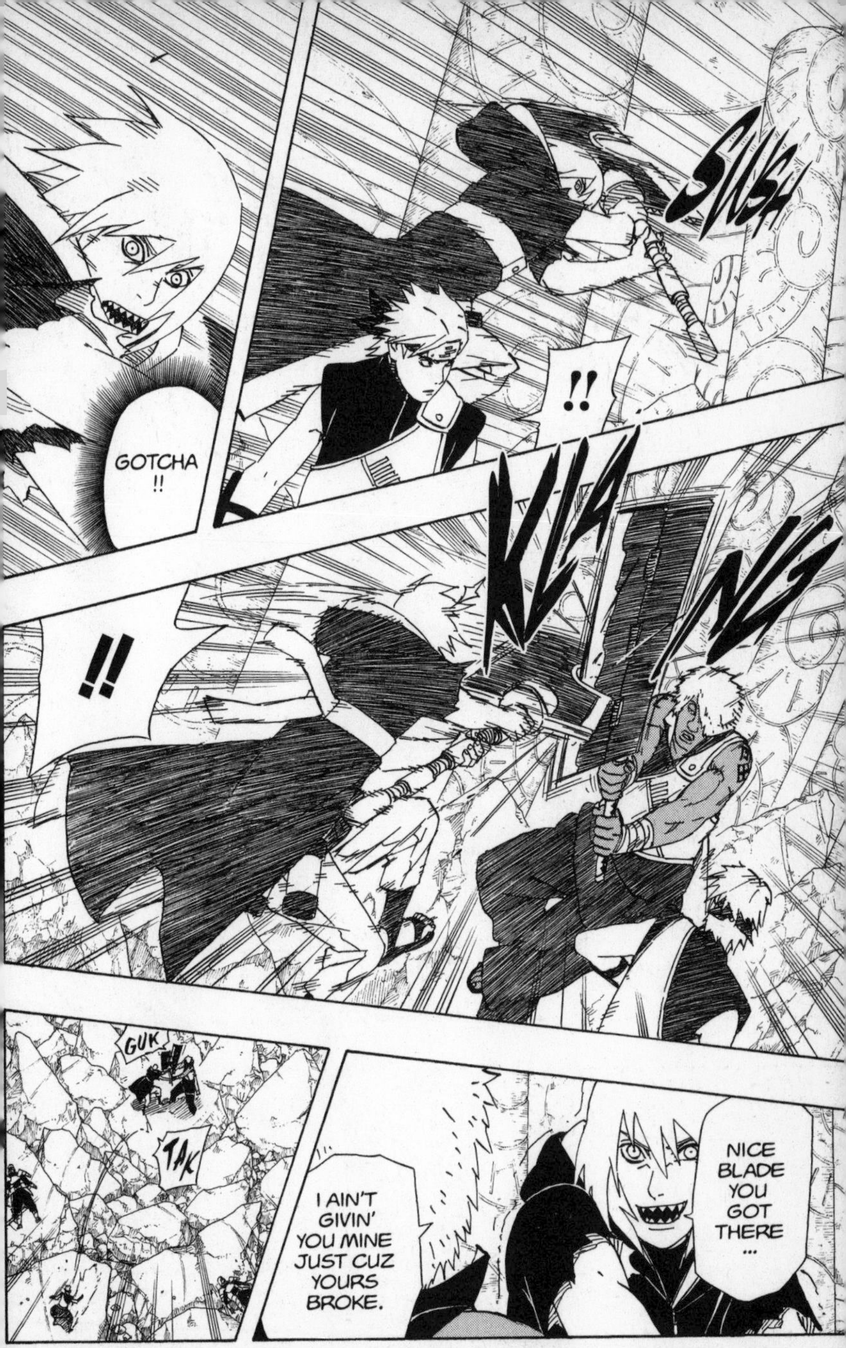
SWISH
!!
GOTCHA !!
KLANG
!!
NICE BLADE YOU GOT THERE ...
I AIN'T GIVIN' YOU MINE JUST CUZ YOURS BROKE.
GUK
TAK

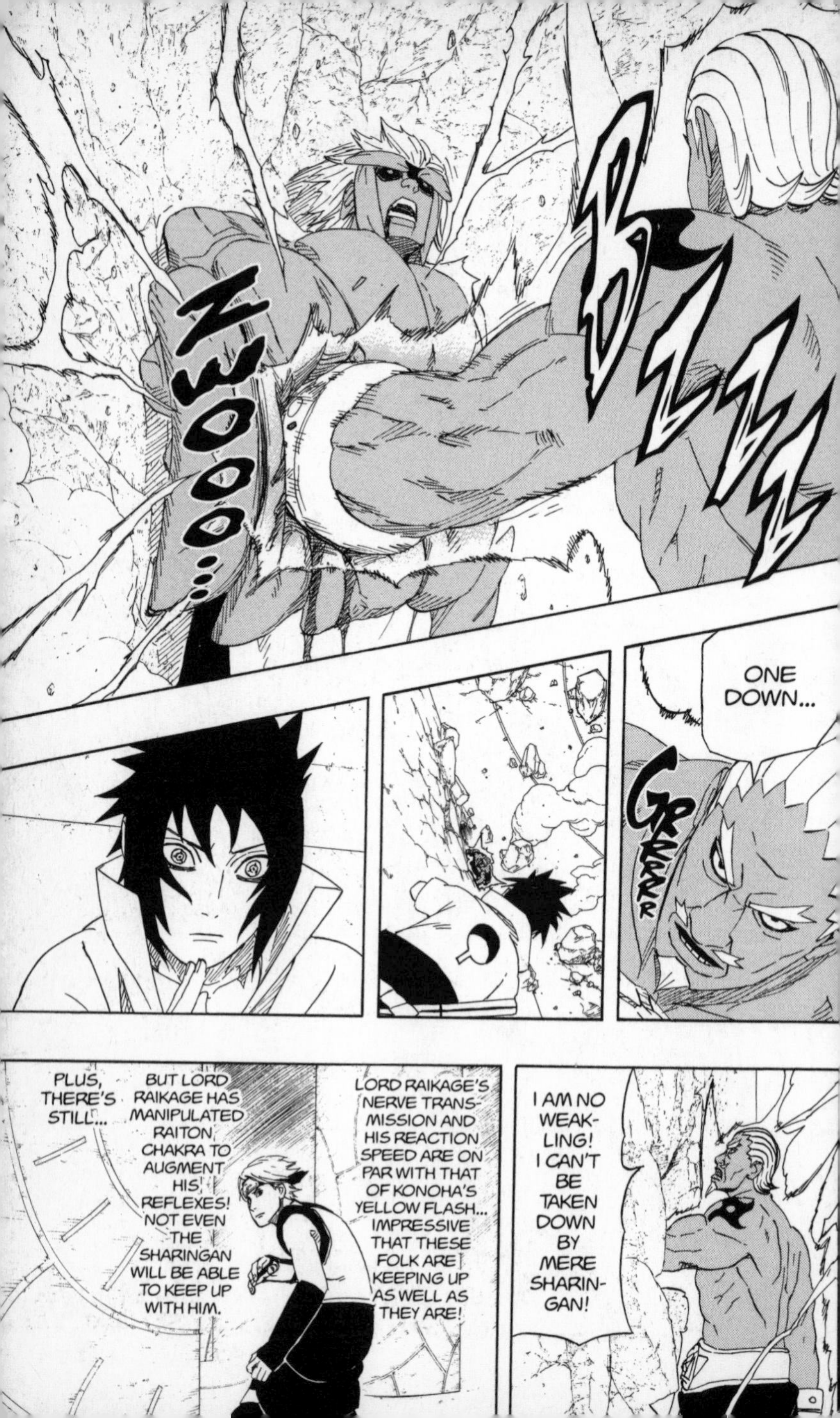
BZZZ
NWOOO...
ONE DOWN...
GRRRRR
I AM NO WEAKLING! I CAN'T BE TAKEN DOWN BY MERE SHARINGAN!
LORD RAIKAGE'S NERVE TRANSMISSION AND HIS REACTION SPEED ARE ON PAR WITH THAT OF KONOHA'S YELLOW FLASH... IMPRESSIVE THAT THESE FOLK ARE KEEPING UP AS WELL AS THEY ARE!
BUT LORD RAIKAGE HAS MANIPULATED RAITON CHAKRA TO AUGMENT HIS REFLEXES! NOT EVEN THE SHARINGAN WILL BE ABLE TO KEEP UP WITH HIM.
PLUS, THERE'S STILL...

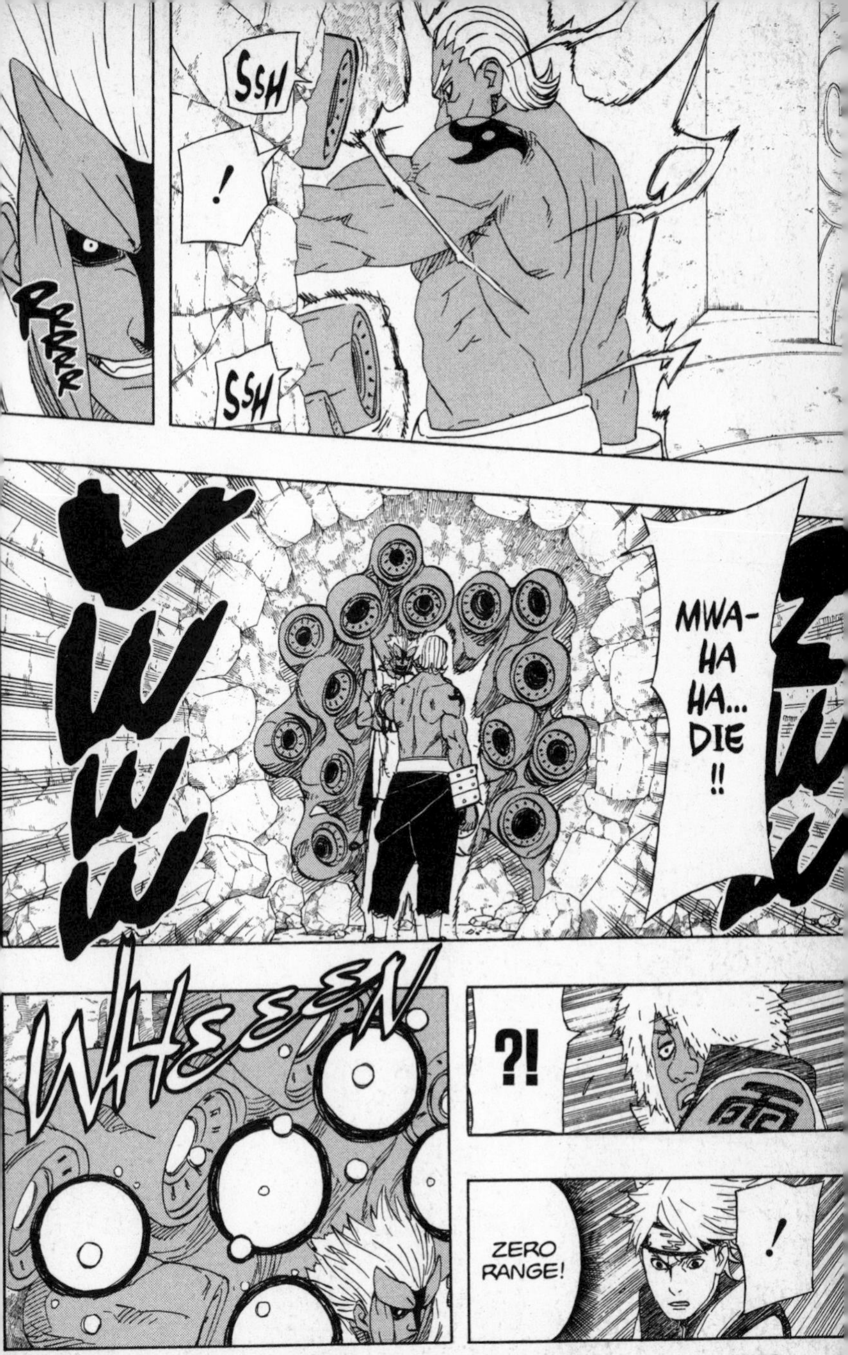

SSH
!
SSH
RRRRR
MWA-HA HA... DIE!!
?!
!
ZERO RANGE!
WHEEEN

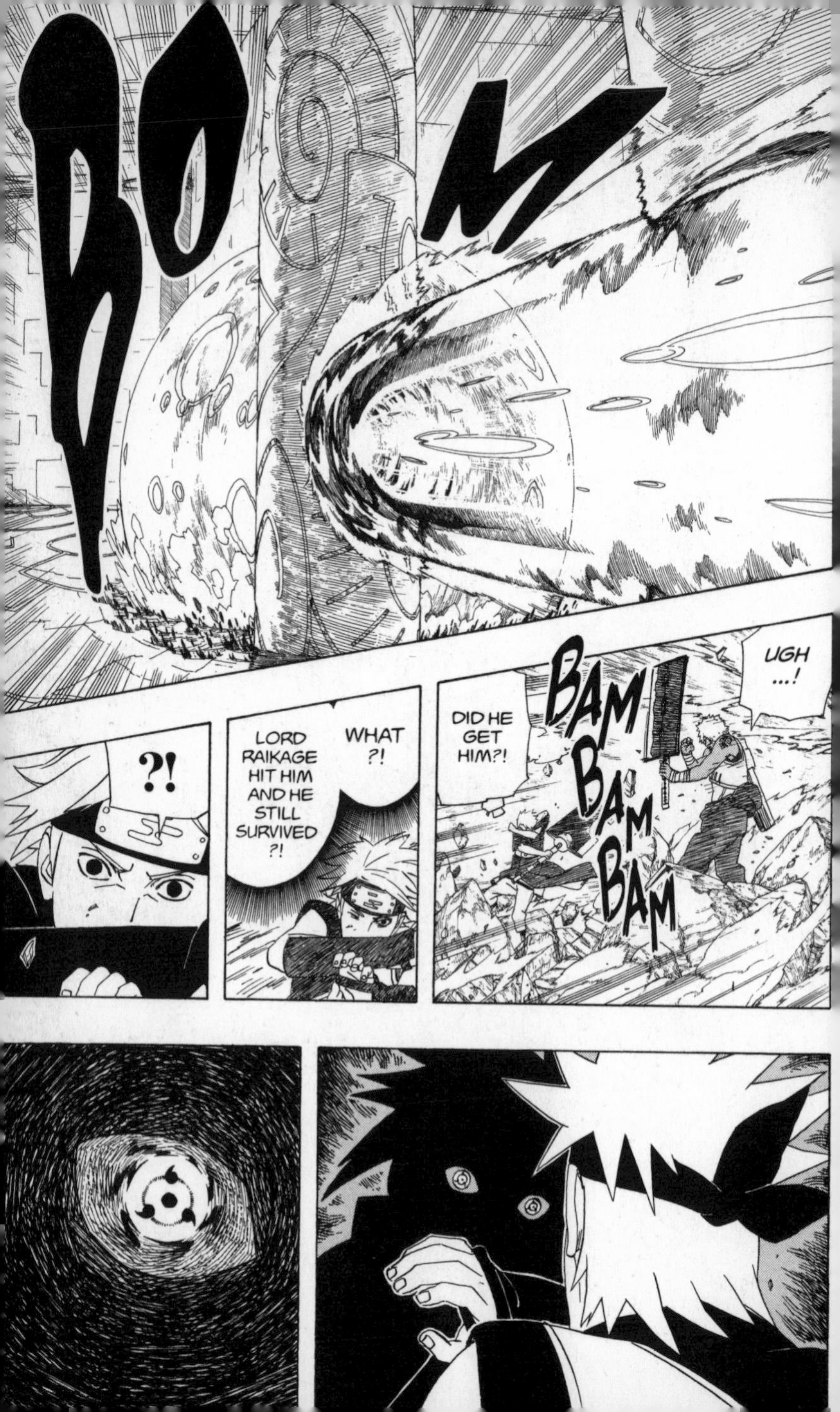
BOOM
UGH ...!
BAM BAM BAM
DID HE GET HIM?!
WHAT ?!
LORD RAIKAGE HIT HIM AND HE STILL SURVIVED ?!
?!

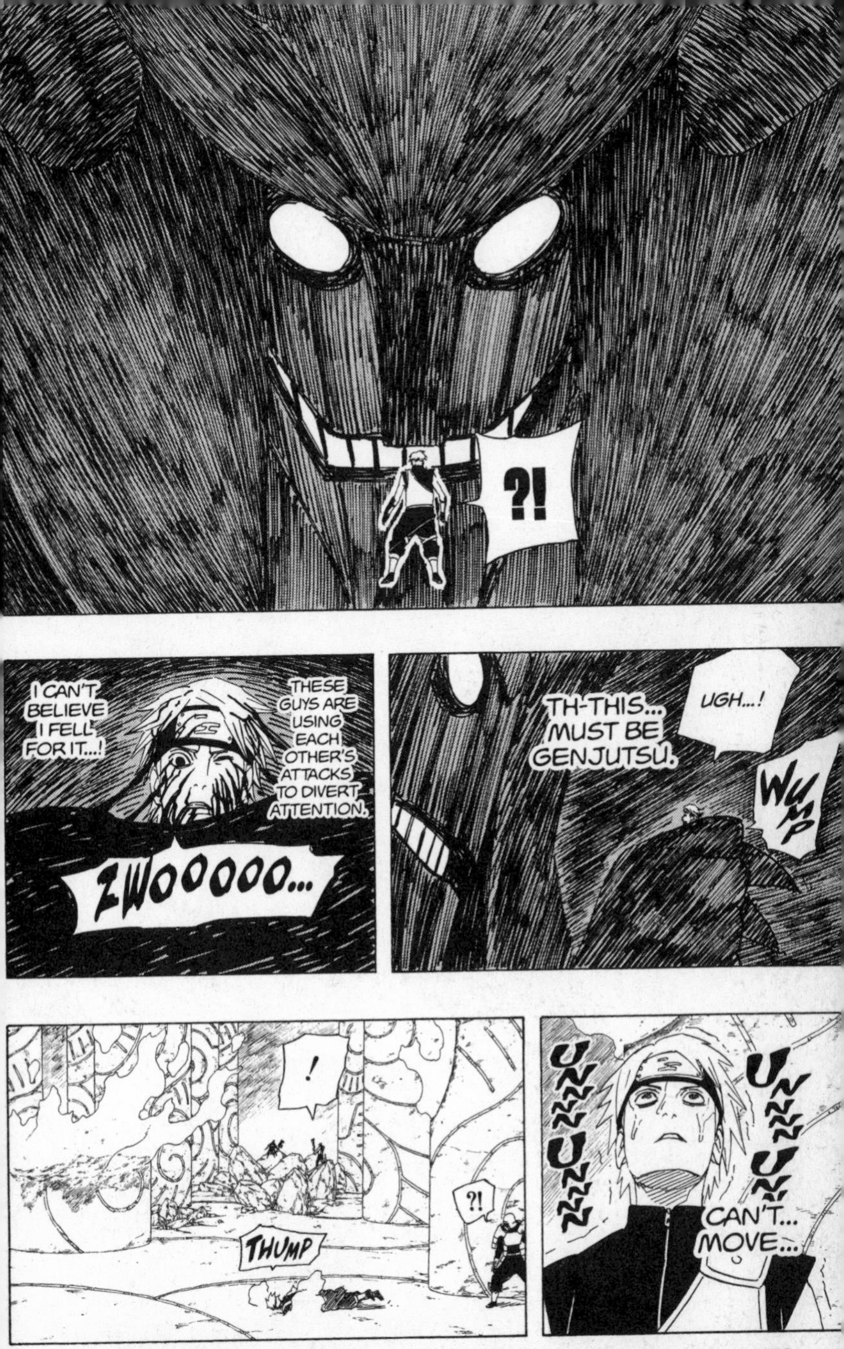
?!
UGH...!
TH-THIS... MUST BE GENJUTSU.
WUMP
THESE GUYS ARE USING EACH OTHER'S ATTACKS TO DIVERT ATTENTION.
I CAN'T BELIEVE I FELL FOR IT...!
ZWOOOOO...
UNNN UNN
UNNN UNNN
CAN'T... MOVE...
!
?!
THUMP

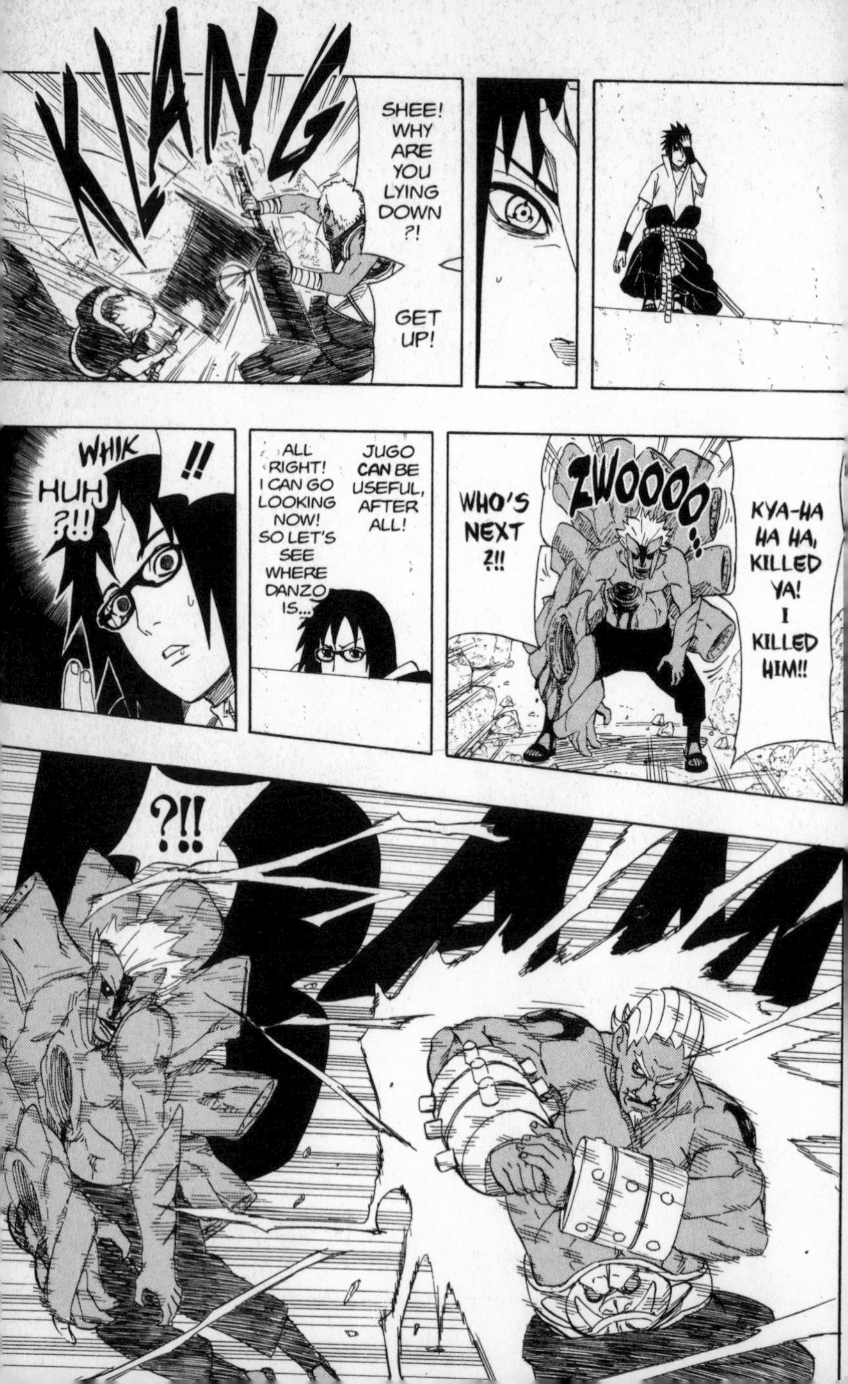
SHEE! WHY ARE YOU LYING DOWN ?!
KLANG
GET UP!
KYA-HA HA HA, KILLED YA! I KILLED HIM!!
ZWOOOO...
WHO'S NEXT ?!!
JUGO CAN BE USEFUL, AFTER ALL!
ALL RIGHT! I CAN GO LOOKING NOW! SO LET'S SEE WHERE DANZO IS...
!!
WHIK
HUH ?!!
?!!

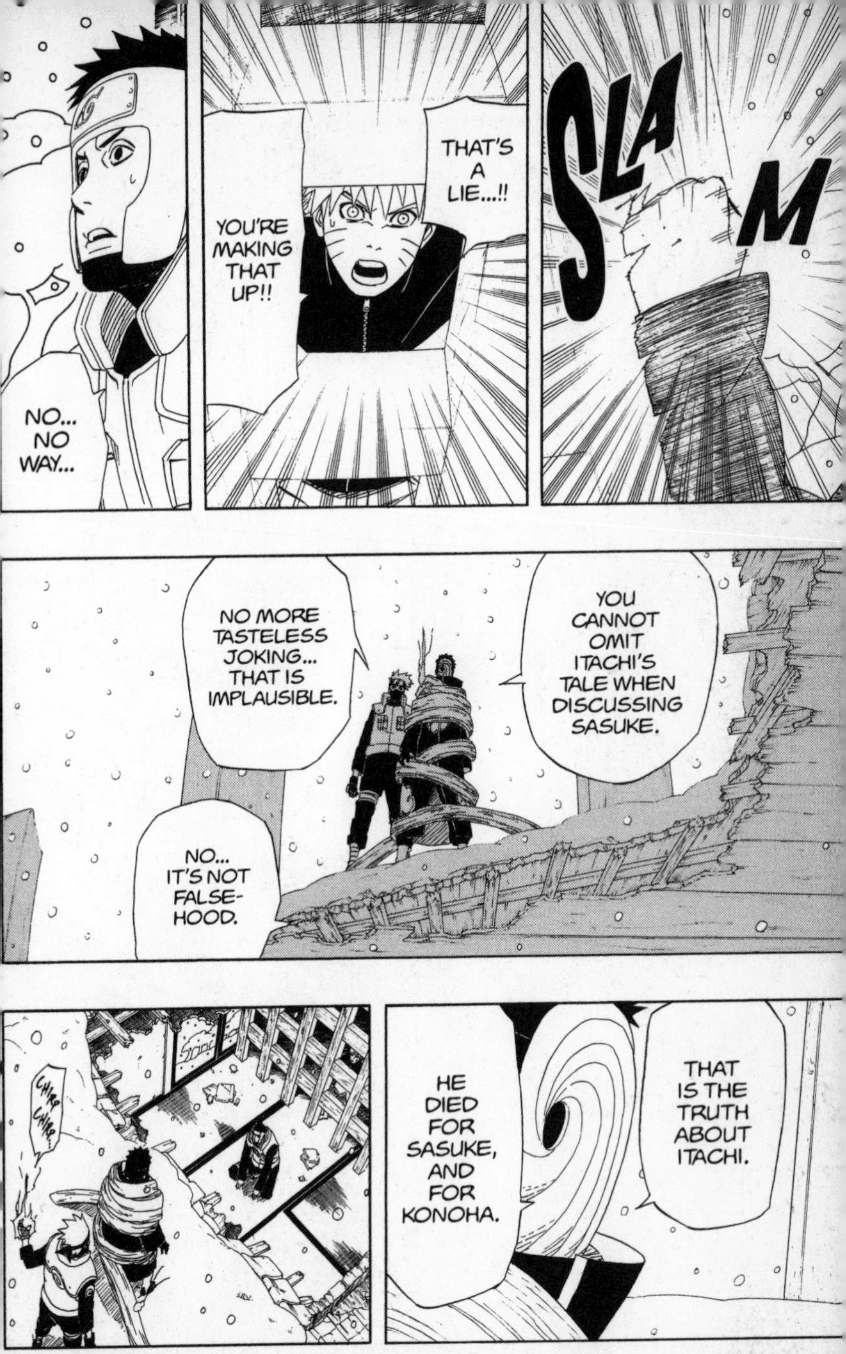
SLAM
THAT'S A LIE...!!
YOU'RE MAKING THAT UP!!
NO... NO WAY...
YOU CANNOT OMIT ITACHI'S TALE WHEN DISCUSSING SASUKE.
NO MORE TASTELESS JOKING... THAT IS IMPLAUSIBLE.
NO... IT'S NOT FALSE-HOOD.
THAT IS THE TRUTH ABOUT ITACHI.
HE DIED FOR SASUKE, AND FOR KONOHA.
CHIRP CHIRP...

READ THIS WAY

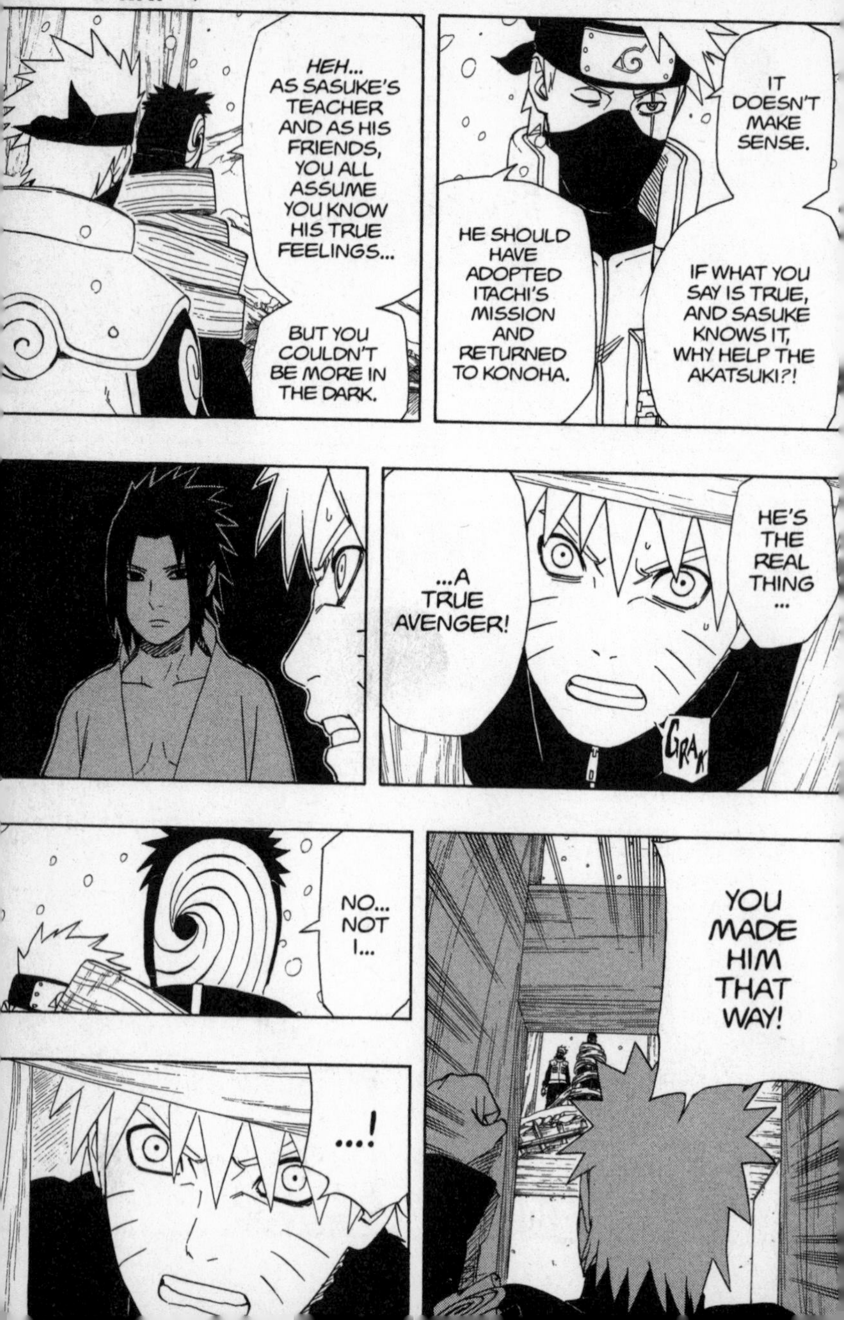
IT DOESN'T MAKE SENSE.
IF WHAT YOU SAY IS TRUE, AND SASUKE KNOWS IT, WHY HELP THE AKATSUKI?!
HE SHOULD HAVE ADOPTED ITACHI'S MISSION AND RETURNED TO KONOHA.
HEH... AS SASUKE'S TEACHER AND AS HIS FRIENDS, YOU ALL ASSUME YOU KNOW HIS TRUE FEELINGS...
BUT YOU COULDN'T BE MORE IN THE DARK.
HE'S THE REAL THING...
...A TRUE AVENGER!
GRAK
YOU MADE HIM THAT WAY!
NO... NOT I...
...!

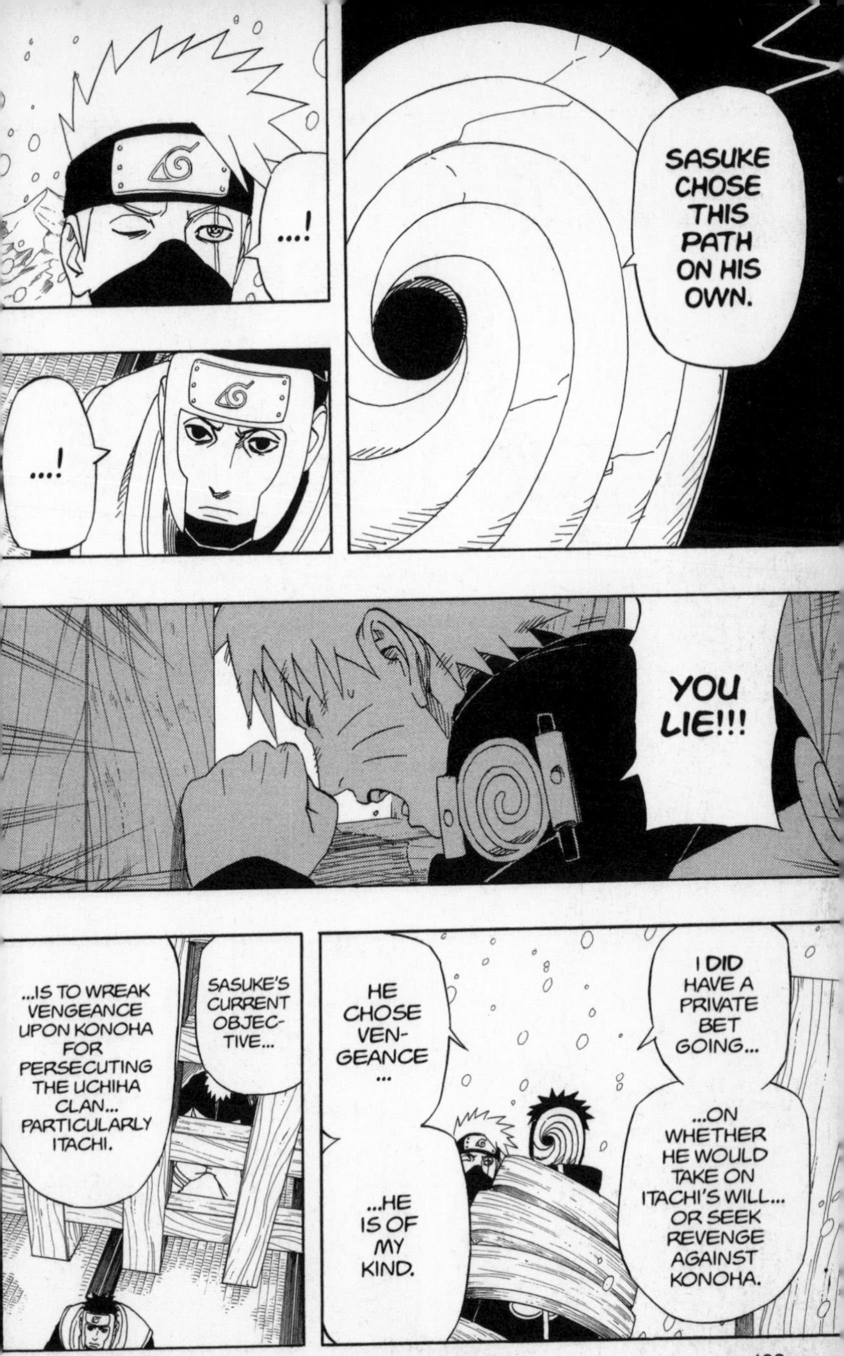
SASUKE CHOSE THIS PATH ON HIS OWN.
...!
...!
YOU LIE!!!
I DID HAVE A PRIVATE BET GOING...
...ON WHETHER HE WOULD TAKE ON ITACHI'S WILL... OR SEEK REVENGE AGAINST KONOHA.
HE CHOSE VENGEANCE...
...HE IS OF MY KIND.
SASUKE'S CURRENT OBJECTIVE...
...IS TO WREAK VENGEANCE UPON KONOHA FOR PERSECUTING THE UCHIHA CLAN... PARTICULARLY ITACHI.

READ THIS WAY

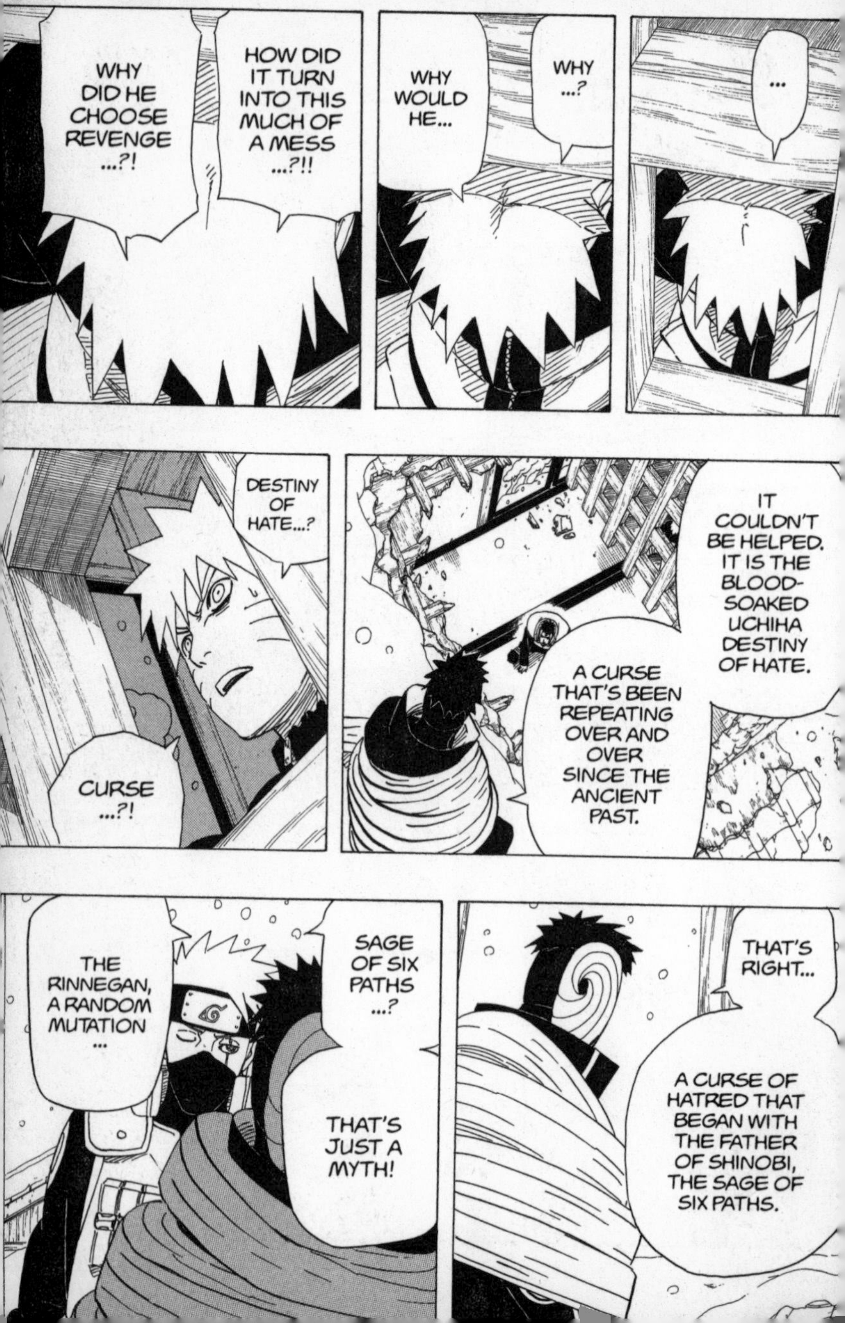
...
WHY ...?
WHY WOULD HE...
HOW DID IT TURN INTO THIS MUCH OF A MESS ...?!!
WHY DID HE CHOOSE REVENGE ...?!
IT COULDN'T BE HELPED. IT IS THE BLOOD-SOAKED UCHIHA DESTINY OF HATE.
A CURSE THAT'S BEEN REPEATING OVER AND OVER SINCE THE ANCIENT PAST.
DESTINY OF HATE...?
CURSE ...?!
THAT'S RIGHT...
A CURSE OF HATRED THAT BEGAN WITH THE FATHER OF SHINOBI, THE SAGE OF SIX PATHS.
SAGE OF SIX PATHS ...?
THE RINNEGAN, A RANDOM MUTATION ...
THAT'S JUST A MYTH!

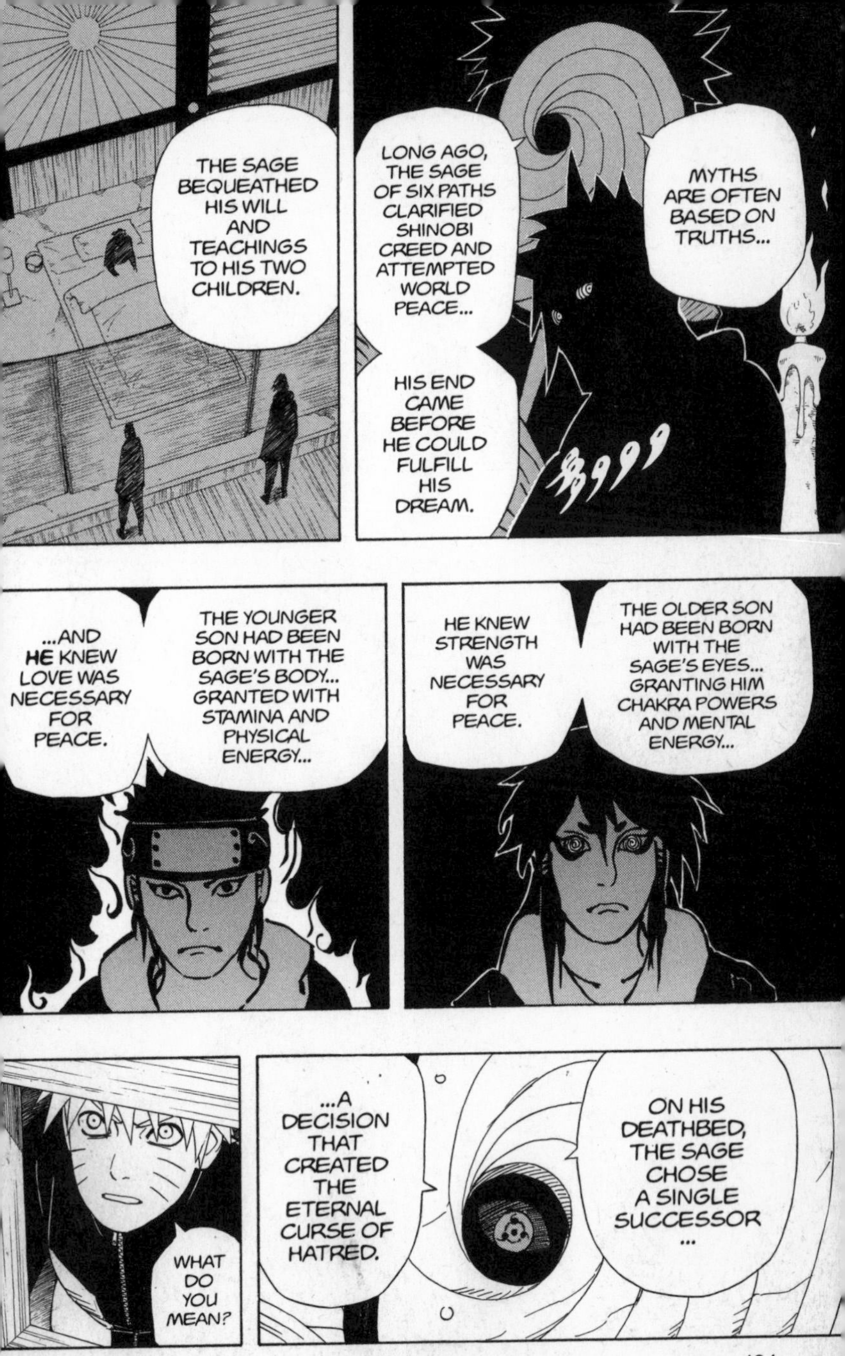
MYTHS ARE OFTEN BASED ON TRUTHS...
LONG AGO, THE SAGE OF SIX PATHS CLARIFIED SHINOBI CREED AND ATTEMPTED WORLD PEACE...
HIS END CAME BEFORE HE COULD FULFILL HIS DREAM.
THE SAGE BEQUEATHED HIS WILL AND TEACHINGS TO HIS TWO CHILDREN.
THE OLDER SON HAD BEEN BORN WITH THE SAGE'S EYES... GRANTING HIM CHAKRA POWERS AND MENTAL ENERGY...
HE KNEW STRENGTH WAS NECESSARY FOR PEACE.
THE YOUNGER SON HAD BEEN BORN WITH THE SAGE'S BODY... GRANTED WITH STAMINA AND PHYSICAL ENERGY...
...AND **HE** KNEW LOVE WAS NECESSARY FOR PEACE.
ON HIS DEATHBED, THE SAGE CHOSE A SINGLE SUCCESSOR ...
...A DECISION THAT CREATED THE ETERNAL CURSE OF HATRED.
WHAT DO YOU MEAN?

READ THIS WAY

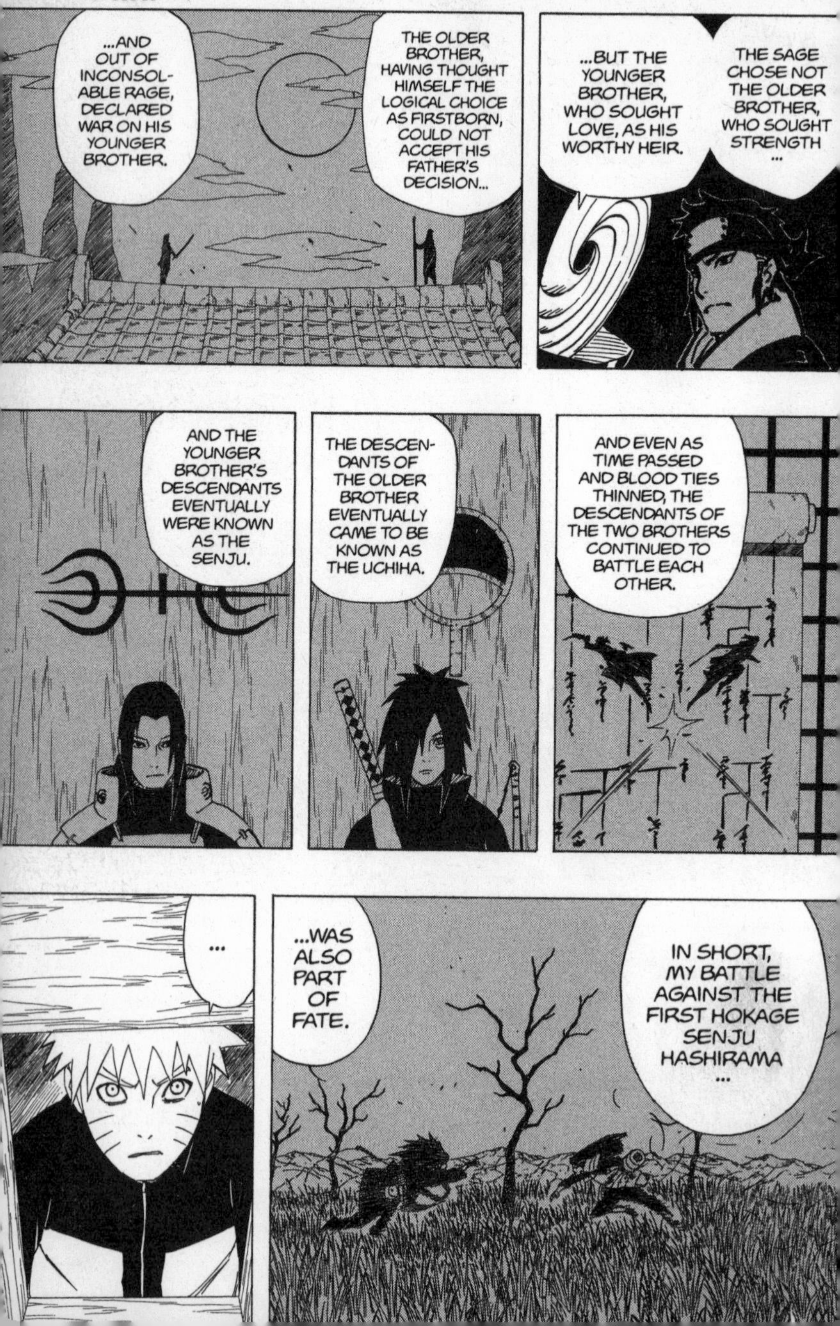

THE SAGE CHOSE NOT THE OLDER BROTHER, WHO SOUGHT STRENGTH ...
...BUT THE YOUNGER BROTHER, WHO SOUGHT LOVE, AS HIS WORTHY HEIR.
THE OLDER BROTHER, HAVING THOUGHT HIMSELF THE LOGICAL CHOICE AS FIRSTBORN, COULD NOT ACCEPT HIS FATHER'S DECISION...
...AND OUT OF INCONSOL-ABLE RAGE, DECLARED WAR ON HIS YOUNGER BROTHER.
AND EVEN AS TIME PASSED AND BLOOD TIES THINNED, THE DESCENDANTS OF THE TWO BROTHERS CONTINUED TO BATTLE EACH OTHER.
THE DESCEN-DANTS OF THE OLDER BROTHER EVENTUALLY CAME TO BE KNOWN AS THE UCHIHA.
AND THE YOUNGER BROTHER'S DESCENDANTS EVENTUALLY WERE KNOWN AS THE SENJU.
IN SHORT, MY BATTLE AGAINST THE FIRST HOKAGE SENJU HASHIRAMA ...
...WAS ALSO PART OF FATE.
...

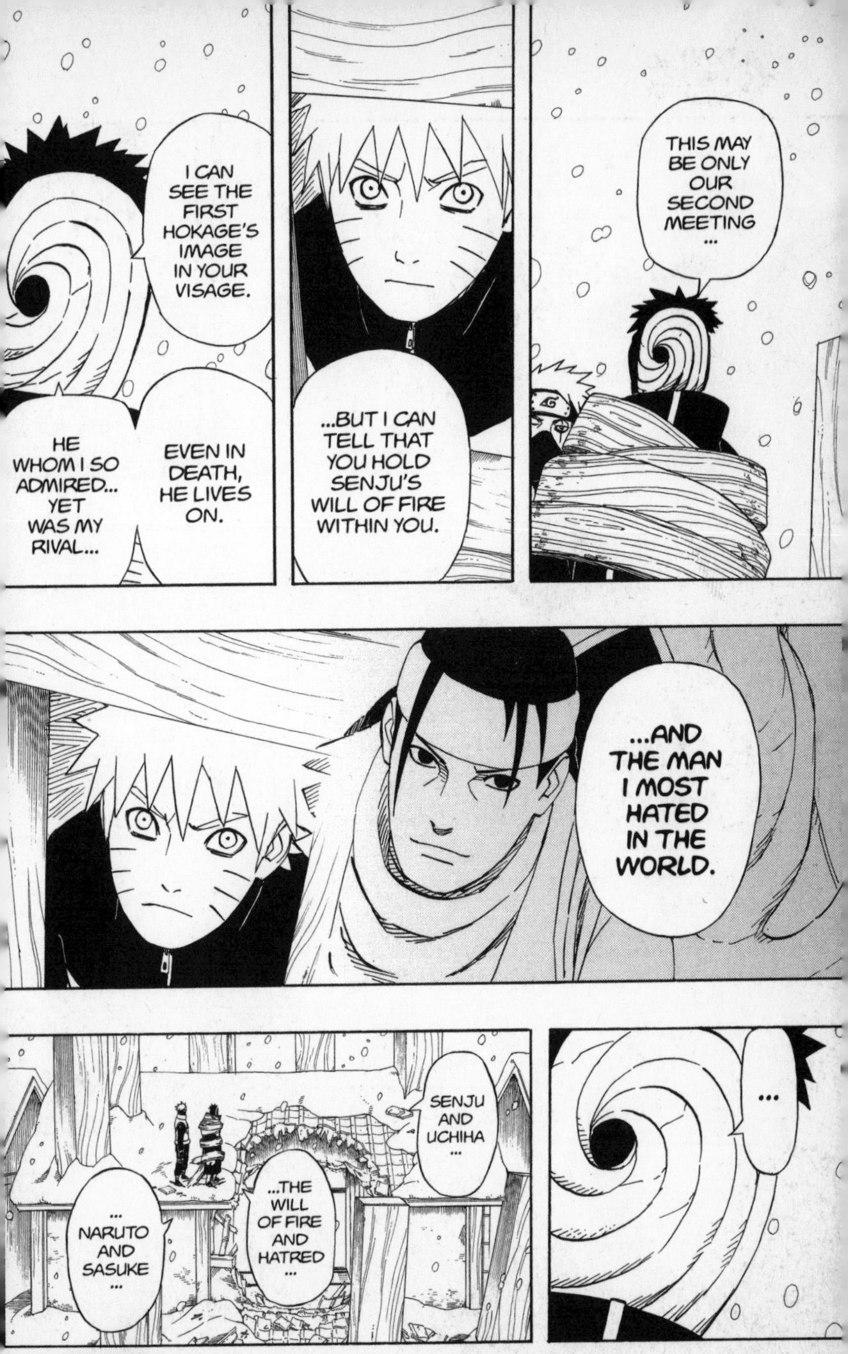

THIS MAY BE ONLY OUR SECOND MEETING ...
...BUT I CAN TELL THAT YOU HOLD SENJU'S WILL OF FIRE WITHIN YOU.
I CAN SEE THE FIRST HOKAGE'S IMAGE IN YOUR VISAGE.
EVEN IN DEATH, HE LIVES ON.
HE WHOM I SO ADMIRED... YET WAS MY RIVAL...
...AND THE MAN I MOST HATED IN THE WORLD.
...
SENJU AND UCHIHA ...
...THE WILL OF FIRE AND HATRED ...
... NARUTO AND SASUKE ...

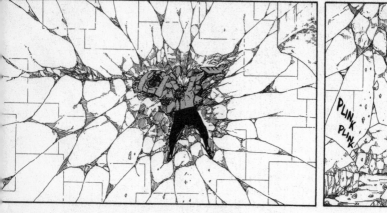

PLINK PLINK

SNOB

YOU ARE JUST THE NEXT IN LINE TO BE CHOSEN BY DESTINY.

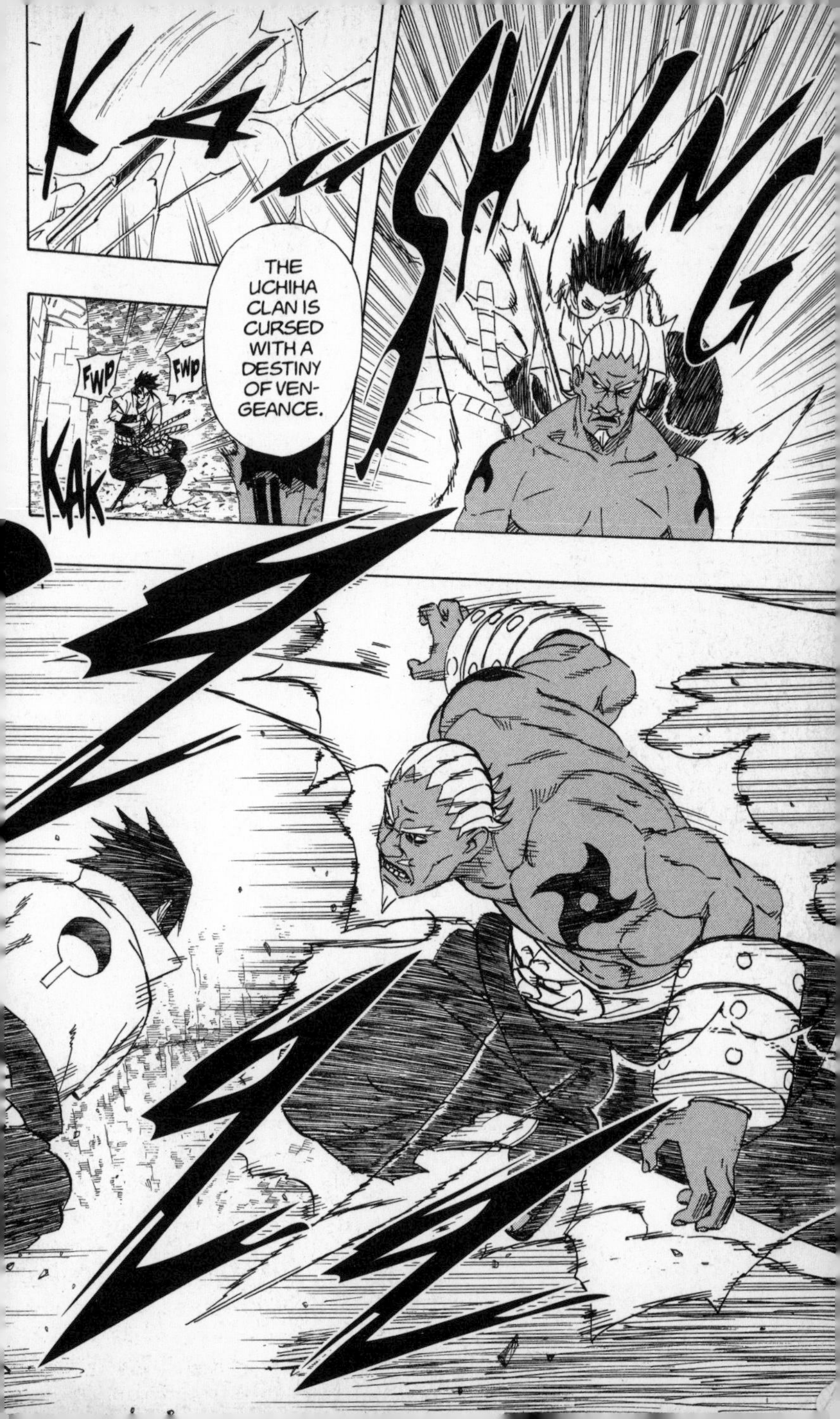
KASHING
THE UCHIHA CLAN IS CURSED WITH A DESTINY OF VENGEANCE.
FWP
FWP
KAK

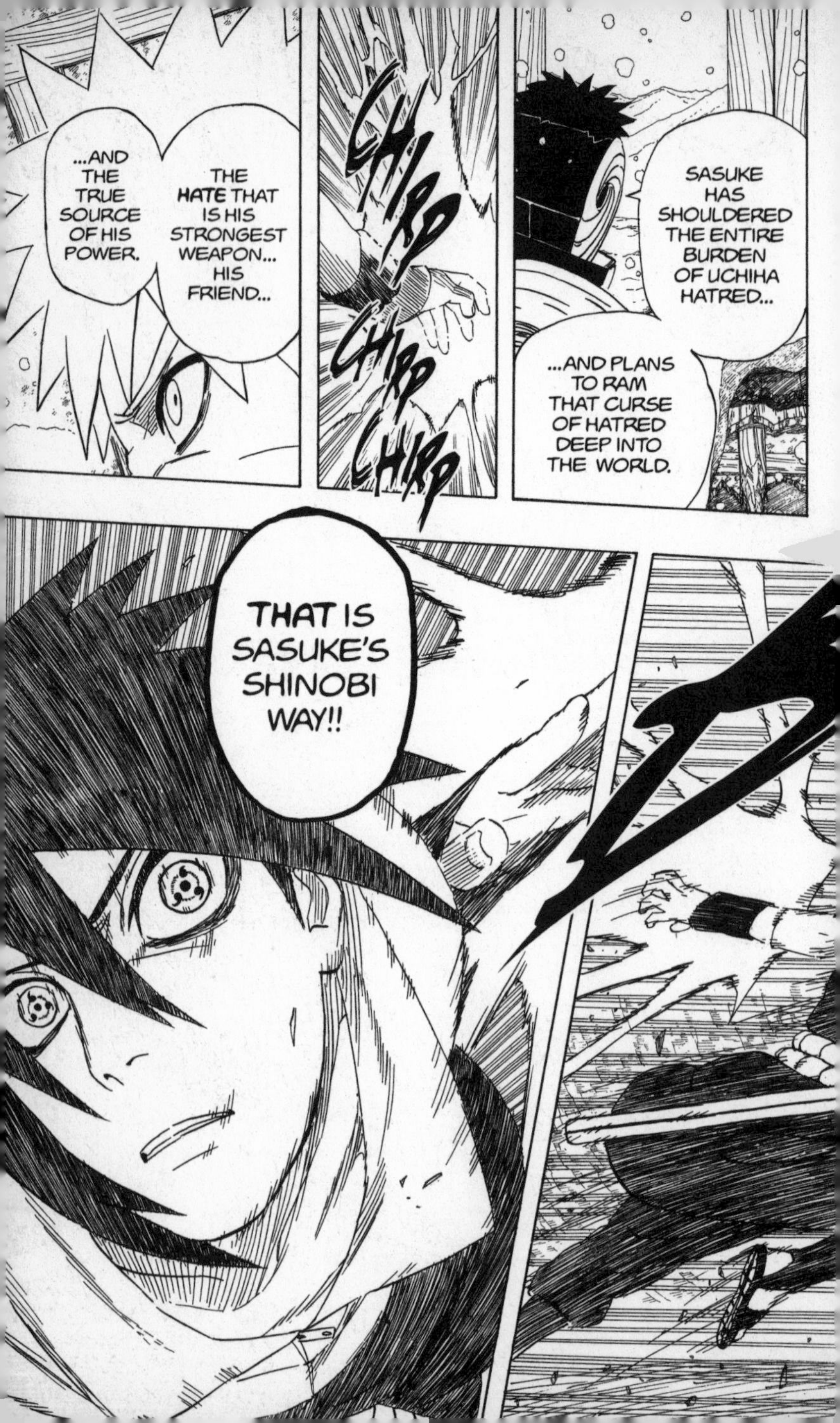

SASUKE HAS SHOULDERED THE ENTIRE BURDEN OF UCHIHA HATRED...
...AND PLANS TO RAM THAT CURSE OF HATRED DEEP INTO THE WORLD.
CHIRP CHIRP CHIRP
THE HATE THAT IS HIS STRONGEST WEAPON... HIS FRIEND...
...AND THE TRUE SOURCE OF HIS POWER.
THAT IS SASUKE'S SHINOBI WAY!!

NARUTO

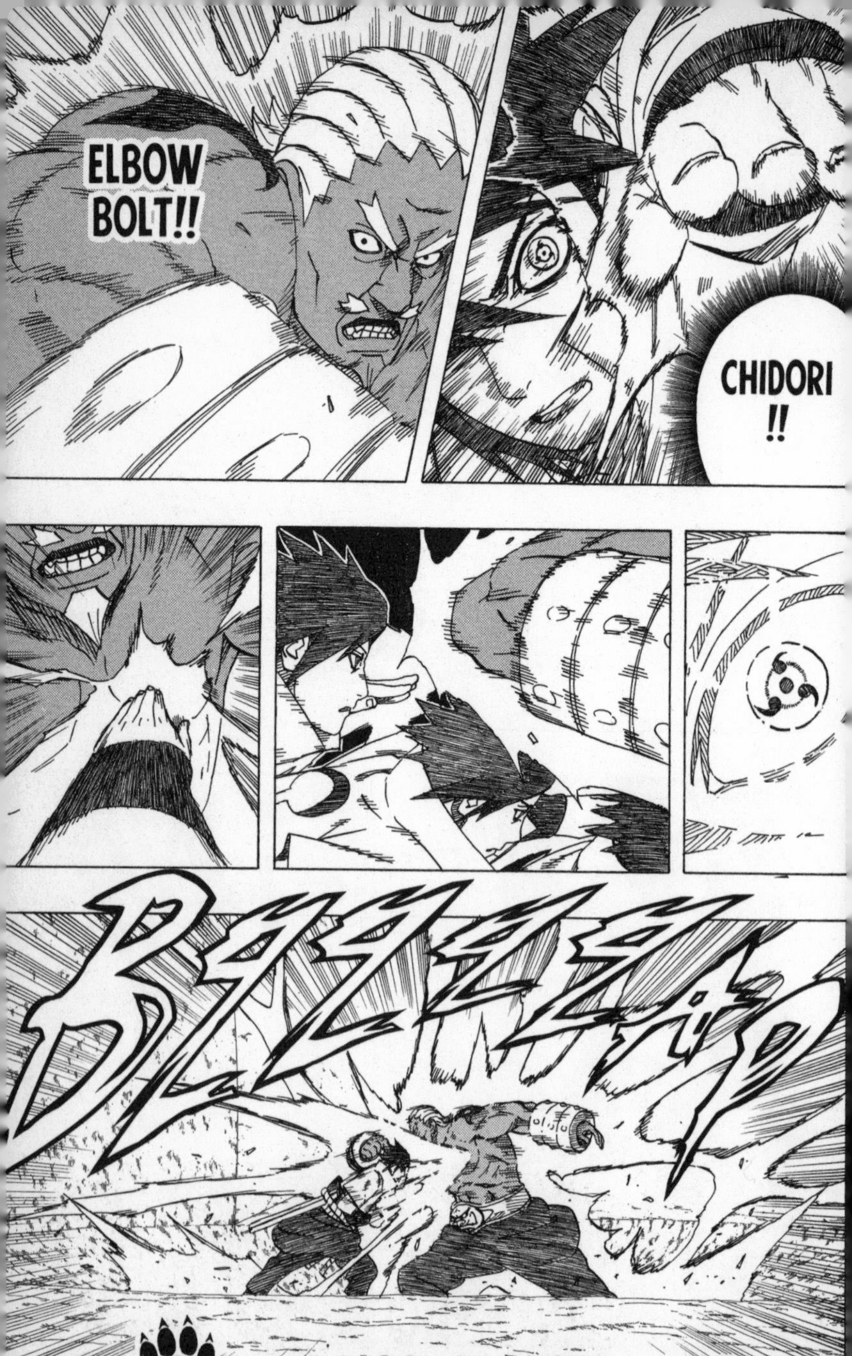
CHIDORI !!
ELBOW BOLT!!

Number 463: Sasuke vs. Raikage!!

Number 463: Sasuke vs. Raikage!!

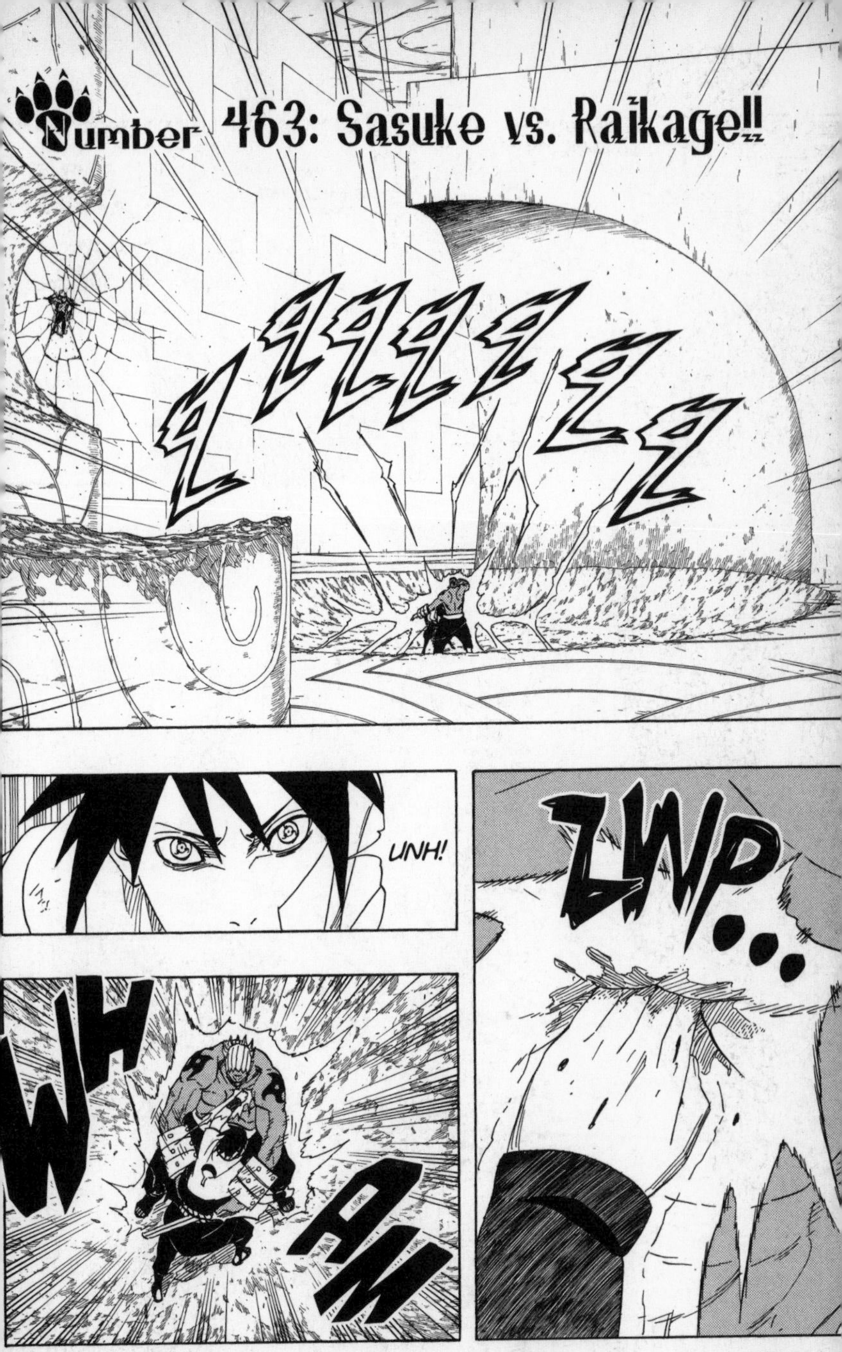
ZWP...
UNH!
WHAM

READ THIS WAY

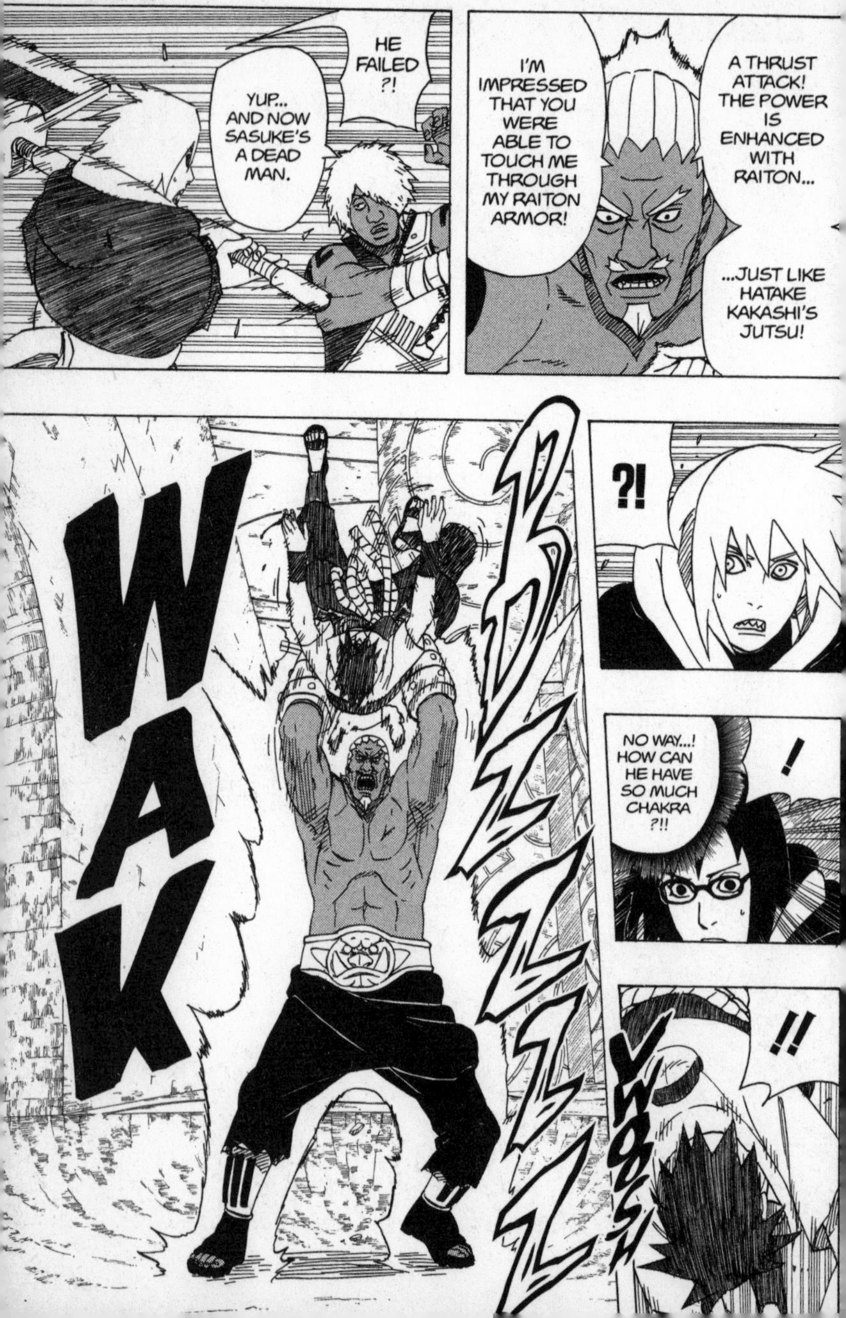

A THRUST ATTACK! THE POWER IS ENHANCED WITH RAITON...
I'M IMPRESSED THAT YOU WERE ABLE TO TOUCH ME THROUGH MY RAITON ARMOR!
...JUST LIKE HATAKE KAKASHI'S JUTSU!
HE FAILED ?!
YUP... AND NOW SASUKE'S A DEAD MAN.
?!
NO WAY...! HOW CAN HE HAVE SO MUCH CHAKRA ?!!
!
!!
WHOOSH
WAK

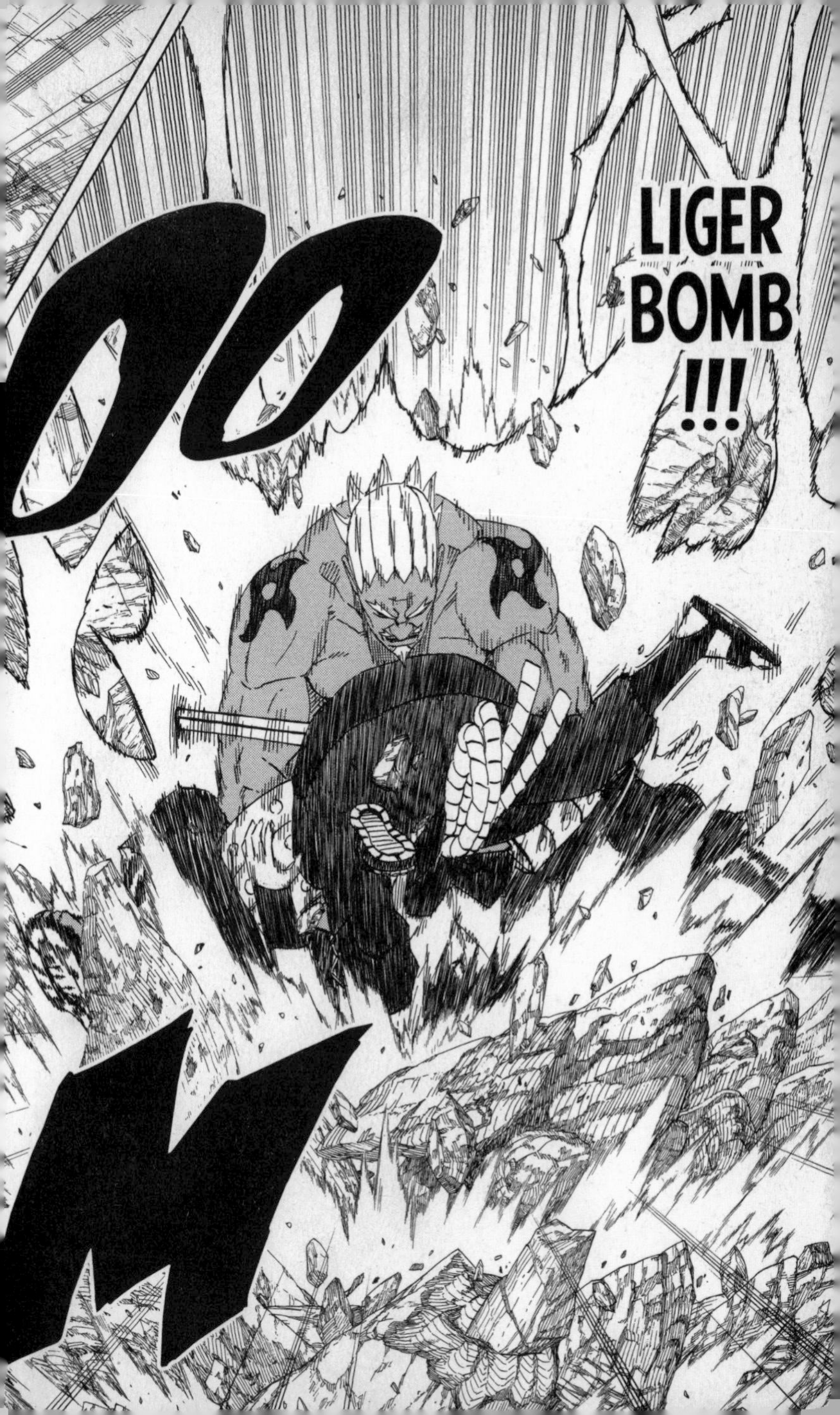
LIGER BOMB!!!

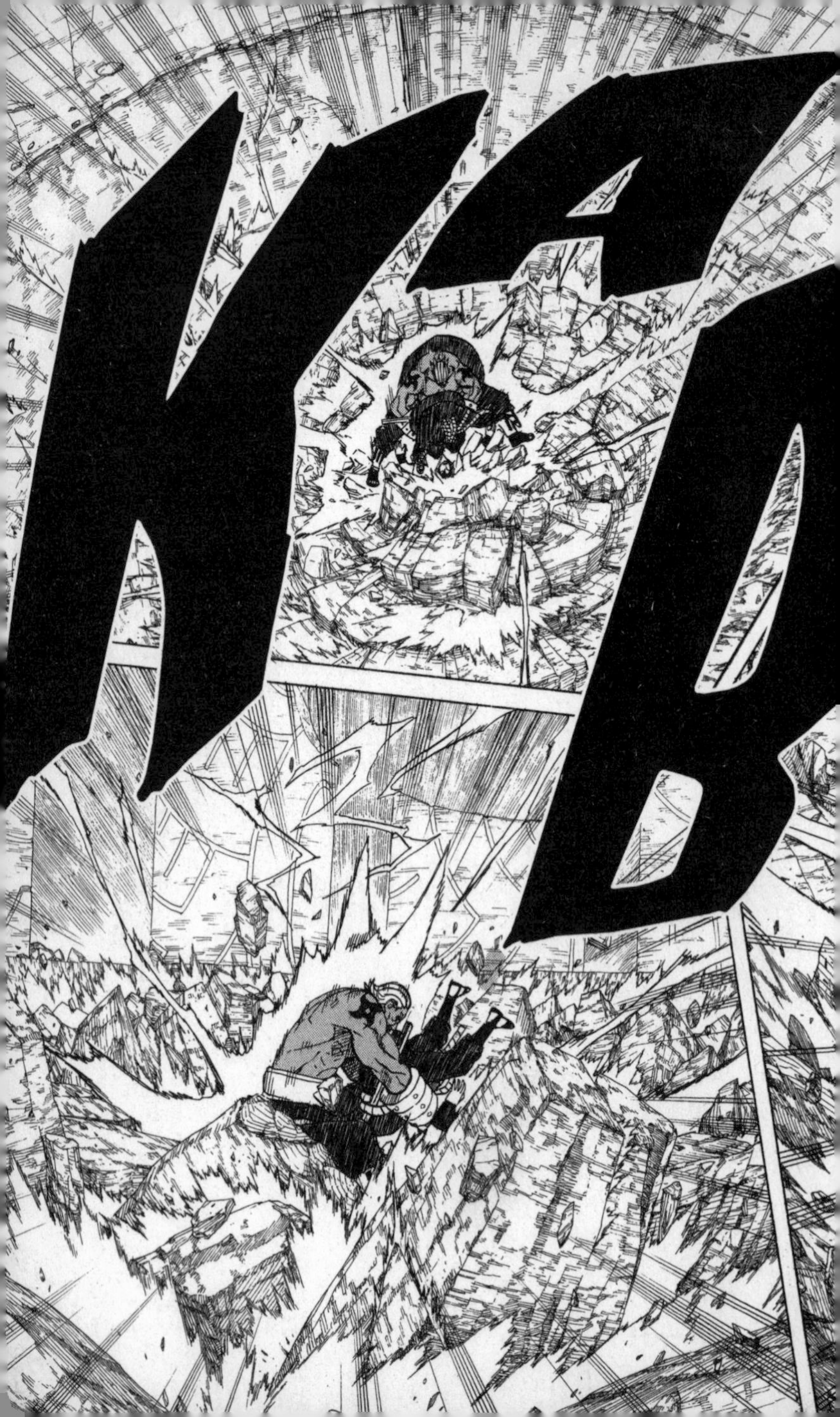

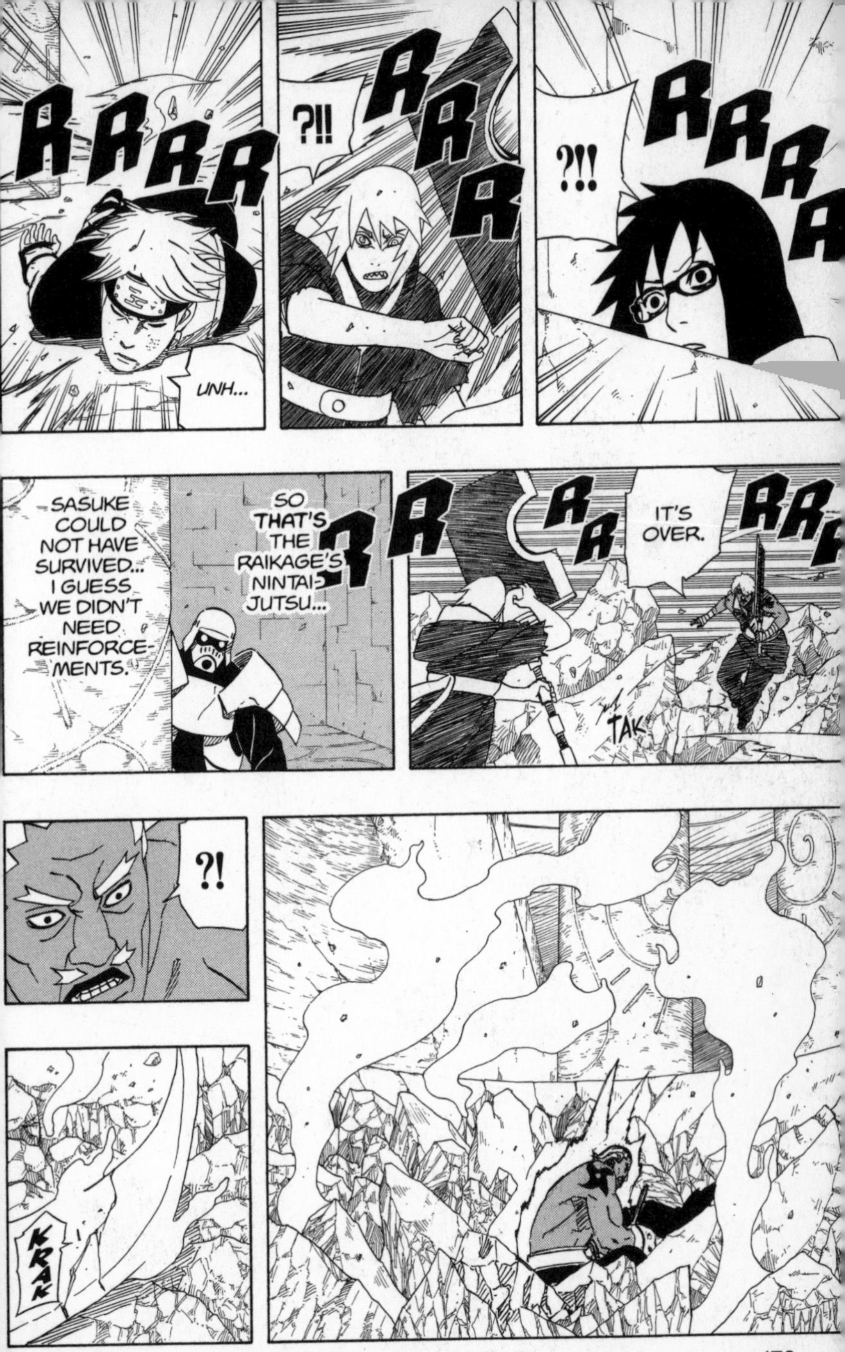
RRRR
?!!
?!!
RRRR
RRRR
UNH...
RRR
IT'S OVER.
RR
TAK
SO THAT'S THE RAIKAGE'S NINTAI-JUTSU...
SASUKE COULD NOT HAVE SURVIVED... I GUESS WE DIDN'T NEED REINFORCE-MENTS.
?!
KRAK

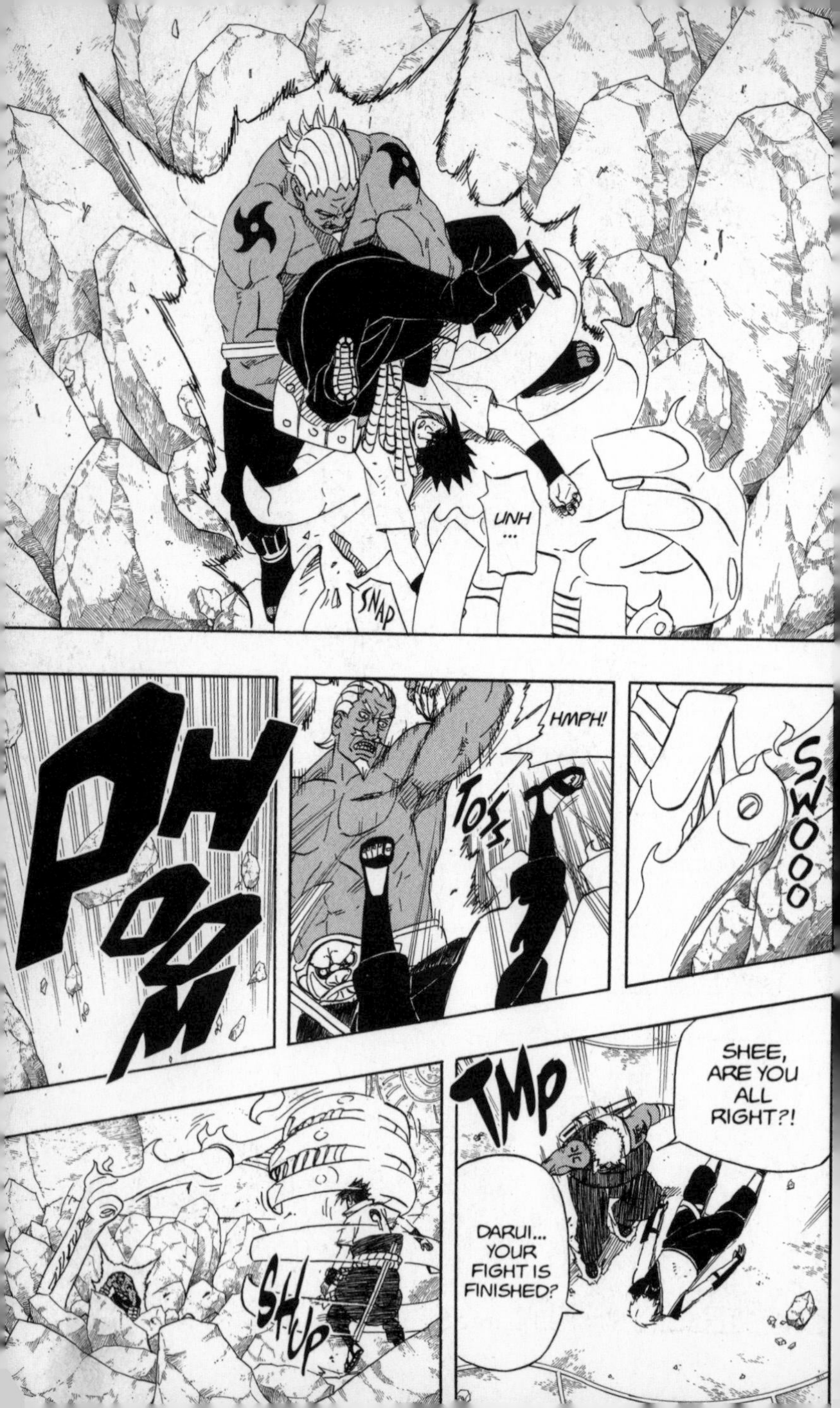

UNH ...
SNAP
SWOOOO
HMPH!
TOSS
DHOOM
TMP
SHEE, ARE YOU ALL RIGHT?!
DARUI... YOUR FIGHT IS FINISHED?
SHUP

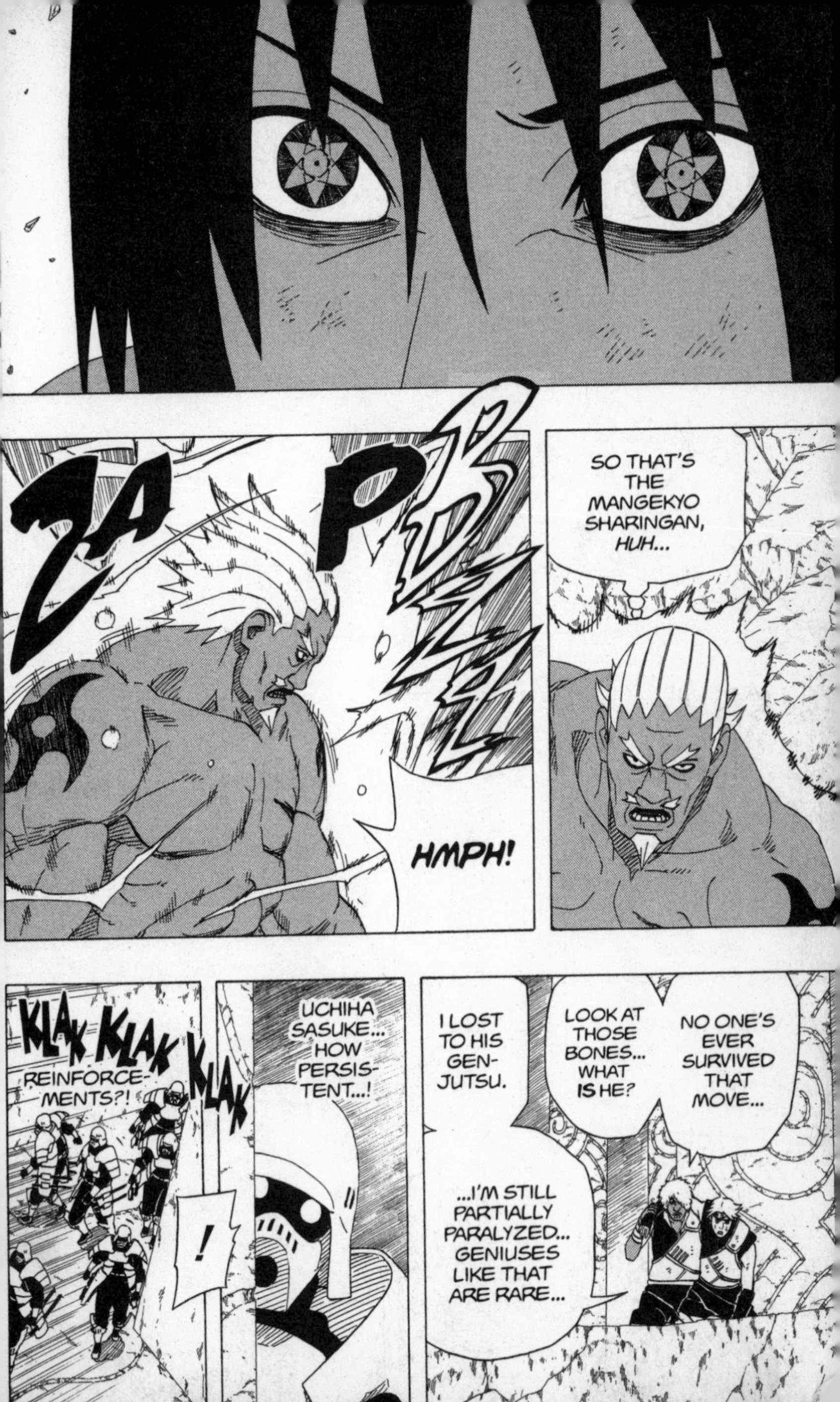

SO THAT'S THE MANGEKYO SHARINGAN, HUH...
ZAP
HMPH!
NO ONE'S EVER SURVIVED THAT MOVE...
LOOK AT THOSE BONES... WHAT **IS** HE?
I LOST TO HIS GEN-JUTSU.
...I'M STILL PARTIALLY PARALYZED... GENIUSES LIKE THAT ARE RARE...
UCHIHA SASUKE... HOW PERSIS-TENT...!
!
KLAK KLAK KLAK
REINFORCE-MENTS?!

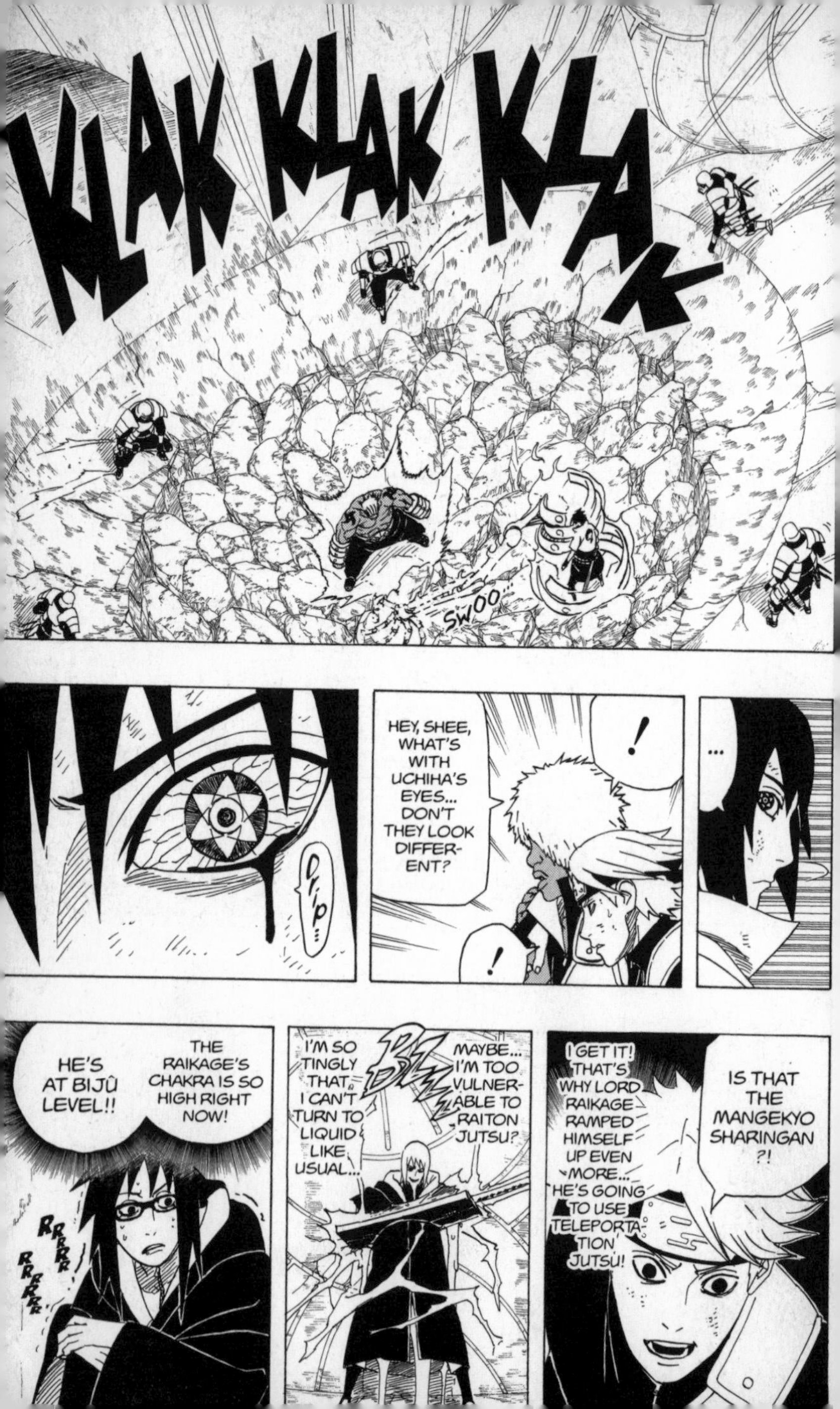
KLAK KLAK KLAK
SWOO...
...
!
HEY, SHEE, WHAT'S WITH UCHIHA'S EYES... DON'T THEY LOOK DIFFER-ENT?
!
DRIP...
IS THAT THE MANGEKYO SHARINGAN?!
I GET IT! THAT'S WHY LORD RAIKAGE RAMPED HIMSELF UP EVEN MORE... HE'S GOING TO USE TELEPORTA-TION JUTSU!
MAYBE... I'M TOO VULNER-ABLE TO RAITON JUTSU?
I'M SO TINGLY THAT I CAN'T TURN TO LIQUID LIKE USUAL...
THE RAIKAGE'S CHAKRA IS SO HIGH RIGHT NOW!
HE'S AT BIJÛ LEVEL!!
RRRRR
RRRRR

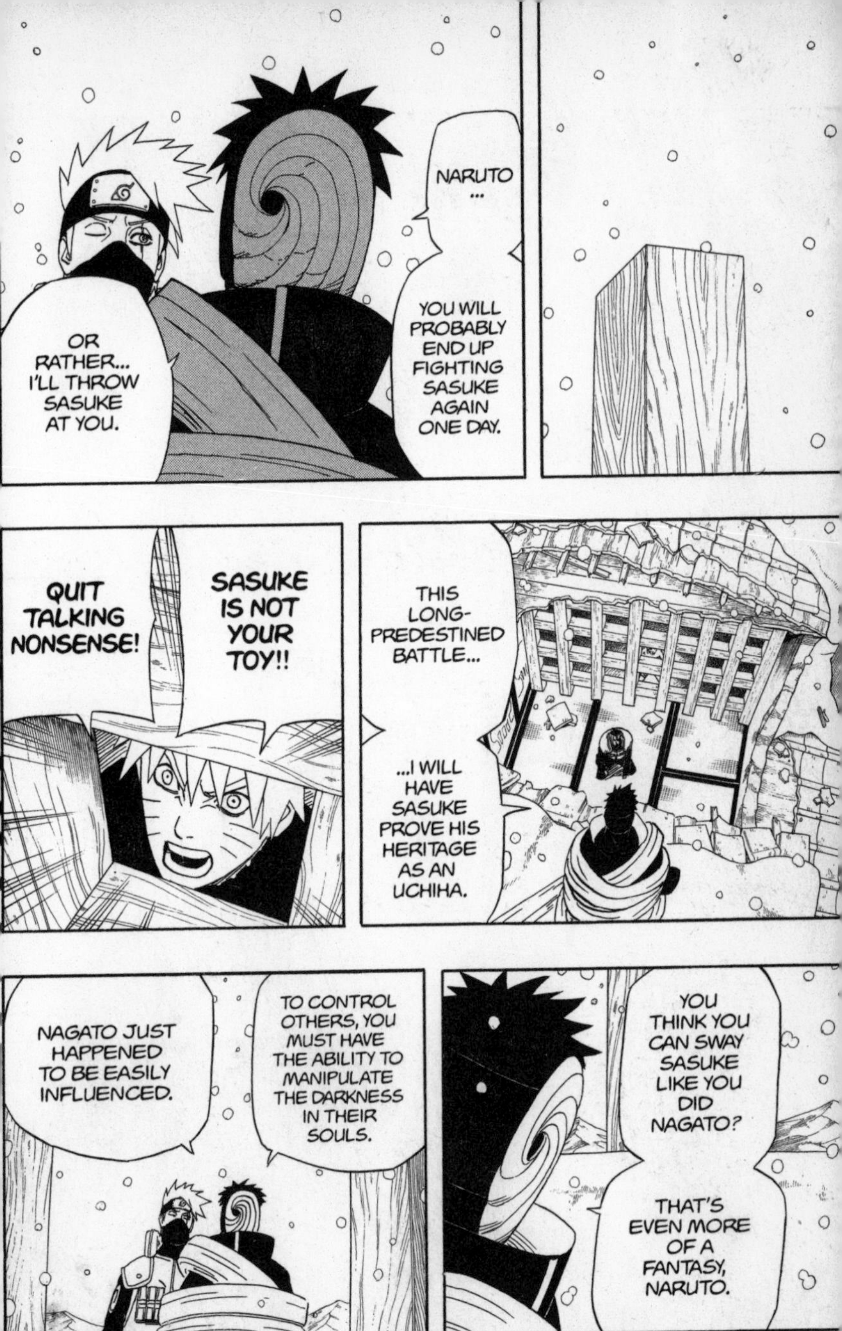
NARUTO ...
YOU WILL PROBABLY END UP FIGHTING SASUKE AGAIN ONE DAY.
OR RATHER... I'LL THROW SASUKE AT YOU.
THIS LONG-PREDESTINED BATTLE...
...I WILL HAVE SASUKE PROVE HIS HERITAGE AS AN UCHIHA.
SASUKE IS NOT YOUR TOY!!
QUIT TALKING NONSENSE!
YOU THINK YOU CAN SWAY SASUKE LIKE YOU DID NAGATO?
THAT'S EVEN MORE OF A FANTASY, NARUTO.
TO CONTROL OTHERS, YOU MUST HAVE THE ABILITY TO MANIPULATE THE DARKNESS IN THEIR SOULS.
NAGATO JUST HAPPENED TO BE EASILY INFLUENCED.

READ THIS WAY

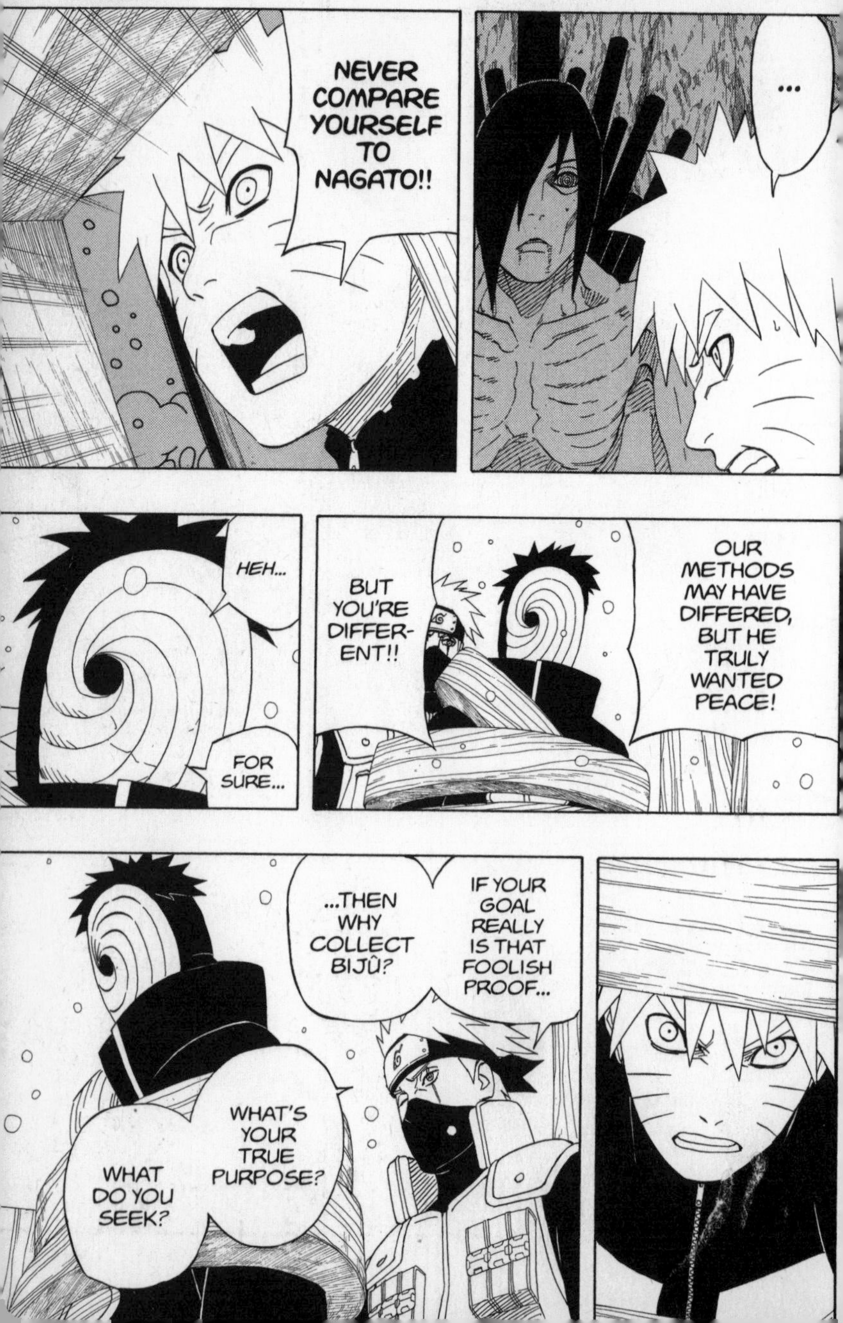
...
NEVER COMPARE YOURSELF TO NAGATO!!
OUR METHODS MAY HAVE DIFFERED, BUT HE TRULY WANTED PEACE!
BUT YOU'RE DIFFER-ENT!!
HEH...
FOR SURE...
IF YOUR GOAL REALLY IS THAT FOOLISH PROOF...
...THEN WHY COLLECT BIJÛ?
WHAT'S YOUR TRUE PURPOSE?
WHAT DO YOU SEEK?

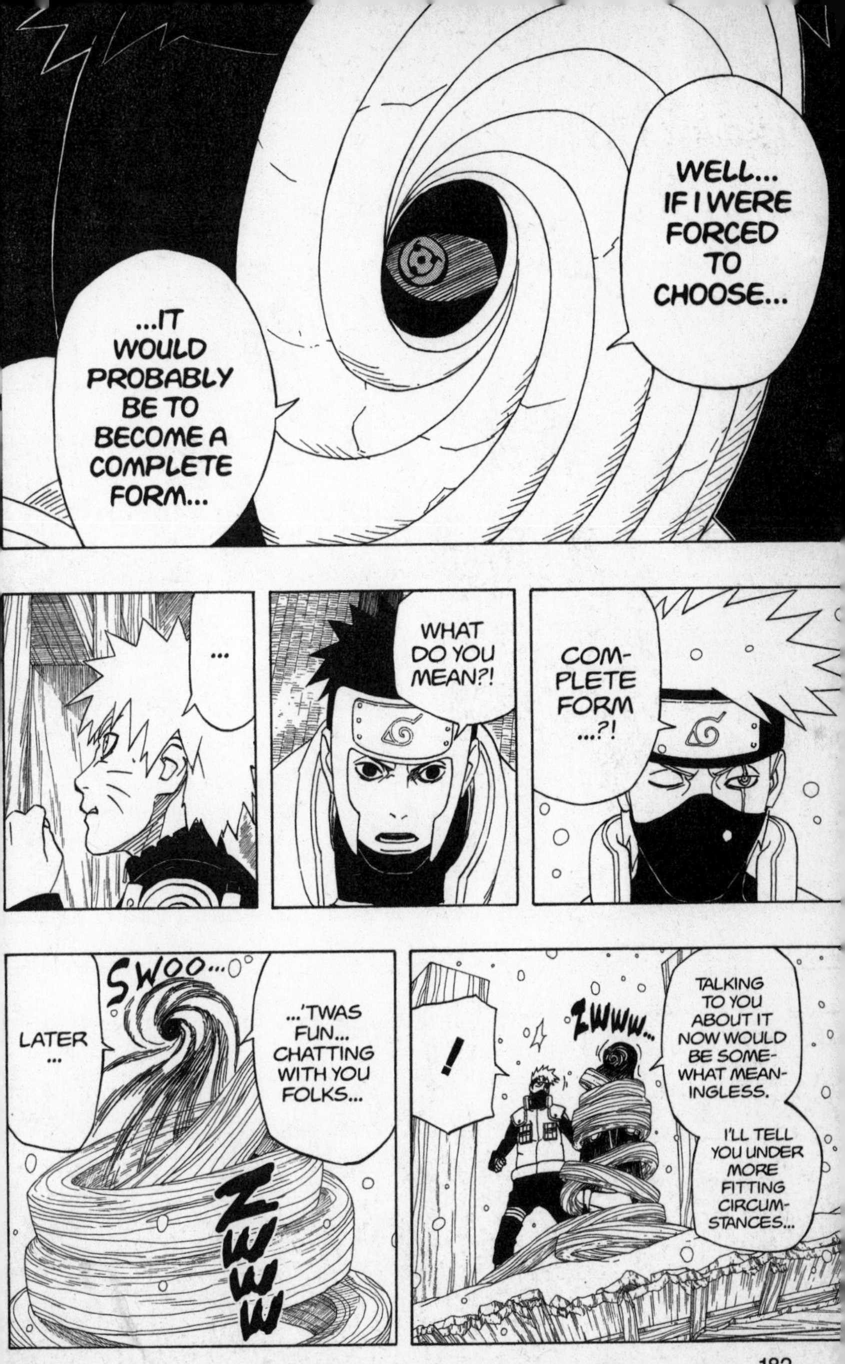
WELL... IF I WERE FORCED TO CHOOSE...
...IT WOULD PROBABLY BE TO BECOME A COMPLETE FORM...
COM-PLETE FORM ...?!
WHAT DO YOU MEAN?!
...
TALKING TO YOU ABOUT IT NOW WOULD BE SOME-WHAT MEAN-INGLESS.
I'LL TELL YOU UNDER MORE FITTING CIRCUM-STANCES...
ZWWW...
!
...'TWAS FUN... CHATTING WITH YOU FOLKS...
SWOO...
LATER...
ZWWW

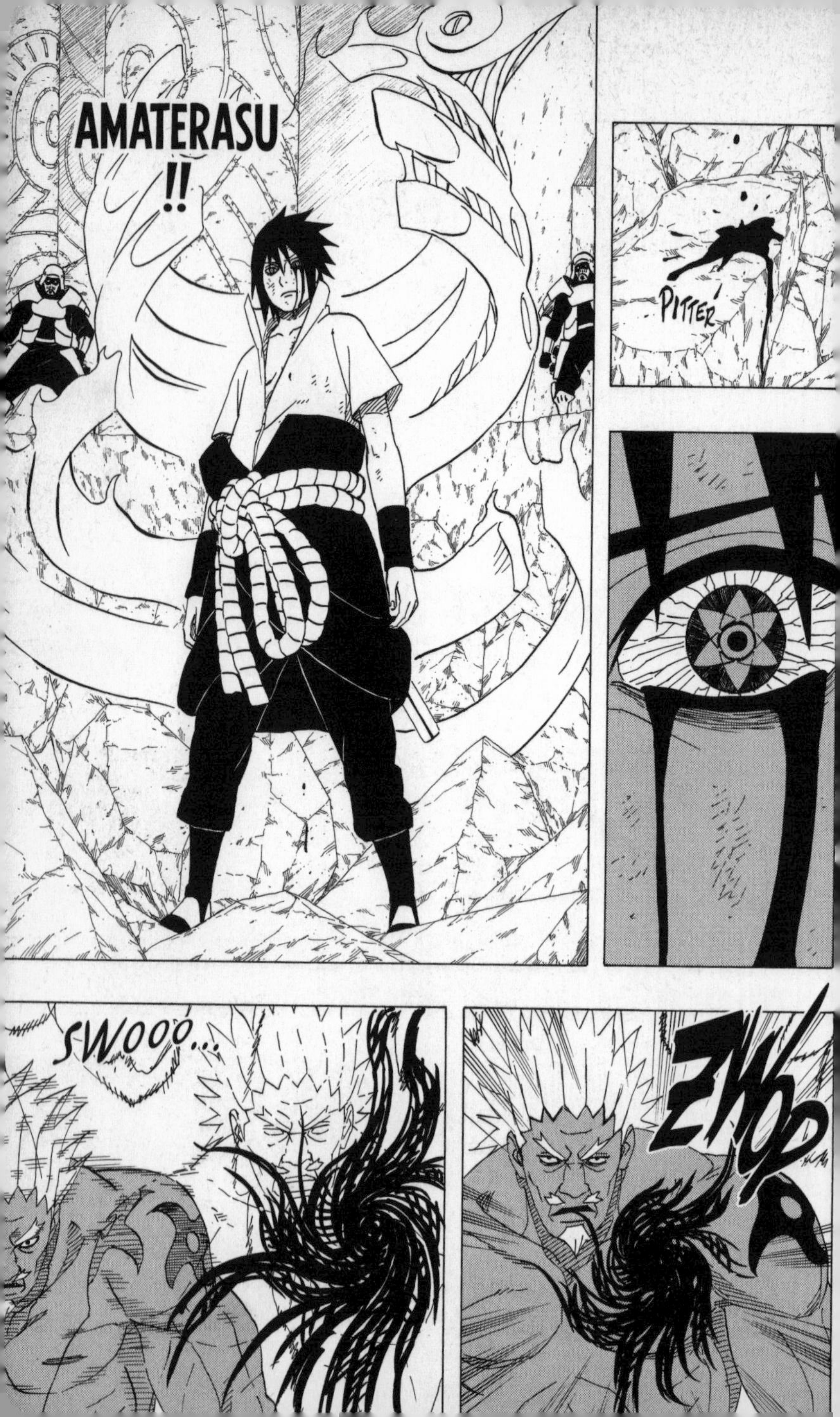
PITTER
AMATERASU !!
ZWOOP
SWOOO...

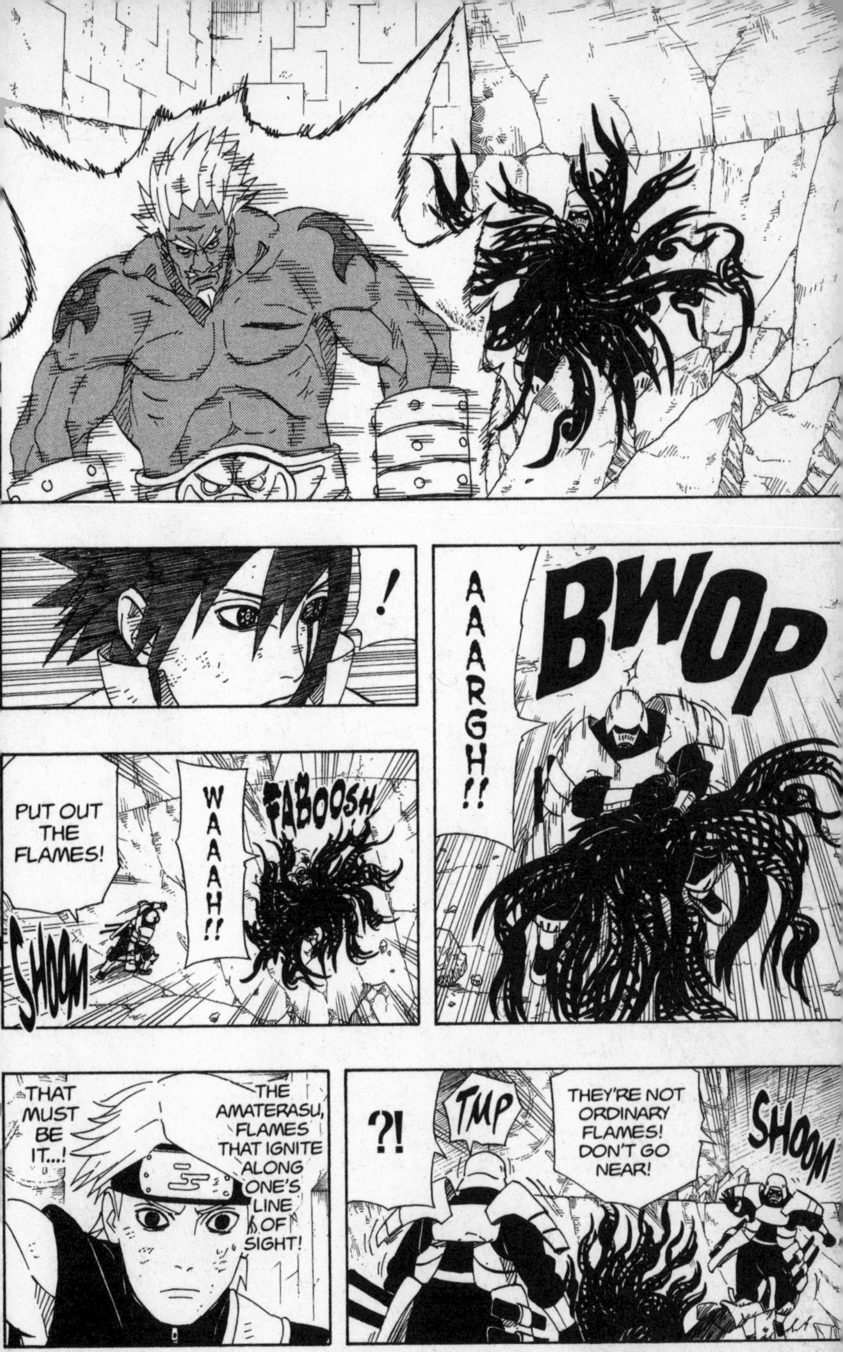
BWOP
AAAARGH!!
!
FABOOSH
WAAAAH!!
PUT OUT THE FLAMES!
SHOOM
SHOOM
THEY'RE NOT ORDINARY FLAMES! DON'T GO NEAR!
TMP
?!
THE AMATERASU, FLAMES THAT IGNITE ALONG ONE'S LINE OF SIGHT!
THAT MUST BE IT...!

READ THIS WAY

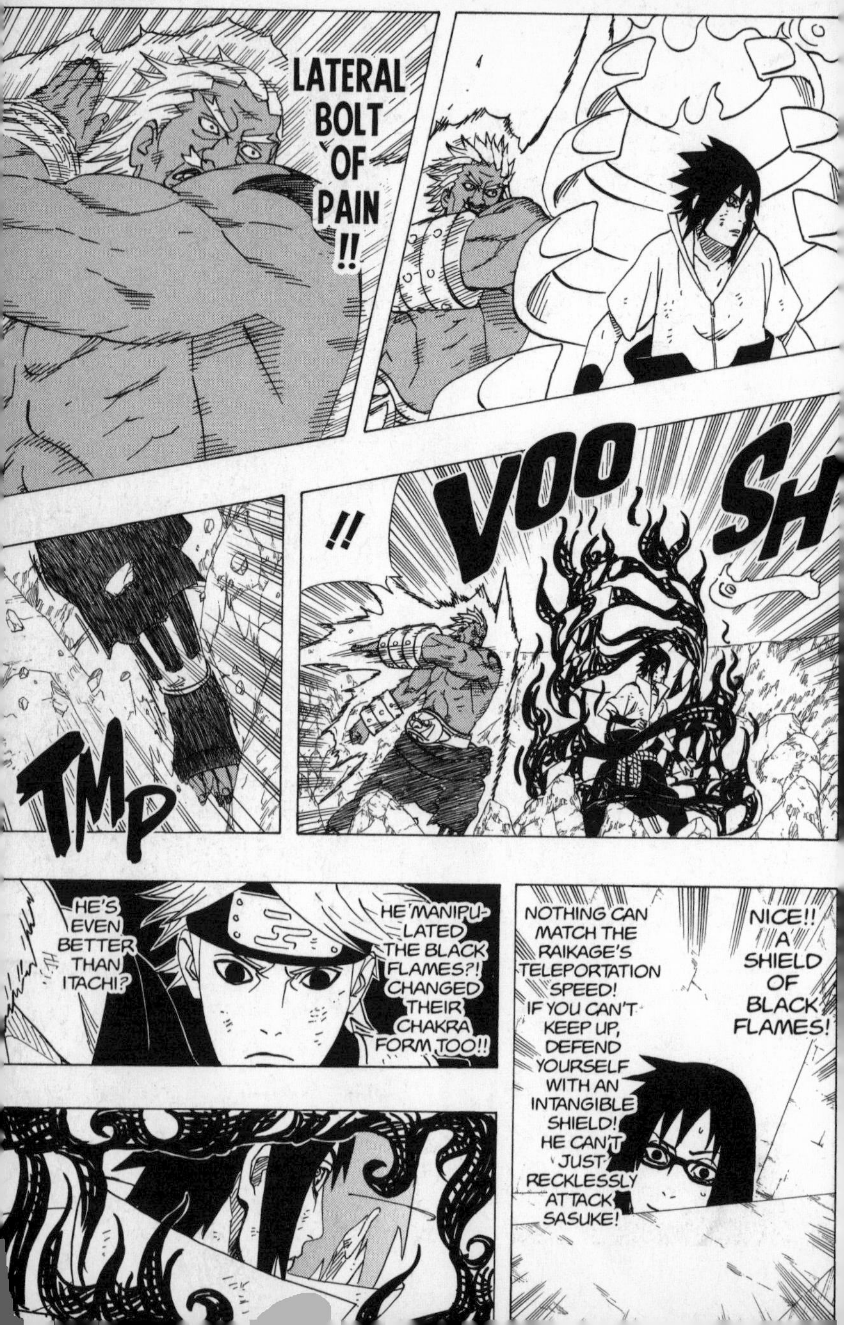
LATERAL BOLT OF PAIN!!
!!
VOOSH
TMP
NICE!! A SHIELD OF BLACK FLAMES!
NOTHING CAN MATCH THE RAIKAGE'S TELEPORTATION SPEED! IF YOU CAN'T KEEP UP, DEFEND YOURSELF WITH AN INTANGIBLE SHIELD! HE CAN'T JUST RECKLESSLY ATTACK SASUKE!
HE MANIPULATED THE BLACK FLAMES?! CHANGED THEIR CHAKRA FORM TOO!!
HE'S EVEN BETTER THAN ITACHI?

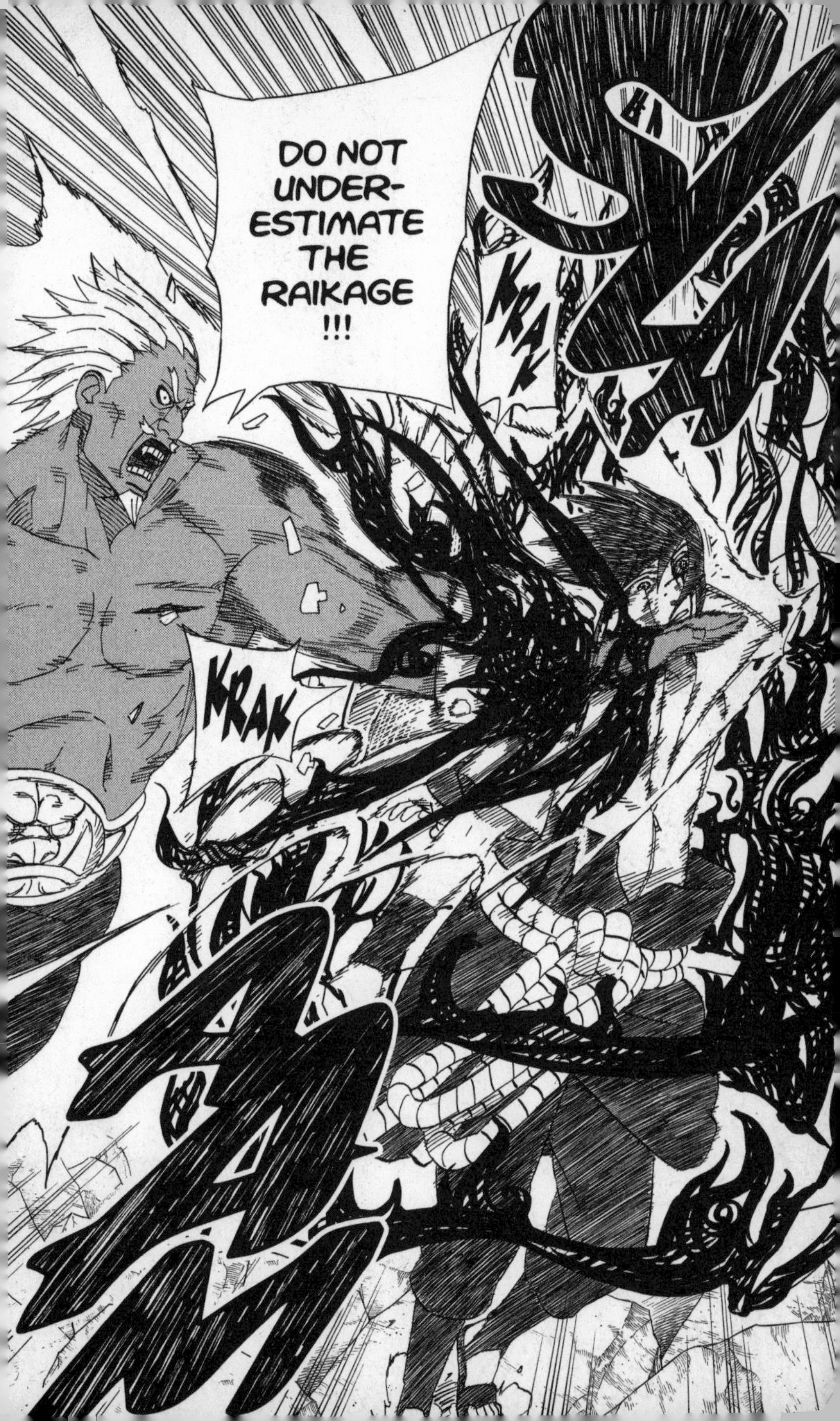
KRAK
DO NOT UNDER-ESTIMATE THE RAIKAGE !!!
KRAK

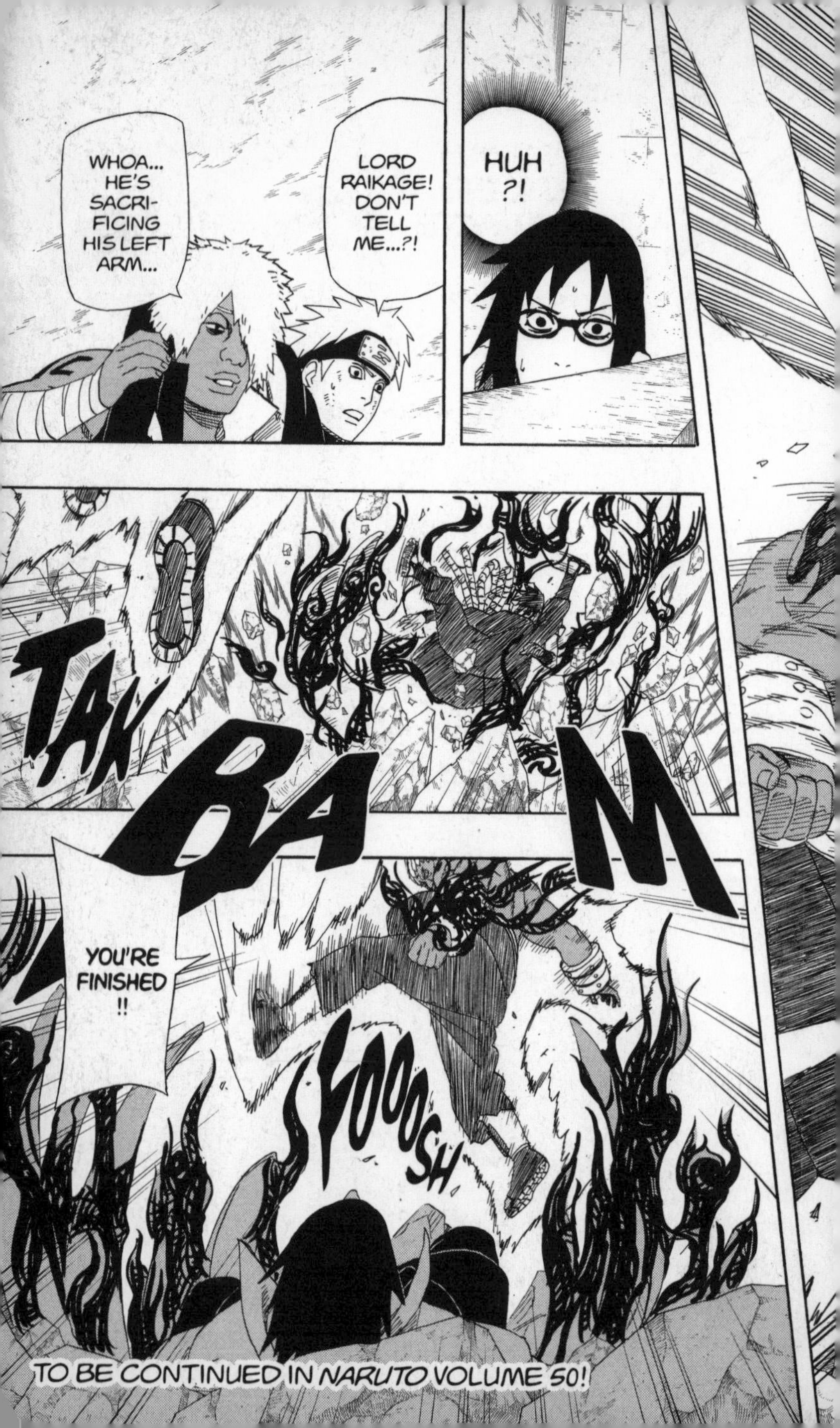
HUH ?!
LORD RAIKAGE! DON'T TELL ME...?!
WHOA... HE'S SACRI-FICING HIS LEFT ARM...
TAK
BAM
YOU'RE FINISHED !!
SWOOOSH
TO BE CONTINUED IN *NARUTO* VOLUME 50!

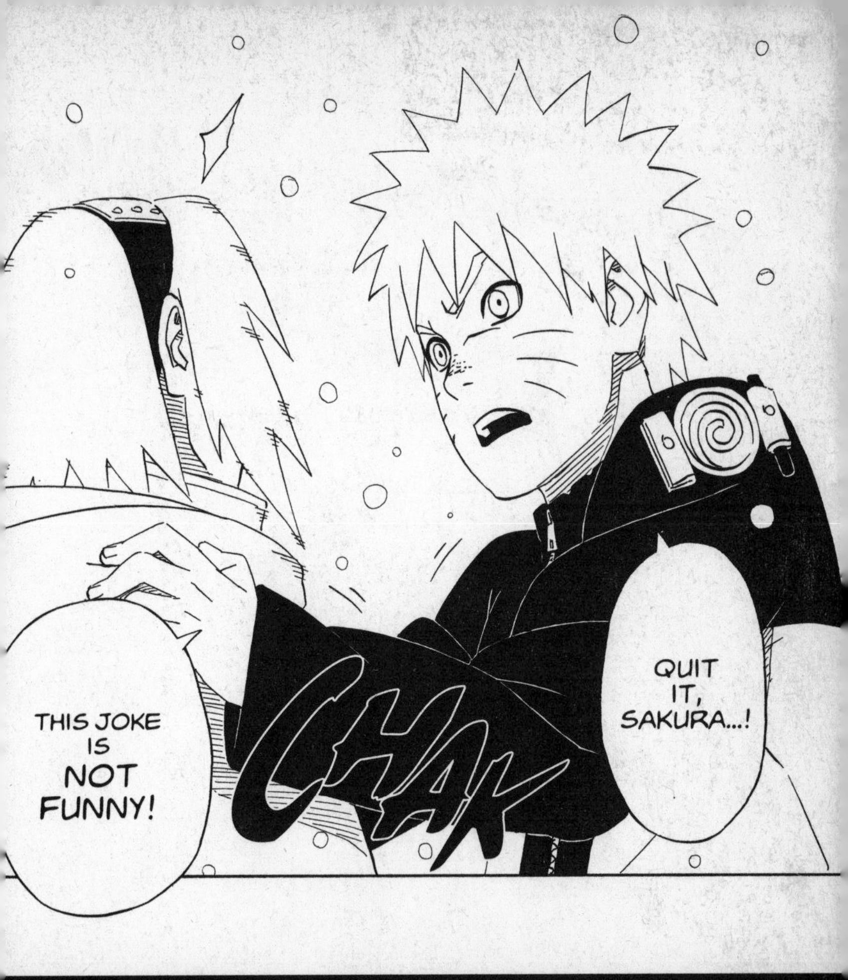
QUIT IT, SAKURA...!
CHAK
THIS JOKE IS NOT FUNNY!

IN THE NEXT VOLUME...

WATER PRISON DEATH MATCH

Naruto's worst nightmare seems to be inevitable as the war he's tried to stop for so long looms on the horizon. Plus, Sakura shocks him with a reveal that's gonna knock him for a serious loop. And a truth behind the modern ninja world sheds new light on Naruto's true role in the fate of his universe.

AVAILABLE FEBRUARY 2011!
READ IT FIRST IN SHONEN JUMP MAGAZINE!

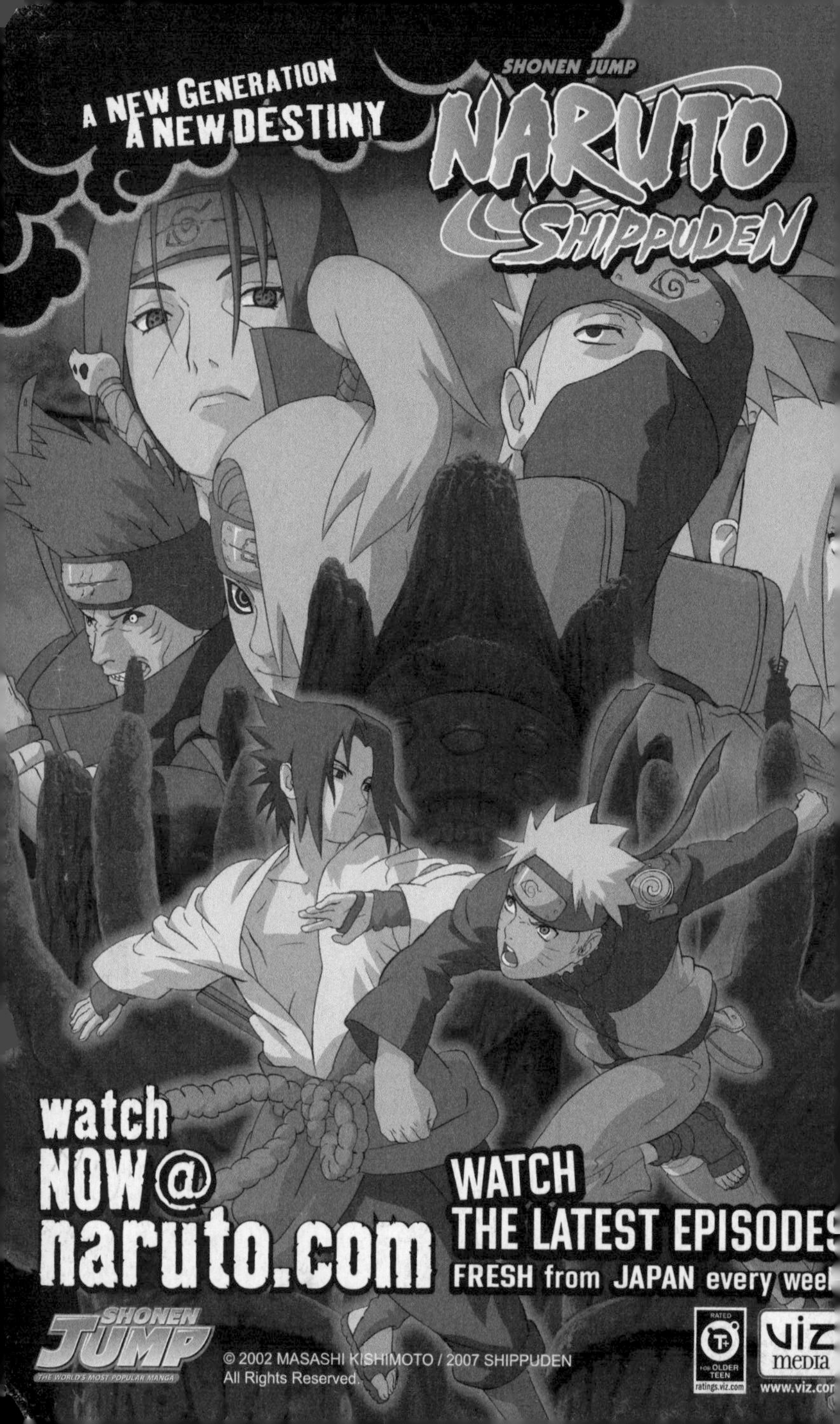

A NEW GENERATION
A NEW DESTINY
SHONEN JUMP
NARUTO SHIPPUDEN
watch NOW @ naruto.com
WATCH THE LATEST EPISODES
FRESH from JAPAN every week
SHONEN JUMP
THE WORLD'S MOST POPULAR MANGA
© 2002 MASASHI KISHIMOTO / 2007 SHIPPUDEN
All Rights Reserved.
RATED T+ FOR OLDER TEEN
ratings.viz.com
VIZ media
www.viz.com

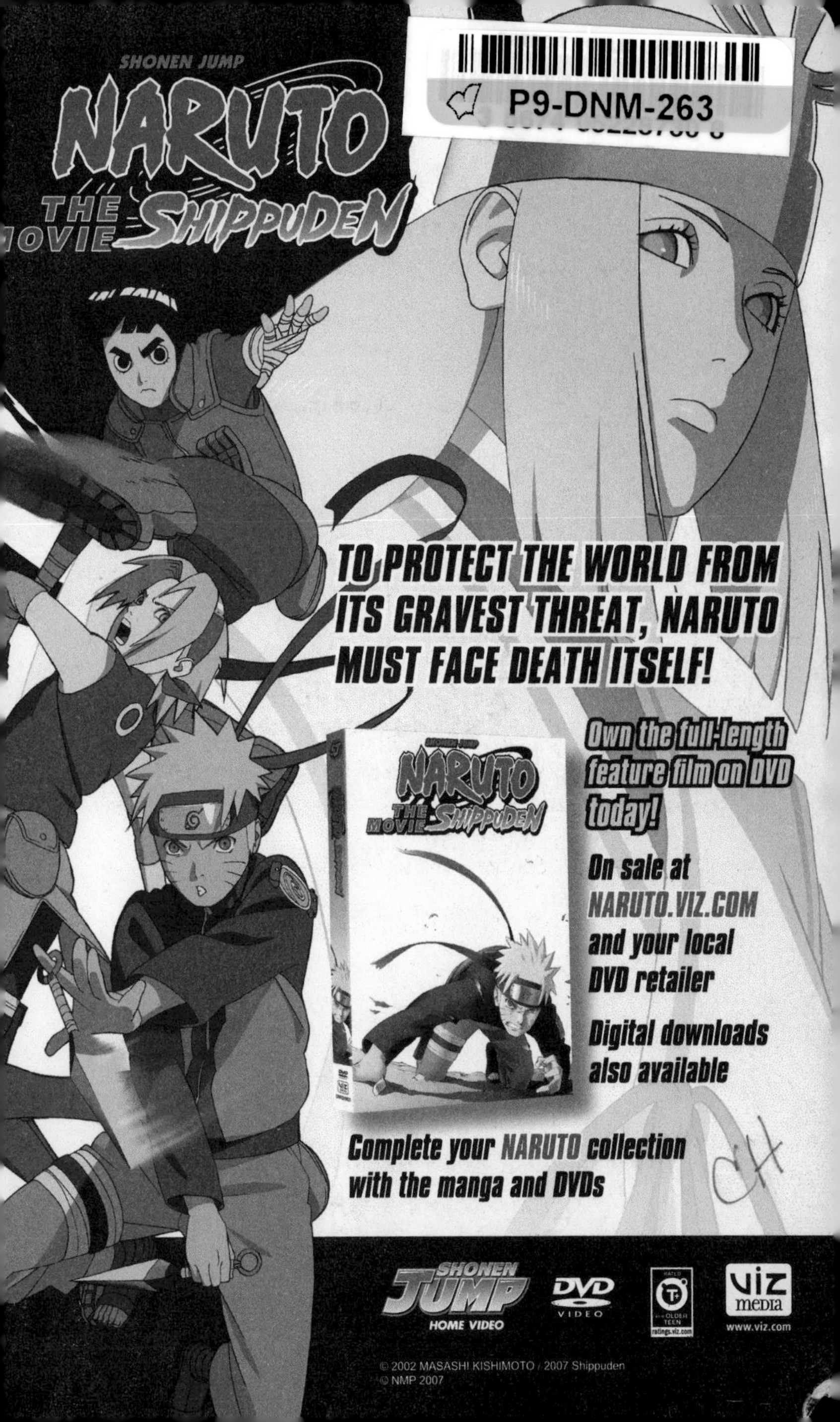
SHONEN JUMP
NARUTO THE MOVIE SHIPPUDEN
TO PROTECT THE WORLD FROM ITS GRAVEST THREAT, NARUTO MUST FACE DEATH ITSELF!
Own the full-length feature film on DVD today!
On sale at NARUTO.VIZ.COM and your local DVD retailer
Digital downloads also available
Complete your NARUTO collection with the manga and DVDs
SHONEN JUMP HOME VIDEO
DVD VIDEO
RATED T+ OLDER TEEN ratings.viz.com
VIZ media
www.viz.com
© 2002 MASASHI KISHIMOTO / 2007 Shippuden
© NMP 2007